PREG: Disabilities

SCOTTISH LAW COMMISSION
(Scot Law Com No 151)

Report on Incapable Adults

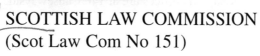
belongs to

Report submitted under section 3(2) of the Law
Commissions Act 1965

Presented to Parliament by the Lord Advocate
by Command of Her Majesty
September 1995

PREG: Disabilities

EDINBURGH: HMSO
Cm 2962   £19.65 net

ISBN 0 10 129622 3

Scottish Law Commission

Item 17 of our Fourth Programme of Law Reform

Judicial Factors, Powers of Attorney and Guardianship of the Incapable

To: The Right Honourable the Lord Rodger of Earlsferry, QC
   Her Majesty's Advocate

We have the honour to submit our Report on Incapable Adults.

(*Signed*)   C K DAVIDSON, *Chairman*
         E M CLIVE
         W A NIMMO SMITH
         N R WHITTY

KENNETH F BARCLAY, *Secretary*
14 July 1995

Contents

PART 4 OTHER TYPES OF EXTRA-JUDICIAL MANAGEMENT

WITHDRAWALS FROM BANK ACCOUNTS

JOINT ACCOUNTS

MANAGEMENT BY ESTABLISHMENTS OF RESIDENTS' FINANCES

PART 5 MEDICAL TREATMENT AND MEDICAL RESEARCH

PART 6 INTERVENTION ORDERS AND GUARDIANSHIP

PART 7 MISCELLANEOUS

PART 8 LIST OF RECOMMENDATIONS

APPENDIX A

APPENDIX B

Part 1   Introduction

Background to the report

1.1   This report follows on our Discussion Paper No. 94 *Mentally Disabled Adults: Legal Arrangements for Managing their Welfare and Finances* which we published in September 1991. In August 1993 we published another Discussion Paper No. 96 *Mentally Disordered and Vulnerable Adults: Public Authority Powers* and have subsequently received many comments on it. That paper was concerned with rationalising the powers public bodies such as local authorities, the Mental Welfare Commission and the police enjoy in order to protect the mentally disabled or those suspected of being mentally disabled. These issues are sufficiently different from those in this present report to justify a separate report. We intend to produce a report following on Discussion Paper No. 96 in the near future.

1.2   Over the last two decades there has been renewed interest in the problems of the mentally disabled. In 1988 the Scottish Health Service Planning Council published a report on *Scottish Health Authorities Review of Priorities for the Eighties and Nineties*[1] which placed services for old people with dementia in the highest category followed by community care for the mentally ill and the mentally handicapped. This assessment of priority was accepted by the then Secretary of State for Scotland. The greater awareness of the needs of the mentally disabled is in part due to the increasing number of elderly people suffering from dementia and similar mentally disabling conditions. The incidence of dementia increases with age. It has been estimated that dementia affects some 3% of the population aged between 65 and 69 years old, but around 20% of those aged 80 or over[2]. The number of people aged 80 or over has risen considerably over the last 15 years from 113,700 in 1977[3] to 175,000 in 1992[4]. The number is expected to rise still further over the next few years[5] due to demographic trends and advances in medicine.

1.3   Another factor is the changing attitudes of society and those professionally caring for the mentally disabled. The policy of care in secure institutions has over the years been replaced by one of providing appropriate support and care so that the mentally disabled can so far as possible live in the community. As the White Paper *Caring for People: Community Care in the Next Decade and Beyond* states:[6]

> "Community care means providing the services and support which people who are affected by problems of ageing, mental illness, mental handicap or physical or sensory disability need to be able to live as independently as possible in their own homes, or in "homely" settings in the community. The Government is firmly committed to a policy of community care which enables such people to achieve their full potential".

The White Paper was implemented by the National Health Service and Community Care Act 1990 which came into force fully in April 1993. Local authorities now charge elderly people for most of the services supplied to them. Private and local authority homes also levy substantial residence charges. This leads to complex financial decisions having to be taken to meet the charges, perhaps by realising assets such as dwellinghouses. These decisions will have to be taken in conjunction with decisions about personal welfare and treatment.

1.4   There is also a greater awareness of the rights of the mentally disabled. The philosophy that lies behind the new approach is one of minimum intervention in their lives, consistent with providing proper care and protection and maximum help to enable individuals to realise their full potential and make the best use of the abilities they have. The United Nations *Declaration on the Rights of Mentally Retarded Persons*[7] encapsulates the new approach and is worth quoting in full:-

> "Article I   The mentally retarded person has, to the maximum degree of feasibility, the same basic rights as other human beings.

---

1. Edinburgh HMSO.
2. Data on Dementia, Scottish Action on Dementia, October 1986.
3. Registrar General Scotland, *Annual Report 1977*, HMSO, Table N 2.3.
4. Registrar General Scotland, *Annual Report 1993*, HMSO, Table N 2.4.
5. 245,000 in 2016. *Annual Report 1993*, Table N 2.4.
6. Cm 849 (1989), para 1.1.
7. 1971 UN General Assembly 26th Session, Resolution 2856.

Article II   The mentally retarded person has a right to proper medical care and physical therapy and to such education, training, rehabilitation and guidance as will enable him to develop his ability and maximum potential.

Article III   The mentally retarded person has a right to economic security and to a decent standard of living. He has a right to perform productive work or to engage in any other meaningful occupation to the fullest possible extent of his capabilities.

Article IV   Whenever possible, the mentally retarded person should live with his own family or with foster parents and participate in different forms of community life. The family with which he lives should receive assistance. If care in an institution becomes necessary, it should be provided in surroundings and other circumstances as close as possible to those of normal life.

Article V   The mentally retarded person has a right to a qualified guardian when this is required to protect his personal wellbeing and interests.

Article VI   The mentally retarded person has a right to protection from exploitation, abuse and degrading treatment. If prosecuted for any offence, he shall have a right to due process of law with full recognition being given to his degree of mental responsibility.

Article VII   Whenever mentally retarded persons are unable, because of the severity of their handicap, to exercise all their rights in a meaningful way or should it become necessary to restrict or deny some or all of these rights, the procedure used for that restriction or denial of rights must contain proper legal safeguards against every form of abuse. This procedure must be based on an evaluation of the social capability of the mentally retarded person by qualified experts and must be subject to periodic review and to the right of appeal to higher authorities."

1.5   In the twenty or so years since the United Nations declaration many countries have enacted legislation embodying its principles. These include Alberta (Dependent Adults Act 1976), United States of America (Uniform Guardianship and Protective Proceedings Act, finalised for adoption by states in 1982), Queensland (Intellectually Handicapped Citizens Act 1985), Victoria (Guardianship and Administration Board Act 1986), Northern Territory, Australia (Adult Guardianship Act 1988), New Zealand (Protection of Personal and Property Rights Act 1988) and West Germany (Betreuungsgesetz 1990). In preparing our discussion paper and this report we have been greatly helped by material from these and other countries. Our discussion paper contained much comparative material to illustrate the different approaches taken on particular issues. Since then we have also benefitted from the comparative and international material, and views on policy, presented at the Council of Europe's Third European Conference on Family Law, which devoted a day to discussion of legal topics relating to incapacitated adults[1]. This wealth of material is not reproduced here for reasons of space and we merely set out succinctly our recommendations for reform of the law of Scotland in this area. We believe that our recommendations are very much in line with recent developments in other countries and with internationally accepted principles.

1.6   The Law Commission for England and Wales has been conducting an examination of the law relating to mentally incapacitated adults along very similar lines to ours. It has published many consultation papers[2] and a report[3]. We have been in close touch with Commissioners and staff of the Law Commission throughout and have had many useful and constructive discussions with them. The general approach of our report is much the same as that of the Law Commission's report. However, there are many differences between the two sets of recommendations and draft Bills. This is partly due to the different responses that each Commission received on consultation, but other factors are the differences in the existing law and court structure between the two jurisdictions.

The present law in outline

1.7   Scottish law has a number of methods which enable decisions to be made or action taken on behalf of adults who are incapable of deciding or acting themselves. In the personal welfare field guardians under the 1984 Act, tutors-dative and tutors-at-law may be appointed by the courts and doctors and other health-care professionals have authority to give incapable patients treatment which is in their best interests to receive. For property and financial affairs there are curators bonis and tutors-at-law appointed by the courts, attorneys appointed by the individuals whose affairs they deal with, many statutory schemes limited to particular property or people in particular situations, and *negotiorum gestio*.

---

1. The Conference was held at Cadiz from 20-22 April 1995. A member of this Commission attended the conference as a Rapporteur on one of the topics at the invitation of the Council of Europe.
2. *Mentally Incapacitated Adults and Decision-Making: An Overview*, No. 119, published April 1991; *Mentally Incapacitated Adults and Decision-Making: A New Jurisdiction*, No. 128 (1993): *Mentally Incapacitated Adults and Decision-Making: Medical Treatment and Research*, No. 129 (1993): *Mentally Incapacitated and Other Vulnerable Adults: Public Law Protection*, No. 130 (1993).
3. *Mental Incapacity*, Law Com No. 231, March 1995.

1.8 **Mental health guardians.** A guardian under the Mental Health (Scotland) Act 1984 (a "mental health guardian") may be appointed to an adult by the sheriff on application by a mental health officer (or occasionally a relative of the adult) of the local authority in whose area the adult lives. The application is supported by two medical reports specifying the form of mental disorder the adult is suffering from and stating that the disorder is such as to warrant guardianship, and a recommendation from the mental health officer that guardianship is necessary in the interests of the welfare of the adult[1]. The mental health guardian may be the local authority or any person chosen, or accepted as suitable, by the local authority[2]. In practice most guardians are the local authority or its Director of Social Work. The powers of a mental health guardian are statutory and three in number; power to require the adult to reside at a specified place, power to require the adult to attend for treatment or training, and power to require access to be given to doctors, mental health officers and others[3].

1.9 **Tutors-dative and tutors-at-law.** Tutors-dative have been recently revived in order to provide a more personal type of guardianship[4]. They are appointed by the Court of Session after consideration of two medical certificates of incapacity. Centuries ago tutors-dative were appointed to act on behalf of incapable adults in all aspects of their lives. In modern practice tutors-dative are granted personal welfare powers only[5]. The appointment of a tutor-dative is not intimated to the Mental Welfare Commission or local authority and these bodies have no statutory duties to visit those subject to tutory. Tutors-at-law are also appointed by the Court of Session using a similar procedure to that used for tutors-dative. Tutors-at-law, like tutors-dative, were common centuries ago but became obsolescent. Recently, after a gap of over 100 years, a tutor-at-law has been appointed[6]. A tutor-at-law has full power over the personal welfare and financial affairs of the adult. The tutor-at-law can only be the nearest male relative. He is entitled to be appointed by virtue of his relationship unless his unsuitability is established. A tutor-at-law supersedes any tutor-dative or curator bonis who has previously been appointed.

1.10 **Medical treatment.** Patients who are unconscious or otherwise temporarily incapable of giving consent may, on the basis of necessity, be given treatment which is necessary and which cannot reasonably be postponed until capacity is recovered[7]. The 1984 Act also contains special provisions on urgent treatment for patients who are detained under that Act[8]. In 1989 in the case of *Re F (Mental Patient: Sterilisation*[9]) the House of Lords clarified the law of England and Wales relating to the treatment of permanently incapacitated patients. Treatment could be given to such patients in their best interests, ie to save their lives or to secure improvement or prevent deterioration in their physical or mental health. The House of Lords' decision would probably be followed in Scotland.

1.11 **Curators bonis.** A curator bonis ("curator" for short) may be appointed to a person who is of unsound mind and incapable of managing his or her affairs or giving instructions for their management[10]. The application for a curator is by way of petition to the Court of Session or the sheriff court. Usually one or more of the incapable adult's relatives will petition, but anyone with an interest may do so[11]. The local authority must, and the Mental Welfare Commission may, petition if no-one else is doing so and a curator is necessary[12]. The petition is supported by two medical certificates to the effect that the grounds for appointment are established. On appointment the curator takes over the management and administration of the incapable adult's affairs completely and acts under the supervision of the Accountant of Court, an official of the Court of Session. The curator must submit an initial inventory and annual accounts of transactions thereafter to the Accountant of Court for audit.

1.12 **Attorneys.** An attorney is a person appointed by another (the granter) under a contract of mandate or agency to deal with some or all aspects of the granter's property and financial affairs. The contract may take the form of a document setting out the powers conferred on the attorney, but oral contracts are also competent. The powers conferred are usually very wide, especially where the purpose of the contract is to enable the attorney to manage the granter's property and financial affairs after the latter's incapacity. All powers of attorney granted since 31 December 1990 continue to be effective after the granter's incapacity unless the contract contains provisions to the contrary[13].

---

1. 1984 Act, ss 37 and 38.
2. 1984 Act, s 37(2).
3. 1984 Act, s 41(2).
4. See Adrian Ward's articles in 1987 SLT (News) 69 and 1992 SLT (News) 325. None of the recent tutor-dative cases have been reported except *Chapman Petrs* 1993 SLT 955.
5. *Chapman Petrs* 1993 SLT 955, but see *Queen Petr* 1992 mentioned in Adrian Ward's article *Tutors to Adults: Some Developments* 1992 SLT (News) 325.
6. *Britton v Britton's CB* 1992 SCLR 947.
7. Mason and McCall-Smith, *Law and Medical Ethics*, (4th edn) p 220; NHS Scotland, *A Guide to Consent to Examination, Investigation, Treatment or Operation* (1992), page 5.
8. S 102.
9. [1990] 2 AC 1.
10. Walker, *Judicial Factors*, p 22.
11. *Mason* (1852) 14 D 761 (adult's solicitor).
12. 1984 Act, ss 92 and 93.
13. Law Reform (Miscellaneous Provisions) (Scotland) Act 1990, s 71.

1.13 Statutory schemes. There are a number of schemes regulated by primary or subordinate legislation. The following are the more common.

(a) The Department of Social Security may appoint a person to claim, receive and deal with any Social Security benefit on behalf of an incapable adult. The application for appointment is made on a prescribed form and medical evidence of the adult's incapacity may be asked for[1].

(b) The managers of a hospital may look after money and valuables belonging to in-patients who have been certified by the doctor in charge as being incapable of managing and administering their property and affairs. The managers may manage amounts up to £5,000 for a particular patient; beyond this sum the consent of the Mental Welfare Commission must be obtained[2].

(c) Government departments[3] and industrial and provident societies[4] may at their discretion pay funds due to a mentally incapable person to an individual who is looking after that person.

1.14 *Negotiorum gestio.* *Negotiorum gestio* is a doctrine whereby one person (the *gestor* or manager) may manage the affairs of another who is absent or incapacitated, without there being any official appointment or contract of mandate. It is based on a sort of legally presumed mandate[5]. It is not limited to urgent or immediate acts of administration. Management by a *gestor* may continue for many years[6]. *Negotiorum gestio* enables a relative or a friend of an incapable adult to manage the adult's property and financial affairs, and recover outlays, without the expense of having a curator appointed.

What's wrong with the present law?

1.15 Each existing method briefly described in the previous section suffers from various defects and is in need of reform. There are however more general criticisms, that the present law is fragmented, archaic and fails to provide an adequate remedy in many common situations.

1.16 The powers of a mental health guardian are fixed by statute[7] and cannot be added to or varied to suit the needs and capabilities of the adult under guardianship. Where, as is commonly the case, the guardian is the local authority or the director of social work, the functions have to be delegated, but it is often unclear which person concerned with the welfare of the adult is actually exercising the guardianship powers[8]. The procedure for appointing a mental health guardian takes some time but there is no power to make an interim appointment to deal with an urgent situation. Other criticisms are that the local authority mental health officer exercises effective control over guardianship since any application must contain his or her recommendation[9], the welfare ground for appointment ("necessary in the interests of the welfare of the patient") is vague and "necessary" is too high a standard.

1.17 Because tutory dative is a recently revived post of considerable antiquity the powers and duties have to be gathered from centuries old cases. It is not clear how far they remain authoritative today in a society with a different outlook and values and different procedures. The local authority and Mental Welfare Commission do not have the same statutory duties in relation to adults subject to tutory as they do in relation to adults under mental health guardianship. Yet the powers of a tutor may be far greater than those of a guardian. Tutors-dative can be appointed only by the Court of Session.

1.18 Tutors-at-law are another recently revived type of guardian whose functions are therefore somewhat uncertain. The fact that the post may be held only by the nearest male relative is incompatible with modern notions of sexual equality. Furthermore, relationship should be only one of a number of factors that should be considered in selecting a suitable person to deal with the personal welfare and financial affairs of an incapable adult.

1.19 A curator bonis takes over the management of the adult's whole estate. The curator's powers are not tailored to the needs and abilities of the adult. There is uncertainty as to the correct balance between conserving the estate and spending it for the adult's benefit, and as a result many curators adopt a conservative approach. Curatory, which is an appointment that lasts until recalled, may be imposed on adults whose needs could be met by a short-term order limited to a particular area of need. Curatory is expensive and the problem of high initial and running costs is particularly acute with small estates.

---

1. Social Security (Claims and Payments) Regulations 1987, reg 33, SI 1987/1968.
2. 1984 Act, s 94.
3. Mental Health Act 1983, s 142.
4. Industrial and Provident Societies Act 1965, s 22.
5. Bell, *Principles*, para 540.
6. *Fernie v Robertson* (1871) 9 M 437.
7. 1984 Act, s 41.
8. See Mental Welfare Commission *Annual Report* 1987, p 24 and *Annual Report* 1989, paras 12.5 and 12.19.
9. 1984 Act, s 37(3).

1.20   The main defect of attorneys is that they are unsupervised. Once the granter becomes incapable there may be no one with sufficient interest to monitor and if necessary challenge the attorney's actings. The court's powers are limited to superseding the attorney by the appointment of a curator[1]. A contract of mandate or agency conferring a power of attorney continues in effect after the granter's incapacity by virtue of the Law Reform (Miscellaneous Provisions) (Scotland) Act 1990[2]. Contracts may therefore confer continuing powers inadvertently through the granter's failure to exclude the statutory provision or to consider carefully whether a continuing power ought to be granted.

1.21   Hospital management of certified in-patient's funds is too informal. A patient's right to deal with his or her own affairs can be taken away by a single doctor certifying incapacity without any court hearing and without any appeal. Many patients could manage their affairs if more help and advice were available to them. Some managers adopt a negative attitude and fail to claim benefits and spend money on behalf of patients so as to enhance their quality of life[3]. Finally, only managers of hospitals may avail themselves of this statutory procedure. Other establishments, such as local authority homes and private nursing and residential homes are unable to manage their residents' finances. This lack of financial management powers is becoming more acute as more and more people with impaired capacity are being moved out of hospitals.

1.22   *Negotiorum gestio* is a useful background doctrine. It provides a legal underpinning for many everyday acts of administration on behalf of incapable adults. However, it suffers from a lack of any document evidencing the appointment or powers of the *gestor*. It is therefore often difficult for *gestors* to persuade third parties to deal with them or accept instructions from them.

1.23   The existing Scottish law is fragmented. With the sole exception of a tutor-at-law all the other methods of dealing with incapacitated adults relate either solely to personal welfare or solely to property and financial affairs. Thus curators have no functions in the personal welfare field while mental health guardians are prohibited by statute from intromitting with the funds of the adults under guardianship[4]. In current practice tutors-dative are restricted to personal welfare matters while attorneys have only financial functions. However, most adults' welfare and finances are inextricably connected and decisions in one area may well have repercussions in the other. Furthermore, for historical reasons various remedies are available only in certain courts. The Court of Session has exclusive jurisdiction to appoint tutors-at-law and tutors-dative while mental health guardians can be appointed only by a sheriff. In order to provide an overall scheme to meet an adult's welfare and financial needs more than one application may have to be made in the same or separate courts.

1.24   Many of the existing methods are inflexible or limited. The law does not allow the remedies to be tailored to the adult's needs. The major exception to this is tutory dative. There is no recognition of the concept of least restrictive action or minimum necessary intervention. A curator takes over the adult's entire estate and financial affairs. A mental health guardian has three limited statutory powers which cannot be added to or subtracted from.

1.25   Much of the law is archaic. Tutors-at-law are appointed under the Curators Act 1585; the law relating to curators rests mainly on the Judicial Factors Act 1849 and even older Acts of Sederunt and practice, and the functions of tutors-dative have to be gleaned from 17th and 18th century cases when such appointments were common. In order to regulate the property and investment powers of curators they have been spatchcocked into the Trusts (Scotland) Acts although they have little in common with trustees. The assets of a trust are made over to and owned by the trustees, whereas the title to an incapable adult's estate remains with the adult, the curator being simply a manager.

1.26   The final general criticism is that Scottish law fails to deal with, or provide adequate remedies in, many common situations. It is not clear whether it is competent to appoint an attorney to make personal welfare decisions on behalf of the granter when he or she becomes incapable. It is not possible to obtain a court order in the financial field limited to a particular area or item of property in order to deal with a particular short-term problem. There is an urgent need for simple schemes not involving the courts for dealing with the finances of those with small or modest estates, such as obtaining authority to use funds in an incapable adult's bank account for the daily needs of that adult. This would be of great benefit to the many carers who are looking after an incapable relative at home. Managers of local authority homes are unable to manage their incapable residents' finances in the same way as managers of hospitals can. The initial and running costs of a curatory are such that it is uneconomic where the estate is modest. The two schemes mentioned previously, together with a system of low cost public management, would go far to address these needs. As far as the authority to give medical treatment to incapable adults is concerned the law in Scotland is uncertain, there is no Scottish authority on advance statements - statements made by patients while capable as to how they wish to be treated when incapable, and the legality of carrying out medical research on those who are incapable of consenting to participate is far from clear.

---

1. See *Fraser v Paterson* 1987 SLT 562.
2. S 71.
3. Scottish Health Service Planning Council, *Report of the Working Party on Incapax Patients' Funds*, (1985) p 14.
4. 1984 Act, s 41(3).

Our reforms in outline

1.27   Many of those responding to our discussion paper commented that the existing law was so patchy and inadequate that a radical reform was the only solution. We have endeavoured to produce recommendations and draft legislation dealing comprehensively with the personal welfare and financial affairs of the incapacitated. At the heart of our recommendations lie certain general principles which are set out in our draft legislation and which should influence every exercise of functions under it. The most important of these principles is that any intervention must be for the benefit of the incapable adult concerned and be the least restrictive to achieve that benefit. Another principle emphasises the need to take the past and present wishes and feelings of the adult into account as well as the views of others close to the adult, such as the nearest relative and primary carer as well as any attorney or guardian. Finally, incapable adults should be encouraged to exercise their existing skills and to acquire and develop new skills.

1.28   Incapacitated adults and their carers should be enabled and encouraged to do as much as possible for themselves and to make their own arrangements for possible future incapacity. Into this category comes the appointment of an attorney for management of property and finances and dealing with personal welfare. Another way in which people could influence their medical treatment after they become incapacitated would be by way of advance statements. The status and legal effect of these in Scotland is set out in our draft legislation. Guardianship by relatives or friends rather than professionals is encouraged, particularly for personal welfare matters and where property of modest value is concerned. In all these schemes there would be a certain degree of oversight by public officials and organisations to ensure that incapable adults are not exploited or abused.

1.29   The various gaps we have identified in the existing law are addressed. We recommend the introduction of schemes whereby a carer looking after an incapable adult at home could be authorised to withdraw money from the adult's bank or building society account to meet the adult's living expenses. In institutional settings the managers of hospitals and other approved establishments would be authorised to manage income and certain other financial matters on behalf of their incapable residents. Authority would be granted by a new public official - the Public Guardian - who would also investigate complaints and carry out spot checks and where necessary terminate the carers' or managers' authority. Our draft legislation also contains provisions dealing with the medical treatment of, and medical research on, the incapable in a more coherent and comprehensive way than the somewhat patchy and uncertain common law. Low cost public management of small estates by the Public Guardian is recommended to deal with the problem that the cost of professional management imposes too great a burden.

1.30   In the absence of satisfactory informal or formal arrangements, such as those described in the previous two paragraphs, the court is to have power to make intervention orders or guardianship orders. These form a flexible system by which powers can be conferred which will be tailored to the incapable adults' needs and incapacity. Intervention orders are intended to deal with single issues or single assets - "one-off" situations. Guardianship is designed for those adults where continuous management or assistance is required over a lengthy period. Intervention orders and guardianship orders would form an integrated and coherent system in that both personal welfare and financial issues could be dealt with in the same proceedings and the guardian could have powers conferred in either or both fields as appropriate in the circumstances.

Scope of the report

1.31   Part 2 of the report sets out the general principles which are to apply to all decisions relating to the mentally disabled in the areas covered by this report. It also contains the proposed general jurisdiction of the sheriff courts in relation to incapable adults and the proposed regulatory and supervisory framework of public officials and organisations. Part 3 is concerned with measures that adults can take to ensure that their personal welfare and financial affairs will be looked after should they become incapable at some future date. We look at continuing powers of attorney and recommend that an attorney should be able to deal with personal welfare as well as property and finances. In Part 4 we recommend various schemes that would enable those caring for incapable adults to assist them without having to apply to the courts. The schemes include management of incapable patients' and residents' financial affairs by the hospital, home or other institution in which they are living and allowing, under safeguards, limited access to an incapable adult's bank or similar account for meeting the adult's living and other expenses. Medical matters are the subject of Part 5. We recommend that doctors and other health-care professionals should have a general statutory authority to treat incapable adults. Any decision about treatment would be governed by the general principles set out in Part 2. Certain treatments, however, would require prior authorisation from the courts or an independent second opinion specialist. Advance statements about future medical treatment ("living wills") are also considered and recommendations are made to put them on a firm legal basis. We also recommend a system of strict controls for medical research on the incapable adults. Part 6 relates to measures that require legal proceedings. The courts would, under our recommendations, be empowered to make various orders in the personal welfare and financial fields, including the appointment of a guardian where the incapable adult's circumstances make a long-term appointment necessary. A scheme for financial management of small estates by the Public Guardian (who would also be the Accountant of Court) is put forward to ease the burden on modest estates. Part 7 deals with appeals, transitional provisions and other miscellaneous matters. Part 8 lists our recommendations. A draft of the legislation required to implement our recommendations forms Appendix A.

1.32   We received a large number of comments on our discussion paper and are grateful to all those who responded. Appendix B to this report lists those organisations and individuals who submitted written comments. Representatives of the Commission participated in many public meetings, seminars and discussion groups organised by some of the bodies involved in the area of mental disability. We found these events extremely useful and derived great benefit from the comments and views expressed at them. We wish to place on record our thanks to the organisations involved and those who attended.

1.33   We have also been greatly assisted in the later stages of this exercise by discussions with the Mental Welfare Commission, the Accountant of Court and his deputy and representatives from the leading Scottish medical bodies. An earlier version of the draft Bill (the final version of which is annexed to this report) was considered in detail by Mr Adrian Ward MBE[1], Mrs Hilary Patrick[2] and Mrs Christine McGregor[3]. We are very grateful to all of them for giving so generously of their time and expertise to assist us with this important project. They are, of course, not responsible for the decisions ultimately taken by us, although their views have always been given very careful consideration.

1.34   In order to shorten commonly occurring references the following abbreviations are used in this report:

(a) "Our discussion paper" for Discussion Paper No. 94 *Mentally Disabled Adults: Legal Arrangements for Managing their Welfare and Finances.*

(b) "The Law Society" for the Law Society of Scotland.

(c) "The Mental Welfare Commission" for the Mental Welfare Commission for Scotland.

(d) "The 1984 Act" for the Mental Health (Scotland) Act 1984.

Two organisations have changed their names since submitting comments on our discussion paper. These are Enable (formerly the Scottish Society for the Mentally Handicapped) and Alzheimer Scotland - Action on Dementia (formerly Scottish Action on Dementia). We use their present names when discussing their comments.

---

1. A solicitor with wide professional experience of the mentally disabled, an author of several books on the subject and Chairman of the Central Scotland Health Care NHS Trust.
2. Legal adviser to the Scottish Association for Mental Health and author, with Professor Blackie, of a book on the 1984 Act.
3. The Social Work Commissioner with the Mental Welfare Commission and author with her predecessor (Mr Huw Richards) of a book on guardianship in Scotland.

Part 2 General Matters

Introduction

2.1   In later sections of this report we recommend the introduction into Scottish law of guardians of incapable adults with powers in the financial and personal welfare fields, attorneys with a similar range of powers exerciseable after the granter's incapacity and other extra-judicial methods of managing some financial assets of incapable adults in order to use the money for their benefit. In this Part we discuss certain general matters such as what the grounds should be for the appointment of a guardian or other intervention in the financial or personal affairs of an adult, what forum (court, tribunal or other body) should appoint guardians and adjudicate on matters falling within the scope of our recommendations, how the various people exercising functions on behalf of adults are to be supervised and the general principles that should be taken into account in order to decide what intervention (if any) should be made and what form any intervention should take. We conclude with a section on the fiduciary relationship between those exercising functions and the incapable adults.

Adults the report deals with

2.2   Our discussion paper was entitled "Mentally Disabled Adults" and dealt with them and not with mentally disabled children. At the time of its publication adults were those who had attained their eighteenth birthday. Shortly afterwards the Age of Legal Capacity (Scotland) Act 1991 came into force. Now individuals attain full capacity in respect of virtually all matters contained in the discussion paper on their sixteenth birthday, at the latest. Parents also lose corresponding parental rights when their child attains 16. Mentally disabled children under 16 will either be in the care of their parents or others or be looked after under existing child-care legislation. There is a slight overlap in that children's hearings continue to have jurisdiction over individuals up to the age of 18 where a supervision requirement was in force before the child was 16[1], but we do not think that this will give rise to any problems. We therefore recommend that:

1. **The recommendations in this report should apply only in relation to individuals aged 16 and over.**

Clause 67(1)

General grounds for intervention

2.3   On what grounds should the court have power to deal with applications involving an intervention in the personal welfare or financial affairs of a mentally disabled adult? We have found this a difficult issue. We have been unable to derive much help from the legislation in other countries as each country adopts a different approach and their provisions seem open to criticism in one respect or another. Under the present Scottish law a guardian may be appointed under the 1984 Act to a patient if[2]:

"(a) he [the patient] is suffering from mental disorder of a nature or degree which warrants his reception into guardianship; and

(b) it is necessary in the interests of the welfare of the patient that he should be so received".

In our discussion paper[3] we criticised these grounds, especially the welfare test in (b). We suggested that it was too vague[4] and that the word "necessary" imposed too stringent a requirement. We did not see these as suitable grounds for the appointment of our proposed new personal guardians. Instead we proposed[5] that a personal guardian should be appointed or some other personal welfare order made only if the court was satisfied that:

"(a) the person in question lacks wholly or partly the capacity to understand the nature of and to foresee the possible implications of personal welfare decisions or has such capacity but is unable to communicate or act consistently in accordance with such decisions, and

---

1. Social Work (Scotland) Act 1968, s 30(1).
2. S 36.
3. Para 2.38.
4. See also Richards and McGregor, *Guardianship in Scotland*, HMSO 1992, p 41.
5. Proposal 5, para 2.62.

(b) the appointment of a personal guardian or the making of some other order would result in a substantial benefit to, or necessary protection of, the person."

In addition we considered that the fact that the person has acted or intends to act in a way an ordinary prudent person would not act should not by itself be evidence of lack of capacity.

2.4   The normal ground for appointment of a curator to a person is that the person is of unsound mind and incapable of managing his or her affairs or giving instructions for their management[1]. Curators have in the past been appointed to physically incapacitated persons. "Giving instructions" includes not only the initial act of appointing someone else, such as an attorney, to manage the affairs but also monitoring the appointee's subsequent actings at least to the extent of being able to recall the appointment if the appointee acts improperly[2]. It is very doubtful whether the court would regard a state of facility as a valid ground for appointment. There are old cases in which appointments were made where the person was of weak mind and very apt to be misled[3]. On the other hand there is later, but by no means recent, authority for the view that facility and undue influence are not in themselves sufficient to justify an appointment[4]. Insane delusions also cause problems. If the delusions do not affect the way in which the person manages his or her affairs, then it has been held that the appointment of a curator is not justified[5]. On the other hand if the delusions do affect the management of affairs with the result that the property is used in a way that the person would not have done had he or she been completely sane, a curator may be appointed[6]. In our discussion paper we proposed[7] grounds for the appointment of a financial manager also based on lack of capacity and very similar to those set out in the previous paragraph in relation to personal guardianship.

2.5   The responses received to these proposals were varied. The Scottish Association for Mental Health strongly welcomed the absence of any reasonableness test but also suggested that further discussion was needed to ensure that personal guardianship or other personal welfare orders could be made for all those who could benefit from them. A similar point was made by the Mental Welfare Commission and some other respondents. Guardianship under the 1984 Act is available, not only to adults who lack capacity but also to those who have capacity but are mentally disordered and are being exploited or ill-treated and require guardianship for their protection. A survey of people on guardianship in 1988 was carried out by Huw Richards and Christine McGregor of the Mental Welfare Commission[8]. This study found that "those on guardianship have multiple and cumulative problems and most have problems of family relationships (83%), general vulnerability (80%) and of financial management (83%) ..... 80% of the group were considered vulnerable, gullible or at risk. Half of those studied were unable to care for themselves[9]." Another study of mental health guardianship found that in practice guardians tended to be social workers and commented that as "guardianship is perceived as a protective order and is therefore often used with clients who do not have suitable carers available to become guardians this outcome is inevitable"[10]. If personal guardians could not be appointed for such people then the respondents mentioned above considered that guardianship under the 1984 Act might have to be retained. In view of the otherwise strong response on consultation to having a new unified system of personal guardianship, we think that the grounds for guardianship should be such as to make it available for those in need of protection rather than retaining guardianship under the 1984 Act for this group.

2.6   A somewhat similar criticism to that made by the Mental Welfare Commission and others in relation to personal guardianship was made by the Law Society, Alzheimer Scotland - Action on Dementia, the Scottish Association for Mental Health and Enable in relation to our proposed grounds of appointment for financial managers. They took the view that financial management or some lesser financial intervention order should be available in respect of those who had capacity yet were unable to look after their own affairs or were at risk from exploitation and abuse.

2.7   Our proposed ground of intervention based on "lack of capacity to understand the nature of .... decisions" was criticised. First, the Mental Welfare Commission thought that capacity should not be defined only as intellectual capacity, but should take into account functional ability and potential for autonomy. Secondly, the Law Commission for England and Wales in a consultation paper published after our discussion paper considered that our proposed formula required the adult to understand the nature of the decision-making process itself[11]. In its view the relevant point was the person's ability

---

1. Walker, *Judicial Factors*, p 22.
2. *Fraser v Paterson* 1987 SLT 562.
3. *Spiers* (1851) 14 D 11; *Dewar v Dewar* (1834) 12 S 315.
4. *Calderwood v Duncan* (1907) 14 SLT 777; *Dowie v Hagart* (1894) 21 R 1052.
5. *Henderson* (1851) 14 D 11.
6. *CB v AB* (1891) 18 R (HL) 40.
7. Proposal 29, para 4.40.
8. *Guardianship in Scotland*, HMSO 1992.
9. P 85.
10. Scottish Office Central Research Unit Paper *"The Hidden Safety Net? Mental Health Guardianship: Achievements and Limitations"*, Carole Moore, Anne Connor, Pauline Martin and John Tibbitt (1992), p 84.
11. *Mentally Incapacitated Adults and Decision Making: A New Jurisdiction*, Consultation Paper No 128 (1993), paras 3.20-3.22.

to understand information relevant to the decision rather than "a decision" and to appreciate the reasonable foreseeable consequences of the decision. Thirdly, the Law Society said that lack of capacity was not adequately defined and more detailed criteria were necessary. There is much force in these criticisms.

2.8   Others criticised our inclusion of those who had capacity but acted inconsistently. It was said that many people may choose to act inconsistently, possibly for the very reason that they do understand the implications of rash or unwise decisions. Having made an unwise decision in the past they do not wish to repeat it. Moreover, it was said that many rational people behave inconsistently from time to time. We accept these points and no longer consider that inconsistency should be an express component of our grounds for intervention. Nevertheless, inconsistent behaviour would be a factor to be taken into account in assessing both mental disorder and the ability to carry out the functions in question.

2.9   We have come to the conclusion that it is not desirable to have one single ground that would apply to all the various applications that could be made under our recommendations. The criteria authorising court intervention in relation to continuing powers of attorney, for example, should be different from those where medical treatment is concerned. Guardianship should have different criteria from those for "one off" intervention orders. Guardianship is intended as a long-term appointment which would normally last for years with the possibility of further extension so that the adult should require to have correspondingly long-term needs or inabilities. Furthermore, guardianship has a protective element and should be available to the mentally disabled who are incapable of protecting themselves from serious risk of financial exploitation or physical abuse, rather than be confined to those who are incapacitated in relation to particular decisions.

2.10   Our earlier suggested criteria for intervention in the personal welfare and financial fields set out above contained no express reference to mental disorder. We now consider that a test using mental disorder (as defined in the next paragraph) as a threshold criterion would be preferable. It would help to delimit more clearly the area with which we are here concerned. Mental disorder would be a necessary condition for intervention but clearly should not be a sufficient condition. To intervene in all cases of mental disorder and in all areas of a mentally disordered adult's life would be to fly in the face of our overall principle of least restriction and would be too crude an approach. It would adopt a "label" or "status approach"; fixing a person with a total lack of faculties simply because of a diagnostic finding. Many, if not most, adults will be able to make certain decisions or perform certain tasks notwithstanding their mental disorder. In order to justify intervention we consider that the adult must also be unable, by reason of mental disorder, to make the decision or perform the act in question. The existence of mental disorder and the coupling of that disorder to the lack of ability are in our view necessary. Inability to make a decision or perform an act is something that affects people who are not considered to be mentally disordered, such as the naturally indecisive or those subject to severe conflicting pressures. The more complex the decision or act, the greater the number of people that will be unable to perform it. Relying solely on inability would permit interference in the lives of many people to an extent that we consider would be unjustified.

2.11   We would adopt the definition of mental disorder used in the 1984 Act. Section 1 defines mental disorder to be "mental illness or mental handicap however caused or manifested" but goes on to provide that no person shall be treated as suffering from mental disorder "by reason only of promiscuity or other immoral conduct, sexual deviancy or dependence on alcohol or drugs". This is a well established[1] definition with which doctors and others are familiar. It covers not only the mentally handicapped or those with learning disabilities and the mentally ill, but also dementia sufferers, the brain injured, and patients in a toxic confusional state where an infection has produced toxins which affect the functioning of the brain. Although people who are drunk or under the influence of drugs are not regarded as mentally disordered, those whose mental faculties are impaired due to past drug or alcohol abuse do come within the definition.

2.12   Inability depends on other factors besides the mental disorder. First, in order to make a decision people need to be provided with relevant information, at a level they can understand, about the likely outcomes of the various courses of action. Providing the relevant information in an appropriate form and manner takes more time and effort when the person concerned is physically disabled (blind or deaf) or mentally disabled. Sense Scotland, the National Deaf-Blind and Rubella Association, commented that "There will need to be a commitment to building a structure which can check out as far as possible the extent to which capacity is impaired, and whether that impaired capacity is the result of lack of access to information rather than to lack of understanding". Second, the surrounding circumstances and help available affect a person's ability. Tasks that people might be able to do in the familiar surroundings of their own home may be beyond them in strange surroundings. Having friends around when matters are discussed often enhances the ability of people to make decisions.

2.13   A test based partly on inability to make a decision or perform an act leads to the question of the required standard. In our discussion paper we proposed that as part of our grounds for appointment of a personal guardian[2] or financial

---

1.   It stems at least from the Mental Health (Scotland) Act 1960. Slight amendments were made by the Mental Health (Scotland) Amendment Act 1983 and consolidated into the 1984 Act, but these were not regarded as having changed the categories of people considered in practice to be mentally disordered.
2.   Proposal 5(2), para 2.62.

manager[1] the fact that the adult had acted or intended to act in a way an ordinary prudent person would not act should not by itself be taken as lack of capacity. Few respondents directly addressed themselves to this part of the overall proposals, but those that did generally agreed with it. The Scottish Association for Mental Health very strongly endorsed grounds based on inability to make a decision rather than making unreasonable decisions. The Senators of the College of Justice remarked that "acts or an intention to act in the way specified [imprudently] could properly be treated as evidence of lack of capacity and it is enough to say that it should not be conclusive". We consider this point to be equally relevant in relation to grounds of intervention based on mental disorder. Under the 1984 Act mental disorder is not to be taken to be present by reason only of promiscuity and other specified factors[2]. We would add acting imprudently to these.

2.14   In our discussion paper we proposed that personal guardianship[3] and financial management[4] should be considered for those who had the capacity to understand the nature and possible implications of decisions in those areas but were unable to communicate. The paradigm case is the unconscious patient. By inability to communicate we mean total inability to communicate in the circumstances. The inability should have to arise from the adult's physical or other disability and not from circumstances such as absence abroad. Some people, the deaf-blind for example, may be able to communicate only if special interpreters or techniques are used. If these methods of communication are not available when a decision has to be made and intervention cannot reasonably be postponed until they are available then the adult should be regarded, but only for this purpose and on this occasion, as being unable to communicate. We would hope that every effort would be made to provide adequate means of communication to those who need them. In order to avoid any suggestion that those unable to communicate are mentally disordered we would place such people in a separate category.

2.15   Summing up we recommend that:

2.   (1)   An intervention should be capable of being made under our recommendations if the adult is:

(a)   mentally disordered, or

**(b)   unable to communicate due to physical or other disability
and by reason of such mental disorder or inability to communicate unable to take the decision or carry out the act in question.**

(2)   Mental disorder should mean mental illness or mental handicap however caused or manifested, but a person should not be regarded as mentally disordered by reason solely of promiscuity or other immoral conduct, sexual deviancy, dependence on alcohol or drugs or acting as no prudent person would act.

Clause 67(2)

2.16   Later in this report in our section on guardianship we recommend slightly different grounds to those recommended above because of the continuing nature of the appointment[5]. However, they too are based on a threshold of mental disorder and inability to perform various functions by reason of such mental disorder.

2.17   In the remainder of this report we use the term incapable adults for those to whom our recommendations apply. In our discussion paper we used the term mentally disabled adults. We do not intend there to be any material difference between the two terms and so, in order to avoid confusion, we also use the term incapable adults when referring to the various proposals in our discussion paper. We would stress that use of the term incapable does not imply that the adult in question is completely incapacitated or cannot manage many aspects of his or her life. As already stated in paragraph 2.9 above mental incapacity has to be evaluated with reference to the task in hand. Thus incapable of making a medical treatment decision means being incapable of making such a decision by reason of mental disorder or inability to communicate.

Which body should authorise interventions?

2.18   In Scotland the vast majority of orders affecting the personal welfare or financial affairs of incapacitated adults are currently made by the courts. Guardianship applications are decided in the sheriff court[6], tutors-dative and tutors-at-law are appointed by the Court of Session, while either court may appoint curators. Some decisions, however, may be made administratively. For example, hospital managers may administer the funds of in-patients who have been certified by the medical officer in charge of treatment as incapable of managing their own property and affairs[7], and persons may be appointed by the Department of Social Security to receive and manage benefits on behalf of incapacitated claimants[8].

---

1.   Proposal 29, para 4.40.
2.   S 1(3).
3.   Proposal 5(1), para 2.62.
4.   Proposal 29, para 4.40.
5.   Recommendation 85, para 6.29.
6.   1984 Act, s 40.
7.   1984 Act, s 94.
8.   The Social Security (Claims and Payments) Regulations 1987, SI 1987/1968, reg 33.

Many other jurisdictions, such as Alberta and New Zealand, give an equally prominent role to the courts. However, others have set up special tribunals to deal with the issues arising out of mental disability. Victoria, for example, has a Guardianship and Administration Board with a legally qualified president[1]. This board is widely regarded within Australia as a system which works well and has recently been adopted in Western Australia. In England and Wales mental health review tribunals review, on application, cases of patients who have been detained or received into guardianship[2].

2.19   Before the publication of our discussion paper Alzheimer Scotland - Action on Dementia, a voluntary organisation set up to promote the interests of dementia sufferers and their carers, proposed a system of mental health hearings along the line of children's hearings to make decisions on behalf of sufferers[3]. Although the organisation's particular concern was with people with dementia, the proposed hearing system was regarded as suitable for all mentally incapable people. In outline the proposals were as follows:-

   (a) A mental health hearing would consist of three people chosen from a list of trained panel members. The members would not necessarily have any legal, medical or social work qualifications. They would be unpaid but would receive allowances for expenses. Panels would be appointed for each region or islands council area.

   (b) Each regional or islands council would appoint an official called a mental health reporter, together with appropriate staff.

   (c) Hospital staff, social workers, relatives, neighbours and others would be able to contact the reporter if they were concerned about the personal welfare or financial affairs of a mentally incapable adult. The reporter would then come under a duty to investigate and to obtain any necessary reports and assessments.

   (d) The reporter could then decide that no action was necessary, dispose of the case informally or refer it to a mental health hearing. He or she would also have power to make interim orders where immediate action was necessary.

   (e) A mental health hearing would consist of three members sitting in private together with the reporter, the allegedly mentally incapable adult and his or her representative and relatives. The hearing would have power to appoint an individual to safeguard the interests of an unrepresented incapable adult. Any assessments and reports obtained by the reporter would be available to the hearing. The proceedings would be conducted informally but the hearing could call for witnesses to attend and for documents to be produced.

   (f) The hearing would have power to make a wide variety of orders in the personal welfare and financial fields, guided by the principle of minimum intervention. For example, a hearing could order supervision by a social worker, require the incapable adult to reside in a particular home or hospital, attend a day centre, consent to treatment on behalf of the incapable adult, make orders relating to the adult's home, finances and other assets, or appoint a guardian. The hearing's decision would be notified to the Mental Welfare Commission. All orders would be reviewed periodically, or at other times on application by the reporter or the incapable adult.

   (g) The reporter or the incapable adult would have a right of appeal to the sheriff in respect of any decision of the hearing.

2.20   In our discussion paper we put forward these three options - court, tribunal, or hearing - outlined their perceived advantages and disadvantages and asked for views as to which would be the most appropriate forum[4]. We were of the view that, whatever forum was adopted, that body should have exclusive jurisdiction over the entire range of matters dealt with in this report and also in relation to applications for detention under the 1984 Act and compulsory removal from home under section 47 of the National Assistance Act 1948 as amended by the National Assistance (Amendment) Act 1951[5].

2.21   The "one door" approach we advocated in our discussion paper was welcomed on consultation. The current need for separate applications (sometimes in different courts) to deal with a mentally incapable adult's personal welfare and financial affairs was deprecated. Tribunals and hearings along the lines proposed were favoured by many respondents, particularly those in the medical and social work field, but the option of using the courts enjoyed majority support. Although, as might be expected, the legal respondents were in favour of courts, support for this option was by no means confined to this category of respondents.

2.22   Those in favour of hearings considered that they would be more user-friendly and approachable than courts. The atmosphere and lay-out of the places where hearings would be likely to be held would put participants more at ease. They also welcomed a non-adversarial approach which would allow incapable adults and their carers, family and others with

---

1. Guardianship and Administration Board Act 1986, s 5.
2. Mental Health Act 1983, ss 65-79.
3. *Dementia and the Law: The Challenge Ahead* (1988).
4. Proposal 84, para 6.09.
5. Compulsory removal is outwith the scope of this report. We intend to deal with it in a separate report to follow on our Discussion Paper No 96 *Mentally Disordered and Vulnerable Adults: Public Authority Powers* (August 1993).

an interest to play a full part in the proceedings. Another feature regarded as attractive was the lay element. The members of the hearing would be trained, but would not normally have legal, medical or social work qualifications. The Social Work Department of Strathclyde Regional Council commented that the establishment of hearings would strengthen "awareness of the problems faced by mentally disabled people and thus hold the potential to facilitate their integration in their local communities."

2.23   Many objections were raised to the introduction of hearings based on the above model. First, and most importantly, it was questioned whether a hearing consisting of lay members, albeit trained, would be regarded as able to deal with all the issues involved. Cases would often involve substantial sums of money or valuable property, disputes as to facts and difficult questions of law. Disputed facts could, as under the children's hearings, be referred to the sheriff for adjudication[1] and the same could be done with questions of law. But in our view involvement of the sheriff would undermine the attractiveness of the hearing system unless confined to a small minority of cases. Many also felt that it was by no means obvious that a system which worked well for children would work equally well for mentally incapable adults. The members in a children's hearing use their commonsense, experience and training to decide how to dispose of a child's case once the grounds of referral have been accepted or established. A mental health hearing would often be faced with more complex tasks and there would be a much wider range of "disposals". Whilst most people have some experience and understanding of children and their problems the same is not true of mental disability. Recruitment of suitable lay members for hearings was thought to pose problems. There is a danger that those putting themselves forward as potential members would have fixed views and perceptions clouded by their own limited experience. Others considered that going from the existing court system to hearings would be too great a leap in the dark. In their view it would be more sensible to try to make the courts a more attractive forum.

2.24   A study published in 1993 investigated the demand for, and feasibility of, hearings for resolving legal and ethical disputes involving people with dementia[2]. Most of the interviews and responses involved professionals (about 150 in the Renfrew and Glasgow areas) such as social workers, residential care workers, community nurses, and a smaller number of doctors, bank and building society managers and lawyers. Four group discussions were also held with people who cared for dementia sufferers. The study found that there were a substantial number of cases which involved legal or ethical conflicts. Existing arrangements for resolving these cases were generally regarded as unsatisfactory or "technically irregular". Most professionals thought that the proposed Mental Health Hearing system would help resolve such disputes. Carers had mixed feelings; fears being expressed about the intrusion of the State into private family affairs and the competence of lay members of the public to make decisions about people with dementia. It should be noted that the cases considered in the study were mainly about an adult's place of residence and general care and that the professionals involved were not presented with a choice between hearings, tribunals or courts.

2.25   Tribunals were perceived to share with hearings the advantages of user-friendliness, informality and lack of adversarial character. Tribunals would differ from hearings in being staffed by professionals with perhaps some lay people, the members being selected as having skills or experience appropriate to the case in question. Professionals, who would be paid for their attendance, would be easier to recruit and would require less in the way of further training. Supporters of tribunals mentioned the benefit of informed debate among the differently qualified members and the likelihood of a multi-disciplinary approach to the problems faced by the incapable adults. Detractors took a more jaundiced view. They thought that one professional might well dominate the others, especially any lay members, and that proceedings could be taken over by technical discussions between the tribunal members and similarly qualified expert witnesses. Another danger that exists with a tribunal staffed by professionals is the blurring of the distinction between their professional role and their decision-making or judicial role. Furthermore, it might be difficult to find suitable properly qualified workers who are not already employed by, or involved with, organisations such as local authorities, hospitals or health boards with the consequence that the tribunal might not be regarded as being independent.

2.26   As has already been mentioned, the option of using the courts as the forum for dealing with matters affecting the mentally incapable attracted most support. Courts were seen to be impartial, respected and authoritative and experienced in conducting hearings properly and producing reasoned written decisions. The other major factor that weighed with their supporters was that some of the matters would involve property and rights of considerable value, as distinct from considerations of the adult's welfare. This demanded a forum capable of adjudicating such matters properly and this in turn pointed to the courts. Finally, the courts have the benefit of continuity; they are already dealing with many of the matters covered by our recommendations so that one would not need to set up new and untried tribunals or hearings.

2.27   Having considered the responses produced by consultation we are firmly of the view that the courts are the appropriate forum and should have exclusive jurisdiction to deal with matters in this report. We are strongly in favour of the "one door" approach whereby one court should be able to deal with all the aspects of mental disability. People should

---

1. Social Work (Scotland) Act 1968, s 42.
2. *Mental Health Hearings for Elderly People with Dementia: A Study of Demand and Feasibility* (Scottish Office Home and Health Department, December 1993), C Davison, M Gilhooly, J Kileen and D Hay.

not be required to go to several different courts or tribunals in order to obtain the desired spread of remedies. As well as the delay and expense of multiple applications there is a danger of gaps between the various jurisdictions and conflicting views being taken by the various forums.

2.28   The support on consultation for tribunals or hearings owes much to the perceived disadvantages of the courts. The courts were regarded by many respondents as intimidating, legalistic, adversarial and only willing to look at the issues put in front of them, lacking in understanding of the needs of the mentally incapable, slow, expensive and associated with criminal proceedings. Some of the criticisms are, we think, unfounded in that many hearings under the 1984 Act are presently handled sensitively by sheriffs and do not give rise to any complaints. The Law Society suggested that if the courts were to be the forum then proceedings should be conducted by specially selected "designated sheriffs". These designated sheriffs should receive training about various aspects of mental incapacity and the needs of the mentally incapable and would specialise in such cases and so develop their expertise further. The concept of nominated or designated judges is not a new one. They exist in the Court of Session in relation to judicial review[1] and in England and Wales for cases under the Children Act 1989[2]. We think the Law Society's suggestion is an excellent one that would go a long way to address the concerns expressed by those opposed to the use of the courts.

2.29   The way the courts deal with the mentally incapable could also be improved by requiring all hearings to be held in chambers. The normal public court rooms should not be used as they are unsuitable for small informal hearings. Indeed, we think it should be made competent for the sheriff to conduct a hearing outwith the court if that would be more convenient for those involved[3]. There seems to us no reason why a hearing should not take place in a small private room in the hospital or other place where the adult is living. The sheriff should be directed to encourage discussion and be prepared in appropriate cases to take a pro-active role in the process, by calling for further information, reports or assessments, for example. Some formality is necessary in legal proceedings. In relation to small claims in the sheriff court, hearings are directed to be conducted so far as practicable in an informal manner[4]. We would adopt this standard for hearing applications recommended in this report.

2.30   In our discussion paper we proposed[5] that if the courts were to be considered the appropriate forum then the sheriff courts should have exclusive jurisdiction, apart from appeals. All those responding agreed with the exception of the Faculty of Advocates. The Faculty were of the opinion that the Court of Session should have concurrent jurisdiction so as to be available to decide cases where large sums of money were at stake or the issues were unusually complex. We would adhere to our original proposal with cases being heard only by specially trained "nominated" sheriffs, who would be experienced in dealing with cases involving mental disability. The Court of Session, situated as it is in Edinburgh, is not convenient for litigants in many parts of Scotland nor does it project an approachable, user-friendly, informal atmosphere. Moreover, giving the Court of Session concurrent jurisdiction would, given our proposal for specially-trained, nominated judges, involve training one or more judges who might rarely, if ever, be called upon. As an exception to this general rule we do however recommend later that applications in relation to withholding or withdrawing of medical treatment from incapable patients should be heard by the Court of Session[6].

2.31   We recommend that:

3.   **(1)   Applications and other proceedings under legislation implementing our recommendations should be dealt with in the sheriff courts. These proceedings as well as proceedings under the Mental Health (Scotland) Act 1984 should be heard, so far as possible, by nominated sheriffs who have received special training.**

(2)   Rules of Court should be made providing that the hearings should take place in chambers, or in another place considered appropriate by the sheriff, rather than in a public court room and should be conducted, so far as practicable, in an informal manner.

Clause 2(5), Schedule 4, paragraph 15(18) and Bill generally

2.32   Many of those responding to our request for views as to the appropriate forum mentioned the need for a reporter, whose functions would be similar to those of a Children's Hearings reporter, even if the chosen forum was the sheriff court. They saw the need for someone to act as a point of contact, investigate the need for action and, if action was needed, to obtain reports, evidence and other matters in preparation for any hearing and to participate in such a hearing. The

---

1.   Rules of Court of Session 1994, rule 58.5.
2.   Children (Allocation of Proceedings) Order 1991, SI 1991/1677 and Family Proceedings (Allocation to Judiciary) Directions 1993.
3.   This is competent in hearings for detention or guardianship under the 1984 Act, see Act of Sederunt (Mental Health (Scotland) Act 1984) 1986, para 2(2).
4.   Small Claim Rules 1988, rule 19.
5.   Proposal 85(1), para 6.12.
6.   See Recommendation 77, para 5.86.

reporter was also envisaged as being entitled to initiate proceedings. We have given this suggestion careful consideration but have come to the conclusion that the advantages of reporters can be achieved in other ways within the existing structure of the courts. Elsewhere in this report we recommend that the Mental Welfare Commission and local authorities should receive and investigate complaints relating to the welfare of incapable adults and should be entitled to make appropriate applications to the court and that the Public Guardian should have similar functions in relation to financial concerns of adults[1]. Furthermore, the sheriff dealing with a case involving an incapable adult should be empowered by rules of court to appoint a safeguarder if the adult is otherwise unrepresented[2]. The safeguarder's duties would include investigating matters and obtaining appropriate reports and evidence. The sheriff should also have a direct power to order such reports and assessments as seem necessary to a proper disposal of the case[3]. Finally, the administrative functions of a reporter could be performed by sheriff clerks and their staff.

Jurisdiction of courts

2.33   In our discussion paper we proposed[4] that the Scottish courts should have jurisdiction to appoint a personal guardian or make other orders relating to a mentally incapable adult who is either resident or domiciled in Scotland, and to make equivalent financial or property orders on the grounds of the adult's domicile or ownership of property in Scotland. The above criteria were also put forward for the selection of the appropriate sheriff court.

2.34   Most of those commenting on our proposals agreed. The Law Society and Enable made the useful suggestion that the adult's residence in Scotland should also ground financial or property orders since there can be difficulties in establishing the domicile of choice of incapable adults who have moved away from their families. On reconsideration we are not now in favour of using domicile as a ground of jurisdiction. In addition to the difficulties mentioned above, the modern approach, particularly in international conventions, is to base jurisdiction on habitual residence. Situations will arise, however, where action will be urgently necessary for those who are in Scotland but not habitually resident there or in any sheriffdom. We think that the courts should have an emergency jurisdiction based on presence similar to that for children under section 12 of the Family Law Act 1986. We have given further thought to jurisdiction on the ground of ownership of property situated in Scotland. We now consider that ownership of Scottish property should give jurisdiction only in relation to that property. For example, ownership of a flat in Dundee by an incapable adult habitually resident in France should give the sheriff court in Dundee jurisdiction to make orders or to appoint a guardian with powers in relation to that flat, but no powers in relation to medical treatment or personal welfare or wider financial affairs. Two commentators pointed out that the Civil Jurisdiction and Judgments Act 1982 contained provisions that possibly determined jurisdiction in relation to some areas of financial management. We think it would be clearer if jurisdiction for all applications and proceedings under our recommendations were based expressly on the grounds that we now recommend. We recommend that:

4. **A sheriff court should have jurisdiction to deal with any application under our recommendations if:**

    (a) **the incapable adult in question is then habitually resident in the sheriffdom, or**

    (b) **the application relates to property belonging to the adult which is situated in the sheriffdom.**

    In addition a sheriff should have jurisdiction to make an order which is immediately necessary for the protection of the adult if the adult is present within the sheriffdom at the date of application.

    Clause 2(2), (3)

2.35   After a guardianship order has been made by the sheriff court of the incapable adult's then habitual residence the adult may become habitually resident outwith Scotland. In most cases it would be more appropriate for the courts of the adult's new residence to deal with further guardianship matters. Situations may arise however where the courts of the new habitual residence have no jurisdiction or where jurisdiction exists but there is no power to make orders relating to existing Scottish guardianship orders. Even if the foreign court has the jurisdiction and the power it may be very inconvenient for the applicant. For example, an adult who was habitually resident in Scotland may go to live in New Zealand. The Public Guardian as a result of investigating a complaint may consider that the existing Scottish guardian should be replaced or the guardianship order recalled. The New Zealand court would probably have no powers to make any such orders and even if it did it would be unreasonable to expect the Public Guardian to apply to that court rather than the original Scottish court. The same problem may occur when adults change their habitual residence within Scotland. Rule 26.1 of the Sheriff Court Ordinary Cause Rules 1993 empowers the sheriff to transfer a case to another sheriff court. Cases on an earlier version of this rule[5] establish that where the court to which it is proposed to transfer the case has no jurisdiction, weighty and compelling reasons for transfer are required[6]. We consider that this test is too stringent for

---

1. Recommendation 21, para 3.36 and Recommendation 110, para 6.129.
2. Recommendation 6, para 2.36.
3. Para 6.36 and Clause 3(2)(c).
4. Proposal 86, para 6.17.
5. Sheriff Courts (Scotland) Act 1907, First Schedule, Rule 20.
6. *Walden v Campbell* 1940 SLT (Sh Ct) 39: *Chiesa v Greenshield* 1958 SLT (Sh Ct) 58.

applications which relate to existing guardianship orders of the other court and that a test based on reasonableness would be better. The same issues arise in relation to intervention orders but to a lesser extent due to their more limited nature. We recommend that:

5. The sheriff court which made a guardianship order or an intervention order should have jurisdiction to deal with an application relating to that order if no other court (Scottish or non-Scottish) has jurisdiction to deal with such an application or if it is unreasonable to expect the applicant to make the application to another court with jurisdiction.

Clause 2(4)

Safeguarders for incapable adults

2.36 Many incapable adults will not be capable of representing themselves in court in connection with applications made by others regarding their welfare or finances. To overcome this lack of capacity we proposed that the court hearing an application should be required to appoint a safeguarder to the adult in question unless satisfied that his or her interests were already adequately safeguarded[1]. While most respondents agreed, some thought that the adult should be entitled to representation by a curator *ad litem*, not merely a safeguarder of their interests. We think that there should be flexibility. Sometimes the adult might need to be represented. At other times an independent look at the papers together with making some further enquiries might be sufficient. A suitable model would appear to be safeguarders appointed to children subject to proceedings relating to the assumption of parental rights by local authorities[2]. Their powers and duties are set out in the Act of Sederunt (Social Work (Scotland) Act 1968) (Safeguarders) 1985[3]. The safeguarder is entitled to see the pleadings and productions, make appropriate enquiries, become a party to the proceedings or lodge a report setting out his or her conclusions as to the interests of the child. A safeguarder who becomes a party to the proceedings has all the powers and duties of a curator *ad litem* to the child, and the safeguarder may appear personally or be represented by an advocate or solicitor. We recommend that:

6. The sheriff should consider whether to appoint a safeguarder to an incapable adult in respect of whom an application has been made. The safeguarder should have similar powers and duties to one appointed under section 18A of the Social Work (Scotland) Act 1968 (safeguarders to children involved in proceedings relating to the assumption of parental rights by local authorities).

Clause 3(4), (5)

Title to apply to the courts

2.37 Who should be entitled to make an application to the court under our recommendations in relation to an incapable adult? The list of those entitled to apply under the existing law for the appointment of a curator bonis is very wide and not confined to those with a pecuniary interest. Most petitioners are the adult's relatives but petitions have been brought by the adult's solicitor[4], banker[5], managers of the hospital in which the adult is a resident patient or a person with whom the adult was staying while in Scotland[6]. The adult himself or herself may petition although this is very unusual[7]. The adult certainly has a title to apply for recall of the curatory. The local authority must, and the Mental Welfare Commission may, petition if no one else is doing so and a curator seems necessary[8]. As far as guardianship under the 1984 Act is concerned only a mental health officer or the adult's nearest relative may submit an application to the sheriff for approval[9]. In the eighteenth and nineteenth centuries title to apply for the appointment of the nearest male relative as tutor-at-law to a mentally disabled adult under the brieve and cognition procedure was limited to relatives[10]. This may still be the position under the present petition procedure. It seems that anyone with an interest could apply for a tutor-dative to be appointed[11].

2.38 In our discussion paper we proposed that anyone with an interest should be entitled to apply for the appointment of a personal guardian[12] or financial manager, or for a property order[13]. We considered that interest should be left to be determined by the court, but should not be confined to pecuniary interest. We specifically mentioned the local authority and the Mental Welfare Commission as qualified applicants. All but one of those responding agreed. The Association of

---

1. Proposal 87(2), para 6.22.
2. Social Work (Scotland) Act 1968, s 18A.
3. SI 1985/780.
4. *Mason* (1852) 14D 761.
5. *Johnstone v Barbé* 1928 SN 86.
6. *Bonar* (1851) 14 D 10.
7. *AB* (1908) 16 SLT 557.
8. 1984 Act, ss 92 and 93.
9. 1984 Act, s 38.
10. Fraser, *Parent and Child*, p 656.
11. Fraser, p 668. A case of friends applying is mentioned on p 669.
12. Proposal 7, para 2.71.
13. Proposal 30, para 4.41.

Directors of Social Work, however, thought that such a wide title could lead to numerous and repeated applications. In their view applications should be made either by the local authority or the nearest relative. We reject such a narrow approach. Some incapable adults need to be protected from their nearest relatives who are exploiting or abusing them. It is not sufficient to rely on local authorities to take protective action. Local authorities are extremely reluctant to apply for a curator to be appointed to adults with modest estates, even though they have a statutory duty to apply, because the estate cannot bear the commission allowed so that the authority would have to act without recovering the full cost of the curatory. Furthermore, we do not accept that casting the net of title to apply wide would lead to numerous and repeated applications. The experience with curators and tutors-dative suggests that once the court has determined an application other applications in respect of the same adult are most unlikely. We prefer the wider title to apply approach taken in relation to curators and tutors-dative than the narrower approach taken by the 1984 Act for mental health guardianship. We also proposed that any person with an interest in the granter's welfare or estate should be entitled to apply to the court for an order relating to a continuing attorney's exercise of his or her functions[1]. Those responding generally approved, but the Sheriffs' Association thought protection was needed against the making of frivolous or maliciously repeated applications. We acknowledge the possibility of such applications, but think that the courts' discretion to award expenses against unsuccessful applicants should be a sufficient deterrent.

2.39   The Law Reform (Parent and Child) (Scotland) Act 1986 entitles "any person claiming interest" to apply to the court for parental rights in respect of a child[2]. In a recent case *D v Grampian Regional Council* 1994 SLT 1038[3] the Inner House considered that "claiming interest" was different from "having interest". The latter suggested that an applicant had to demonstrate his or her interested status before the court could consider the application. Claiming interest seems to us to be the correct approach for applications that could result in benefit to incapable adults. Any relative, friend, professional involved, carer, manager of the establishment in which the adult lives, an organisation involved with incapable adults, and public bodies such as the local authority, Mental Welfare Commission and Public Guardian should be entitled to apply to the courts. The latter three bodies play an important part in our recommended supervisory structure and should have a clear title to apply. We imagine that there will be few applications for the appointment of a guardian to an incapable adult by the adult himself or herself, but applications by an adult for variation or recall of his or her own guardianship could be more numerous. To put the adult's position beyond question we think that an express title to apply should be granted. We recommend later that in connection with certain applications title to apply should be limited. For example, an additional guardian may be appointed to act jointly with the existing guardian. In this situation the only applicant would be the proposed additional guardian.[4] We therefore recommend that:

7. **The Public Guardian, Mental Welfare Commission, local authority and any individual (including the adult himself or herself) or organisation claiming an interest in the welfare or financial affairs of an incapable adult should be entitled to apply to the court under our recommendations, except in relation to matters where a more restricted title is recommended.**

Clause 67(1) and Clauses generally

The supervisory framework

2.40   We recommend in later Parts of this report various ways in which the personal welfare or property and financial affairs of incapable adults can be dealt with by others for the benefit of the adults concerned. Here we look at the overall supervisory structure; the organisations involved and their powers and duties, which are the subject of specific recommendations throughout the report. The courts have a central role in appointing guardians and others, giving directions to the various people with functions under our recommendations and recalling or varying the terms of appointment. However, there is also a need for monitoring and supervision either generally or for specific cases only and also for investigating complaints and taking necessary action. The courts cannot undertake such tasks because they need to remain impartial should matters lead to legal proceedings. Moreover, they do not have the staff to undertake these additional functions, which nevertheless ought to be carried out by some public bodies or officials. Our general approach is to confer additional functions on existing public bodies with expertise in this area. The Accountant of Court already supervises curators bonis, the Mental Welfare Commission has general protective functions in relation to the mentally disordered and specific functions as regards those subject to mental health guardianship under the 1984 Act and the local authority (or their social work staff) act as mental health guardians and monitor non-local authority guardians.

2.41   **The Public Guardian**. Under our recommendations the Accountant of Court's existing role would be considerably expanded. A new post of Public Guardian would be created which would be held by the Accountant of Court. In addition to being guardian when appointed to act as such by the court[5], the Public Guardian would have the following general functions under our recommendations:

---

1. Proposals 68-70.
2   S 3(1). The Children (Scotland) Act 1995, s 11(3) uses the phrase "claiming an interest".
3. Reversed in the House of Lords on different grounds 1995 SLT 519.
4. Clause 47(1)(b).
5. Recommendation 94(2), para 6.60.

(a) registering all continuing and welfare attorneys[1], individuals authorised to withdraw from an incapable adult's bank or building society accounts[2], intervention orders[3] and guardianship orders[4]. Any subsequent court orders and events brought to the Public Guardian's attention affecting registered entries would also be noted. The Public Guardian would not supervise appointees in connection with their personal welfare powers, but would pass on details of such appointees to the Mental Welfare Commission and local authority who are more directly concerned.

(b) supervising and monitoring the performance of guardians in relation to their financial powers in much the same way as the Accountant of Court presently supervises curators bonis and other judicial factors[5]. The Public Guardian would have an increased role since we recommend that many functions in connection with the administration of guardianship estates should be exercised by the Public Guardian rather than the courts[6]. Although continuing attorneys would not normally be subject to the same supervisory regime as guardians, the court could, on application, order this where an attorney's actings give rise to concern[7].

(c) investigating complaints relating to the exercise of financial functions by guardians, continuing attorneys, withdrawers, interveners or managers of establishments managing residents' finances. The Public Guardian would also be entitled to look into circumstances which give rise to concern and make spot checks even in the absence of any complaints. As a result of investigations or otherwise the Public Guardian should be entitled to apply to the court for appropriate orders for the protection of incapable adults. In some cases the Public Guardian may be able to take direct action, for example, by suspending or terminating the authority of a withdrawer or giving directions to a guardian.

2.42 The Public Guardian may need to initiate legal proceedings in order to protect an incapable adult's property. For example, as a result of a complaint and investigation the Public Guardian may consider that an unsuitable continuing attorney ought to be superseded and may make an application to the sheriff for the appointment of a guardian. The Public Guardian may also wish to become involved in existing proceedings to argue for the adoption of a particular course of action or to put forward his or her views based on official experience. Where the Public Guardian initiates legal proceedings to protect an incapable adult, the Public Guardian should generally be entitled to expenses if successful. Such expenses should be awardable out of the adult's estate or against any person whose conduct necessitated the application. The court should also have a discretion to award expenses to the Public Guardian when intervening. We recommend that:

8. The court should have a discretionary power to award expenses to the Public Guardian if he or she has initiated or entered proceedings in order to protect an incapable adult's property or to represent the public interest.

Clause 6

2.43 **The Mental Welfare Commission**. The Mental Welfare Commission has general protective functions towards the mentally disordered under the 1984 Act. The functions we recommend in this report are to be seen as additional to those existing statutory functions. Our recommendations would make the Mental Welfare Commission, along with the local authority, the main supervisory and monitoring organisation where the personal welfare of incapable adults was concerned. The Public Guardian would have the main role in financial matters. The Mental Welfare Commission would:

(a) monitor guardians in the exercise of their personal welfare powers in much the same way as it presently monitors guardians appointed under the 1984 Act[8].

(b) investigate complaints relating to the exercise of personal welfare functions by guardians, welfare attorneys[9] and others. The Mental Welfare Commission would also be able to investigate suspicious circumstances, even in the absence of complaints. As a result of such investigations or otherwise the Mental Welfare Commission would be entitled to initiate legal proceedings or take other action in order to protect the welfare of the adults concerned[10].

The Mental Welfare Commission would also have power to recall personal welfare powers previously conferred on a guardian by the court where such powers were no longer appropriate[11].

2.44 **The local authority**. The local authority would have a major role in looking after the personal welfare of incapable

---

1. Recommendation 21, para 3.36.
2. Recommendation 37, para 4.12.
3. Recommendation 84, para 6.23.
4. Recommendation 91, para 6.40.
5. Recommendations in Part 6 generally.
6. For example, approving a management plan and authorising the making of gifts by the guardian.
7. Recommendations 27 and 28, paras 3.65 and 3.66.
8. Recommendation 106, para 6.118.
9. Recommendation 21(6), para 3.36.
10. Recommendation 111, para 6.129.
11. Recommendation 136, para 6.196.

adults under our recommendations. It would have a duty to apply for an intervention or guardianship order if such an order appeared to be necessary and no other suitable person was applying[1]. The local authority's chief social work officer could be appointed guardian with welfare powers in appropriate cases[2] and the local authority via its mental health officers would be involved in investigating and supplying reports in connection with applications for intervention or guardianship orders[3]. As well as these specific functions the local authority would also have general supervisory functions-

(a) supervising guardians in the exercise of their personal welfare functions in much the same way as it presently supervises non-local authority mental health guardians under the 1984 Act[4]. It would also supervise welfare attorneys and those acting under intervention orders, but only where the court had ordered such supervision[5]. The local authority would be able to give directions to guardians in the exercise of their personal welfare functions, which the guardian would be bound to comply with[6].

(b) investigating complaints relating to guardians, welfare attorneys and others in the exercise of their personal welfare functions. The local authority would also be able to investigate suspicious circumstances even in the absence of complaints. As a result of such investigations or otherwise the local authority would be entitled to initiate legal proceedings in order to protect the welfare of the adults concerned[7].

The local authority, like the Mental Welfare Commission, would also have power to recall the personal welfare powers previously conferred on a guardian by the court where such powers were no longer appropriate[8].

2.45 **Cooperation and provision of information**. Many complaints and investigations will involve matters in the personal welfare field and in the financial field. Close co-operation between the various supervisory bodies (the Public Guardian, Mental Welfare Commission and local authority) and a free exchange of information will be required to carry out "a mixed" investigation properly. For example, a complaint may be made to the Mental Welfare Commission about the actings of a guardian. If initial investigations by the Commission lead to suspicion of financial irregularities it should alert the Public Guardian to these and the two bodies could then come to a mutually acceptable arrangement for further investigations on the financial side. If the irregularities appeared to be minor it might be more sensible for the Commission to include these in its investigation, but serious matters would best be handed over to the Public Guardian. We recommend that:

9. The Public Guardian, the Mental Welfare Commission and the local authority should be under a duty to collaborate and liaise with each other in relation to investigations.

Clause 9(2)

2.46 The Public Guardian, the Mental Welfare Commission and the local authority should also have a role in providing information and advice to guardians, attorneys and others exercising personal welfare or financial functions in relation to incapable adults. One method of doing this would be by means of publications. The Accountant of Court presently produces a very helpful booklet for families where a relation is under curatory[9] and the Mental Welfare Commission issues a series of leaflets about guardianship under the 1984 Act. The Accountant also produces more technical Notes for the Guidance of Judicial Factors[10]. We think there will be a need for more material to help those involved with the changes in the law and practice, by way of publications, guidance notes or otherwise. Information and advice should also be capable of being given in specific cases. For example, a guardian or attorney should be able to contact the Public Guardian, the Mental Welfare Commission or local authority for information and advice according to whether financial or welfare advice was being sought. We recommend that:

10. The Public Guardian should be required to provide advice and information, on request, to those exercising functions under our recommendations relating to incapable adults' property and financial affairs. The Mental Welfare Commission and the local authority should be under a similar obligation in relation to personal welfare functions.

Clauses 4(2)(g), 7(1)(e) and 8(1)(e)

General principles governing interventions

2.47 In our discussion paper when considering the introduction of new style personal guardians we set out the main

---

1. Recommendation 86(2), para 6.33.
2. Recommendation 94, para 6.60.
3. Recommendation 87, para 6.36.
4. Recommendation 106, para 6.118.
5. Recommendation 29, para 3.67.
6. Recommendation 107, para 6.119.
7. Recommendation 111, para 6.129.
8. Recommendation 136, para 6.196.
9. *Information for Families of Persons Subject to Curatory*, (1989).
10. Parliament House Book, M 301.

principles underlying similar types of guardianship in other jurisdictions[1] and adopted them for our proposed scheme. The principles were:

(a) restricting a guardian's powers in order to make the minimum necessary intervention;

(b) the guardian being under a statutory duty to encourage the incapable adult to do as much as possible for himself or herself;

(c) the guardian being under a statutory duty to consult and give effect to the wishes of the adult and his or her family so far as possible;

(d) mandatory periodic review of the need for a guardian's appointment to continue.

Very similar principles were set out for our proposed new scheme of financial management[2].

2.48   These principles were also contained or alluded to in many of the subsequent proposals dealing with the details of the proposed new schemes of personal guardianship and financial management. In relation to personal guardians we proposed that:

(a) the court considering an application for a personal welfare order or the appointment of a personal guardian should have to be satisfied that it would result in a substantial benefit to, or necessary protection of, the incapable adult (Proposal 5(1)(b));

(b) in considering whom to appoint as guardian the court should take the wishes of the incapable adult into account in so far as it was reasonable and practicable to do so (Proposal 6(a));

(c) the court should be under a duty to choose the least restrictive remedy consistent with safeguarding the rights of the incapable adult and accordingly should not appoint a guardian unless one or more personal orders were insufficient to meet the needs of the adult, and when appointing a guardian should specify the minimum number of powers necessary (Proposal 8(4));

(d) personal guardians should exercise their powers in the adult's best interests. They should consult as far as practicable the adult, family and carers and any financial appointee and have regard to views expressed by the adult while capable (Proposal 11).

Similar proposals were made in relation to the court's powers when considering applications for property orders or the appointment of a financial manager and the powers of financial managers[3].

2.49   In general these proposals and the principles they embodied were agreed by those who responded. Many expressly mentioned in response to a particular proposal which dealt with one of the principles that some or all of the other principles should apply as well. Thus, for example, in connection with our proposal that the court in deciding whether to make a property order or appoint a guardian should be required to make the least restrictive order, the Scottish Association for Mental Health commented that our other principles should also apply. The favourable responses have led us to formulate a set of general principles that should apply throughout the legislation implementing our recommendations.

2.50   Our general principles do not rely on the concept of best interests of the incapable adult. Proposals 11 and 38 suggested that the personal guardian and financial manager respectively should act in the best interests of the adult, these being established after consultation with the adult, family and others interested in the adult's welfare or finances and any personal guardian or financial manager. Although the majority of those responding agreed, others were more critical. The proprietors of a Lothian home for mentally disabled people thought that best interests was too paternalistic, and many others considered that the wishes and feelings of the incapable adult should be given greater weight. The Scottish Association for Mental Health in response to Proposal 11 and the Law Society and Enable in response to Proposal 38 took the view that guidelines were required in order to establish what the best interests of the incapable adults were. The Scottish Association for Mental Health in response to Proposal 38 commented that a best interests test was not always acceptable and a financial manager should override the express wishes of the adult only in exceptional circumstances and where there is no reasonable alternative. Best interests was also rejected in the context of medical treatment. The majority of those responding to Proposal 24 which asked for views as to the criteria the court should adopt in deciding disputes about medical treatment preferred more detailed guidelines instead. We consider that "best interests" by itself is too vague and would require to be supplemented by further factors which have to be taken into account. We also consider that "best interests" does not give due weight to the views of the adult, particularly to wishes and feeling which he or she had expressed while capable of doing so. The concept of best interests was developed in the context of child law where a

---

1.   Para 2.50.
2.   Para 4.30.
3.   Proposals 29(b), 31(2), 34 and 38 respectively.

child's level of understanding may not be high and will usually have been lower in the past. Incapable adults such as those who are mentally ill, head injured or suffering from dementia at the time when a decision has to be made in connection with them, will have possessed full mental powers before their present incapacity. We think it is wrong to equate such adults with children and for that reason would avoid extending child law concepts to them. Accordingly, the general principles we set out below are framed without express reference to best interests.

2.51   **Benefit to adult**. Our first general principle is based on benefit to the incapable adult. The person intervening should be satisfied that the intervention will benefit the adult and that the benefit cannot reasonably be obtained without the intervention. By intervention we mean any decision by a court, a guardian or any other person on whom functions are conferred under our recommendations which directly affects the welfare or affairs of the incapable adult. The category of "any other person" would include the Public Guardian and managers of establishments who are looking after the finances of their incapacitated patients or residents. In our discussion paper we proposed that the courts should make personal or property orders or appoint a personal guardian or financial manager only if that would result "in a substantial benefit" to the adult[1]. Some commentators thought that the word "substantial" should be omitted, because it raised the question as to what constituted a substantial benefit. We agree. The intervener should have to weigh the intervention against the benefit; the more serious the intervention the greater the benefit that should have to result from it. A requirement of substantial benefit distorts this exercise of discretion and could well result in adults being denied assistance which would produce a modest, but nevertheless worthwhile, benefit to them.

2.52   As well as an intervener being satisfied that the intervention proposed will produce a benefit to the incapable adult he or she should also be satisfied that such benefit cannot be reasonably achieved in another, less intrusive, way. Thus, an adult should not be removed from home (by means of an intervention order or guardianship) if extra help could be made available so as to enable the adult to carry on at home. Again, the appointment of a guardian to manage financial affairs could perhaps be avoided if informal advice and assistance were available or the affairs were reorganised so as to make them easier for the adult to handle. Consideration of other reasonable ways of achieving the benefit does not mean that they have to be tried first and found wanting. That could give rise to unacceptable delay. If a court was involved in considering whether to intervene it should be up to the applicant to satisfy the court that other methods are either impracticable or unlikely to produce the same benefit as the proposed intervention.

2.53   The Law Society and Alzheimer Scotland - Action for Dementia in response to our proposal that a personal guardian should not be appointed if one or more personal orders would suffice and that any guardian should be appointed with the minimum powers necessary[2] were concerned lest the principle of minimum necessary intervention denied guardianship to those who could benefit from it. An incapable adult's welfare and affairs might be being looked after informally by his or her family or others, but the informal controls might be so extensive that they should be placed on a formal footing. Formal guardianship involves independent monitoring of the guardian's actings and also incorporates a series of principles and guidelines which guardians have to have regard to. Informal management lacks these elements. We accept this point but take the view that a court should take it into account in assessing the benefits that will accrue to the incapable adult by reason of the proposed intervention.

2.54   We recommend that:

11.   **Any intervention in the welfare or financial affairs of an incapable adult under or in pursuance of the proposed new legislation should be required to produce a benefit for that adult. Any person proposing to intervene should have to be satisfied that the intended benefit cannot be reasonably achieved otherwise than by the intervention.**

Clause 1(2)

2.55   **Least restrictive intervention**. The second of our general principles is that any intervention must be that which is least restrictive of the adult's freedom having regard to the need to achieve the purpose of that intervention. An alternative formula often used is "minimum necessary intervention". We prefer least restriction in that it focuses on the practical results of an intervention. This was generally approved by those who responded to our various proposals, but concern was expressed as to how it would work in practice. If a property order was granted or a guardian with limited financial powers was appointed and then the mentally disordered adult's capacity took a turn for the worse then a fresh application to the court with its attendant worry and expense might be needed. We think that in these circumstances an additional application to the court would be inevitable, although less might be required in the way of procedure for extending the powers of an existing guardian than for appointing a guardian for the first time. We would not be in favour of some administrative body (such as the Public Guardian or the Mental Welfare Commission) being entitled to increase the powers that have been granted to a guardian by the court. Considerations of civil liberties and the European Convention on Human

---

1. Proposals 5 and 29, paras 2.62 and 4.40 respectively.
2. Proposal 8(4), para 2.80.

Rights require that any restriction of rights be done by an independent and impartial tribunal established by law after a fair and public hearing[1]. However, where the incapable adult is known to have variable capacity or rapidly deteriorating capacity the court would be entitled to take this into account and appoint a guardian with the powers he or she is likely to need then and in the reasonably foreseeable future. The fact that the principle of least restriction also applies to the guardian in exercising the powers conferred should prevent him or her from exercising powers that were not in fact needed at the time in question.

2.56   The Sheriffs' Association pointed out that a court can proceed only on information presented to it and suggested that the applicant should be under a duty to satisfy the court that the remedy sought was the least restrictive. We are grateful for this observation and have altered the wording of our principle accordingly. In the case of the intervention taking the form of a decision by the guardian or some other person on whom functions have been conferred, the decision-maker would be required to satisfy himself or herself that the proposed course of action was the least restrictive.

2.57   The former Accountant of Court in his general comments on the discussion paper thought that the principles of least restrictive order and encouraging the incapable adult to use existing skills and develop new skills might not be consistent with the adult's need for protection. We would meet this point by making it clear that the purpose of the intervention has to be considered in deciding what the least restrictive remedy is. For example, if a guardian is appointed to manage the incapable adult's bank account because the adult is frittering money away on unnecessary items the principles of least restrictive intervention and use and development of skills point towards the guardian allowing the adult to operate the account under supervision. But the need for protection, which is the purpose of the appointment, requires the guardian to sign (or at least countersign) every cheque.

2.58   We recommend that:

> **12. Any proposed intervention in the welfare or finances of an incapable adult under or in pursuance of the proposed new legislation should be that which is least restrictive of the adult's freedom having regard to the purpose of the intervention.**
>
> Clause 1(3)

2.59   **Encouraging use and development of skills**. Our third general principle is that those with authority in terms of our recommendations over an incapable adult should encourage the adult to use his or her existing skills and develop new skills. It would be all too easy for a guardian appointed to manage the affairs of an adult simply to take over. But someone like a young mentally handicapped person will never develop unless encouraged to deal with his or her own affairs and run his or her own life as far as possible. Even with dementia sufferers the rate of decline may be lessened by encouraging use of their existing faculties. This principle is also founded on respect for the autonomy of the individual. Proposal 39 in our discussion paper embodied the principle by entitling a financial manager to allow the incapable adult to deal with any part of the property under management. The proposal was agreed by all those who commented although some raised queries about protection of third parties dealing with the adult[2]. Two respondents considered that merely entitling the guardian did not go far enough. In their view guardians should be under an explicit statutory duty to encourage incapable adults to exercise their existing skills and develop capacity where there is scope for so doing. We think that expressing the principle as a statutory requirement would enhance its effectiveness. We consider that the requirement should exist not only in relation to financial guardians but to guardians in general, continuing and welfare attorneys and the managers of establishments, all of whom exercise authority over the financial or personal affairs of incapable adults. The requirement cannot be made absolute. It would be unreasonable to require guardians to encourage adults with rapidly deteriorating capacity to acquire new skills, and impracticable for comatose patients and others with virtually no capacity to exercise existing skills. Furthermore, some adults grant continuing powers of attorney in order to be relieved of the burden of managing their affairs. They would not welcome being encouraged to exercise their existing skills, let alone to acquire new skills. We recommend that:

> **13. Any guardian, continuing or welfare attorney or the managers of an establishment managing an adult's finances under our recommendations should be required to encourage the adult to use existing financial and welfare skills and acquire new skills, but only in so far as it is reasonable and practicable to do so.**
>
> Clause 1(5)

2.60   **Consultation and consideration of views**. Our fourth and final general principle is consultation with those who have an interest in the proposed intervention or its effects. The Scottish Association for Mental Health in response to Proposal 38 in our discussion paper[3] (consultation by financial manager when exercising powers) commented that "Whilst

---

1. Article 6 of the Convention.
2. See para 6.153 for further details of protection of third parties.
3. Para 4.76.

the duty to consult is very important, we would not wish to see the duty so onerous as to be unworkable". We agree with this sentiment and put forward a scheme which we hope will prove workable. We would stress that the principle of consultation applies only to those exercising authority or making decisions under our recommendations. It is not intended that every person dealing with an incapable adult should be required to consult before taking any step. Another important limitation is that the degree of consultation should be appropriate to the scale of the proposed intervention. Consulting incapable adults, their nearest relatives, primary carers and others would be unduly burdensome if it had to be done for every minor matter, such as a guardian allowing an adult to buy small items or go out with some friends.

2.61   We proposed in our discussion paper[1] that a personal guardian before exercising a power conferred should be under a duty to consult, so far as it was practicable to do so, the incapable adult, his or her family and carers and any person appointed to look after the adult's financial affairs and to have regard to the views expressed by the adult when mentally capable. A very similar proposal was made in relation to the exercise of powers by a financial manager[2]. There was strong support for consulting the adult and many considered that the adult's views should always be taken into account although the guardian should also take the disability into account. Enable commented that there may be cases where the adult should not be consulted as that might produce adverse consequences for his or her health. We agree and consider that the duty to consult the adult should not be an absolute one. The intervener should be required to take account of the adult's views so far as they can be ascertained and would be entitled to take into account the difficulties and dangers of trying to ascertain them. For example, the adult may be so disabled as to make consultation pointless. The intervener should still be required to have regard to any known present and past feelings and wishes of the adult because these can often be obtained from others closely associated with the adult or from written material.

2.62   One respondent suggested that the views of an incapable adult which he or she expressed while mentally capable should be followed unless they could be presumed to be no longer applicable. We consider that such views or even instructions should indeed be given great weight but should not be treated as conclusive. As we point out elsewhere in this report in relation to advance refusal of medical treatment[3], the views may be outdated, have been made without adequate information or as a result of pressure or the situation may have changed radically since they were expressed. The same is equally true of instructions in documents conferring a continuing power of attorney. In our view the best approach is to emphasise the importance of the adult's wishes but give the intervener a discretion not to follow them in appropriate cases. We suggested in our discussion paper that a personal guardian should have regard among other things to any wishes expressed by the adult "while mentally capable".[4] We now consider that such a restriction is both unwarranted and unworkable. Even if the adult is or was incapable he or she may express views or react in some way to the proposed intervention and that that should be taken into account. Furthermore, it would be very difficult for an intervener to evaluate the past mental capacity of the adult at a time when the views were expressed.

2.63   The requirement to consult the adult, in so far as it is reasonable and practicable to do so, and to take account of the views expressed should not be confined to a proposed exercise of powers by guardians or determination of applications by courts. We regard this as a principle that should apply throughout this report and to all those having to make a decision under or in pursuance of the proposed new legislation; the Public Guardian, the managers of establishments, doctors in respect of medical treatment as well as guardians and courts. In our discussion paper we proposed[5] that the court should be required to appoint a safeguarder to an adult who was not otherwise adequately represented. Part of the safeguarder's role would be to ascertain the views of the adult and ensure that they were put before the court. Our proposal was supported by all those who commented. The Senators of the College of Justice were of the opinion in connection with the adult's wishes as to a proposed guardian[6] that it would be preferable for the views of the adult to be put before the court via a third party rather than by personal interview. We appreciate this concern but consider that incapable adults should be encouraged to participate in court proceedings affecting them unless they clearly cannot understand the proceedings or are disruptive. To this end we have recommended that the proceedings should be conducted informally in a private room rather than in the normal public court room[7]. Rules of court will require to be made providing for the intimation of all applications to the adult concerned and perhaps any known representative as well.

2.64   We turn now to deal with the role of guardians, continuing attorneys, relatives, carers and others in the decision-making process. Anyone who thinks they have relevant views or information should be entitled to communicate them to the decision-making power or authority and the decision-maker should then take them into account. The more difficult issue is to what extent (if any) the decision-maker should be under a duty to adopt a pro-active role and seek out the views of persons other than the mentally disabled adult concerned? We stress that these others would not simply be

---

1. Proposal 11, para 2.87.
2. Proposal 38, para 4.76.
3. Para 5.52.
4. Proposal 11, para 2.87.
5. Proposal 87(2), para 6.22.
6. Proposal 6(a), para 2.69.
7. Recommendation 3, para 2.31.

consulted in order that they might pass on any information about the adult and his or her views and wishes, although they would naturally be entitled to do so. We see them as having an independent contribution to the decision-making process. Decisions will usually affect those looking after the adult and his or her close family and it seems to us that their legitimate concerns should be taken into account.

2.65   As far as consultation by other decision-makers is concerned, guardians appointed by the court and continuing attorneys appointed by the adult are in a special category. We think they should always be entitled to be consulted by the decision-maker on matters lying within the scope of their powers since they are to be regarded as legal representatives - standing in the adult's own shoes. We also think that the nearest relative and primary carer of the adult should be entitled to be consulted, but that there should be no obligation on the part of the decision-maker to seek out the views of others who might have an interest in the adult's welfare. This would often be onerous or impracticable, and could place the adult's welfare at risk. However, anyone with an interest who knew of a proposed intervention should be able to make his or her own views known to the intervener, and where they were made known they should be taken into account. In the following paragraphs we discuss further the role of relatives and carers.

2.66   Numerous proposals in our discussion paper mentioned the role of the incapable adult's family, nearest relatives or carers. Proposal 11 suggested that a personal guardian should consult the adult's family and carers. A similar proposal was made in relation to financial managers[1]. These proposals were generally supported but it was pointed out that the interests of adults and their families do not always coincide. For example, the adult might wish to be placed in a well-appointed but expensive home while the family, perhaps with their eye on their eventual succession prospects, might incline to a cheaper alternative. The Scottish Association for Mental Health commented that in some cases the adult would not wish his or her family to be consulted. We deal with this point later[2]. A strong expression of views from the adult against consulting the family might make it unreasonable for them to be consulted.

2.67   The Elms, a registered care home for the mentally handicapped, welcomed our inclusion of carers. It pointed out that welfare decisions may have a devastating effect on primary carers, whilst having minimal effect on physically distant nearest relatives. In its view primary carers should be on a par for consultation purposes with the nearest relative. We agree and have framed our recommendations in terms of equality. Where the adult is living at home the primary carer and the nearest relative may well be the same person.

2.68   "Family" is too imprecise a term for the purposes of consultation. In connection with medical treatment and research we used the concept of nearest relative[3]. Rather than the extended list in the 1984 Act we proposed a shorter list comprising spouse, adult children, parents and siblings. The Law Society, together with some other respondents, thought that the 1984 Act's list of relatives should be used throughout so as to achieve consistency throughout the mental health field. In its view the 1984 Act's list of relatives together with its other provisions for ascertaining the nearest relative or acting nearest relative should continue to be used and be extended to the legislation implementing our recommendations. The National Schizophrenia Fellowship (Scotland) pointed out that many elderly dementia sufferers are cared for by nieces who would be excluded by our proposed abbreviated list but are within the 1984 Act list. We accept the force of these comments and now favour using the list in the 1984 Act.

2.69   We have been made aware of some dissatisfaction with the nearest relative provisions of the 1984 Act. First, some incapable adults have become alienated from their relatives and do not wish them to be consulted. The relatives in turn may not wish to be consulted and would probably have little to offer to the decision-makers were they to be consulted. In these circumstances the adult may well prefer a trusted friend or companion to be consulted. Secondly, the adult may have been cohabiting with a partner or sharing accommodation with a companion on a non-sexual basis. Section 53(6) of the 1984 Act permits such a partner or companion to be regarded as the adult's nearest relative, but only if they had been living together for at least five years. In the case of a married adult there is a further condition that he or she must be permanently separated from his or her spouse. It has been represented to us that a partner or companion of say three years standing is more likely to be aware of the adult's wishes and views than a parent or brother and sister living in some other part of the country. A possible solution to both these problems would be to allow people while capable, to nominate an individual to be consulted in place of their nearest relative. We mention this possibility but do not make a recommendation here for the reasons given in paragraph 2.71 below.

2.70   Should there be a procedure for excluding unsuitable nearest relatives from the consultation process? We put forward such an idea in connection with consultations about an incapable adult's medical treatment[4]. This was generally agreed, although some thought it was unnecessary since doctors simply had to take into account the nearest relative's views and could take into account the unsuitability of nearest relatives in weighing up their views. However, the doctors

---

1.   Proposal 38, para 4.76.
2.   See para 2.69 below.
3.   Proposals 21 and 26.
4.   Proposal 21(3), para 3.21.

or others consulting may be unaware of the unsuitability. Moreover, it is a waste of time and effort to consult those who do not deserve to be consulted. The Law Society supported our proposal as it was aware of many cases where the nearest relative was an abuser or otherwise seriously unsuitable. It expressed the view that some of the existing provisions in section 56 of the 1984 Act, whereby the sheriff may appoint an acting nearest relative in place of the nearest relative were not satisfactory. The sheriff may replace a nearest relative who is incapable of acting by reason of mental disorder and the application may be made by any relative, any person with whom the patient is or was residing or a mental health officer[1]. The nearest relative (and only the nearest relative) may also apply if "he is unwilling or considers it undesirable to continue to act as such [nearest relative]"[2]. There is no mechanism for replacing a relative who is unsuitable but wishes to continue to act or does not consider it undesirable that he or she should continue to act. Moreover, even if a nearest relative does fall into either of these categories, he or she is not usually prepared to incur the trouble and expense of legal proceedings to seek a replacement.

2.71　Although there seems merit in the suggestions in the preceding paragraphs that a nominee could replace a nearest relative and that it should be made easier to replace an unsuitable nearest relative we have decided not to recommend any reforms. It seems to us highly desirable, if not essential, that the same person should be the nearest relative for the purposes of the 1984 Act and for the purposes of our recommendations, given the close similarity of the subject matter. Amendments to the 1984 Act in this area should be preceded by further consultation by the appropriate authorities. Accordingly we have decided to adopt without amendment the nearest relative provisions in the 1984 Act.

2.72　It was suggested to us that the sheriff on appointing a guardian or making some other order should have power to nominate a person other than a nearest relative or primary carer who should be required to be consulted by the guardian or other intervener. For example, a particular social worker or a close friend may have valuable views to offer in connection with all or some specific parts of the adult's welfare or financial affairs. We consider this to be a useful suggestion and have accordingly adopted it.

2.73　Summing up we recommend that:

14. (1) A person proposing to make an intervention in the welfare or financial affairs of an incapable adult under or in pursuance of the proposed new legislation should be required to take account of the present and past wishes of the adult.

(2) An intervener should also be required to consult with the incapable adult's nearest relative, primary carer, any guardian or continuing attorney or welfare attorney with relevant powers, but only in so far as it is reasonable and practicable to do so. The intervener should take account of the views expressed.

(3) An intervener should also be required to take into account the views of any other person appearing to have an interest in the incapable adult's welfare or the proposed intervention, but should not be under a duty to seek out such views.

(4) The sheriff should, on application, have power to direct that a specified person should have to be consulted and their views taken into account in relation to every or any particular intervention (under consideration or in the future) relating to the incapable adult.

(5) An adult's nearest relative should be determined by the provisions of sections 53 to 57 of the Mental Health (Scotland) Act 1984.

Clauses 1(4) and 67(1)

Fiduciary duties in relation to adults

2.74　Certain categories of people who are appointed to look after the affairs of others are regarded as standing in a fiduciary relationship to them or as having fiduciary duties in relation to them.

"It is a rule of universal application that a person having fiduciary duties to discharge (as, for example, an executor, guardian, judicial factor, agent, promoter or director of a company as well as a trustee in the strict sense) is not allowed to enter into engagements in which he has or can have a personal interest conflicting, or which may possibly conflict, with the interests of those whom he is bound to protect[3]".

A fiduciary who enters into conflicting or potentially conflicting engagements is said to be acting as *auctor in rem suam*[4].

---

1. S 56(2), (3)(b).
2. S 56(3)(c).
3. Gloag and Henderson, *Introduction to the Law of Scotland*, 9th edn, pp 770-771.
4. Trayner, *Latin Maxims and Phrases* translates it as "one who acts for his own behoof"; *Aberdeen Railway Co v Blaikie Brothers* (1854) 1 Macq 461.

The engagement is voidable[1] and any profit made has to be held for the beneficiary[2]. Another aspect of the *auctor in rem suam* rule is that a fiduciary cannot make any profit out of the position unless this is authorised by the appointment or the beneficiary. Illustrations of these rules are that a curator bonis appointed to manage the affairs of an incapable adult may not buy the adult's property[3] nor sell his or her own property to the adult or lend to, or borrow from, the adult's estate[4]. The curator is allowed commission which is paid by the Accountant of Court for managing the adult's affairs, but all other commissions and discounts received by the curator in that capacity have to be accounted for to the adult's estate[5].

2.75   Other fiduciary duties are the undivided loyalty rule and the confidentiality rule. The undivided loyalty rule requires fiduciaries not to place themselves in a position where their duty towards one beneficiary conflicts with a duty owed to another[6]. A fiduciary must make available to a beneficiary all the information that is relevant to the beneficiary's affairs. The confidentiality rule requires that a fiduciary must use information obtained in confidence from a beneficiary for the benefit of that beneficiary and must not use it for his or her own advantage or for the benefit of others[7]. These rules are of more importance where a professional curator or judicial factor manages the affairs of several incapable adults.

2.76   Many people who have functions under our recommendations in later Parts of this report will stand in a fiduciary relationship to the incapable adults in question. Guardians and continuing attorneys[8] are clear examples of fiduciaries. Those authorised to use money from an incapable adult's bank accounts for the adult's benefit, managers of establishments who manage their incapable residents' finances and persons appointed to carry out intervention orders would also be regarded as standing in a fiduciary relationship with the adults concerned. Breach of a fiduciary duty gives rise to liability on the part of the fiduciary. It is therefore important that such people are aware of these duties and the consequences of failing to observe them. Professional guardians such as solicitors and accountants ought to be aware of them, but the same may not be true for lay guardians or continuing attorneys. We have suggested that the Public Guardian should produce notes of guidance for guardians and others[9]. These notes should include material relating to fiduciary duties. The various Codes of Practice which we recommend[10] should also deal with this issue.

2.77   Where the fiduciary is a member of the incapable adult's family it may be very difficult or even impossible to avoid breaches of fiduciary duty. Suppose, for example, a woman appoints her husband to be her continuing attorney. Many actions by him such as the apportionment of household expenses between them or deciding whether to invest her estate for maximum income or for income and capital growth involve a conflict or potential conflict between his own interests and those of his incapacitated wife. Again, a daughter who has been appointed guardian to her father faces a conflict of interest between herself as successor to his estate and herself as his guardian in deciding whether or not to place her father in a private nursing home. Actings in breach of a fiduciary duty may be authorised by the appointer of the fiduciary or be consented to by the beneficiary concerned. For example, a trustee is allowed to claim only out-of-pocket expenses, but either the trust deed or the beneficiaries can authorise payment of fees. Neither of these methods would apply in the case of guardianship or most of the other fiduciary relationships under our recommendations.

2.78   Some other method of excusing breaches of fiduciary duty has to be devised. We do not think it possible to set out all the circumstances where a breach of fiduciary duty should be overlooked. The circumstances are too many and too varied. We would also reject the courts being required to grant dispensations for such breaches[11]. Repeated applications would be necessary since in some situations almost every action would be in breach of a fiduciary duty. Moreover, applications to the court would be likely to be numerous and would increase the expense of continuing attorneyship or guardianship, especially where relatives rather than professionals were involved.

2.79   In our view the solution lies in the requirements of reasonableness, good faith and adherence to the general principles. Suppose, for example, a daughter is continuing attorney for her incapable father. It becomes impossible to look after the father at home and he has to go into a residential home. In order to pay for this the father's share of the home which he owns jointly with the daughter has to be realised. The daughter should be able to purchase this share provided she does so openly at a price fixed by an independent professional valuer. Summing up we recommend that:

---

1. *Fraser v Hankey and Co* (1847) 9 D 415
2. *Inglis v Inglis* 1983 SLT 437.
3. *Dunn v Chambers* (1897) 25R 247.
4. *Perston v Perston's Trs* (1863) 1M 245 (borrowing from trust); *Wilson v Smith's Trs* 1939 SLT 120 (loan to trust). These cases involved trustees but were decided on the basis of fiduciary duty.
5. *AB's CB* 1927 SC 902.
6. *North and South Trust Co v Berkeley* [1971] 1 WLR 470 at 484-5. There may be a term implied permitting this where an agent (such as an estate agent) acts for several principals *Kelly v Cooper* [1993] AC 205.
7. *Brown's Trs v Hay* (1898) 25R 1112.
8. *Robertson v Dennistoun* (1865) 3M 829; *Maffett v Stewart* (1887) 14R 506.
9. Para 2.46.
10. Such as the code for guardians, Recommendation 106, para 6.118.
11. Under s 32 of the Trusts (Scotland) Act 1921 the court may excuse trustees from personal liability for breach of trust if satisfied that they have acted honestly and reasonably and ought fairly to be excused.

15. (1) A guardian, continuing or welfare attorney, person authorised to withdraw funds from accounts under Recommendation 37, managers of an establishment authorised to manage residents' affairs under Recommendation 47 and a person carrying out an intervention order who has acted reasonably, in good faith and in accordance with the general principles should not be liable for any breach of fiduciary duty to the incapable adult in question.

(2) Codes of Practice and other publications should make guardians and others aware of their fiduciary duties and the need to avoid acting in breach of them.

Clause 64(1)

Ill-treatment and neglect of incapable adults

2.80   Section 105 of the 1984 Act provides that it is to be a criminal offence for managers or staff in a hospital or for guardians to ill-treat or wilfully neglect their patients. Those convicted are liable to imprisonment for up to six months or to a fine not exceeding the statutory maximum or both (summary conviction) and to imprisonment for up to two years or an unlimited fine or both (conviction on indictment). We consider that this offence should be extended to all those exercising welfare powers under our recommendations; welfare attorneys, persons acting under intervention orders and guardians. We recommend that:

16. Any person exercising welfare powers under our recommendations who ill-treats or wilfully neglects an incapable adult should be guilty of an offence and liable to imprisonment and/or payment of a fine.

Clause 65

Part 3   Continuing and Welfare Powers of Attorney

Introduction

3.1   In this Part we look at powers of attorney. The term "power of attorney" is used in two senses. Strictly speaking, it refers to a power of legal representation conferred by one person on another by means of a contract of mandate or agency. However, the term is also frequently used to refer to the document in which the power is granted. In the interests of clarity we use the term in the sense of the power conferred rather than in the sense of the document in which it is conferred. In this sense a power of attorney is a power granted by one individual (the granter) to another (the attorney) to act on his or her behalf in relation to various matters specified. The contract of mandate or agency conferring a power of attorney usually takes the form of a document setting out the powers conferred, but oral contracts are also competent. Contracts of mandate or agency appointing others to manage one's financial affairs and property have been available in Scotland for many centuries and there is a well-developed common law relating to them. Those appointed were known as factors or factors and commissioners, but nowadays the term attorney is more usual and we adopt this for the rest of the report[1]. Attorneys with powers over the granter's personal welfare or health care do not feature to any great extent in current Scottish practice. Their legal status is unclear in Scotland although many other jurisdictions have introduced them recently by legislation[2].

3.2   Powers of attorney are used in various ways that are relevant to this report[3]. Elderly or ill people anticipating likely future incapacity may wish to hand over all or part of their financial affairs to an attorney although at that time they are mentally capable of managing their affairs themselves. Should they become incapable later they wish and expect the attorney to carry on acting. Powers of attorney are also used to a lesser extent as an "insurance policy" by those who are perfectly physically and mentally well but who wish to provide against an unforeseen future loss of capacity. Attorneys appointed by contract are an alternative to the tutors, curators, guardians and others appointed by the court to look after an incapable adult's finances and welfare.

3.3   The main advantage of contractually conferred powers of attorney is that they are relatively cheap and flexible compared with court appointed guardians. The granter can decide whom to appoint as attorney and what powers to confer on him or her. Furthermore, the granting of a power of attorney does not require the acknowledgement by the granter or his or her family of possible future incapacity, its certification by medical practitioners and its publication in legal proceedings. The main disadvantage is that the attorney, unlike a court appointed guardian, is not supervised and monitored by some public official. As long as the granter remains mentally capable he or she can keep an eye on the attorney's actions. Once the granter becomes incapable he or she cannot monitor the attorney's actings or recall the power of attorney. The satisfactory operation of powers of attorney depends to a large extent on the honesty and integrity of the attorneys appointed. Sadly but inevitably a small minority of attorneys take advantage of this lack of supervision and abuse their position. We consider that powers of attorney which have effect after the granter's incapacity should be encouraged as they promote personal autonomy and prevent legal proceedings. However, there must be adequate protection for granters if powers of attorney are to continue to play a useful role in this area.

3.4   In our discussion paper[4] we suggested that it might be possible to regard attorneys as privately appointed guardians. However, we have found that there would have to be too many differences between court appointed guardians and privately appointed guardians/attorneys if the latter were to remain relatively informal and flexible. For example, the supervision, monitoring and auditing of the accounts of court-appointed guardians by the Public Guardian could not be applied to attorneys without destroying the benefits of this way of proceeding. We therefore continue to use the term "attorney" for

---

1. Samples of documents registered in the Books of Council and Session in 1977 and 1987 showed that nearly all were called power of attorney. A few were termed "power of attorney or factory and commission" or "factory and commission or power of attorney". The last is used in the Law Reform (Miscellaneous Provisions) (Scotland) Act 1990, s 71.
2. California, Durable Power of Attorney Health Care Act 1983; New Zealand, Protection of Personal and Property Rights Act 1988; Ontario, Substitute Decisions Act 1992.
3. Powers of attorney are also used in commercial transactions and by those going abroad wishing to leave someone at home with authority to cope with their affairs during their absence. About half the powers of attorney in 1977 were estimated to have been granted for this reason, the other half were by "infirm" granters. D Nichols, *Legal Arrangements for Managing the Finances of Mentally Disabled Adults in Scotland*, 1992, Journal of Social Welfare and Family Law, 193.
4. Para 8.3.

the appointees who would be subject to our new recommended regime, although we call them "continuing attorneys" to emphasise that their authority in relation to financial matters continues after the incapacity of the granter. Use of the term attorney or continuing attorney brings in much useful Scottish common law, such as the fiduciary relationship between granter and attorney, the events which terminate the attorney's authority and the effect of termination on the attorney and any third party dealing with the attorney. Adoption of a term other than attorney or continuing attorney would involve setting out all these common law rules in new statutory provisions.

3.5   In our discussion paper we dealt with powers of attorney for property and financial affairs separately from powers of attorney relating to personal welfare. While it is, and has for many centuries been, accepted that people can delegate management of their financial affairs it was, we thought, questionable whether and if so to what extent delegation of personal welfare decisions should be permitted. Delegation of personal welfare decisions raises ethical issues which are absent from the financial management area. Our proposal[1] that legislation should be introduced permitting attorneys to take welfare and health care decisions on behalf of granters after the granters' incapacity was widely welcomed, although some respondents questioned the need for welfare attorneys as well as court-appointed guardians with welfare powers. We consider the two posts to be complementary in the same way as financial attorneys and guardians with financial powers are. Later on in this Part[2] we recommend that a power of attorney in relation to personal welfare matters should not become effective until the granter becomes incapable of making the personal welfare decision in question. Such a power is not a continuing power for it never had effect prior to the granter's incapacity. We therefore use the term "welfare power of attorney" for it, with the person appointed being termed a "welfare attorney". The term "continuing power of attorney" is confined to a power of attorney relating to the granter's financial affairs, since such a power may be operable before incapacity and continues to be effective after incapacity if completed in accordance with our recommended requirements. The appointee we call a "continuing attorney". Apart from this nearly all our recommendations as to the form of the contracts of mandate or agency conferring continuing or welfare powers of attorney and the functions of the continuing or welfare attorney appointed are identical. It would be possible for a granter to appoint a continuing attorney who is a different person from the welfare attorney and to do so by separate contracts in different documents. We imagine, however, that in most cases a single document will be employed and the same person will be appointed as welfare and continuing attorney.

Effectiveness after incapacity to be express or implied?

3.6   A power of attorney granted on or after 1 January 1991 does not lapse by operation of law on the subsequent mental incapacity of the granter. Section 71(1) of the Law Reform (Miscellaneous Provisions) (Scotland) Act 1990, which came into force on that date, provides:-

"Any rule of law by which a factory and commission or power of attorney ceases to have effect in the event of the mental incapacity of the granter shall not apply to a factory and commission or power of attorney granted on or after the date on which this section comes into force".

Granters who do not wish their powers of attorney to continue must insert an express clause "opting-out" of the statutory rule. The above statutory provision was intended as an interim measure pending our consideration of the issue[3]. In our discussion paper we proposed[4] that granters who wished their attorneys to continue to have authority after incapacity should be required to insert an express clause to that effect in the document conferring the power. They should have to "opt-in" rather than "opt-out". To put it another way the general rule should be that powers of attorney do not continue after the granter's incapacity, but it should be competent for granters by express provision to grant continuing authority after incapacity on their attorneys. An opting-in system enables appropriate safeguards to be incorporated for those contracts expressly providing for continuing powers of attorney without extending them to powers of attorney in general. It also ensures that granters have to consider carefully the desirability of granting a continuing power and prevents them inadvertently conferring a continuing power through ignorance or forgetfulness of the need to opt-out. Many powers of attorney are granted for commercial reasons or for a limited purpose and it is doubtful whether such granters intend the attorneys appointed to operate after their incapacity.

3.7   Most of the many respondents who commented on the opting-in proposal were in favour of a new statutory regime for powers of attorney with increased protection for granters and thought that that purpose would be better achieved by an "opting-in" system. Two of those consulted preferred the existing system because of its simplicity. Some of those supporting the new regime urged us to adopt a flexible scheme which did not contain too many restrictions and conditions. We consider that the balance between simplicity and protection of granters falls on the side of the latter and that the present system of automatically conferring continuing authority on attorneys without much in the way of protective

---

1. Proposal 76, para 5.101.
2. Recommendation 23, para 3.42.
3.   HL Debs, Vol 522 Col 1651 (25 Oct 1990).
4. Proposal 58(2), para 5.12.

measures is unsatisfactory. We have, however, endeavoured to build in protection without undue rigidity, bureaucracy and expense.

3.8   Should the clause which has the effect of imparting a continuing effect to a power of attorney be prescribed? The advantages of a prescribed style are that third parties can readily see that the document confers a continuing power and that granters and their advisers are more likely to use continuing powers of attorney if there is a prescribed style whose effect is laid down by statute and hence is certain. The disadvantage is that any deviation from the prescribed style would deny effect to the granter's intention, unless there was a further provision allowing minor deviations. In our discussion paper we proposed[1] that a style should be prescribed but that it should not be mandatory to use it. Any words showing that the granter clearly intended the document to confer continuing authority should suffice. There was little comment from those consulted on this aspect of continuing powers of attorney. One commentator with wide experience of enduring powers of attorney in England and Wales said that while prescribed forms were easier for third parties they created difficulties for granters in situations that were out of the ordinary. On reconsideration we think the form of words is best left unprescribed. The only requirement should be that the document clearly shows that the granter intended the attorney to have continuing power.

3.9   In our discussion paper we proposed that granters of welfare powers of attorney should also have to "opt-in"[2]. Our later recommendation that a welfare power of attorney only becomes effective on the granter's incapacity[3] requires this to be reconsidered. Strictly speaking, a contract of mandate or agency conferring a welfare power of attorney need not contain an express clause conferring power on the welfare attorney to act after the granter's incapacity since that is the only period during which the welfare powers could be exercised. Nevertheless, we consider that it would be better to have the same "opt-in" rule for both continuing attorneys and welfare attorneys. An express clause would make it obvious to granters what they were doing in granting a welfare power of attorney.

3.10   We therefore recommend that:

17. (1) A person having a power of attorney granted after the commencement date of legislation implementing our recommendations should have power to act after the granter's incapacity only if the contract of mandate or agency conferring the power of attorney clearly shows that that was the granter's intention.

(2) There should be no style prescribed for conferring a power of attorney which is to have effect after the granter's incapacity.

(3) Section 71 of the Law Reform (Miscellaneous Provisions) (Scotland) Act 1990 should be repealed with respect to powers of attorney granted on or after the commencement date of legislation implementing our recommendations.

Clauses 11(1),(3)(b) and 12(1), (3)(b) and Schedule 5

Execution of continuing or welfare powers of attorney

3.11   At present a power of attorney may be conferred orally or in writing and in the latter case may be simply signed by the granter. As a matter of practice a document conferring a power of attorney is almost invariably subscribed by the granter and witnessed in accordance with the statutory requirements for attestation[4]. It is then presumed to be authentic and formally valid until the contrary is established in court proceedings. In our discussion paper we proposed[5] that a document conferring a continuing power of attorney should have to be in writing and signed by the granter at the end in order to be valid. Oral grants of powers would therefore be ineffective. This was agreed by all those who responded. Section 2(1) of the Requirements of Writing (Scotland) Act 1995 now provides that the granter's subscription is sufficient for formal validity. In practice documents providing for continuing or welfare powers of attorney will continue to be attested for evidential purposes. Not only would the Public Guardian wish some presumption of formal validity before registering the document[6] but also the strong presumption of authenticity would be very useful in a document which is going to be relied on for an indefinite future period at a time when evidence from the granter would be unavailable.

3.12   We also proposed that there should be a statutory prohibition on the attorney acting as a witness to the granter's signature of a document conferring a continuing power of attorney[7]. Although there was unanimous agreement on consultation we now consider that there is no need for a statutory provision. Attestation is a matter of evidence, not validity

---

1. Proposal 58(2), para 5.12.
2. Proposal 77(1), para 5.103.
3. Recommendation 23, para 3.42.
4. The Requirements of Writing (Scotland) Act 1995, s 3 provides for a single witness in documents executed after commencement (1 August 1995). Before then two witnesses were required.
5. Proposal 59(1), para 5.21, extended to welfare powers in Proposal 77(2), para 5.103.
6. See Clause 14(2) of the draft Bill.
7. Proposal 60, para 5.22.

and current practice is to obtain completely independent witnesses wherever possible in order to minimise the risk of future challenge and we consider that this is unlikely to change in the future. We therefore recommend that:

18. A contract of mandate or agency conferring a continuing or welfare power of attorney should be required to be in a written document and subscribed by the granter in order to be formally valid.

Clauses 11(3)(a) and 12(3)(a)

Signature by attorney?

3.13   At present attorneys do not sign the document conferring the power of attorney to signify their consent to appointment. In our discussion paper we proposed[1] that it should not become a requirement for formal validity that a document conferring a continuing power of attorney was signed by the attorney. Most of those who responded agreed with our proposal, but some took the view that an attorney should sign to indicate acceptance. We think, however, that the stage at which a formal indication of acceptance should be required is when the document is presented to the Public Guardian for registration. It is at that stage, when the power is about to be used, that attorneys are in a position to know whether or not they can accept the appointment. It does not seem reasonable to require those named as attorney to bind themselves to act at some indeterminate time in the future, when circumstances might be very different. If the attorney's subscription is not binding, it is merely confusing to require it for formal validity. Why should an unnecessary signature, signifying at most that the signatory has read the document, be necessary for formal validity? Another disadvantage of requiring the attorney's signature for formal validity is that this would open up a difference between continuing or welfare powers of attorney and other powers of attorney. This we are reluctant to do unless it is necessary. It would create further problems such as whether the attorney's subscription would have to be attested for evidential purposes and, if so, whether the statutory provisions on attestation of the signatures of granters of documents applied to a person who was signing not as a granter but in some vague and unspecified capacity. For all these reasons we do not recommend that subscription by the attorney should be necessary for the formal validity of a continuing or welfare power of attorney.

Ensuring granters understand document when signing

3.14   Continuing powers of attorney by their very nature continue to have effect after their granters have lost capacity. Welfare powers of attorney become effective then. Granters should be fully aware of what they are doing in signing a document conferring a continuing power of attorney or a welfare power of attorney. They are handing over the future management of their affairs or personal welfare to individuals they will be unable to supervise and if necessary dismiss. There may well be no-one sufficiently interested to monitor the attorney's actings and take steps to terminate the appointment if the attorney acts improperly. We consider that proper measures of protection should be introduced at the earliest possible stage - when the document conferring the power of attorney is signed. The formalities of execution should be such as to ensure that granters are fully aware of the consequences of creating a continuing or welfare power and that they are not subject to any pressure to do so. We note that the Alberta Law Reform Institute has come to a similar conclusion[2]. A research report into the workings of enduring powers of attorney in England and Wales suggested that certification of capacity at the time of execution might be a more effective safeguard for granters than the current notification and registration procedures contained in the Enduring Powers of Attorney Act 1985[3]. In our discussion paper we asked whether over and above signature by the granter there should be other requirements for formal validity in order to ensure that granters were aware of the long term consequences of granting a continuing financial power[4]. We suggested three such requirements:

(a) a signed statement by the granter that he or she had read a prescribed form of explanatory notes.

(b) a certificate by a solicitor that the effects of the document conferring a continuing power had been explained and the granter appeared to understand the explanation, or

(c) a certificate by a doctor or other appropriate person that the granter had capacity to understand the consequences of signing the document conferring a continuing power of attorney.

We also proposed that the requirements for valid execution of a welfare power of attorney should be the same as those for a financial power with continuing effect[5].

3.15   There was little support amongst those responding for granters having to certify that they had read prescribed form explanatory notes. This was regarded as an ineffective safeguard; people who signed documents without fully understanding their effects would in all likelihood not read and take in the explanatory notes either. They would simply sign the document conferring the power of attorney and any accompanying certificate. Nevertheless we think many

---

1. Proposal 61, para 5.24.
2. *Enduring Powers of Attorney*, Report No 59, p 3.
3. S Cretney and others, *Enduring Powers of Attorney: A Report to the Lord Chancellor* (1991), para 2.40.
4. Proposal 59(2), para 5.21.
5. Proposal 77(2), para 5.103.

granters would find brief explanatory notes helpful and we suggest that the appropriate authorities should consider issuing them.

3.16 Certification by a solicitor that the granter had had the effect of a continuing power of attorney explained and appeared to understand it was generally welcomed by those consulted[1]. This would not give rise to extra expense in most cases since most powers of attorney are prepared with the involvement of lawyers. The Scottish Association for Mental Health suggested that other independent people of standing in the community should also be able to certify, as otherwise granters using printed form powers would be put to the expense of employing a solicitor just to have their understanding certified. We would adopt this helpful suggestion because it would encourage the use of continuing and welfare powers of attorney if forms were provided by voluntary organisations and the granter's understanding could be certified by a minister of religion, doctor or other member of a prescribed class. "Appearing to understand" the explanation of the effect of a power of attorney is perhaps somewhat vague. We are now in favour of a slightly stricter test - that the solicitor or other certifying individual should be satisfied that the granter understood the nature and effect of the document conferring the power. The certifier would be expected, as a matter of course, to question the granter and make such other enquiries as seemed necessary in order to be in a position to give the certificate.

3.17 Many granters of continuing or welfare powers will be failing in their mental and physical faculties and suggestible to pressure from others. We consider that the solicitor or other certifying individual should also have to state that he or she had no reason to believe that the document conferring the power was being signed as a result of anything (such as undue influence) which would vitiate the granting of the power.

3.18 Respondents were not in favour of a medical certificate of capacity being mandatory in all cases, partly on grounds of expense and partly because those with undoubted full capacity would find a compulsory medical assessment insulting. However, many saw a role for such a certificate where the solicitor was unable to certify the granter's understanding. Others doubted whether a medical practitioner was the appropriate person to certify an individual's capacity to understand the meaning of a legal document; capacity is as much a legal concept as a medical one[2]. We consider that a certificate of capacity should not be a mandatory requirement, but if there were doubts as to the granter's capacity an assessment of the granter's capacity by a medical or other specialist should be sought. A report indicating that the granter had capacity would enable the solicitor or other certifier to certify the granter's understanding. We received a suggestion that the sheriff should have power to declare that an intending granter of a continuing or welfare power of attorney had capacity to grant it so that the validity of the document could be established. After careful consideration we have decided not to recommend this. First, there is a presumption of capacity at common law which those challenging the power of attorney later would have to rebut[3]. This presumption would be greatly strengthened if the granter had been assessed as capable at or around the time of signing by a medical or other specialist. Second, to prevent a later challenge the declarator would have to be conclusive. We do not think that a declarator should be given this effect since all those likely to be affected by the validity or otherwise of the document could not be identified in advance and called as contradictors. A declarator which merely created a presumption would add nothing to the existing law.

3.19 Summing up we recommend that:

19. In order to be formally valid a document conferring a continuing or welfare power of attorney should:

   (a) **contain a certificate by a solicitor (or a member of some other class of persons to be prescribed by the Secretary of State) that, after interviewing the granter and obtaining any necessary reports, he or she is satisfied that the granter understood the nature and effect of the document, and**

   (b) **contain a certificate by a solicitor or other certifying person that he or she has no reason to believe that the document was being signed as a result of anything which would vitiate the granting of the power.**

   Clauses 11(3)(c) and 12(3)(c)

Who may be appointed a continuing or welfare attorney?

3.20 Under the present law an attorney must be over 16[4], mentally capable and not bankrupt at the time of appointment in order for the appointment to be valid. An initially valid appointment falls on the attorney's later bankruptcy or mental incapacity[5]. In our discussion paper we proposed that these personal attributes should continue to be required for both

---

1. This is done in New South Wales; Conveyancing Act 1919, s 163F(2) added by the Conveyancing (Powers of Attorney) Amendment Act 1983. Barristers and clerks of petty sessions may also certify the granter's understanding.
2. The British Medical Association and the Law Society of England and Wales are currently producing a booklet about assessment of capacity in relation to legal matters.
3. *Lindsay v Watson* (1843) 5D 1194.
4. Age of Legal Capacity (Scotland) Act 1991.
5. Halliday, *Conveyancing Law and Practice*, Vol I, para 13-11.

financial[1] and welfare[2] continuing attorneys. There was almost unanimous acceptance of our proposals for financial attorneys, but many questioned the exclusion of bankrupts from acting as welfare attorneys. Close relatives who had been appointed attorney and who would be in the best position to decide personal welfare matters might become bankrupt and so have to be replaced by court-appointed guardians. It was said that in times of recession bankruptcy did not necessarily imply dishonesty or a lack of probity. While we would prefer to minimise distinctions between continuing attorneys and welfare attorneys we consider that a distinction is justified in relation to bankruptcy. Those whose financial affairs are taken out of their own hands should not be permitted to manage the financial affairs of others, but purely personal welfare powers should be exercisable by a bankrupt welfare attorney unless the power of attorney provides otherwise. This may give rise to problems where the same individual is appointed continuing attorney and welfare attorney, but careful drafting of the document of appointment with possible future bankruptcy in mind should mitigate such problems.

3.21   The bankruptcy of the granter of a power of attorney automatically terminates the authority of the attorney[3]. On sequestration the trustee is vested in the estate of the bankrupt[4] and clearly must supersede the attorney in relation to matters affecting the estate. We consider that a welfare attorney's authority should not be terminated automatically since there would be no direct conflict between the welfare attorney and the trustee.

3.22   In current practice an attorney is almost invariably an individual although there is no prohibition against a corporate appointment. We asked in our discussion paper whether it should be competent to appoint a corporation as continuing financial[5] attorney, but proposed confining continuing welfare attorneys to individuals[6]. This approach was approved by the majority of those who responded although some considered that corporate attorneys should not be allowed even in the financial field. We consider that granters should be free to appoint a corporate attorney to exercise financial powers should they wish to do so, although we do not anticipate this being done to any great extent. Enable have set up a trustee scheme whereby a company limited by guarantee can act as trustee for trusts created for mentally handicapped individuals. It or other organisations may wish to set up similar schemes for continuing attorneys. As far as welfare powers are concerned we consider that it should be competent to grant them only to one or more individuals.

3.23   The Law Society in its response said that the provider of services or facilities to the granter or the employee of such a provider should not be permitted to be a continuing attorney, while Alzheimer Scotland- Action on Dementia considered that the proprietors of private residential and nursing homes should also be excluded in respect of their residents. We recognise the possibility of abuse and concentration of power in such appointments. This, however, could also occur with individuals looking after the affairs of their incapacitated relatives at home and would be more difficult to detect because such carers are not subject to the local authority registration and inspection that residential homes are subject to. Moreover, somebody in a residential home may be the most appropriate person to be appointed as an attorney by a resident who has been in the home for many years and who is without close family. We recommend below[7] that all continuing and welfare powers of attorney should be registered with the Public Guardian so that it would be possible for the local authority charged with carrying out inspections of residential homes and the Public Guardian to monitor situations which might give rise to concern.

3.24   Joint attorneys and substitute attorneys are frequently met with in current practice. Our proposal to permit such appointments with financial[8] and welfare[9] attorneys was agreed by all those who commented. Joint attorneys have many advantages. It is helpful for an attorney to have someone to discuss problems with and share the responsibility. The functions could be divided up informally between the appointees according to their wishes and abilities. For example, a son looking after his elderly mother could look after her day-to-day finances while her investments could be managed by someone with more experience and aptitude for such business. Joint attorneys also cater for the situation where one attorney is temporarily unable to act. The main disadvantage is that the joint attorneys may disagree so leading to stalemate, but this only happens when all the joint attorneys have to agree to any act. It is more usual for the appointment of more than one attorney to be made joint and several, in which case any one can act without the others[10]. Irreconcilable differences between joint attorneys might have to be resolved by the court (or the granter if still capable). This adjudication would be part of the court's recommended general power to give directions to continuing or welfare attorneys[11].

---

1. Proposal 63(1), para 5.33.
2. Proposal 77(3), para 5.103.
3. *McKenzie v Campbell* (1894) 21R 904.
4. Bankruptcy (Scotland) Act 1985, s 31.
5. Proposal 63(2), para 5.33.
6. Proposal 77(3), para 5.103.
7. Recommendation 21, para 3.36.
8. Proposal 63(1), para 5.33.
9. Proposal 77(4), para 5.103.
10. Halliday, *Conveyancing Law and Practice*, Vol 1, para 13.08.
11. Recommendation 30, para 3.68.

3.25   A substitute attorney allows for succession to the post should the original attorney die or wish to resign. Without a substitute a continuing or welfare power of attorney would come to an end so that an application would have to be made to the court for the appointment of a guardian. The granter might wish to specify events other than death or resignation of the original attorney that would trigger the substitute taking over and this should be permitted. The Public Guardian as registration authority should require to be notified that the substitute had taken over.

3.26   As most of the above points are already covered by the existing law on powers of attorney it is necessary for us to make only the following recommendations:

> **20. (1) A welfare attorney should be permitted to exercise welfare powers notwithstanding his or her bankruptcy or the bankruptcy of the granter.**
>
> **(2) Welfare powers under a welfare power of attorney should be exercisable only by individuals.**
>
> Clause 12(4), (6)

Registration of continuing or welfare powers

3.27   At present there is no requirement for documents conferring powers of attorney to be registered or made public in any way. As a matter of prudent professional practice, in order to guard against loss of the document, solicitors invariably register documents conferring powers of attorney in the Books of Council and Session (a national public register of documents situated in Edinburgh) or similar public registers kept at sheriff courts. Registration may take place immediately after completion of the document or it may be delayed until the attorney needs to exercise the powers.

3.28   In our discussion paper we put forward three options for a possible registration system[1]. The first, and most elaborate, was registration with some public authority that supervised and monitored the registered attorneys and required annual accounts for auditing. The second was modelled on that used in England and Wales under the Enduring Powers of Attorney Act 1985. The attorney would be under a duty to register the document with some public authority when the granter is, or is becoming, mentally incapable. Before applying for registration the attorney would have to give notice of the intended application to the granter and the granter's nearest relatives who would be entitled to object. The registration authority or the court would adjudicate on any objections. The third option was to make publication by registration in the Books of Council and Session mandatory by rendering ineffective a document conferring a power of attorney that was not registered within a specified period from the date of signature. Our provisional conclusion was that none of the options should be adopted and that the existing practice of voluntary registration should continue.

3.29   Many of those consulted agreed with our provisional conclusion that there should be no requirement of registration. Many others, however, favoured the introduction of a simple registration system so that possible abuse could be detected and notified to the appropriate authority. For example, one individual being registered as an attorney for a number of granters (apart from solicitors or accountants for their clients) might give rise to suspicion. We now think there would be merit in having a simple registration system. An open public register would bring continuing or welfare powers of attorney into the public domain and this, coupled with the requirement to present documents to public officials, would act to some extent as a deterrent to unscrupulous attorneys. We would stress that registration of a document conferring a continuing or welfare power would not imply any mental incapacity on the part of the granter or affect the granter's capacity to enter into transactions. The question of the granter's capacity would be one of fact both before and after registration. We would reject the first option of the registration authority also being a supervising and monitoring authority since that would be too complex and duplicate our recommended system of guardianship. The second option, a registration authority and procedure along the lines of that in England and Wales under the Enduring Powers of Attorney Act 1985 also seems to us to be too complex. Registration should be an administrative act rather than a procedure which gives an opportunity to air family feuds by way of relatives' objections. The Law Commission of England and Wales have come to a similar conclusion in their *Report on Mental Incapacity*[2]. The third option, compulsory registration in the Books of Council and Session would achieve only publication but most powers of attorney are registered there already. Those respondents who were in favour of a simple registration system undoubtedly wished to see something more than mandatory publication.

3.30   Continuing and welfare attorneys would lose their advantages, and would indeed become redundant, if such attorneys were to be subject to the same statutory regime as guardians. In order to be effective a registration system should have to be:

(a) compulsory;

(b) in a single national register open to public inspection;

(c) not more expensive than registration in the Books of Council and Session; and

---

1. Paras 5.44-5.49.
2. Law Com No 231 (March 1995), paras 7.37 and 7.38.

(d) kept by some public authority which would be under a duty to investigate complaints or circumstances giving rise to concern and to pass on information to other investigating bodies on request.

3.31   We envisage that the overwhelming majority of attorneys will be appointed with financial powers, either solely or in addition to welfare powers, so that the registration authority should be an organisation familiar with the management of finances and property. The Accountant of Court's office is the most obviously appropriate registration authority because of its existing functions in supervising and monitoring curators bonis and other judicial factors. Furthermore, the office would have staff familiar with carrying out investigations and capable of carrying out spot-checks. We do not think that those responsible for the Books of Council and Session should be given investigative functions into the conduct of attorneys. Their task is to maintain an accurate register of documents presented to them. Investigating the legal efficacy of continuing or welfare powers of attorney and the conduct of attorneys would be a radical and substantial new function. Elsewhere in this report we recommend that the Accountant of Court should be the Public Guardian and as such should maintain a register of guardians appointed by the court to incapable adults[1] and a register of people entitled to withdraw funds from incapable adults' bank accounts[2]. The Public Guardian would also have investigative functions in relation to these registered appointees. There seems to us to be considerable merit in having all these registration and investigatory functions undertaken by the same body. It is not worth creating a separate registration authority for welfare attorneys who are appointed solely with welfare powers. The Public Guardian should register them but any investigation should be carried out by the Mental Welfare Commission or the local authority. We envisage that registration of continuing or welfare powers of attorney would be a simple administrative process. The Public Guardian would be expected to check the documents to see that they complied with the requirements for formal validity we recommended earlier[3]. In practice, attestation would be the normal way of establishing the authenticity of the granter's subscription[4]. Acceptance for registration would not preclude a later challenge to the document's validity. We also think that the Public Guardian should not be required to register a document unless satisfied that the attorney accepts the appointment. There would be no point in registering documents which were never likely to be used.

3.32   The Books of Council and Session and the sheriff court registers are public registers. Documents registered there may be inspected by any member of the public during normal office hours on payment of the appropriate fee. We think it would be a retrograde step to make the Public Guardian's register of continuing and welfare attorneys a closed one. Many organisations and individuals involved with incapable adults or their attorneys have a legitimate interest in details of the attorneys and their powers. Registration in a public register may not be sufficient in itself to alert people to the continuing or welfare power of attorney. It should be open to the granter in the document conferring the power to add a clause requiring the Public Guardian to send a copy of the registered document to no more than two specified individuals or office holders. The Public Guardian should automatically send a copy of the registered document to the granter.

3.33   Registration would have to be compulsory if it were to achieve the results desired by those consultees in favour of registration. The only sensible sanction for non-registration is that the continuing or welfare power of attorney should be ineffective unless the document conferring it is registered. Any document conferring a continuing power of attorney that was expressed to be effective after incapacity would therefore have to be registered in a register kept by the Public Guardian before the attorney could competently use the powers conferred, even while the granter remained mentally capable. Welfare powers of attorney, however, would not become effective merely by virtue of registration because welfare powers are exerciseable only if the granter is incapable. Financial powers of attorney that are granted because the granter is going abroad or for some other commercial purpose would, we imagine, not normally contain an express continuation clause. Our recommendations as to registration and the other recommendations in this Part would not apply to such powers of attorney.

3.34   An attorney under an ordinary power of attorney granted after the commencement of the new legislation recommended here might be able to continue to act after the granter's incapacity since there is no clear rule in Scottish law that the power of attorney lapses then. Repeal of section 71(1) of the Law Reform (Miscellaneous Provisions) (Scotland) Act 1990[5] would leave the law doubtful. Documents conferring powers of attorney without an express continuation clause might therefore be used to circumvent our recommended registration provisions. In order to avoid this there should be a new statutory provision rendering ineffective during the granter's incapacity a power of attorney which does not contain an express continuation clause.

3.35   One of the purposes of the register is to enable those with an interest in the incapable granter to find out current details of the continuing or welfare attorney. Any significant changes should therefore be required to be notified to the Public Guardian so that the register can be amended. Such changes should include a permanent change of address of either the granter or the attorney, the death of the granter and the resignation or removal by the sheriff of the attorney.

---

1.   Recommendation 91, para 6.40.
2.   Recommendation 37, para 4.12.
3.   Recommendations 18 and 19, paras 3.12 and 3.19.
4.   See para 3.11 above. An alternative would be a certificate or decree under section 4 of the Requirements of Writing (Scotland) Act 1995.
5.   See para 3.6.

3.36 We recommend that:

21. (1) The Public Guardian should set up and maintain a register of documents conferring continuing or welfare powers of attorney.

(2) The Public Guardian should not be required to register a document conferring continuing or welfare powers of attorney unless the document appears to comply with the requirements of Recommendations 18 and 19 (signature by granter and certification of granter's understanding and absence of vitiating factors) and he or she is satisfied that the attorney accepts the appointment.

(3) The register should be open to inspection by any member of the public. On registration the Public Guardian should give a copy of the document to the attorney or other ingiver with a certificate of registration and also send a copy to the granter and, if the document requests this to be done, to up to two other specified individuals.

(4) A continuing or welfare attorney should have no authority by virtue of the power of attorney until the document conferring such a power is registered with the Public Guardian.

(5) Once the document conferring the power has been registered the Public Guardian should be notified of any permanent change of address of the granter or continuing or welfare attorney or the death of the granter.

(6) The Public Guardian should be required to investigate complaints made about the actings of continuing attorneys and alert the competent authorities in order to prevent further abuse. The Mental Welfare Commission and the local authority should have similar functions in relation to welfare attorneys.

(7) A power of attorney conferred after the commencement of the new legislation otherwise than in accordance with our recommendations should lapse on the granter's incapacity.

Clauses 4(2)(c), 4(2)(d), 7(1)(c), 8(1)(c), 13, 14(1), (2), (5), and 16

Springing powers of attorney

3.37 Normal contracts of mandate or agency conferring powers of attorney confer immediate authority on the attorney. Under our recommendations registration of the document conferring a continuing power would be required before continuing attorneys could exercise their powers. Nevertheless, the document could be registered immediately after its signature by the granter. Many granters do not wish to confer immediate authority on their attorneys. At the date of signing they are perfectly capable of managing their affairs and are merely making prudent provision should incapacity occur later. Such people may be deterred from granting a power of attorney by its immediate effect.

3.38 In our discussion paper we asked[1] whether there should be new statutory provisions for springing powers - powers of attorney that would spring into effect only on the occurrence of an event specified in the document conferring a power of attorney. The most common springing event is likely to be the granter's incapacity, but others could be imagined such as moving from home into permanent residential care. Most respondents were in favour of new statutory provisions, but some questioned the need for them. We understand that some solicitors are preparing springing powers for their clients at the moment and the Scottish Association for Mental Health was of the view that practice should be allowed to develop, rather than rules being laid down in legislation.

3.39 Taking account of the views expressed we have decided to deal with the matter slightly differently using our recommended registration system. We consider that the Public Guardian should be required to register any document conferring a continuing or welfare power of attorney unless the document contains a clause prohibiting registration until the occurrence of a specified event. Where such a clause exists the person presenting the document for registration would have to satisfy the Public Guardian that the event had occurred. This approach allows granters to confer springing powers on their continuing or welfare attorneys without regulating such powers in detail by statute. Welfare powers of attorney are in a sense always springing powers since the powers conferred may not be exercised until the granter becomes incapable. But the welfare power should be registrable at any time after granting unless the granter stipulates otherwise.

3.40 We recommend that:

22. Where the terms of a document conferring a continuing or welfare power of attorney prohibit registration until the occurrence of a specified event, the Public Guardian should not register it unless satisfied that the event has occurred.

Clause 14(3)

---

1. Proposal 73, para 5.86.

When should welfare powers be exercisable?

3.41   In our discussion paper we proposed[1] that a personal welfare attorney should not have authority to make a decision in respect of a personal welfare matter while the granter was capable of making that decision. This proposal was strongly supported on consultation. Immediate authority while the granter remains capable may be desirable in the financial field but does not seem sensible in the personal welfare field. For example, a doctor requesting consent to medical treatment would naturally ask the patient if capable rather than a welfare attorney, even if the latter had registered the document conferring the welfare power. The welfare attorney should therefore have authority to make a personal welfare decision if the granter is unable to make that decision by reason of mental disorder or an inability to communicate. The welfare attorney should also have authority to take a personal welfare decision if he or she reasonably believes the granter to be incapable, but the third party involved could take a different view of the granter's capacity, refuse to recognise the attorney's authority and deal directly with the granter. Irreconcilable differences of opinion between welfare attorneys and third parties as to capacity might have to be resolved by the courts. In its response Sense in Scotland considered that an attorney should always take account of the express wishes of the granter. We agree and deal with this by means of the general principles that we recommend should govern all decision-makers. One of these principles[2] requires a decision-maker to take account of the past and present wishes and feelings of the incapable adult. Past instructions or wishes might be contained in the document conferring the welfare power of attorney. The greater the granter's capacity the more weight the attorney should give to the granter's present wishes and feelings.

3.42   We recommend that:

   23. A welfare attorney should not be entitled to exercise a welfare power contained in the document conferring the power of attorney unless the granter is incapable of making a decision regarding the welfare matter in question, or the attorney reasonably believes the granter to be incapable.

Clause 12(4)

Powers of continuing and welfare attorneys

3.43   The authority of a continuing or welfare attorney is delimited by the powers conferred by the granter in the document of appointment. There are also restrictions imposed by the common law both as to what an attorney cannot competently do (such as make a will for the granter) and the manner in which the attorney exercises the powers[3]. In our discussion paper we looked at limitations in the financial and welfare fields. In the financial field we proposed[4] following the existing common law relating to attorneys so that a continuing attorney should in general not be entitled to remuneration or to make gifts or use the granter's estate for the benefit of others unless the granter was under an obligation to them (such as an obligation of aliment). We considered that the granter should, however, be able to expressly authorise the continuing attorney to receive remuneration or to do any of the other acts. There was no dissent on consultation, but one body did suggest that a continuing attorney should be entitled to make gifts even in the absence of any power to do so in the document of appointment, provided that the entitlement was appropriately restricted. We do not favour this even though enduring attorneys in England and Wales have statutory power to make reasonable birthday, seasonal and charitable gifts[5]. If the granter wishes the attorney to be able to make gifts, such as birthday and Christmas gifts to grandchildren or donations to charities, then this should be expressly provided in the continuing power of attorney. "Reasonable" and "seasonal" are vague terms that a less than scrupulous attorney could exploit. We prefer a simple straightforward rule that prohibits gifts unless the granter expressly provides for them. If the continuing attorney wished to make gifts and had no power to do so he or she could resign and apply to the court for appointment as guardian. Under our recommendations a guardian has power to make such gifts as are approved by the Public Guardian[6]. The attorney's authority to benefit others should as under the existing law be limited to alimenting those whom the granter is obliged to aliment. This would allow a wife looking after her incapable husband to keep the household going.

3.44   Entitlement to remuneration should have to be conferred expressly or by clear implication. Professional attorneys, such as solicitors or accountants, expect to be paid but relatives and close friends generally do not. This should be something that should be decided by the granter, but we would adopt the existing position in relation to powers of attorney that remuneration is not due unless authorised by the granter[7].

3.45   Another matter we raised was whether a continuing attorney should be entitled to see the granter's will. Doing so would help the attorney manage the estate in a way that would avoid difficulties on the granter's death. In our discussion

---

1.   Proposal 82, para 5.124.
2.   See Part 2, paras 2.61 to 2.63.
3.   Attorneys also have fiduciary duties to their granters, see paras 2.74 to 2.79.
4.   Proposal 64, para 5.39.
5.   Enduring Powers of Attorney Act 1985, s 3.
6.   Recommendation 104, para 6.110.
7.   *Orbiston* v *Hamilton* (1736) Mor 4063.

paper we proposed[1] that the power to see the will should be one that had to be expressly conferred. This was agreed. In connection with guardianship we consider that a guardian should not be empowered to make a will on behalf of an incapable adult[2]. The common law already prohibits such action on the part of an attorney. The existing law as to the extent to which a granter can delegate to an attorney his or her functions as a trustee, executor or other fiduciary is unclear. Discretionary functions cannot be delegated[3], but administrative acts like voting at a company meeting and perhaps signing documents can be performed by an attorney[4]. In our discussion paper we proposed[5] that it should not be competent for a trustee or other fiduciary to appoint an attorney to act in his or her place on incapacity. All those who responded agreed with our proposal. The purpose of continuing powers of attorney is to enable the attorney to manage the granter's affairs not the affairs of others which have been entrusted to the granter on the basis of his or her personal qualities. We also suggested that, in order to avoid legal proceedings to remove an incapable trustee[6], a continuing attorney for the trustee could be given power to resign the trusteeship on behalf of the trustee. Although our suggestion met with no dissent on consultation we now think it is an unnecessary refinement. If it were to be introduced there would have to be an exception where the granter was the sole trustee, since a sole trustee cannot generally resign without the leave of the court[7]. The number of cases where it would be useful would be small and the extra statutory provisions required would complicate the law relating to continuing powers of attorney.

3.46   Again, we do not need to make any recommendations for reform in this area as the existing law on powers of attorney will apply to continuing attorneys.

3.47   In connection with welfare attorneys we asked in our discussion paper[8] whether the attorney should have power to consent to the granter's admission to hospital for treatment of mental disorder, and if so whether such a power could be implied from a general power to take personal welfare and medical treatment decisions or whether it should have to be expressly conferred. There was a wide variety of opinions expressed on consultation, ranging from outright prohibition of such a power to acceptance that such a power would be useful and could be implied from a general power to take welfare decisions. A welfare attorney would normally be involved only if an incapable granter was refusing to go to hospital, for unprotesting granters could simply be taken there and treated. Where some measure of compulsion is needed we consider that the detention provisions of the 1984 Act should be used rather than obtaining the consent of a welfare attorney with appropriate powers. The Mental Welfare Commission foresaw difficulties in the status of patients if welfare attorneys could commit them to hospital against their will. Would the patient be detained in terms of the 1984 Act or not? It suggested as one possible solution that the welfare attorney could have the same powers as the nearest relative has under the 1984 Act in connection with detention. Thus if the welfare attorney had appropriate powers under the power of attorney he or she could apply for admission, require a mental health officer to consider the case for admission or consent to an emergency admission. We would adopt this suggestion, but would stress that any action by the attorney would not by itself result in detention. Further action by doctors, mental health officers or the courts would also be required. The welfare attorney could also have the same powers as the nearest relative in connection with discharge from detention. In Part 5 of this report we recommend that certain treatments for incapable patients (such as sterilisation or ECT) should require prior authorisation by the sheriff or a favourable second opinion from an independent specialist and that restraint should be used only in an emergency[9]. It should not be possible for a welfare attorney to circumvent these protective measures by consenting to such treatment or restraint. The views of the attorney would of course be taken into account by the doctors and he or she would be entitled to make representations to the sheriff or second opinion specialist.

3.48   We recommend that:

24. (1) A welfare attorney should not be entitled to place the granter in a hospital for treatment of mental disorder against the granter's will. However, the welfare attorney should, if the power of attorney confers such powers, have the same rights in relation to detention as the granter's nearest relative has under the Mental Health (Scotland) Act 1984.

(2) A welfare attorney should not be entitled to authorise any of the prescribed treatments in Recommendations 59 to 64 or consent to the adult being restrained.

Clause 12(5) and Schedule 4, paragraph 15

---

1. Proposal 64(2), para 5.39.
2. Para 6.105.
3. *Freen v Beveridge* (1832) 10S 727.
4. *Wolfe v Richardson* 1927 SLT 490.
5. Proposal 65, para 5.42.
6. Trusts (Scotland) Act 1921, s 23.
7. 1921 Act, s 3(1). The incapable granter would not, and the attorney should not, be able to appoint a new trustee.
8. Proposal 79, para 5.120.
9. Paras 5.21 to 5.32.

A duty to act?

3.49   We now turn to consider whether a continuing or welfare attorney should be under a statutory duty to use the powers conferred by the document of appointment and be liable for loss caused by failure to use them. At present the position depends on the terms of the power of attorney, but the usual styles confer various powers on the attorney without imposing any express obligation to use them, and indeed often give the attorney a discretion whether to act[1]. It is difficult to imply an obligation to act in such circumstances, or the existence of a delictual remedy for failure to act, except where professionals such as solicitors or accountants are employed to look after the granter's affairs on a remunerated basis.

3.50   In our discussion paper we proposed that continuing financial attorneys should be under a statutory duty to carry out the functions set out in the document of appointment[2] and asked for views as to whether a similar duty should be imposed on welfare attorneys[3]. These proposals were agreed by almost all those who commented on them, subject to the proviso that the duty should arise only after the attorney had accepted the appointment. The main argument in favour of imposing a duty to act is that it would be in line with the granter's expectations. Continuing powers of attorney are created so that there will be someone to manage the granter's affairs when the granter is incapable or wishes to hand over financial matters to an attorney, or in the case of welfare powers to make decisions in the welfare field when the granter is incapable of doing so. The granter's intentions would be frustrated if the attorney simply did nothing. In connection with welfare attorneys the Senators of the College of Justice thought, however, that such a duty would be difficult to enforce and the possibility of being sued in respect of some failure to act might be a deterrent against agreeing to act as welfare attorney.

3.51   On reconsideration we have come to the conclusion that a statutory duty should not be imposed on either continuing or welfare attorneys. A statutory duty would pose particular difficulties in the welfare field where an attorney may be reluctant or unable to come to a decision. For example, if the power of attorney included power to consent to surgery should the attorney be forced, on pain of liability to damages, to come to a decision about the proposed operation? Another argument against imposing a duty to act is that relatives and friends might be unwilling to be appointed continuing attorneys in such circumstances. Moreover, any duty to act would be qualified once the granter was incapable by our recommended general principles of least restrictive action and having regard to the present wishes and feelings of the granter. We would point out that as far as paid professional attorneys are concerned the absence of a statutory duty to act would not make much difference since there would be an implied obligation on them to carry out the functions to the normal professional standard. We discuss the duties arising out of the fiduciary relationship between granter and attorney in Part 2[4].

3.52   We think that granters are best protected against inaction by choosing people who can be relied on to take appropriate action rather than the imposition of any statutory duty. Although we reject the imposition of an express statutory duty to act on continuing or welfare attorneys, such attorneys should consider exercising the powers conferred in appropriate circumstances. Making attorneys aware of this is something that should be included in the Code of Practice[5], a copy of which might be issued by the Public Guardian to continuing or welfare attorneys on registration.

Should there be official supervision of continuing or welfare attorneys?

3.53   In dealing with financial continuing attorneys in our discussion paper we rejected a scheme whereby some public authority should register continuing attorneys and monitor the performance of their functions[6]. As we pointed out regular monitoring would require a considerable number of new officials to be appointed since there could be somewhere in the region of 10,000 continuing attorneys active at any one time. Duplication of the monitoring system presently used for curators bonis and recommended by us for guardians appointed by the court would deprive continuing powers of attorney of much of their utility and make them much more expensive than they are at present. These points were accepted by those consulted and we received no evidence of widespread abuse by attorneys which would justify setting up a monitoring authority for all attorneys. Many respondents did, however, wish to see a simple registration system and we have already recommended[7] that the Public Guardian should register all documents conferring continuing or welfare powers of attorney and investigate complaints against registered attorneys.

3.54   In our discussion paper we asked whether welfare attorneys should be supervised by the Mental Welfare Commission in much the same way as mental health guardians appointed under the 1984 Act are as at present[8]. This includes periodical

---

1.   Halliday, *Conveyancing Law and Practice*, Vol 1, para 13.12; Journal of the Law Society of Scotland 1981, W209.
2.   Proposal 71(1), para 5.74.
3.   Proposal 81(1), para 5.122.
4.   Paras 2.74 to 2.79.
5.   Recommendation 25, para 3.56.
6.   Proposal 66(a), para 5.50.
7.   Recommendation 21, para 3.36.
8.   Proposal 83, para 5.126.

visits to those under guardianship as well as dealing with any problems and complaints as and when they arise[1]. Responses on this issue were divided. Some considered that welfare attorneys should be so supervised and monitored but questioned whether the Mental Welfare Commission would be able to offer the same supervisory service as it presently does for mental health guardianship without an enormous increase in resources. At present there are 81 active cases of guardianship[2]. If even a modest proportion of all future attorneys were to be granted welfare powers the case load could increase by a factor of ten. Others thought that the Mental Welfare Commission's existing protective role in relation to the welfare (and property) of the mentally disordered should suffice, so that the Commission would be under a duty to investigate complaints. We prefer this latter approach. There should be a difference in the degree of supervision between continuing or welfare attorneys and guardians that have been appointed by the court. Attorneys have been freely appointed by granters when capable and have been chosen on the basis of their knowledge of the granter and their reliability and honesty; guardians are appointed by a court to incapable adults on the basis of need. Moreover, attorneys are privately appointed so that there should not be extensive intervention by public agencies. One body suggested that local authorities, via their social work departments, should have the same functions (periodical visits and supervision of non-local authority guardians) in relation to welfare attorneys as they do for mental health guardians[3]. We disagree for the same reasons as we have put forward for not conferring such functions on the Mental Welfare Commission.

3.55   Although the Public Guardian, the Mental Welfare Commission and local authorities would not supervise or monitor the performance of every continuing or welfare attorney they would in terms of our earlier recommendations be under a duty to investigate where there was a complaint or cause for concern[4]. Furthermore, the court could, on the application of any interested person subject a continuing or welfare attorney to supervision and monitoring by one of the appropriate bodies. As a result of such investigations or otherwise any one of these bodies is to be entitled to apply to the court for various orders in relation to continuing or welfare attorneys[5]. A Code of Practice would help in making continuing and welfare attorneys aware of their duties and responsibilities. This in turn should cut down the number of complaints and investigations. Registration of the document conferring the power of attorney provides an opportunity to hand every attorney a copy of the Code.

3.56   We recommend that:

> **25. (1) Continuing and welfare attorneys should not be monitored or supervised either by the Public Guardian, Mental Welfare Commission or local authority except where a court order is made to this effect under Recommendation 26. This should be without prejudice to the existing and recommended investigative and protective functions of the Public Guardian, Mental Welfare Commission and local authority.**
>
> **(2) The Secretary of State should prepare and publish a Code of Practice containing guidance to continuing and welfare attorneys as to the exercise of their functions.**

Clause 10(1)(b)

Court orders relating to continuing or welfare attorneys

3.57   In our discussion paper we put forward various powers which could be conferred on the courts in order to improve the protection of granters[6]. We saw increased court powers as a less intrusive alternative to the continuous supervision and monitoring of attorneys by some public authority, and the possibility of court intervention would tend to make attorneys more careful. Before discussing the powers in detail we consider the general grounds for making an application to the court.

3.58   In our discussion paper we proposed that an application for production of accounts by an attorney[7] or for removal of a continuing attorney[8] should not be competent as long as the granter remained mentally capable. We considered that intervention while the granter remained capable would be an unwarranted intrusion into the granter's affairs. The granter and the attorney may have agreed to dispense with accounts or the granter may have agreed with, or acquiesced in, the attorney's actions. Moreover, a capable granter could defeat any court order by granting a fresh power of attorney or reappointing the attorney. On the other hand basing competence on the granter's capacity means that an applicant must first satisfy the court that the granter is incapable and this could cause practical difficulties.

3.59   Although there was general agreement with our proposals, some respondents pointed out that the effect would be that vulnerable or facile granters with limited capacity would be denied protection unless they took the necessary action

---

1.   1984 Act, s 3.
2.   Mental Welfare Commission, *Annual Report, 1993/94*, p 14.
3.   The Mental Health (Specified Treatments, Guardianship Duties etc) (Scotland) Regulations 1984, SI 1984/1494.
4.   Recommendation 21(6), para 3.36.
5.   Recommendation 26, para 3.60.
6.   Paras 5.51 to 5.63.
7.   Proposal 68(1), para 5.57.
8.   Proposal 69(1), para 5.63.

themselves. We appreciate the concerns of these respondents but intervening in every case of vulnerability would go too far. Vulnerable is a vague concept as is facile. In Part 6 we recommend that a guardianship order may be granted if the court is satisfied that the adult is incapable of making decisions or is incapable of acting to promote or safeguard his or her interests[1]. We think the same test should apply to court orders for continuing and welfare attorneys, except that the incapacity should have to exist in relation to the matters covered by the power of attorney. In addition the court should have to be satisfied that the making of an order is necessary to safeguard or promote the interests of the granter in the matters to which the power of attorney relates. This additional requirement prevents the court from revoking the power of attorney and replacing the attorney with a guardian simply because the granter has become incapable. As far as welfare attorneys are concerned it is most unlikely that any application would need to be made to the court in advance of the granter's incapacity. This is because of our previous recommendation that a welfare power should not be exerciseable by a welfare attorney until he or she considers that the granter is no longer capable of making the welfare decision in question[2].

3.60   We recommend that:

26. In order to better protect granters of continuing or welfare powers of attorney, the court should have power, on application by any person claiming an interest in the granter's welfare or finances, to make various orders relating to the attorney. The power should be exercisable only if the court is satisfied that the granter is incapable of giving directions to the attorney or of safeguarding his or her own interests in relation to the matters covered by the power of attorney and that the making of the order is necessary to safeguard the granter.

Clause 15(1), (2)

3.61   **Accounting.** In our discussion paper we proposed that the court should be empowered to order a continuing attorney to produce accounts and receipts for all or any part of the period since the date of execution of the continuing power of attorney[3]. The accounts produced were to be audited by the Public Guardian. We pointed out the difficulties that had arisen in Ontario where a similar power is limited to accounts for the period after incapacity. Because of the difficulty in deciding when incapacity occurs the power is rarely used.

3.62   Those responding to this proposal were generally in favour. The Accountant of Court, however, commented that attorneys would have to be under a statutory duty to keep accounts during their period of acting as attorney so that they would be available for production if the court so ordered. We see the force of this comment but think it would be unduly onerous to impose a duty to keep accounts on every continuing attorney. Many attorneys will be relatives or friends who could not prepare formal accounts and would have to pay for this to be done. Attorneys should simply keep a record of their transactions. These records could then be used to prepare the accounts if the court ordered production of accounts. Of course, if accounts had been prepared, as might be the case where a solicitor or accountant was acting as continuing attorney on a paid basis, then such accounts could be produced to the court.

3.63   Under our recommended registration scheme a continuing attorney has no authority to act as such until the document of appointment is registered with the Public Guardian[4]. The earliest date from which the court should be able to order accounts or records to be produced should be the date of registration rather than the date of execution of the continuing power of attorney as we had originally proposed.

3.64   One respondent questioned the desirability of disclosing the accounts and the Public Guardian's audit report to the applicant and others. We consider this is best left to the discretion of the court. The accounts and audit report should always be lodged with the court which thereafter would decide whether to disclose them and if so to whom they should be disclosed. Any further action would also be a matter for the court on receipt of an application made to it.

3.65   We recommend that:

27. The court should have power under Recommendation 26 to order a continuing attorney to produce accounts of his or her transactions with the granter's estate. Accounts should be ordered in respect of all or any of the period from the date of registration of the document conferring the continuing power to the date of the order. The accounts should be audited by the Public Guardian and the accounts and audit report thereafter lodged in court.

Clause 15(2)(b)

3.66   **Supervision by Public Guardian.** Some of those responding to our proposal that the court should have power to order a continuing attorney to produce accounts for auditing suggested that future supervision of the attorney might be

---

1. Recommendation 85, para 6.29.
2. Recommendation 23, para 3.42.
3. Proposal 68(2), para 5.57.
4. Recommendation 21(4), para 3.36.

D

appropriate. We are attracted to this suggestion. It could be a useful halfway house between letting the attorney carry on unchecked and revoking the appointment with the substitution of a fully supervised court-appointed guardian. For example, the court might order that the granter's dwellinghouse and other valuable assets should be disposed of only with the Public Guardian's consent. We recommend that:

28. **The court should have power under Recommendation 26 to order that a continuing attorney should in future be subject to such supervision by the Public Guardian as it thinks fit.**

Clause 15(2)(a)

3.67 **Reporting to court and supervision by local authority.** Some equivalent of a financial audit is needed in relation to a welfare attorney's powers. We consider that the court should be empowered to order the attorney to produce a report on how the welfare powers have been exercised. The report should be made to the court in the first place. Thereafter it may decide to ask the local authority Social Work Department to consider the report, investigate as necessary and report back to the court. As a result of these proceedings the court should, we consider, have power to order the attorney to be supervised in the exercise of his or her welfare functions. We recommend that:

29. (1) **The court should have power under Recommendation 26 to order a welfare attorney to produce a report as to how any welfare powers have been exercised in all or any of the period between registration of the document conferring the welfare power and the date of the order.**

(2) **As a result of the report or otherwise the court should have power to order the welfare attorney to be subject in future to such supervision by the local authority in respect of any welfare powers as it thinks fit.**

Clause 15(2)(c), (d)

3.68 **Directions to attorney.** Some jurisdictions have conferred on their courts the power to give directions to the attorney as to the exercise of his or her functions, and we proposed that a similar power be introduced to Scotland[1]. All those responding agreed. A directory power would be useful for an attorney faced with a difficult decision since a ruling could be obtained from the court after all those interested had been given an opportunity to make representations and be heard. Others with an interest in the granter's welfare and estate could also apply, either to prevent an attorney carrying out some proposed transaction or to have the attorney directed to do something. We recommend that:

30. **The court should have power under Recommendation 26 to give directions to a continuing or welfare attorney as to the exercise of his or her functions.**

Clause 3(3)

3.69 **Removal of continuing or welfare attorney and revocation of power.** As long as the granter retains capacity he or she may remove the attorney and appoint another or revoke the continuing or welfare power of attorney already granted. Once the granter becomes incapable removal or revocation by the granter is no longer possible. At present the court has no express power to remove an attorney or revoke a power of attorney. The court can, however, appoint a curator who supersedes the attorney in the management of the granter's financial affairs[2]. Appointment of a guardian under our recommendations in Part 6 would have the same effect but only in so far as the guardian's financial or welfare powers coincided with those of the attorney.

3.70 We proposed in our discussion paper that the court should have an express power of removal[3]. This would be useful where the continuing or welfare attorney ought to be removed but the granter's estate and welfare could be managed without the appointment of a guardian. Removal of the acting attorney might also be sought in order to allow the substitute attorney specified in the power of attorney to take over, or to remove one of two joint attorneys. All those consulted agreed, but it was pointed out that the court should have power to remove the substitute attorney as well since the terms of the power of attorney might be inappropriate rather than the way in which a particular attorney has exercised the functions. We agree and consider that this is best achieved by giving the court an express power to revoke the power of attorney (wholly or partially) as well as to remove the attorney. For removal of an attorney we proposed a simple general formula that removal was in the best interests of the granter rather than detailed guidelines. While this was agreed we now consider that the general principles recommended in Part 2 above should guide the court in the exercise of its powers of revocation and removal. The Public Guardian as registration authority should be informed of any revocation or removal so that the register of attorneys could be amended.

3.71 The overlap between guardians and continuing or welfare attorneys needs to be considered. In most cases we imagine that the appointment of a guardian will be sought in order to supersede the attorney completely. The effect of the appointment of a guardian should be to terminate the authority of the attorney in relation to matters within the scope

---

1. Proposal 70(2)(a), para 5.68.
2. See, for example, *Fraser v Paterson* 1987 SLT 562.
3. Proposal 69, para 5.63.

of the guardian's powers[1]. But it ought to be possible to appoint a guardian with powers that do not impinge on those of the attorney. For example, another person could seek appointment as guardian with welfare powers and thereafter collaborate with the financial continuing attorney in promoting the overall welfare of the granter or the continuing attorney himself or herself could seek appointment as welfare guardian. There might even be situations where a guardian is appointed with financial powers in an area where the continuing attorney has no authority. Where the attorney is to remain functioning along with a guardian directions might need to be given by the court as to how each appointee is to exercise their functions.

3.72   We recommend that:

31. The court should have power under Recommendation 26 to revoke a continuing or welfare attorney's appointment (including one or more joint attorneys or a substitute attorney) and to revoke in whole or in part the continuing or welfare power of attorney. The revocation should be notified to the Public Guardian.

Clause 15(2)(e), (3)

3.73   **Variation of continuing or welfare power of attorney.** Should the court have power to vary the power of attorney? The attorney may find that he or she lacks a power to deal with something that was not anticipated by the granter. We did not favour conferring a power of variation on the courts in our discussion paper[2] and most of those consulted agreed. The Senators of the College of Justice commented that variation would be worthwhile to deal with cases where carrying out the granter's instructions had become impossible, unduly burdensome or expensive. But the general principles that we have recommended should govern all decision-makers, including continuing or welfare attorneys, would not require the exercise of powers after the granter's incapacity in these circumstances. Two bodies considered that variation should be available to deal with drafting errors. New statutory provisions however seem unnecessary to deal with errors which stem from the failure of the document to express accurately the intentions of the granter. Such errors can be rectified by the court under section 8 of the Law Reform (Miscellaneous Provisions) (Scotland) Act 1985.

3.74   Some flexibility is necessary: granters should not be left without anyone able to help or protect them because their powers of attorney turn out to be inadequate in the circumstances. However, we remain of the view that this aim should not be achieved by court variation of the power of attorney. Variation involves interfering with the expressed wishes of the granter and the court in re-writing the document could only guess at what the granter would have decided in the circumstances. We consider that an appropriate remedy would be available under our other recommendations. Where the granter's instructions were such that to carry them out would be unduly burdensome or expensive the attorney would be justified in not following them under our recommended general principles. In extreme cases the attorney might have to resign and seek appointment as a guardian with more appropriate powers. Where extra powers over and above those conferred by the granter seemed to be needed the attorney could apply to the court for an intervention order or a limited guardianship order conferring such powers. This would not be a variation of the contract of mandate or agency conferring the continuing or welfare power of attorney because the attorney would continue to exercise the existing power of attorney according to the contract and would exercise the other powers conferred by the court in terms of the intervention order or guardianship order. Accordingly we recommend that:

32. The court should not have power to vary the terms of a contract of mandate or agency conferring a continuing or welfare power of attorney.

Resignation of continuing or welfare attorneys

3.75   An attorney acting under an ordinary power of attorney may resign at any time. Resignation by a continuing or welfare attorney at a time when the granter is incapable would leave the granter without anybody to take financial or welfare decisions. In our discussion paper we asked whether a sole or remaining continuing attorney should be required to notify his or her intention to resign to the granter if capable and, where the granter was not capable, to the granter's nearest relative and the local authority[3]. This proposal was put forward in order to avoid any undesirable hiatus in the granter's affairs since steps could be taken after notification to ensure that a guardian was appointed before the attorney's resignation became effective.

3.76   All those responding agreed that continuing attorneys should be required to notify their intention to resign, although it makes continuing powers of attorney a little more complex. Several suggestions were made which we consider useful. First, that if continuing powers of attorney were to be registered then notice of intention to resign should be given to the registration authority. In our scheme the register is to be kept by the Public Guardian. Our recommended resignation procedure should apply only to continuing or welfare powers of attorney conferred in documents which have been registered with the Public Guardian, since before registration the powers cannot be exercised. Secondly, that there should

---

1.   Recommendation 34(2), para 3.79.
2.   Proposal 70(1), para 5.68.
3.   Proposal 72, para 5.79.

be a period before the resignation took effect in order to allow time for alternative arrangements to be made. 28 days seems to us to be an appropriate period. This period would not be necessary where there were other joint attorneys willing to continue to act or a substitute attorney willing to take over. Thirdly, notification to the local authority and the granter's nearest relative was queried. It was pointed out that the granter may not have wished the nearest relative to be involved and may have deliberately appointed someone else as attorney. We would substitute the granter's primary carer, the individual or organisation primarily responsible for looking after the granter. Notification to the local authority was proposed since that body had under our proposals a duty to apply for appointment as a financial manager if no one else applied. We recognise the force of the criticism that powers of attorney are meant to be private documents and that there should be minimum involvement by public authorities. Notification to one public official, the Public Guardian, should suffice unless a welfare attorney was being supervised by the local authority in accordance with a court order. A duty to notify only capable granters could cause problems for attorneys, especially where capacity fluctuates. We now think that the granter should always be notified of the attorney's intention to resign. In the rare case where a guardian has been appointed to act alongside the attorney, the attorney should also notify the guardian. The above resignation procedure should also apply to welfare attorneys.

3.77   We recommend that:

33. (1)   In order to prevent a lapse in arrangements made for the safeguarding of the granter's welfare and financial affairs a continuing or welfare attorney acting under a registered power of attorney should have to give notice of his or her intention to resign to the granter, the Public Guardian, the granter's primary carer, and, if the local authority was supervising the attorney or a guardian had been appointed, also to the local authority or guardian.

(2)   The resignation should become effective 28 days after notification to the Public Guardian. But where the attorney's resignation would still leave at least one continuing or welfare attorney (joint or substitute) in post the resignation should be effective as soon as the Public Guardian is satisfied that the remaining joint attorney(s) will continue to act or the substitute attorney is willing to act.

Clause 17

Termination of continuing or welfare powers of attorney

3.78   Termination of continuing powers of attorney on the occurrence of certain events and the protection of good faith attorneys and third parties who engage in transactions in ignorance of the termination were considered in our discussion paper. We came to the provisional conclusion that the common law rules were adequate and no reform was needed[1]. No contrary comments were made by those consulted. However, we consider that it would be helpful for the new legislation to contain an express provision making it clear that the common law rule that the appointment of a curator terminates the authority of an attorney[2] applies to the appointment of a guardian in so far as their powers coincide.

3.79   A new statutory provision also seems necessary to deal with the situation where the granter appoints his or her spouse to be continuing or welfare attorney and the couple subsequently separate or divorce or their purported marriage is annulled. We imagine that most granters would not wish their spouses to continue to act, and accordingly consider that the appointment should fall automatically. Granters who wish their spouses to continue to act after a decree of separation divorce or nullity may insert a provision to that effect in the contract of mandate or agency conferring the continuing or welfare power of attorney. We recommend that:

34. (1)   The appointment by the granter of his or her spouse as continuing or welfare attorney should be revoked automatically by a decree of separation, divorce or nullity relating to the granter and his or her spouse, unless the granter provides otherwise in the contract of mandate or agency conferring the continuing or welfare power of attorney.

(2)   Where a guardian is appointed with certain powers the authority of a continuing or welfare attorney in relation to matters within the scope of those powers should automatically terminate.

Clause 18(1), (2)

Disposal by attorney of special legacies

3.80   A special legacy is adeemed if the item bequeathed is not part of the deceased's estate at death because it had been disposed of earlier. The intended beneficiary receives nothing in lieu[3]. This could cause problems with continuing attorneys. Suppose, for example, a granter leaves by will her shares in British Gas to her son and her shares in British Petroleum to her daughter. The continuing attorney sells the British Gas shares to raise cash or invest elsewhere. As a result the

---

1. Paras 5.87 to 5.90.
2. *Fraser v Paterson* 1987 SLT 562.
3. Gloag and Henderson, *An Introduction to the Law of Scotland* (9th edn), para 43.16.
4. Proposal 70(3), para 5.68.

special legacy is adeemed and the son receives nothing. In our discussion paper we considered whether the court should have power to award the disappointed beneficiary something in lieu. In order to avoid litigation we proposed[4] that the present rule for disposals by curators should be adopted ie disposal of a specially bequeathed item does not result in ademption unless disposal was necessary[1].

3.81   While most of those responding agreed with our proposal, the Law Society was not in favour. The problem was in its opinion best solved by granters giving instructions in the document containing the power of attorney as to what the attorney should do with items that were the subject of special legacies and by the attorney being aware of the granter's will. There is also the practical difficulty of deciding years later whether it had been necessary for the attorney to dispose of a particular item. On reconsideration we have concluded that this report is not the appropriate place to deal with the problem of ademption of legacies. The problem is one of succession law since people other than attorneys and guardians may dispose of items specifically bequeathed.

Private international law aspects

3.82   Our discussion paper dealt with the authority in Scotland of non-Scottish powers of attorney. As far as formal validity is concerned a document conferring a power of attorney will be regarded as valid in Scotland if it is executed in accordance with the law of the country in which it was executed or, it is thought, in accordance with the rules of the proper law[2]. The more difficult issue is the authority in Scotland of an attorney appointed by an enduring, durable or continuing power of attorney granted in another jurisdiction whose internal law would confer authority on the attorney during the granter's incapacity. With the increasing mobility of people and possession of property in more than one country this and similar issues are becoming increasingly important. In order to clarify the matter we proposed[3] that the authority of such an attorney to act after the granter's incapacity should be governed by the proper law of the power of attorney. The proper law is the law which the granter either expressly or impliedly indicates to be the applicable law in the document conferring the power of attorney or the one which has the closest or most real connection with the power of attorney. All those who responded agreed. The Contracts (Applicable Law) Act 1990 does not apply to the question whether an agent is able to bind a principal to a third party[4]. As we recommend in the next paragraph non-Scottish attorneys should be subject to the same restrictions relating to personal welfare powers and the same protective jurisdiction as Scottish continuing or welfare attorneys. We recommend that:

35.   Subject to Recommendation 36 the effect during the granter's incapacity in Scotland of a mandate or agency conferring a continuing or welfare power of attorney (however expressed) should be determined according to the proper law of the mandate or agency.

Clause 19

3.83   To what extent should non-Scottish attorneys be equated with Scottish attorneys for the purposes of our previous recommendations? In Part 6 we deal with a similar question in relation to guardianship[5]. Our general approach there is that the registration, supervision and regulatory provisions should apply only to Scottish guardians, but that the investigation of complaints, the taking of protective action and making protective orders and obtaining and considering the views of guardians in relation to proposed courses of action should apply to non-Scottish guardians as well. We would adopt the same approach in relation to continuing and welfare attorneys. The special execution requirements we recommend for Scottish continuing and welfare powers of attorney clearly should not be applied to non-Scottish documents conferring similar powers; such documents should be treated as formally valid if executed according to the applicable foreign requirements. We therefore recommend that:

36.   The following recommendations in Part 3 relating to Scottish continuing or welfare attorneys should apply to their equivalents appointed under the law of any other country:

(a)   Recommendation 23 (welfare powers exerciseable only during granter's incapacity),

(b)   Recommendation 24 (welfare attorney not to place granter in hospital for treatment of mental disorder against granter's will),

(c)   Recommendations 26-31 (various court orders relating to continuing or welfare attorneys), and

(d)   Recommendation 34(2) (appointment of guardian terminates attorney's authority in so far as powers coincide).

Clauses 12(7), 15(5) and 18(3)

---

1.   *McFarlane's Trs v McFarlane* 1910 SC 325.
2.   Anton, *Private International Law*, (2nd edn) p 305.
3.   Proposal 74, para 5.93.
4.   Sch 1, Article 1(2)(f).
5.   Paras 6.218 to 6.225.

Part 4   Other Types of Extra-Judicial Management

Introduction

4.1   Our investigations have revealed that there is an unmet need for simple inexpensive ways of managing the property or financial affairs of incapable adults with modest means. The expense of appointing a curator bonis often rules out this solution and it is unlikely that our recommended guardianship will be substantially cheaper. Continuing attorneys would be a solution but only a small proportion of incapable adults currently take steps before incapacity to appoint an attorney to act should they become incapable later. Even if this proportion increases substantially there would still be a very large number of incapable adults without attorneys.

4.2   The affairs of incapable adults may be managed informally using the concept of *negotiorum gestio*. This, according to Bell is "the management of the affairs of one who is absent, spontaneously undertaken without his knowledge, and on the presumption that he would, if aware of the circumstances, have given a mandate for such interference"[1]. Absence includes absence of mind through mental incapacity[2]. *Negotiorum gestio* is not limited to urgent or immediate acts of administration and management by a *gestor* may continue for many years[3]. *Negotiorum gestio* enables a husband, wife, parent, child or other relative or close friend to look after the affairs of an incapable adult without the expense of having a curator appointed. The main disadvantage is the lack of any document evidencing the powers of the *gestor*. Because of this and the doubts about the limits of a *gestor's* powers it is often difficult for *gestors* to persuade third parties to deal with them or accept instructions from them. Nevertheless, we think *negotiorum gestio* has a useful role to play in the management of the affairs of the incapable and we do not make any express recommendations for curtailing it. However, some of our recommendations, by providing new statutory procedures for some matters that currently fall within the scope of *negotiorum gestio*, will to that extent make reliance on it unnecessary.

4.3   In this Part we put forward three schemes for dealing with the financial affairs of incapable adults in terms of which authority may be obtained otherwise than from the courts. The first would allow an individual caring for an incapable adult at home to obtain authority from the Public Guardian to withdraw money from the adult's bank or building society account to meet household and other necessary expenditure for the adult. The second would authorise hospitals and other residential establishments approved by the Public Guardian to set up properly run and accountable systems for managing the finances of their incapable residents up to a specified monetary limit. Both schemes build upon existing statutory and extra-statutory methods but extend them to other organisations and add an element of accounting to, and scrutiny by, a public official - the Public Guardian. The third scheme would entitle one account holder of a joint account to carry on operating the account when the other became incapacitated.

WITHDRAWALS FROM BANK ACCOUNTS

The scheme in outline

4.4   In our discussion paper we pointed out that some of the financial problems of incapable adults, especially the dementing elderly, could be solved if access could be given to their bank or building society account otherwise than by the appointment of a curator[4]. Income such as a pension, dividends and social security benefits payable to the adult can readily be paid into his or her account, but there is often difficulty in obtaining money from the account to pay for food, clothing and household expenses for an incapable adult being cared for at home. Informal arrangements can sometimes be made with the bank whereby the carer is permitted to withdraw money, but even where such an arrangement is made it is often only a temporary facility pending the appointment of a curator. Some building societies have in their rules a more formal, but nevertheless non-statutory, procedure for allowing access by a carer to an incapable adult's account.

4.5   In our discussion paper we proposed an administrative system whereby a named individual could obtain authority to withdraw money from an adult's bank account[5]. The individual was required to present -

---

1. *Principles*, para 540.
2. *Fernie v Robertson* (1871) 9M 437.
3. *Maule v Graham* (1757) Mor 3529; *Fernie v Robertson*; *Dunbar v Wilson and Dunlop's Tr* (1887) 15 R 210.
4. Para 4.173.
5. Proposal 57, para 4.178.

(a) a medical certificate that the adult was mentally disabled to a substantial extent,

(b) a certificate from a solicitor or social worker that the named individual was looking after the adult, and

(c) an undertaking from the individual to use any money withdrawn for the benefit of the adult.

On presentation of the certificates and undertaking the bank was to be entitled, but not bound, to allow the individual to withdraw. The bank might terminate the arrangement at any time on becoming aware of circumstances making it inappropriate for the arrangement to continue. Termination could also have been ordered by the court on application by any interested person.

4.6   Our proposal was welcomed in principle by nearly all those who replied. Respondents considered there was a need for a fairly simple method of withdrawing money from an incapable adult's bank account. One dissenting organisation commented that it was sadly the case that people sometimes exploited their incapacitated relatives and that the proposals would make it easier for them to do so. Many other respondents also voiced concern about abuse and put forward helpful suggestions for improvements to minimise abuse. We accept that any scheme not involving close supervision by a public official could lead to increased abuse. It is a question of balancing this against the undoubted benefits to be gained from making access by the vast majority of honest and reliable carers easier and cheaper.

4.7   The Scottish Association for Mental Health suggested that the arrangements should have to be reported to the Accountant of Court or the Mental Welfare Commission who would maintain a register and could identify potential abuse if an individual was found to have obtained access to several adults' accounts. We agree with this suggestion and have taken it further. We have also had the benefit of further consultation with the Accountant and Deputy Accountant of Court, the Committee of Scottish Clearing Bankers and the Building Societies Association. We are grateful to them for their comments and suggestions which have greatly assisted us in preparing a new scheme. We now consider that the Public Guardian (whose functions would be carried out by the Accountant of Court) should not only keep a register but should also act as the authorising body. In our view any scheme for managing the financial affairs of an incapable adult which is imposed without that adult's advance consent ought to be controlled and monitored to some extent by a public official. The outline of the scheme we now put forward is as follows. Individuals wishing to obtain authority to withdraw should have to apply to the Public Guardian for such authority. The application should be accompanied by a medical certificate that the adult is incapable of operating the account. The application would be countersigned by a member of a prescribed class of persons that to the best of the countersigner's knowledge and belief the applicant was a fit and proper person to be given authority to withdraw. The Public Guardian would then notify the adult and his or her nearest relative and primary carer and give them an opportunity to object. If there were no objections or the Public Guardian was satisfied that any objection was groundless the Public Guardian should grant authority. Details of the authorisation would then be recorded in a public register kept by the Public Guardian. The Public Guardian's certificate of authority would then be handed to the applicant, for presentation to the bank concerned.

4.8   The scheme outlined in the previous paragraph also meets concerns expressed by the Committee of Scottish Clearing Bankers about our proposed certificates. It queried how a bank manager could ensure that the certificates had indeed been given by the account-holder's general practitioner, solicitor or social worker and whether the bank would be liable for failing to carry out adequate checks on the certificates and any further information provided by the individual applying for authority to withdraw. The Building Societies Association informed us that many of its members operating in Scotland would also prefer not to have to decide the suitability of applicants and the appropriateness of allowing withdrawals themselves lest they leave themselves open to claims. Under our new scheme the bank or building society would be entitled to rely on a document from the Public Guardian showing that authority to withdraw had been granted. We do not regard this scheme as duplicating guardianship or intervention orders which we recommend later[1]. Guardians are appointed to safeguard and promote all or part of an incapable adult's welfare and finances over an extended period. Because of the range of their powers, and the effect of their appointment on the adult's own legal capacity, they are to be appointed by the court after checks to ensure that guardianship is needed and the proposed guardian is suitable. Where the question at issue is a limited power to withdraw from a bank account, which has no effect on the adult's own legal capacity, a simpler administrative procedure is justified. Intervention orders are designed for "one-off" situations where a decision has to be made or a consent granted. They are not intended to continue for a considerable period of time, unlike authority to withdraw from accounts.

4.9   Registration in a public register held by the Public Guardian of individuals having authority to withdraw would also have other benefits. The fact that the authorisation is in the public domain would serve as some check on abuse. Bodies such as the Mental Welfare Commission with statutory duties to protect the property of the mentally disordered and others with an interest in the welfare of incapable adults (either generally or in relation to particular individuals) would have ready access to information about those authorised to withdraw and could take the appropriate action if abuse

---

1. See Part 6.

was suspected. The Public Guardian's office would also act as a place to which complaints could be made or possible abuse reported. If there seemed to be any substance in a complaint the Public Guardian should be entitled to suspend or terminate the authority to withdraw, in either case immediately notifying the withdrawer and the bank concerned.

4.10   What degree of incapacity should have to exist before authority to withdraw should be granted? We consider the incapacity should be such as to render the adult incapable of operating the account. Those incapable of operating the account should include adults who can physically sign cheques or perform other tasks in connection with the account, but do so without any understanding, and also adults who are unable to communicate in any way due to their physical condition. A definition tied to the particular area in which authority is sought is necessary otherwise there would be too great an interference in the financial affairs of those who, while having some degree of incapacity, could still manage their banking arrangements. A functional test is also easier for applicants and those certifying incapacity to work with.

4.11   The scheme we are putting forward should be limited to Scotland in some way. This should be done using two criteria. First, the incapable adult account holder should have to be habitually resident in Scotland. Second, the account should have to be held at a branch situated in Scotland, but the bank need not be a Scottish bank.

4.12   We recommend that:

> **37. (1) The Public Guardian, on application, should be empowered to authorise the applicant to withdraw money, or arrange for payments to be made, from a specified bank account held at a branch situated in Scotland of an adult who is incapable of operating the account and habitually resident in Scotland.**
>
> **(2) The Public Guardian should keep a public register of individuals authorised to withdraw.**
>
> Clauses 4(2)(c)(iii) and 20(1), (2)(a), (3)

When scheme applies

4.13   The recommended scheme is intended to enable named individuals to obtain authority to withdraw money from an incapable adult's bank account without having to go to court for an intervention order or the appointment of a guardian. The scheme should not be capable of being used where other persons have already been appointed with powers over the account[1]. For example, if the adult has appointed a continuing attorney with powers over his or her bank account or the court has appointed a guardian with similar powers or made an intervention order, then the Public Guardian should not grant authority to withdraw to the applicant. The Public Guardian would be aware of the existence of a continuing attorney or guardian or an intervention order since these would have been registered with the Public Guardian. Non-Scottish attorneys or guardians would not be so registered, but the bank ought to be aware of their existence if their powers extended to such accounts. If so, they should decline to allow withdrawals. Our recommendations would allow them to do this since the scheme merely entitles, but does not oblige, the bank to allow withdrawals. Those who operate the scheme in good faith and without knowledge of a prior appointment should be protected. We recommend that:

> **38. (1) The withdrawal scheme recommended in Recommendation 37 should not apply if the incapable adult's bank account was subject to an existing intervention order or powers granted to a guardian or continuing attorney or similar appointee under the law of any other country.**
>
> **(2) No liability should be incurred by any person who acts in good faith and in ignorance of any grant or appointment.**
>
> Clause 26

Procedure in obtaining authority to withdraw

4.14   Our proposed certificates, one from the adult's general practitioner certifying incapacity and the other from a solicitor or social worker who knew the incapable adult and the individual caring for him or her were criticised by many of those who responded. The British Medical Association (Scottish Branch) thought that certifying incapacity for this purpose was not an appropriate use of a doctor's time and Enable doubted whether a general practitioner necessarily had sufficiently detailed knowledge of the patient's degree of disorder and the extent to which it affected his or her ability to manage finances. It was also pointed out that certification by a solicitor or social worker who knew the adult and his or her circumstances would not be possible for many people who had neither a solicitor nor a social worker. Other respondents thought that the certification scheme was too complex and suggested a countersigning procedure by persons of standing in the community similar to that used for authenticating passport photographs. We are most grateful for this helpful suggestion and have adopted it. We now recommend that an applicant for authority to withdraw should provide information about himself or herself, the incapable adult and the bank account by filling in a prescribed application form. The form would contain an undertaking by the applicant to use money withdrawn only for the purposes sanctioned by the scheme[2]. The applicant would also be required to provide a medical certificate that the adult was incapable of operating the account.

---

1. See para 4.24 for the effect of the subsequent appointment of a guardian or the making of an intervention order.
2. See paras 4.16 and 4.17.

The form should include a statement by a person of standing in the community, (such as a doctor, social worker or police officer, being a member of a class prescribed by regulations made by the Secretary of State) that, to the best of his or her knowledge and belief, the information given in the form by the applicant was true and that the individual applicant was a fit and proper person to be granted authority to withdraw. The form should contain a prominent warning that making false statements was a serious offence. We consider that those wishing to obtain authority to withdraw should be able to find a countersigner without undue difficulty. Accordingly we recommend that:

39. (1) An applicant for authority to withdraw should have to apply on a prescribed form. The form should require details of the applicant, the incapable adult and the bank account to be provided. It should also contain a declaration by a member of a prescribed class of persons that to the best of his or her knowledge and belief the applicant was a fit and proper person to be granted authority to withdraw.

(2) The application should be accompanied by a certificate from a medical practitioner or other person qualified to assess incapacity that the adult was incapable of operating his or her bank account.

Clause 21(1)

4.15   On receipt of the application the Public Guardian should intimate it to the incapable adult, and his or her nearest relative and primary carer if they exist and their whereabouts are known. The applicant would have to give the names and addresses of these individuals in the application form. We envisage that in most cases no objections would be made so that the Public Guardian would grant authority. The Public Guardian should be empowered to grant the application even if objections were made. In this case the Public Guardian should give the applicant and any objector an opportunity to lodge further material and if the objection is still persisted in an opportunity to make oral representations. Where an objection raised complex issues or testimony from others seemed necessary to deal with the objection then the Public Guardian should be empowered to remit the application to the sheriff for a determination. Any objector should also be entitled to ask the Public Guardian to remit to the sheriff. An appeal would lie to the sheriff against the Public Guardian's decision on the application and also against a refusal to remit[1].

40.   The Public Guardian should give the incapable adult and his or her nearest relative and primary carer an opportunity to object to the application. The Public Guardian should have power to grant the application after considering any objections and any further representations by the applicant and any objector, or to remit the matter to the sheriff.

Clause 22(3)-(6)

Limits on amounts withdrawable

4.16   In our discussion paper we considered whether to propose limits on the amount that could be withdrawn under the scheme in order to cut down abuse[2]. We pointed out that cash limits would be difficult to operate since household needs and expenditure vary so much from one person to another. Many of those responding were in favour of some limitation of the right to withdraw. It was pointed out that a deposit account could contain many thousands of pounds representing the adult's entire savings. We have accordingly reconsidered the question of financial limits. The idea behind the scheme is to enable money in an incapable adult's bank account to be made available to meet living expenses. Many regular household expenses can be paid for by standing order or direct debit. Gas and electricity bills, council tax, rent, mortgage or accommodation charges and household insurance are familiar examples. There should be a statutory list of items which the withdrawer's normal authority should cover. Withdrawals of cash should be kept to a modest level to minimise the risk of abuse, but some cash purchases will always be necessary for items such as food. We consider that at present a weekly cash limit of £50 should be adequate, but this figure should be reviewed periodically and altered as necessary by the Secretary of State.

4.17   The statutory list of items payable by standing order or direct debit together with the weekly cash should suffice for many households. Others may require goods and services outwith the list or which cannot be paid for by standing order or direct debit. We do not think the withdrawer should be given a cash card or chequing facilities since there is no effective control over the use of these. We consider that the Public Guardian should be given a discretion, to be exercised where appropriate, to extend the withdrawer's normal authority. This could be done by specifying extra goods or services or payment by the bank (on request by the withdrawer) directly to specified suppliers. We see authorisation of these extras by the Public Guardian as having a number of advantages. First, it gives the adult and the nearest relative and primary carer an opportunity to object. Secondly, it introduces an element of public control and, thirdly, it removes from the bank staff the burden of having to decide whether or not to accede to requests by the withdrawer for extra-statutory payments.

4.18   The authority granted by the Public Guardian should apply only to a specified account held in the sole name of the adult at a specified branch of the bank[3]. We would not be in favour of withdrawals being made simultaneously from

---

1. See Recommendation 146, para 7.3.
2. Para 4.175.
3. See para 4.28 for joint accounts.

several different branches or banks because that would render the recommended financial limits meaningless. To cater for those people who keep modest sums in several branches or banks we think that it should be competent to reapply to the Public Guardian for authority to withdraw from a different organisation if funds in the initially authorised one had been exhausted. Extra caution would no doubt be exercised by the Public Guardian in dealing with serial applications. We recommend that:

41. (1) The Public Guardian's authorisation should entitle (but not oblige) the bank to allow the applicant to:

(a) withdraw £50 per week (or such other sum as may be prescribed by the Secretary of State) in cash, and

(b) authorise the bank to pay by direct debit or standing order for fuel, accommodation, clothing, sustenance and related goods and services;

in order to meet the living expenses of the incapable account holder. The authorisation should not entitle the withdrawer to overdraw the account.

(2) The Public Guardian should be empowered, if satisfied that an extension of authority is needed, to authorise:

(a) payment otherwise than by direct debit, standing order or cash to specified suppliers of goods and services, or

(b) payment for specified goods and services outwith those listed in paragraph (1)(b) above.

Clause 22(1), (2), (7)

Further safeguards for incapable adults

4.19   The scheme which we are recommending is designed to make an incapable adult's money in his or her own bank account available to meet the daily needs of that adult. The withdrawer should therefore be under a statutory duty to apply any money withdrawn only for the benefit of the adult, and be liable to repay any money spent on other matters. It would be difficult to apply this rule strictly where the withdrawer was living in the same household as the incapable adult, especially if the adult owed the withdrawer an obligation for aliment. Suppose, for example, a wife was looking after her demented husband. Is she supposed to pay her own share of the bills? We consider that the Public Guardian should have a discretionary power to authorise in appropriate cases the withdrawer to use money from the adult's account on household expenses. It follows from the fact that money must generally be spent only for the benefit of the adult that no gifts may be made out of the money withdrawn either to charities that the adult used to support or birthday or other seasonal gifts to members of the adult's family. The scheme is intended to be a simple one. If such gifts are desired then an application should be made for the appointment of a guardian who would, under our recommendations, have power to make such gifts with the consent of the Public Guardian[1]. Simple repayment of money misspent by the withdrawer would not be sufficient recompense to the account holder. We would therefore recommend repayment with interest at a rate substantially higher than the withdrawer could have obtained from misappropriating the money for his or her own benefit. A suitable enhanced interest rate would in our opinion be 5% above the rate from time to time applicable to a sheriff court decree in the absence of any rate specified in the decree[2]. This rate is readily ascertainable and does not change so frequently that interest calculations become laborious. At present the enhanced rate would be 13%.

4.20   We have considered whether the withdrawer should be under a statutory duty to keep accounts or records of what the money withdrawn has been spent on. Having to keep accounts or records for possible later examination would help to prevent abuse, but a duty to keep accounts would we think be too onerous, as many of the withdrawers would be unable to prepare accounts without professional assistance. Even a statutory duty to keep records is in our opinion too heavy a duty to impose on ordinary family carers. Many of the transactions will be on a cash basis, buying food and other household items. Withdrawers might wish to keep records for their own protection should their actings be challenged. A Code of Practice containing guidance to withdrawers as to how to operate the scheme would help develop good practice. The Secretary of State should prepare and issue such a code. If it appears after the scheme has been operating that withdrawers should be required to keep records of expenditure then this should be introduced. To avoid new primary legislation the Secretary of State should have power to introduce such a requirement by way of regulations. The Public Guardian could also have a role in policing the scheme by investigating complaints about withdrawers and carrying out "spot checks" even in the absence of complaints. The Public Guardian should be empowered to require a withdrawer to produce such records and vouchers as exist. Failure to comply could lead to termination of the withdrawer's authority to withdraw[3]. We recommend that:

42. (1) The withdrawer should use money withdrawn under the scheme only for the benefit of the incapable

---

1. Recommendation 104, para 6.110.
2. Sheriff Court (Scotland) Extracts Act 1892, s 9.
3. See Recommendation 44(2), para 4.25.

account holder except in so far as otherwise authorised by the Public Guardian. If money is used otherwise the withdrawer should be obliged to repay it with interest at 5% above the rate from time to time applicable to a sheriff court decree in the absence of any rate specified in the decree.

(2) The Public Guardian should be entitled to receive and investigate complaints and carry out checks on individual withdrawers even in the absence of complaints.

(3) The Secretary of State should issue a Code of Practice containing guidance to withdrawers and banks as to how they should exercise their functions.

(4) The Secretary of State should have power to make regulations requiring withdrawers to keep records of their expenditure under the scheme and to produce them to the Public Guardian on demand.

Clauses 4(2)(d)(ii), 10(1)(d), (e), 22(4)-(6), and 23

Liability of the bank

4.21   We now turn to consider the liability of the bank in respect of payments made to, or on the instructions of, authorised withdrawers. Payment of cash within the weekly limit should give rise to no liability. The bank cannot know whether or not the money had been spent for the benefit of the incapable adult and any detailed questioning of, or accounting from, the withdrawer would render the scheme unduly complex and impose an inappropriate burden on the bank. On the other hand liability should, we think, arise where the bank allows cash withdrawals over the weekly statutory limit. The bank should be aware of the limit and any amount already withdrawn that week. It would also be impracticable for a bank to have to satisfy itself that every third party to whom payments were made by standing order, direct debit or otherwise had indeed supplied goods and services within the scope of the withdrawer's authority in order to avoid liability for misuse of the sums so paid[1]. Banks should be entitled to rely on the probity of withdrawers who have been authorised by the Public Guardian. But if the bank staff were suspicious they could decline to make the payment. The scheme only entitles them to make payments, it does not oblige them to do so. We recommend that:

43. (1) The bank should be liable for allowing cash withdrawals over the weekly limit but on restoring the money to the incapable adult's account it should be entitled to claim against the withdrawer.

(2) The bank should not be liable for making payments for goods and services that were outwith the ambit of the withdrawer's authority.

Clause 22(3)(a)

Termination of authority to withdraw

4.22   In our discussion paper we asked whether the scheme should be reviewed periodically[2]. Those whose responded to this question were in favour of some limit to the duration of authority to withdraw and some mentioned a period of two years. Some asked what sort of review we had envisaged and who should be charged with carrying it out. On looking at this issue again we have come to the view that the authority to withdraw granted by the Public Guardian should last for two years unless terminated earlier. The Law Society thought that thereafter the person seeking further authority to withdraw should have to apply to the court. We think that to limit the life of the scheme to a maximum of two years would deprive it of much of its usefulness. Many elderly people with dementia live for longer than two years after becoming incapable of operating their bank accounts. We think that it should be competent for the withdrawer to present a fresh application for authority to withdraw to the Public Guardian which, if granted, would authorise withdrawal for a further two years. The Public Guardian might decide to see the withdrawer's records from the previous period before granting the application in respect of a new period.

4.23   Another protection against abuse is that the Public Guardian should be entitled to suspend or terminate the authority already granted at any time. The Public Guardian might become aware of facts giving rise to concern either through complaints, spot-checks of records of expenditure or otherwise. As urgent action may be necessary the Public Guardian should not be required to inform the withdrawer of an intention to suspend or terminate or to give the withdrawer any right to make representations beforehand. The Public Guardian's decision would, however, be appealable to the sheriff[3].

4.24   The authority to withdraw should also come to an end if a guardian is appointed to the incapable adult with powers over matters that include the adult's bank account. A guardian might for example be necessary because of the need for wider financial management than the scheme permits or a guardian might be appointed specifically to supersede an unsatisfactory withdrawer. As the Public Guardian is, under our recommendations, the registration authority both for guardians appointed by the Scottish courts and for withdrawers he or she would be in a position to notify the bank and the withdrawer that the latter's authority had terminated on appointment of a guardian. The same action should be taken when the court makes an intervention order in relation to the bank account which is incompatible with the withdrawer's

---

1.   See para 4.24 for withdrawals after termination of the withdrawer's authority.
2.   Proposal 57(4), para 4.178.
3.   Recommendation 146, para 7.3.

authority. A suspension or termination should be notified by the Public Guardian to the withdrawer and the branch of the bank concerned. Pending receipt of the notification neither the withdrawer nor the bank should be liable for continuing to operate the scheme provided they acted in good faith and in ignorance of the suspension or termination. The bank should be liable for any withdrawals made by the branch after it received notification, but on making good the amount withdrawn should be entitled to recover from the withdrawer.

4.25   We recommend that:

44. (1) A withdrawer's authority should cease two years after the date of its grant, but the withdrawer should be able thereafter to make a fresh application to the Public Guardian.

(2) The Public Guardian should be empowered at his or her sole discretion to suspend or terminate the authority. The authority should automatically terminate on the appointment of a guardian or continuing attorney or the making of an intervention order in relation to the account.

(3) Notification of suspension or termination should be given by the Public Guardian to the withdrawer and the branch of the bank at which the account is held. The withdrawer and bank should not be liable for withdrawals made in good faith and in ignorance of the suspension or termination.

Clauses 22(3)(b) and 24(1)-(3), (5)

Extension to other organisations

4.26   So far we have dealt with withdrawals from bank accounts of incapable adults, but the scheme outlined above might be suitable for other sources of money that could be accessed for the adults' benefit. In our discussion paper we asked for views on extending the scheme[1]. Many respondents mentioned building society accounts. As we have noted in paragraph 4.4, many building societies have somewhat similar schemes already under their rules. Furthermore, many people have building society accounts which they use in much the same way as a bank account; having pensions, dividends and other income paid in and making withdrawals to meet current expenditure. We favour extension to building society accounts.

4.27   Other extensions mentioned by those consulted included payments due under life or accident insurance policies, small legacies and compensation payments. These lump sum payments would require a different scheme from that proposed for bank accounts. It would not be appropriate, for example, to require an insurance company to make payments of cash weekly or pay third party suppliers. We consider it would be better to see how our recommended scheme for bank and building society accounts works before deciding whether to extend it to other sources of money. The Secretary of State should however have power to extend the scheme by regulations to other organisations with which adults had accounts. We therefore recommend that:

45. The scheme set out in Recommendations 37 to 44 should be applicable to building society accounts in the same way as it applies to bank accounts. The Secretary of State should have power by regulations to extend the scheme to other organisations similar to banks or building societies.

Clause 20(2)(b), (c)

JOINT ACCOUNTS

4.28   A useful extra-judicial method for managing the affairs of an adult who is becoming incapable is for a close relative or carer and the adult to open an "either or survivor" joint account. A joint account enables either account holder to operate the account without a signature being required from the other. As the adult becomes more incapacitated so the other holder can take over operating the account to a greater extent, until the stage is reached where the adult is wholly unable to operate the account and the other holder becomes the sole user. Many married couples already have a joint bank or building society account which could be used in the same way if one of them becomes incapable. We understand, however, that many banks take the view that if one holder of a joint account becomes incapacitated then that has the effect of bringing to an end the holders' instructions to the bank. Thus, once the bank becomes aware of the adult's incapacity it may freeze the account preventing further withdrawals, so that a curator bonis usually has to be appointed.

4.29   The law as to the termination of joint mandates and similar arrangements on the incapacity of one party is somewhat uncertain where that party has no obligations to perform[2]. Whatever the law may be, the practice of freezing joint accounts has unfortunate consequences for many incapable adults and their carers. Although we did not raise this issue in our discussion paper it has since been represented to us that enabling a joint account holder to continue to operate the bank or building society account notwithstanding the incapacity of the other holder would be a useful reform. We agree, although

---

1. Proposal 57(4), para 4.178.
2. McBryde, *Contract*, 8-45.

it has to be recognised that the facility will occasionally be abused. While the adult remains capable he or she can monitor withdrawals by the other account holder, but this would cease on incapacity. Any person who considers that the joint account holder is operating the account to the detriment of an incapable adult would, under our recommendations made in Part 6 of this report, be entitled to apply to the court for an intervention order in relation to the account or a guardian to be appointed to the adult, or to raise the matter with the Public Guardian[1].

4.30   We would stress that our recommendation is not intended to apply to joint accounts where all the joint account holders have to sign every cheque or withdrawal document. Furthermore, it should be competent for joint account holders in an "either or survivor" joint account to opt out of our scheme by agreeing with the bank or building society that the incapacity of one of them should terminate the authority of the other account holder to operate the account. The scheme should apply only to accounts held at a branch situated in Scotland of a bank or building society. The bank or building society, however, need not be Scottish.

4.31   Where a curator bonis is appointed to an individual who has a joint account with others the account is frozen until the curator establishes the rights of all the account holders. After this the others are allowed to withdraw their shares (if any). It has been pointed out to us that this process, which inevitably takes some time, can have an extremely serious effect on the other joint account holders. Married couples often have joint accounts which they rely on for meeting household expenses. A wife to whose husband the curator is appointed may be left without access to money for weeks or even months until the joint account is unfrozen. The problem is not confined to married couples because others living together may have joint accounts too. We have considered whether the sheriff in appointing a guardian to one joint account holder should have a discretionary power to allow the other holder to continue to operate the account, but we have decided against it. We think it would make the job of the guardian (and the Public Guardian supervising the guardian) very difficult if others had uncontrolled access to joint accounts. Guidance notes prepared by the Public Guardian should alert guardians to the problems faced by joint account holders and suggest that they be resolved as a matter of urgency immediately after appointment.

4.32   We recommend that:

46. (1) **If two or more individuals are holders of a joint bank or building society account at a branch situated in Scotland whose terms allow any one individual to operate it and one individual becomes incapable of operating the account, then the other account holder or holders should continue to have authority to operate the account.**

   (2) **The continued authority to operate should not apply if the account holders have agreed, or the court has ordered, otherwise, or a guardian or continuing attorney has been appointed or an intervention order made in relation to the account.**

Clauses 25 and 26

MANAGEMENT BY ESTABLISHMENTS OF RESIDENTS' FINANCES

The existing system and criticisms of it

4.33   Section 94 of the 1984 Act empowers the managers of a hospital to receive and hold money and valuables belonging to a patient if the doctor in charge of the patient certifies that he or she is incapable, by reason of mental disorder, of managing and administering his or her own financial affairs. A hospital may spend the money for the patient's benefit and dispose of the valuables but must have regard to their sentimental value[2]. Once the funds of a particular patient exceed £5,000[3] the hospital requires the consent of the Mental Welfare Commission in order to continue to manage them. Whether consent is given depends on the type of assets in the patient's estate and their capital value[4], consideration of a possible curatory and the extent of the involvement of family members in current management. The hospital is not entitled to manage the funds of a patient who already has a curator. Similarly the hospital managers cease to be entitled to manage as soon as a curator is appointed, although curators sometimes delegate some expenditure decisions to the hospital[5].

4.34   The management of patients' affairs under section 94 was investigated by a Working Party (Chairman Mr W S Crosby) set up by the Scottish Health Service Planning Council. Its report, the *Report of the Working Party on Incapax Patients' Funds* ("the Crosby Report"), was published in 1985. The report stated that in 1985 most of the funds held on behalf of patients were fairly small. One-quarter of the balances were less than £50 and three-quarters were less than £500[6]. The amounts may be larger now as the Crosby Report recommended that reduction or termination of allowances

---

1. Para 2.41(c).
2. 1984 Act, s 94(3).
3. This figure is set by the Secretary of State and increased from time to time, s 94(2). It was raised to the present amount in January 1993.
4. Mental Welfare Commission, *Annual Report 1992/3* p 14. Further guidance is given as to whether a curator should be appointed on p 15.
5. 1984 Act, s 94(6).
6. Appendix II, Table 4.

should be sought only in very exceptional circumstances[1]. One hospital financial manager in responding to our discussion paper remarked that the management of incapable patients' finances was a growing problem as they could be in receipt of considerable sums of money.

4.35   In our discussion paper we set out several criticisms of the current management scheme under section 94[2]. First, a hospital can take over the management of a patient's funds if the medical officer in charge of the treatment certifies that the patient is incapable, by reason of mental disorder, of managing and administering his property and affairs[3]. This administrative procedure compares unfavourably with that for appointing a curator where two medical certificates are required, the "incapable" person is given an opportunity to challenge averments of incapacity and the appointment is made by a court after consideration of the evidence. Many in-patients could manage their affairs if more help and advice was available to them, yet the current procedure pays no attention to this possibility. Moreover, the present procedure is possibly in breach of the European Convention of Human Rights. Article 6(1) stipulates that determinations of civil rights (which include the right to manage one's own property and financial affairs) should be decided by an independent and impartial tribunal established by law after a fair and public hearing.

4.36   Secondly, the hospital managers' statutory duty is to hold and receive the money and personal possessions. They have a discretion to spend money held for a patient on his or her behalf. The Crosby Report noted and deprecated the negative attitude that incapable patients have no need for money because they cannot appreciate the benefits[4]. This may lead to hospitals seeking termination of state benefits or not claiming them on behalf of patients, allowing money to accumulate, or spending only small amounts on items such as sweets or cigarettes. The Crosby Report recommended that all income should be claimed and a more active policy should be adopted towards spending it to enhance the quality of life of in-patients[5].

4.37   Thirdly, it is not clear whether the hospital managers' duty to receive money extends to withdrawing money from a patient's bank or building society account which the patient had before admission in order to spend it on the patient's welfare. Practice varies but all too often small balances have to lie untouched if the advice received is that a curator would have to be appointed.

4.38   Fourthly, there is a danger that patients' funds are used to buy items that the National Health Service should provide free of charge. The Crosby Report[6] and the Mental Welfare Commission[7] have drawn attention to misuses of patients' funds in this way.

4.39   Fifthly, management of patients' funds by hospital central management may lead to a remote and impersonal service. Unlike curatory there is no single individual responsible for the funds of particular patients. The family of an in-patient who helped him or her to manage money before admission to hospital are superseded by the hospital administration and may feel excluded.

4.40   In the light of the various criticisms we proposed that hospital managers should be entitled to manage funds only up to a prescribed limit for each individual patient, above which either the Public Manager (whom we now term the Public Guardian) or a financial manager (now a guardian) supervised by the Public Manager should be appointed to manage them[8]. We also proposed that the doctor in deciding whether to certify a patient as incapable of managing his or her affairs and so entitling the hospital to manage them should consider the help that was available to the patient or could reasonably be made available to the patient in this respect[9], and that the hospital managers should be entitled to access funds held by the patient in an existing bank or building society account[10].

4.41   Those responding to the proposals in our discussion paper were generally in favour of continuing with the present system whereby hospital managers may manage the affairs of patients certified as incapable of managing them. There was no pressure for wholesale replacement of hospital management by curators bonis. However, many stated that the present system was in urgent need of reform and there was a general view that more guidelines and external monitoring were needed. It is against this background of qualified approval of the present system that we put forward recommendations for its reform.

---

1. Recommendation 8, p 37.
2. Paras 4.156-4.161.
3. 1984 Act, s 94(1).
4. P 14.
5. Recommendation 1.
6. Recommendation 6.
7. *Annual Report 1988*, pp 11-13.
8. Proposal 53(1), (3), para 4.167.
9. Proposal 53(4), para 4.167.
10. Proposal 53(2), para 4.167.

Which establishments?

4.42   In terms of section 94 of the 1984 Act certified patients in a hospital can have their affairs managed if they are liable to be detained there under the 1984 Act or are receiving treatment for mental disorder as a patient there. "Hospital" means an NHS hospital, an NHS Trust hospital, the State hospital, and any private hospital registered under Part IV of the 1984 Act. This leaves out many categories of establishments with incapable patients or residents, such as private hospitals not registered under the 1984 Act, residential establishments run by the local authority under the Social Work (Scotland) Act 1968, private residential homes registered with and inspected by the local authority under that Act and nursing homes registered under the Nursing Homes Registration (Scotland) Act 1938. This gives rise to difficulty where residents of such establishments have finances which require more management than a DSS appointeeship yet where the sums involved are not large enough to make it worthwhile appointing a curator. These difficulties are becoming more acute with the increasing number of people in private nursing and residential homes. In our discussion paper we proposed extending the management scheme under section 94 to the above establishments presently excluded from its scope[1].

4.43   Our proposal received by and large a favourable response. Two respondents were opposed to allowing the managers of private hospitals and homes to manage residents' finances because of the potential conflict of interest due to the charging of fees and the system being too open to abuse. In their view current problems, such as absorbing residents' DSS personal allowances into the fees, would be intensified and other similar problems created. The other respondents were in favour of such an extension but only if there was strict external monitoring and control of the system. Enable saw no reason why hospitals should be specially favoured and observed that there were examples of good and bad practice in the public sector as well as in the private sector. The Scottish Association for Mental Health considered that there was no reason in principle to limit management of residents' finances to public hospitals. The controls suggested by respondents included approval of the establishment by the Accountant of Court, the drawing up of a Code of Practice that would require to be followed, spot-checks of individual residents' accounts, indemnity by the managers against loss caused by mismanagement and proper separation of residents' funds from those of the establishment.

4.44   The Law Society and some other respondents suggested that the management scheme should be available to hospitals, nursing homes and other residential establishments provided they had been approved on an individual basis by the Accountant of Court as Public Manager (now Public Guardian). Approval should be granted provided the arrangements made by the establishment in respect of patients' funds and their use were satisfactory. We consider this to be a very worthwhile suggestion and have adopted it with some modifications. A distinction can be drawn between NHS hospitals (including NHS trust hospitals and the State hospital) and other establishments since no fees are charged for the former and hence any conflict of financial interest between the managers and the patients is less than in private establishments. Moreover, NHS hospitals have been operating section 94 for many years. We do not suggest that NHS hospitals should be exempt from all external monitoring and observance of Codes of Practice but we do think that they should be automatically approved to run the new management scheme we recommend[2]. Other establishments should have to apply to the Public Guardian for approval. In order to lessen the administrative burden we would permit a local authority or other person that had more than one establishment to apply for approval in respect of all of them in a single application. Other classes of residential establishment may emerge in the future. We consider that the Secretary of State should be empowered to extend our recommended management scheme to them. All establishments should have to be situated in Scotland to be within the scheme.

4.45   Summing up the previous paragraphs we recommend that:

47. (1) The management of patients' finances by the managers of hospitals under section 94 of the Mental Health (Scotland) Act 1984 should be replaced by a new scheme as set out in Recommendations 48 to 57.

(2) The new scheme should apply to NHS hospitals in Scotland (including NHS trust hospitals and the State hospital), unless the sheriff terminates their authority to manage.

(3) The new scheme should also apply to residential establishments in Scotland run by, or registered with, the local authority under the Social Work (Scotland) Act 1968, private hospitals and nursing homes in Scotland registered under the Nursing Homes Registration (Scotland) Act 1938; but only if the Public Guardian so permits after an application for approval made by the managers of the establishment. The managers of one or more establishments seeking approval for them should be entitled to submit a single application in respect of all of them.

(4) The Secretary of State should have power to make regulations amending the list of establishments in paragraphs (2) and (3) above.

Clauses 4(2)(f), 27(1)-(4) and 28(1) and Schedule 5

---

1. Proposal 56, para 4.172.
2. This approval may be withdrawn later by the sheriff, see para 4.71.

4.46　In their comments the Law Society stated that an adequate and satisfactory service of managing residents' finances should be an essential part of the total provision made by hospitals and other institutions caring for incapable people. If an institution was neither able nor willing to provide such a service then it should be provided by the Public Guardian and the institution charged for it. We do not agree with these views. Hospitals, nursing homes and other residential establishments are primarily concerned with the treatment and personal welfare of their patients or residents. Managing finances is a facility which an establishment may wish to provide but which should not be imposed on it. Residents in establishments which do not offer a financial management scheme could have their affairs looked after in other ways, for example DSS appointeeships, authority to withdraw from bank accounts or guardianship by a relative on an unpaid basis. Guardianship by a solicitor or the Public Guardian on a paid basis would also be available.

Which residents?

4.47　At present section 94 of the 1984 Act covers patients who are liable to be detained under that Act in a hospital or who are receiving treatment for mental disorder as a patient in a hospital. Those liable to be detained include patients on leave of absence under section 27 of the 1984 Act. Patients resident in private establishments where contractual arrangements exist with an NHS trust hospital or health board in respect of their medical treatment are also regarded as coming within section 94 so that the managers of those establishments can manage the patients' finances in the same way as the managers of hospitals can[1]. The management scheme should also cover in-patients in long stay wards who are not detained and are not being treated for mental disorder, although of course to qualify they would have to be certified as incapable of managing their finances. The kind of patients we have in mind are those suffering from dementia or severe head injuries. For nursing homes and other residential establishments we consider that the scheme should apply to people whose main residence is the establishment. We recommend that:

48.　The management scheme should be available for managing the financial affairs of:

　　(a)　**persons who are liable to be detained in a hospital under the provisions of the Mental Health (Scotland) Act 1984 or who are receiving treatment for mental disorder as resident patients in a hospital, and**

　　(b)　**persons who are resident patients in an NHS hospital, an NHS Trust hospital or the State Hospital,**

　　(c)　**persons who have as their main residence an establishment approved by the Public Guardian under Recommendation 47.**

Clause 27(5)

In the remainder of this Part we use the term "residents" for individuals to whom the new scheme applies.

Certification of residents as incapable

4.48　A hospital can at present hold money and valuables on behalf of a patient if the medical officer in charge of his or her treatment certifies that the patient is incapable, by reason of mental disorder, of managing and administering his or her property and affairs[2]. As we pointed out in our discussion paper[3] this administrative procedure compares unfavourably with that for appointing a curator to a person, where two medical certificates are required, the person has an opportunity to challenge averments of incapacity and the appointment is made by a court after consideration of the evidence. The certification procedure under section 94 of the 1984 Act may well be in breach of the European Convention on Human Rights. Article 6(1) of the Convention provides that:

> "In the determination of his civil rights and obligations or of any criminal charge against him, everyone is entitled to a fair and public hearing within a reasonable time by an independent and impartial tribunal established by law".

Furthermore, there is no appeal against certification under section 94 whereas the appointment of a curator can be challenged by means of an appeal to a higher court. The Law Society, Alzheimer Scotland - Action on Dementia, the Scottish Association for Mental Health and Enable all regarded the present certification procedure as unacceptable.

4.49　Introducing more complex certifying procedures and invoking a court would lose all the simplicity and ease of operation of the present administrative scheme. Moreover, there seems to be little point in having a procedure to authorise managers of establishments to manage their residents' finances that mirrors that for the appointment of a curator or our recommended replacement, a guardian. The law would be unnecessarily complicated by having two management schemes with very similar procedures and effects. Accordingly, we do not favour introducing a judicial element at the initial stage, although for reasons set out later[4] we think that the decision to certify incapacity should be challengeable by way of an application to the sheriff.

1.　Mental Welfare Commission, *Annual Report 1992/93*, p 15.
2.　S 94(1), 1984 Act.
3.　Para 4.156.
4.　Para 4.52 below.

4.50   We have also decided against introducing a requirement for two certificates of incapacity. A certificate from a single doctor should be sufficient provided he or she is suitably qualified to assess the resident's capacity to manage finances and has no financial interest in the establishment. Those incapable of managing their finances should include residents who are unable to communicate in any way due to their physical condition. Where the establishment has no attached medical staff with the required qualifications then a resident should have to be certified by an outside doctor. But we do not consider that outside doctors should always have to be used. If a hospital or other establishment does have suitably qualified persons on its staff with no financial interest then certification by such persons should be allowed. When considering whether to certify a resident the doctor should have to take into account the help that is available, or that could reasonably be made available, to the resident in managing his or her financial affairs. Where the family had been helping the resident at home before the move to the establishment they should be encouraged to continue to help and not be excluded by the establishment managers using our scheme. This can happen at present with hospitals[1]. Some initial reorganisation and simplification of a resident's finances might enable him or her to manage them in future. Consideration should also be given as to whether the resident has sufficient capacity to grant a continuing power of attorney[2].

4.51   The Mental Welfare Commission in their 1993/94 Annual Report[3] have urged that more use should be made of section 94 of the 1984 Act in relation to patients whose incapacity to manage their affairs is only temporary. Cases arise of functional psychoses, most notably hypomanic illness, where patients spend money recklessly or dispose of their property in a manner which later causes them considerable regret and hardship. We intend our scheme to apply both to temporary and permanent incapacity to manage. In the case of recovery of capacity it would be a simple matter for a doctor to certify this. The effect of such a certificate should be to terminate the managers' authority to manage that resident's affairs.

4.52   The lack of a right to appeal against certification was adversely commented on in our discussion paper and also by the Law Society, Alzheimer Scotland - Action on Dementia, the Scottish Association for Mental Health and Enable in their responses. In our opinion the right to apply to an "independent and impartial tribunal established by law" would make the administrative certification procedure by a single doctor more acceptable. The application should be for a determination of the current capacity of the resident rather than an appeal against the granting of the original certificate. The application should be heard by the sheriff because under our other recommendations nearly all applications would be heard in the sheriff courts. It would involve obtaining fresh reports from independent specialists and other evidence as appropriate. The sheriff should also have to consider the help that is, or could reasonably be made, available to the resident.

4.53   We recommend that:

49. (1)   The managers of an approved establishment should have authority to manage the financial affairs specified in Recommendation 53 of a resident who has been certified as incapable of managing them by a doctor suitably qualified to assess capacity who does not possess a financial interest in the establishment.

(2)   Where a certificate has been issued under paragraph (1) above an application may be made to the sheriff, by any person claiming an interest in the resident's welfare or finances, for a determination of the resident's mental capacity to manage his or her financial affairs.

(3)   The managers should cease to have authority when the resident is certified as capable of managing them by a suitably qualified doctor or declared to be so capable by the sheriff.

(4)   In deciding whether a resident is incapable of managing his or her own affairs account should be taken of assistance that is available or that could reasonably be made available.

Clauses 29 and 35

4.54   The management scheme we recommend for managers of establishments clearly should not apply where a guardian (or equivalent from another legal system) had previously been appointed with powers over the resident's financial affairs or an intervention order had been granted in relation to any of them. Judicial appointees should take precedence over administrative ones. A similar policy exists at present under section 94(6) of the 1984 Act in relation to hospital managers when a curator is appointed. We also consider that a continuing attorney who has been registered with the Public Guardian should be allowed to continue to act in the financial field rather than be superseded by the managers of the establishment. The management scheme is designed for those adults whose affairs are not being managed already by other means and should apply only in so far as no other person with authority to manage financial affairs is in existence. Thus, for example, if the resident has a DSS appointee to deal with his or her social security benefits the managers of the establishment should not have authority in that area. A similar restriction should apply if an individual had already obtained authority

---

1.   Adrian Ward, *The Power to Act* (published by Enable 1990), p 112.
2.   See Part 3 above.
3.   P 29.

E

to withdraw funds from the resident's bank or building society account. The managers of the establishment could, however, take steps to have the continuing attorneyship, DSS appointeeship or authority to withdraw revoked if they considered that this would be of benefit to the resident. We recommend that:

50. **The authority of the managers of an establishment should be subject to any existing intervention order or to the existing authority of a previously appointed guardian or continuing attorney (or their equivalents under other legal systems), a DSS appointee or an individual authorised to withdraw from the resident's bank or building society account.**

Clause 36

4.55   Where a guardian is appointed after the managers of an establishment have become authorised to manage a resident's financial affairs, then we consider that the guardian should supersede the managers. However, the guardian would be entitled to delegate appropriate financial matters to the managers. For example, a guardian may permit hospital managers to continue to receive and spend the resident's DSS personal allowance or the guardian could periodically hand over money to be spent by the managers on the resident's welfare. The hospital managers would, however, be acting as delegates or agents of the guardian and would have to account for money received and spent. A similar solution should be adopted if a continuing attorney appointed before certification of incapacity is registered with the Public Guardian afterwards. Accordingly we recommend that:

51. **The authority of the managers of an establishment should be subordinated to the authority of a guardian or continuing attorney (or their equivalents under other legal systems) appointed or registered after the managers have commenced to act, but the guardian or continuing attorney may appoint the managers to act as his or her agent.**

Clause 31

4.56   We do not make any recommendations for dealing with the potential clash of authority between the managers of an establishment and subsequently appointed DSS appointees or withdrawers from bank or building society accounts. This is because we consider such a situation to be most unlikely to occur. The managers would be in contact with the Department of Social Security in relation to benefits so that the Department would be aware of their authority and should not appoint someone else. If the managers were managing a resident's financial affairs it is unlikely that any individual would need to apply for authority to withdraw and if it were granted we consider the bank or building society should decline to give effect to it if aware of the managers' authority.

4.57   At present incapable patients in hospital can have their financial affairs managed by the managers of that hospital. On discharge, however, the managers' authority ceases. There is a lack of any system for looking after the finances of discharged patients unless they are rich enough to merit the appointment of a curator. Our recommendations relating to withdrawals from bank accounts would go some way towards meeting the problem as would public management of small estates by the Public Guardian. But we think there would still be a substantial number of incapable residents without close relatives whose affairs would benefit from continued management after discharge. It was suggested to us that hospital managers should continue to have authority to manage the affairs of discharged patients at least until other satisfactory methods have been found. We endorse this useful suggestion and would extend it to other approved establishments. The continuing authority of managers after discharge should be a facility and not something they should be under a statutory duty to provide. We do not think it would be acceptable to impose such a duty especially on private nursing and residential homes. The likelihood of being bound to continue managing the affairs of former residents might deter many homes from entering into financial management at all. We therefore recommend that:

52. **The managers of an establishment should be entitled, but not bound, to continue managing the financial affairs of a former resident if no other adequate arrangements appear to have been made.**

Clause 32(6)

What matters may be managed?

4.58   Hospital managers acting under section 94 are authorised to "receive and hold money and valuables" of a patient and may "expend that money or dispose of those valuables for the benefit of that person". The extent of this authority is unclear particularly in relation to items outwith the hospital such as the patient's own bank account. We do not consider that managers of an establishment should be given the same wide powers as a curator has or that a guardian with full financial powers would have under our recommendations. Management by establishments is intended to operate without extensive supervision by the Public Guardian and so should be confined to fairly straightforward matters. If acquiring accommodation for a resident or disposing of it or making investments in shares is needed, then a guardian ought to be appointed or an intervention order made.

4.59   The managers of an establishment should be entitled to hold, on behalf of the resident, items brought into the establishment by the resident. Likely items include personal possessions, a television set or other furniture. The managers should, we think, also be able to claim, receive and manage on behalf of the resident any pensions and benefits whether from the Department of Social Security, the resident's former employment or otherwise. The Crosby Report deprecated the negative attitude adopted by some hospitals that certified patients were unable to appreciate money spent on them and therefore had no need of any money. It recommended that all income should be claimed and a more active policy adopted towards spending it to enhance the patients' quality of life[1]. The Code of Practice which we recommend later would address this problem. There are many sources of money falling due to the resident while certified other than pensions and benefits that we think should also be available to the managers. These include therapeutic earnings from participation in industrial therapies[2], compensation and insurance claim payments, proceeds of a life policy and legacies. The managers should be entitled to claim and receive these on the resident's behalf. The managers should also be entitled to withdraw money from an existing bank or building society account in the sole name of the resident in order to use it for the benefit of the patient[3]. We recommend below[4] an aggregate monetary limit on management by managers of establishments which would prevent managers acquiring large lump sums from these sources.

4.60   Once the money or items are in the possession of the managers they should be empowered to hold, spend or dispose of them for the benefit of the resident. Decisions in relation to substantial assets and the general course of management to be adopted would be governed by the general principles set out in Part 2 and by the Code of Practice which we recommend later[5]. Subject to these considerations the managers should follow a general policy of spending the money received for the resident's benefit and to enhance his or her quality of life rather than saving it. However, there will be situations where saving would be appropriate, for example, when the resident is to be discharged in the near future or where some costly item is wanted. The managers should be permitted to spend capital as well as income but further guidance on expenditure is best left to the Code of Practice.

4.61   We recommend that:

53. The managers of an establishment should be entitled to:

   (a) claim and receive any pension or benefit due to the resident while certified and any sums falling due to the resident while certified and to hold them along with any other money brought by the resident into the establishment.

   (b) spend any money so held by them on behalf of the resident in order to enhance his or her quality of life in accordance with the provisions of the Code of Practice recommended in Recommendation 56.

   (c) hold or dispose of items which the resident brought into the establishment or which have been acquired by or on behalf of the resident subsequently.

   (d) withdraw money from an existing bank or building society account in the name of the resident.

Clauses 30 and 32(3)

Safeguards for residents

4.62   At present hospital managers are entitled to hold money and valuables up to an aggregate value of £5,000 for each patient by virtue of their general authority under section 94[6]. They may hold in excess of this value with the consent of the Mental Welfare Commission. The current guidelines used by the Mental Welfare Commission[7] are that for sums between £5,000 and £10,000 there should have to be a good reason for replacing hospital management by curatory and for estates over £20,000 there should have to be a good reason for not appointing a curator. For estates between £10,000 and £20,000 there is no presumption either for or against curatory.

4.63   In our discussion paper we suggested[8] that managers of hospitals should be permitted to manage funds only up to a specified limit over which management would have to be undertaken by a financial manager (now a guardian) or the Public Manager (now the Public Guardian). Views were invited as to what the specified limit should be. There was a wide variety of views expressed on consultation. A few respondents favoured a figure of about £3,000[9], but most favoured the now current limit of £5,000. Others mentioned a substantially higher figure of £10,000. Most of those responding wished the existing system to continue whereby permission could be given to manage sums over the specified limit rather than, as we proposed, making the limit an absolute ceiling. On reconsideration we now favour flexibility and think that the Public Guardian should be entitled to approve management of funds in excess of the specified limit. In approving management in excess of the limit the Public Guardian should have power to impose conditions such as submission of

1. Recommendation 1.
2. Crosby Report, p 18.
3. See para 4.37.
4. Recommendation 54, para 4.64.
5. Recommendation 56, para 4.70.
6. Direction issued by Secretary of State under s 94(2) of the 1984 Act dated 7 January 1993.
7. *Annual Report 1992/93*, pp 14 to 16, see also para 4.33 above.
8. Proposal 53(1), para 4.167.
9. The limit at the date of publication of our discussion paper.

reports or even accounts from time to time. Approval of management over the specified limit is presently entrusted to the Mental Welfare Commission[1]. We recommend that this function should be carried out in future by the Public Guardian instead, as it is more in line with that official's current duties and responsibilities in relation to curators and our recommendations that guardians, continuing attorneys and others with financial powers should be supervised by the Public Guardian. We would stress that our recommendation does not imply any criticism of the way the Mental Welfare Commission has carried out this function in the past. The specified limit should, we think, remain at its current level of £5,000 for hospitals, but other lower limits may be appropriate for other classes of establishment. Hospitals have been managing substantial funds for many years, but this would be a new venture for local authority establishments and private nursing and residential homes. The Secretary of State should be empowered to prescribe different limits for different classes of establishments as well as changing the monetary limits from time to time to take account of changes in the value of money.

4.64   We recommend that:

54. (1) **The managers of an establishment should be entitled to manage money and items up to £5,000 in total value, or such other sum as may be prescribed, for each individual certified resident.**

   (2) **The power to permit the management of money and items in excess of the above limit should be transferred from the Mental Welfare Commission to the Public Guardian. The Public Guardian should be empowered to grant approval subject to conditions.**

   (3) **The Secretary of State should be empowered to make regulations prescribing a limit or limits other than £5,000 for establishments other than NHS hospitals and altering the £5,000 limit and other limits from time to time.**

Clause 32(1), (2) and (7)

Oversight by the Public Guardian

4.65   We have recommended in the previous section that the Public Guardian should be charged with approving management of residents' funds over a specified limit. In our discussion paper[2] we proposed that the Public Manager (now the Public Guardian) should be entitled to require the managers of the establishment to produce accounts of their transactions with specified individual residents' money and personal possessions. This "spot-check" system was approved by all those responding. One body commented that such accounts should always be produced, but we consider that this would be too expensive and unnecessary. Most managers will have already carried out an internal audit of residents' accounts and there is no point in the Public Guardian duplicating that work. Of course, if serious deficiencies are revealed by a spot check then the accounts of all residents in that establishment could be called for. Another body commented that management services might be provided by a private contractor. Our recommendations are framed so that the managers of establishments remain liable for the performance of their statutory management functions whether they perform them personally or by agents. In addition we consider that the Public Guardian should also have a general supervisory role in relation to approved establishments and be the authority to whom complaints could be made. The Public Guardian would be under a duty to investigate any complaints or other circumstances giving rise to concern, but we do not thereby intend to exclude the Mental Welfare Commission from exercising their general protective statutory functions in relation to the mentally disordered. Accordingly we recommend that:

55. **The Public Guardian should be under a duty to receive and investigate complaints about the management of certified residents' funds by managers of approved establishments and be entitled to question the managers regarding their transactions with funds of specified residents, and require them to produce accounts and records even in the absence of complaints.**

Clauses 4(2)(d)(iii) and 33

Duties of establishments under scheme

4.66   The Crosby Report made many recommendations in relation to a proper system of accounting for patients' funds and preventing such funds being used to purchase items that hospitals should provide free of charge. The Mental Welfare Commission in their subsequent Annual Reports[3] have drawn attention to continuing deficiencies in these areas. We consider that the basic responsibilities of managers of establishments should be set down in statute and be fleshed out by a Code of Practice prepared by the Secretary of State.

4.67   Residents' funds clearly should have to be kept separate from the funds of the establishment. The managers should be entitled to open individual accounts for all their residents, but they should also have the option of a block account for all the residents. Block accounts are currently run by some hospital managers for patients' funds. They offer the advantage

---

1. 1984 Act, s 94.
2. Proposal 55, para 4.169.
3. 1987, p 13 and 1988, pp 11-13.

of reduced administration costs and better terms from the bank. For example, higher rates of interest can be obtained on say £100,000 in a block account than on several hundred accounts with the same aggregate value. If block accounts are to be used then the establishment's records must be such as to enable the balance (including interest) due to each participating resident to be identified at all times. Money belonging to a particular patient above a prescribed limit (which we suggest should be £50) should have to be placed in an interest-bearing account (block or individual).

4.68 There should in our opinion also be a statutory duty on the managers of an establishment to spend a resident's money only on items which benefit that particular resident and which are not provided as part of the service provided free under the NHS or included in normal fees charged by the establishment. We think this duty is of prime importance in relation to private nursing and residential homes where the proprietors could gain a direct pecuniary advantage by failing to comply with it. Many of those responding to our proposal to extend the present system of hospital management to other establishments expressed concern over possible misuse of funds, particularly in using them to meet any shortfall in fees. Other instances of which we have become aware include buying extra furniture for the resident's room from his or her funds which stays there when the resident moves. Some of the misuse occurring at present may well result from uncertainty as to what is allowable. The Code of Practice should therefore give clear guidance on this issue.

4.69 The managers should not be liable for any loss to a resident's funds if they act reasonably, in good faith and in accordance with the recommended general principles in Part 2. A similar restriction of liability has been recommended for breach of fiduciary duty[1]. The Public Guardian should be empowered, as a condition of granting approval, to require the managers of an establishment to provide a satisfactory indemnity by way of insurance or otherwise against such losses. NHS hospitals should normally be exempt from such a requirement as health boards and NHS trusts should have access to funds to meet any such claims that might be made against them.

4.70 Summing up the previous paragraphs we recommend that:

56. (1) The managers of an approved establishment should be under a statutory duty to:

   (a) keep certified residents' funds separate from those of the establishment.

   (b) if the funds are not in separate bank or building society accounts for each individual resident, maintain records enabling the balance due to each resident at any time to be ascertained.

   (c) place sums over £50 (or such other amount as may be prescribed by the Secretary of State) in an interest-bearing account.

   (d) spend a resident's money only on goods and services that are of benefit to that resident, not including items which should be provided by the establishment as part of the normal service to residents.

   (e) adhere to a Code of Practice drawn up and published by the Secretary of State.

   (2) The managers should be liable for any loss to a resident's funds arising from a breach of the duty of care or any misuse of funds, only if they fail to act reasonably, in good faith and in accordance with the general principles set out in Recommendations 11 to 14, and should be under a duty to make proper provision for indemnification for losses for which they are liable.

   Clauses 10(1)(f), 32(4) and 64

Withdrawal of approval of establishments

4.71 The duties laid on managers of approved establishments in managing the funds of certified residents, either directly by statute or under the Code of Practice, require to be backed up by sanctions. One sanction, liability to make good losses arising from a breach of duty, has already been mentioned. We consider that in appropriate cases the approval of the establishment should be withdrawn by the sheriff or continued only on conditions. Withdrawal of approval would prevent further management by an establishment that was demonstrably unfit to manage its residents' funds, while the threat of withdrawal of approval or attaching conditions to continued approval should be sufficient to secure future compliance in other cases.

4.72 Withdrawal of approval should, we think, be a judicial act involving the sheriff courts. We do not consider that the Public Guardian can properly decide whether contested allegations of mismanagement are substantiated since this would involve hearing evidence. That official's role should be to investigate and make the application to the court. Moreover, withdrawal of approval would have serious consequences for the standing of an establishment and it is right that the issue should be decided by an independent public tribunal. The process should start by an application to the sheriff by the Public Guardian who would have been involved in the initial investigations. The sheriff, on being satisfied that the managers of the establishment have failed to comply with any statutory requirement (including adherence to the Code of

---

1. Recommendation 15, para 2.79.

Practice) or are otherwise unsuitable, should be empowered either to withdraw approval or attach conditions to the continued approval. Unsuitability could, for example, arise where the proprietor of a residential home had been convicted of a crime involving dishonesty but unconnected with the running of the home. Another reason for withdrawing approval should be that the establishment no longer falls within the terms of the scheme, such as a nursing home losing its registration under the Nursing Homes Registration (Scotland) Act 1938. Any conditions imposed should be capable of being subsequently varied or removed. The sheriff should also have power to make interim orders since action might be urgently needed to protect residents' funds.

4.73   If the sheriff withdraws approval from an establishment to manage the funds of the certified residents the managers will lose their authority to manage those funds. In order to provide short term management until some more permanent arrangements are made, the Public Guardian should be appointed interim guardian with the same powers as the managers enjoyed.

4.74   We recommend that:

57. (1) The sheriff should have power, on application by the Public Guardian, to withdraw approval from an establishment or to impose conditions on its continued approval. The sheriff should have to be satisfied that the managers had failed to carry out any statutory requirements relating to the management of certified residents' funds or that the managers or the establishment were otherwise no longer suitable.

(2) Any conditions imposed should be capable of being subsequently removed, varied or added to.

(3) On withdrawing approval the sheriff should have power to appoint the Public Guardian as interim guardian of the funds of the certified residents of that establishment with the same powers that the managers had.

(4) The sheriff should have power to make any appropriate interim order (including the suspension of approval) pending the determination of the application by the Public Guardian.

Clauses 3(2)(d) and 34

Part 5   Medical Treatment and Medical Research

Introduction

5.1   This Part is concerned with health-care issues, particularly the giving of treatment to those incapable of consenting to it, when such treatment can be lawfully given and what treatments, if any, should require special authorisation. Other allied topics are participation in medical research, taking organs from a living incapable person for the purpose of transplanting them into another person, and withholding or withdrawing treatment from patients who are unlikely to benefit from it. Proxy decision-makers, either guardians appointed by the court or attorneys appointed by the adults themselves, are discussed elsewhere[1], but we look in this Part at the role of such proxies in the health-care area. The effect to be given to statements by patients when capable as to their treatment if they become incapable (sometimes known as "advance directives" or "living wills") is also considered. Treatment is used in the remainder of this Part in a wide sense to include surgery, prescribing and administering drugs, preliminary examinations, nursing care, physiotherapy, taking samples, psychological and psychiatric procedures, dental and optical treatment and also procedures to promote and safeguard health such as screening and preventative medicine. "Doctor" is used to mean any person giving or proposing to give such treatment.

5.2   An incapable patient is one who is unable to make a decision relating to the treatment by reason of mental disorder or being wholly unable to communicate. Certain patients with learning difficulties, severe head injuries or dementia would be examples of the first category, while patients in a coma or unconscious would come into the second category. The inability to decide also must be related to the treatment in question. People who are able to decide whether to undergo some minor surgical operation may not be able to decide about sterilisation, abortion or cosmetic surgery where many conflicting factors have to be considered. The ability to come to a decision on the treatment in question depends to some extent on the person's ability to comprehend, from information supplied by the doctor or others, the nature of the proposed treatment and its effects and risks. The patient does not need to have been given an exhaustive evaluation of the treatment. In particular minimal risks need not be mentioned. What is required is that the patient is informed in broad terms of the nature of the proposed treatment[2].

Authority to treat incapable patients

5.3   Where a patient is unconscious, drunk or otherwise incapable of giving consent and is not known to have objected to receiving treatment it is widely accepted that doctors may give necessary treatment which cannot be reasonably delayed until the patient recovers capacity[3]. In addition the 1984 Act authorises certain categories of urgent treatment for mental disorder to be given to detained patients without their consent or a second opinion[4]. This doctrine of necessity applies in emergencies and to the temporarily incapacitated. Appropriate treatment had always been afforded to other incapable patients but the legal basis on which it was provided was somewhat uncertain. In 1989 in the case of *Re F* (*Mental Patient: Sterilisation*)[5] the House of Lords clarified the law relating to the treatment of permanently mentally incapacitated patients in England and Wales and considered the legal justification for such treatment.

5.4   The *F* case concerned the sterilisation of a 35 year old woman resident in a mental hospital who had the mental capacity of a very young child. Sterilisation was regarded as being in her best interests because she was having a sexual relationship with a fellow inmate. Pregnancy and birth of a child would, the doctors considered, cause her severe psychological harm. Other contraceptive methods were considered inappropriate. It was held that doctors were entitled under the common law to give treatment to patients who were incapable of consenting. As Lord Brandon said[6]:

---

1. See Part 6 (guardians) and Part 3 (attorneys).
2. *Chatterton v Gerson* [1981] QB 432; see also *Sidaway v Governors of Bethlem Royal Hospital* [1985] AC 871 and *Moyes v Lothian Health Board* 1990 SLT 444.
3. Hoggett, *Mental Health Law*, (2nd edn) p 202; Mason and McCall-Smith, *Law and Medical Ethics* 4th edn p 220; British Medical Association, *Medical Treatment and Incapable Adults: Interim Guidelines for the Medical Profession* (1990), p 2; NHS Scotland, *A Guide to Consent to Examination, Investigation, Treatment or Operation* (1992), para 16.1.
4. S 102.
5. [1990] 2 AC 1.
6. At p 55.

"A doctor can lawfully operate on, or give other treatment to, adult patients who are incapable, for one reason or another, of consenting to his doing so, provided that the operation or other treatment concerned is in the best interests of such patients. The operation or other treatment will be in their best interests if, but only if, it is carried out in order either to save their lives or to ensure improvement or prevent deterioration in their physical or mental health".

In our discussion paper we were of the view that the House of Lords' decision would probably be followed in Scotland even though it is not necessary to invoke the concept of necessity here[1]. In English law there is no person capable of taking medical treatment decisions on behalf of a mentally incapacitated adult[2], so of necessity the court had to declare certain treatment to be lawful, but in Scotland a tutor-dative can be appointed with power to consent to treatment[3].

5.5   In our discussion paper[4] we unhesitatingly rejected the notion that the courts or some other body should always be involved in all treatment decisions for incapacitated patients, either directly or indirectly via the appointment of a tutor-dative with appropriate powers[5]. Nothing was said on consultation to require us to reconsider this. The courts or other body would be deluged with applications and necessary treatment would be delayed and made more expensive by such requirements. We then went on to consider what reforms, if any, were needed. One possibility discussed was that doctors should simply be left to treat patients in their best interests according to clinical judgment. This would be to adopt the line taken by the House of Lords in *Re F*. In our discussion paper in order to elicit views we put forward another option which included as an additional element involvement of the patient's nearest available relative from a short list of such relatives[6]. The nearest relative would have to be consulted in so far as it was reasonably practical to do so and the doctors would be required to take account of the relatives' views. The discussion paper also asked whether the court should have power to disqualify relatives who were unsuitable to be consulted. Requiring consultation with the nearest relative would not prevent the doctors from seeking the views of others with an interest in the patient's welfare and taking them into account also in deciding what treatment, if any, to give.

5.6   The Mental Welfare Commission and the Law Society commented that our proposal should not affect the statutory provisions relating to the treatment of mental disorder of patients liable to be detained[7]. These are contained in Part X of the 1984 Act and may be summarised as follows. A patient may be treated for his or her mental disorder without consent[8]. A patient may also be given urgent treatment where life or serious danger to health is at stake without consent or a second opinion[9]. Electro-convulsive therapy and medicines for mental disorder given for a period in excess of three months require either the patient's consent or a formal second opinion[10]. Psycho-surgery and implantation of hormones to reduce male sex drive require the patient's consent and a formal second opinion[11]. We fully agree and had intended that the proposals in our discussion paper relating to medical treatment should not apply to situations regulated by the 1984 Act, although this reservation appeared in the introduction to the section on medical treatment[12] rather than explicitly in each of our proposals. We deal later with "Part X treatments" in relation to incapable patients who are not detained. Other situations we also intended to exclude, since they were the subject of other different proposals were:-

(a) treatments specified by the Secretary of State as requiring the approval of a court.

(b) participation in medical research.

(c) transplantation of organs.

We discuss these and other exceptions later in this Part.

5.7   Consultation revealed a division of opinion. Although the majority of those responding were in favour of consulted relatives' views merely being taken into account some were in favour of the relatives' consent being required. The latter would not give relatives an absolute veto since it was accepted that doctors faced with a refusal to consent by the relatives concerned could go to the court for an order authorising them to proceed with treatment. Those favouring a requirement of consent argued that in the case of a competent patient his or her consent was required. In their view there should not

---

1. Para 3.8.
2. The *parens patriae* jurisdiction of the courts there was abolished in 1960.
3. *Usher's CB Petr* 1989 (unreported).
4. Para 3.13.
5. *Usher's CB Petr*; Adrian Ward, *Tutors to Adults: Developments*, 1992 SLT (News) 325.
6. Proposal 21, para 3.21.
7. These include those on leave of absence, but exclude certain short term detainees, see s 96.
8. S 103. This may include feeding by naso-gastric tube to prevent physical deterioration so that treatment for the mental disorder could be carried out; *B v Croydon Health Authority*, [1995] 1 All ER 683.
9. S 102.
10. S 98 and the Mental Health (Specified Treatments, Guardianship Duties etc) (Scotland) Regulations 1984; SI 1984/1494. The second opinion is given by a consultant nominated by the Mental Welfare Commission.
11. S 97 and the 1984 Regulations.
12. Para 3.2.

be a different requirement for patients incapable of consenting; a consent should have to be obtained from someone on the incapable patient's behalf. Another concern was that merely being required to take the relatives' views into account left the decision in the hands of the doctors. They might merely go through the motions of consultation since there were no sanctions proposed to compel them to take account of the views of those consulted. The Law Society suggested that consulted relatives should be entitled to register disagreement with the doctor but allow the treatment to go ahead nevertheless, or to disagree and require the matter to be referred to the court for a decision. The consulted relative should be given a standard form setting out the two options described above which the relative would complete and return to the doctor with the selected option indicated.

5.8   We would adhere to our proposal in the discussion paper that the views of relatives and others consulted should only be taken into account. Those consulted may have exploited or abused the patient, may have conflicting interests or may unreasonably withhold consent. Exploiters and abusers may not have been disqualified from acting as nearest relative nor may the doctors be aware of their behaviour or conflicting interests. We imagine that cases of irreconcilable differences between doctors and relatives would be rare because doctors would strive to achieve a consensus with relatives and others with an interest in the patients' welfare. If there was disagreement then we consider that it should be for the objectors to apply to the court for an order prohibiting treatment rather than for the doctors to have to apply for authority to proceed. Placing the onus on the objectors recognises the clinical judgement and professionalism of the doctors and their medical, ethical and legal duty to care for the patient as best they can. We note that our recommendation is consistent with the guidelines *Medical Treatment and Incapable Adults: Interim Guidelines for the Medical Profession* published by the British Medical Association in October 1990 in taking the views of the health-care team, relatives and friends of the patient into account.

5.9   Alzheimer Scotland - Action on Dementia and some others responding to our proposal observed that the doctors should also be required to take the patient's own views as to the proposed treatment into account. We agree wholeheartedly where communication with the patient is feasible. This requirement was implicit as part of our general approach to the mentally disabled. Even though the patient is unable to take a decision as to the treatment in question he or she may have wishes and feelings, current or past, that should be taken into account[1]. The situation where an incapable patient refuses treatment is a difficult one. We consider that if the doctors are satisfied that the patient is truly incapable of making a decision and that the refusal is irrational or mindless then they should be entitled to give appropriate treatment notwithstanding the patient's refusal. One organisation suggested that in such situations doctors should be required to go to court to seek authority to give treatment. We think that this would be unduly burdensome.

5.10   The issue of doctor-patient confidentiality was raised by a number of respondents. If the nearest relatives and others with an interest are to be consulted in a meaningful way then they will have to be adequately informed as to the patient's medical condition and other circumstances. This, it may be said, disadvantages mentally incapable patients compared with competent patients who are entitled to confidentiality. This distinction is inevitable unless doctors, contrary to our views, are to take decisions unaided. Doctors should, however, reveal to relatives only as much as is necessary for them to reach an informed decision upon the matter they are being consulted about.

5.11   The Mental Welfare Commission commented that our proposal gave doctors too much autonomy for serious treatments. It suggested that for a serious treatment the doctors should be required to obtain a second opinion from an independent practitioner skilled in that treatment, as recommended by the British Medical Association's *Interim Guidelines*[2]. In these guidelines a serious treatment is defined as having one or more of the following characteristics:-

"(a) Any treatment that contemplates an irreversible change in the patient;

(b) Any treatment that is a serious hazard;

(c) Any experimental treatment and all types of research;

(d) Any intervention which as a consequence may shorten the life of the patient;

(e) Any long term regime/intervention designed to effect a change in the mood or behaviour of the patient;

(f) Any treatment, notwithstanding that it does not possess one or more of the above characteristics, which should be regarded as serious."

We are not in favour of making a second opinion a legal requirement for the treatment of incapable adult patients except in certain cases, which we discuss later[3]. Our preference is for second opinions and consultations with colleagues to be regulated by guidelines or codes of practice issued by the medical and other professional organisations concerned. Furthermore, we doubt whether "serious treatments" could be defined with sufficient precision for legislative purposes.

---

1. In certain circumstances previous statements may be determinative, see paras 5.41 to 5.59.
2. At p 6, see para 5.8 above.
3. Paras 5.25 and 5.26 for example.

5.12   Another suggestion to emerge from consultation was that the doctors should consult a mental health officer. This would provide a non-medical input where relatives were not reasonably available to be consulted or were unwilling to express a view. The views of a mental health officer could on occasion be very helpful, particularly where he or she knew the patient and the circumstances well. However, we are not in favour of making such consultation a statutory requirement in all cases. Doctors should be free to consult a mental health officer as someone with an interest in the patient's welfare, but should not be bound to do so.

5.13   One respondent suggested that the individual or organisation caring for the patient as well as the nearest relative should be required to be consulted and the views expressed taken into account. We welcome this helpful suggestion. The carer is likely to be as good a source of useful information and views as the nearest relative and the carer would also be a useful and indeed a natural person to consult in connection with those patients who had no reasonably available relatives or whose relatives were unconcerned with their treatment.

5.14   In our discussion paper we asked for views as to whether the existing common law relating to the medical treatment of incapable adults should be put into a new statute[1]. A majority of those responding were in favour of legislation even if no change were to be made. Many doctors were said to be ignorant of the current law and decisions such as *Re F (Mental Patient: Sterilisation)*[2] were not readily accessible to give guidance to those involved in treating patients. The law would, it was argued, be more available and succinct in legislation. Some of the medical respondents were concerned that legislation would be too restrictive. Legislation could prevent appropriate treatment being given and deficiencies in the statutory provisions would take some time to correct since Parliamentary proceedings would be required. The Scottish Council of the Royal College of General Practitioners suggested that non-binding professional guidelines and codes of practice would be of assistance in this area as an adjunct to legislation.

5.15   The approach we now favour takes the form of a new general statutory authority to doctors to give treatment to incapable patients. This authority, like all other authority directly affecting incapable adults within the scope of our report, would be exercisable in accordance with the general principles set out in Part 2 of our report. These general principles require any intervention to be for the benefit of the incapable adult in question and to be the option which is least restrictive of the adult's freedom consistent with achieving the purpose of the intervention. The intervenor would be required (in so far as was reasonable and practicable) to consult the adult, his or her nearest relative and primary carer and any guardian or attorney and take their views[3] into account as well as the views of any other person who seemed to have an interest and who made the views known to the intervenor. This approach confers some of the benefits of legislation without its restrictive effects and is broadly in line with the views of those responding to our proposals.

5.16   The assessment of a patient's capacity to give or withhold consent to a proposed treatment is a matter for the doctor concerned, using his or her own judgment guided by legal requirements and professional practice. Different doctors may reasonably come to a different view as to a particular patient's capacity. Authority to treat patients which was based on an objective test - whether the patient was incapable - would give little protection to doctors and might make them reluctant to give treatment lest another doctor or a court should come to the opposite conclusion later. We therefore consider that our recommended general authority should be available if, in the opinion of the doctor, the patient is incapable of making a decision regarding the treatment in question. The Age of Legal Capacity (Scotland) Act 1991 adopts a similar approach in relation to the capacity of children to consent to treatment[4].

5.17   We recommend that:

58. (1) A doctor should have authority to give treatment which is reasonable in the circumstances in order to safeguard or promote the health of a patient who, in the doctor's opinion, is incapable of making a decision relating to it.

(2) Treatment should include any surgical, medical, nursing, psychiatric, psychological, optical or dental treatment, procedure, examination or assessment. Treatment for mental disorder of incapable patients liable to be detained under the Mental Health (Scotland) Act 1984 should continue to be governed by Part X of that Act with the exception of psychosurgery which could be authorised by the sheriff under Recommendation 62.

(3) The general authority in paragraph (1) above should not apply to those matters more specifically dealt with in Recommendations 59 to 68.

Clause 37(1), (2)

---

1. Proposal 20, para 3.11.
2. See para 5.4.
3. We discuss the effect of a written or oral statement made by the adult while capable as to future medical treatment when incapable at paras 5.41 to 5.59.
4. S 2(4).

Consulting the patient's nearest relative

5.18   In deciding whether to give treatment doctors would be required to consult (so far as reasonable and practicable) the nearest relative of a patient about proposed treatment which the patient is mentally incapable of deciding whether or not to accept[1]. In our discussion paper we noted that the 1984 Act contains detailed provisions about relatives in relation to detention in hospital or guardianship. Section 53(1) provides that "relative" means:-

(a) spouse

(b) child

(c) father or mother

(d) brother or sister

(e) grandparent

(f) grandchild

(g) uncle or aunt

(h) nephew or niece.

Briefly the nearest relative is the first listed relative who is caring for the patient or who was caring for the patient before admission to hospital or guardianship[2]. If no relative is or was caring for the patient the first listed relative is the nearest relative (and within the class of children or siblings priority depends on age)[3]. Relatives not resident in the British Islands, spouses living apart and persons under 18 are disregarded[4]. A spouse includes a cohabitant[5]. The sheriff may appoint one of the other relatives or any other person to act as nearest relative on cause shown[6].

5.19   Our provisional view in the discussion paper was that these provisions were unduly complex for the purposes of medical treatment and we put forward a shorter list[7]. Under our proposal the patient's nearest relative would be the first person reasonably available on the following list (in order of priority):-

(a) husband, wife or cohabiting partner

(b) a child over 18 years of age

(c) a parent

(d) a brother or sister.

Where the first available relative declined to give any views then the doctor was to be entitled to go to the next reasonably available relative in the list.

5.20   Many of those responding agreed with our proposed short list of relatives or suggested minor modifications. However, the Law Society and the National Schizophrenia Fellowship (Scotland) considered that the more detailed provisions in the 1984 Act should be applied. On reconsideration, we think there is considerable force in their view that consistency across the whole area of mental disability is very desirable. Adoption of the 1984 Act provisions would also meet the criticisms voiced by some respondents about our list that a definition of cohabiting partner and provisions regulating the order in which cohabiting partners and spouses should be consulted were also needed. Sections 53(4) and (5) of the 1984 Act deal with such matters. In Part 2 of this report we recommend[8] that the 1984 Act's provisions relating to nearest relatives and acting nearest relatives should be adopted for the purposes of consultation in relation to an intervention in the welfare or affairs of an incapable adult. There is no reason to adopt a different approach for medical treatment of incapable patients.

Treatments outwith the general authority

5.21   In the previous section we recommended that doctors and other health care professionals should have a general statutory authority to give treatment or to take steps to safeguard and promote the health of incapable patients. This general authority was however to be subject to various exceptions, which we now consider. Participation in research, organ

---

1. See para 5.15.
2. S 53(3).
3. S 53(3).
4. S 53(4).
5. S 53(5).
6. S 56.
7. Proposal 21(2) at para 3.21.
8. Recommendation 14, para 2.73.

transplants from incapable donors and withdrawal of life-support measures from patients in a persistent vegetative state are discussed separately. These matters would not fall within the general authority, since they are neither treatments nor do they safeguard or promote the patient's health.

5.22 In our discussion paper[1] we noted that many jurisdictions had recently introduced new legislation or practices to ensure that certain treatments on incapable patients had to be agreed by a court or similar body before they could be given. Examples include sterilisation (England and Wales, Germany, Victoria), abortion (Victoria) and any treatment carrying a risk of death or severe injury (Germany). Since our discussion paper was published the Parliamentary Assembly of the Council of Europe has published a recommendation[2] inviting the Committee of Ministers to adopt a recommendation on this subject based on rules designed to guarantee respect for the human rights of psychiatric patients. The rules deal, among other things, with "lobotomies" and electro-convulsive therapy. In Scotland there is no statutory or common law requirement that certain treatments require the consent of a court or similar body.

5.23 The justification for involving the courts or some similar body is that the specified treatments are controversial. The need for such treatment should be examined in a public forum where opposing views can be presented and evidence tested and evaluated. The decision to use such treatment should not simply be left to the doctors and the patient's family; there is a public interest in monitoring the use of such treatments and protecting those unable to protect themselves. In our discussion paper we were of the opinion that merely appointing a tutor-dative or some other proxy to consent to the treatment was insufficient, at least without procedure to ensure proper consideration and debate[3]. We proposed that a treatment prescribed by the Secretary of State should require the consent of a court before it could be carried out on an incapable patient (except in an emergency), and that the prescribed treatments should include sterilisation (other than for therapeutic reasons), abortion, electro-convulsive therapy, psychosurgery and the implantation of foetal tissue[4]. Views were invited on whether any other treatments should be specified. Our proposal was supported in principle by all those who commented. We have no hesitation in adhering to it. There are certain treatments or procedures which involve questions of value, fundamental human rights and social policy rather than mere medical views.

5.24 **Sterilisation**. There was no dissent about including sterilisation as a prescribed treatment requiring authorisation by a court. In the last few years some tutors-dative have been appointed to consent to the sterilisation of incapable women (other than for treatment of a medical condition)[5]. Some concern was expressed at the vagueness of our proposed exclusion of therapeutic sterilisations and it was suggested that more precision was necessary in describing the class of sterilisations that should not be required to be authorised by a court. Although sterilisation is normally thought of in terms of female sterilisation the same issues arise for male sterilisation. Since *Re F (Mental Patient: Sterilisation)* there have been cases in England and Wales where a declaration by the High Court was held unnecessary to authorise a hysterectomy because the patient suffered from heavy painful menstrual periods[6]. The hysterectomy was held to be a necessary operation for therapeutic purposes. The distinction we had in mind in using the term therapeutic was between sterilisations for avoidance of possible pregnancy or other social reasons and those to cure an existing disease of the reproductive organs. The distinction between therapeutic and non-therapeutic is not an easy one to draw and has been stated to be likely to lead to an arid semantic debate[7]. We conclude that focusing on treatment of an existing serious malfunction or disease would exclude those cases which should be allowed to proceed without prior authorisation by the court. Accordingly we recommend that:

59. **Sterilisation of an adult incapable of consenting to it should require prior authorisation by a sheriff, unless the procedure is to be carried out to treat an existing serious malfunction or disease of the adult's reproductive organs.**

Clause 37(4)(c)

5.25 **Electro-convulsive therapy**. Our proposal that electro-convulsive therapy (ECT) should require authorisation from the court before being carried out on a patient incapable of consenting to it was criticised by many respondents. Many medical commentators pointed out that ECT is a well-established, effective and safe treatment that has no irreversible effects when used in accordance with modern procedures. The Mental Welfare Commission said that there was no evidence that ECT causes any long-term tissue damage but it may impair past memories. It considered that it should be regarded as a serious treatment requiring a second opinion. On reconsideration we would agree that ECT should not require prior court approval. It would be anomalous if ECT for incapable informal patients required court approval while a second opinion was sufficient for detained patients[8]. Moreover, ECT is so frequently used that requiring court approval would

---

1. Para 3.24.
2. Recommendation 1235 (1994).
3. Para 3.25.
4. Proposal 22, para 3.28.
5. *D Petr* and *G Petr*: Adrian Ward *Tutors to Adults: Developments*, 1992 SLT (News) 325.
6. *Re E (a minor)* Times Law Reports, 22 February 1991; *Re G F (Medical Treatment)* [1992] 1 FLR 293.
7. *Re B* [1988] AC 199 Lord Bridge at p 205.
8. Under s 98, 1984 Act.

either lead to its use being curtailed or the courts being deluged with applications for approval. However, ECT on incapable patients should, in our view, be subject to some control. The fact that many respondents supported our proposal suggests that there is concern about unregulated use of ECT on incapable patients[1]. We note that section 98(1)(a)[2] of the 1984 Act provides that detained patients who are either incapable of consenting or refuse to consent may be given ECT provided a medical practitioner approved by the Mental Welfare Commission certifies, that having regard to the likelihood of its alleviating or preventing a deterioration of the patient's condition, it should be given. The Scottish Association for Mental Health suggested that if a person needs treatment for mental disorder but is incapable of consenting then he or she should be detained so that the safeguards in the 1984 Act would apply. We think it should not be necessary for incapable patients to be detained before treatment and that it would be better simply to extend section 98 to them. This would be in line with best current practice. The Royal College of Psychiatrists have recommended[3] that detention should be used for those incapable patients who resist being given ECT but that those who passively accept it may either be detained or given ECT after obtaining a second opinion and discussing the situation with the relatives. Extending section 98 would also result in a second opinion being required for drugs for mental disorder if more than three months has elapsed since the patient started taking them. A second opinion should be obtained whether or not the patient resists ECT or the drugs. We recommend that:

60. Section 98 of the Mental Health (Scotland) Act 1984, providing for an independent medical practitioner appointed by the Mental Welfare Commission to certify that electro-convulsive therapy and the giving of medicines for mental disorder for more than three months is an appropriate treatment, should be extended to incapable patients who are not liable to be detained under the Act.

Clause 37(5)

ECT is not mentioned specifically in the draft Bill but would be a treatment that the Secretary of State should prescribe. This is how it is dealt with in section 98 of the 1984 Act.

5.26 **Abortion.** Although there was support on consultation for including abortion in the list of treatments requiring prior court authorisation, we do not now favour this approach. We note that in the English case of *Re G (Mental Patient: Termination of Pregnancy)*[4] it was decided that a declaration from the High Court was not necessary for abortions because the Abortion Act 1967 contains appropriate safeguards. We agree with that general approach. There is also the practical considerations that abortion will generally have to be performed within a certain period. If court authority had to be sought the procedures for obtaining it would have to be speedy or (as we proposed in the discussion paper) there would have to be an exclusion for those abortions which were urgently necessary on medical grounds. Proper consideration of an application for authority to terminate a pregnancy with discussion of all the issues and alternatives is not likely to be consistent with speedy procedure. However, whilst we do not think that court authority should be required we think that some extra safeguard would be justifiable in the case of women incapable of consenting. We consider that the second opinion procedure recommended for electro-convulsive therapy and long term medication for mental disorder should be applied. We accordingly recommend that:

61. The termination of a pregnancy of a woman incapable of consenting to termination should be carried out only if it would be lawful under the Abortion Act 1967 in the case of a consenting patient and an independent medical practitioner appointed by the Mental Welfare Commission certifies that termination is appropriate.

Clause 37(5)(b)

5.27 **Psychosurgery.** Psychosurgery may at present be carried out on patients liable to be detained under the 1984 Act only if they are capable of consenting to it[5]. As far as non-detained incapable patients are concerned it is possible that psychosurgery could be performed on the basis of the doctors' common law authority (if the decision in *Re F (Mental Patient: Sterilisation)* were to be followed in Scotland) or the consent of a tutor-dative. In practice doctors would not perform psychosurgery on incapable patients without some specific authority and we doubt whether the court would appoint a tutor-dative for this purpose. In our discussion paper we considered that a prohibition on psychosurgery for incapable patients seemed too absolute and proposed that the treatment should be able to be carried out with the court's approval[6]. Since our discussion paper there have been a small number of operations carried out in Scotland; some on detained patients, the others on non-detained patients, all of whom have consented to such treatment.

---

1. The recommendation of the Parliamentary Assembly of the Council of Europe mentioned in para 5.22 above suggests that ECT (and lobotomies) should require (a) the consent of the patient or a person chosen by him as his representative and (b) confirmation of the decision by a committee not composed exclusively of psychiatric experts. This seems unduly restrictive but it illustrates the concern felt on this topic.
2. In conjunction with the Mental Health (Specified Treatments, Guardianship Duties etc) (Scotland) Regulations 1984, SI 1984/1494, reg 3(2).
3. *The Practical Administration of ECT*, 1989.
4. Times Law Reports, 31 January 1991.
5. S 97. A medical practitioner appointed by the Mental Welfare Commission has to certify that the patient understands the nature and likely effects of the operation and consents to it and the patient's understanding and consent also has to be certified by two lay people appointed by the Commission.
6. Proposal 22, para 3.26.

5.28   The only dissent on consultation was from the Scottish Association for Mental Health. In its view if a person needs treatment for mental disorder and cannot consent to it because of mental incapacity, then he or she should be compulsorily detained in hospital and treated under the provisions of Part X of the 1984 Act. Compulsory detention under the 1984 Act would not advance matters in the case of psychosurgery, however, because in terms of section 97 a detained patient's consent is required. If the Association's comment is to be taken to mean an absolute prohibition of psychosurgery for all incapable patients then we would disagree. Those who are so profoundly mentally disordered that they are incapable of consenting to psychosurgery may well include patients who would most benefit from the operation. The operation should however never be performed on those who oppose or resist it. We note that a similar view has been expressed by a Scottish Office Good Practice Group (Chairman, Dr David Nichols) in its draft *Neurosurgery for Mental Disorder* report published in September 1994. New South Wales has recently enacted legislation[1] allowing psychosurgery to be carried out on incapable patients if a review board and the court approve. We have already noted the recommendation of the Parliamentary Assembly of the Council of Europe on this subject[2]. We recommend that:

62. Psychosurgery should be able to be carried out on a patient incapable of consenting to it (whether or not detained under the Mental Health (Scotland) Act 1984) but only if the court authorises it and the patient does not resist it.

Clause 37(4)(b)

5.29   **Other treatments**. We proposed that the implantation of foetal tissue into mentally incapable patients' brains should require authorisation from the court. While the majority of those responding agreed, some queried this treatment's inclusion as it was neither particularly risky nor posed ethical problems as far as the mentally incapable recipient was concerned. The controversy over its use is whether it is ethical to use material from foetuses for any patient. This ethical issue is not one which it is appropriate to address in this report.

5.30   In putting forward our proposal that certain treatments should require prior authorisation from the court we asked for views on what treatments should fall into this category besides sterilisation, psychosurgery, electro-convulsive therapy, abortion and implantation of foetal tissue[3]. Other treatments suggested by respondents included:

(a) long term contraception

(b) cosmetic surgery

(c) psychotropic drugs

(d) withdrawal of nutrition and hydration from a patient in a persistent vegetative state

(e) removal of teeth for biting

(f) continuation or withdrawal of narcotic drugs from mentally disabled addicts

(g) hormonal treatment for patient's libido

(h) physical restraint in connection with behaviour modification.

We have recommended earlier that giving drugs for the treatment of mental disorder for more than three months should require a second opinion[4]. We do not think that giving such drugs for a shorter period should warrant a second opinion, much less prior approval by the court. Hormonal treatment for the patient's libido given by means of an implant is governed by section 97 of the Mental Health (Scotland) Act 1984 and requires the patient's consent in the same way as psychosurgery[5]. We consider implant treatment should be available to incapable patients in the same way as we have recommended for psychosurgery[6]. Hormonal treatment given by injection or orally requires a second opinion under section 98 of the 1984 Act if the treatment extends for more than three months and we consider this should remain the position for detained patients and have recommended that section 98 be extended to informal incapable patients[7]. Withdrawal or withholding of life-support measures from incapable patients, such as those in a persistent vegetative state, is a complex and sensitive subject which we discuss at length later[8]. Long term contraception, cosmetic surgery, removal of teeth for biting and the withdrawal or continuation or narcotic drugs from incapable adults are not in our view sufficiently exceptional or problematic to warrant court involvement. However, the Secretary of State should be empowered to make

---

1. Mental Health Act 1990.
2. See footnote 2 to para 5.25 above.
3. Proposal 22(2), para 3.27.
4. Recommendation 60, para 5.25.
5. The Mental Health (Specified Treatments, Guardianship Duties etc) (Scotland) Regulations 1984 (SI 1984/1494), reg 3(1).
6. Recommendation 62, para 5.28.
7. Recommendation 60, para 5.25.
8. See paras 5.77-5.86.

regulations varying the list of prescribed treatments that require either prior court authority or a formal second opinion from an independent specialist. This would enable other treatments to be added to those we recommend if that was thought appropriate. We recommend that:

63. (1) Hormonal treatment for the patient's libido by means of an implant should be carried out on an incapable patient only if a court authorises it and the patient does not resist it.

(2) The Secretary of State should have power to make regulations prescribing other treatments which should require court approval or a second opinion.

Clause 37(4)(a), (5)(b)

5.31   Enable in responding to our proposal was concerned lest restraint and detention could be justified as treatment or therapy. The Centre for Studies in Mental Handicap also mentioned behaviour modification programmes as a possible special treatment requiring authorisation from the court. We consider that the general authority we recommend above for health care professionals should not include such action. If detention or forcible treatment is considered appropriate then the 1984 Act should be used. There should be an exemption to cover cases where forcible detention is necessary to avert serious harm to the patient. This should be a temporary power to be used in urgent situations, where there is no opportunity to use even the emergency detention provisions in the 1984 Act.

5.32   We recommend that:

64. The general authority to treat so as to safeguard and promote health in Recommendation 58 should not authorise restraint or detention of an incapable patient, except where urgently necessary to prevent serious harm to that patient.

Clause 37(3)(a)

5.33   In our discussion paper we saw a role for the courts in adjudicating disputes as to medical treatment for incapable patients, although we hoped that litigation would be rare. While the court is dealing with the dispute patients should be given treatment necessary to keep them alive and in a stable condition. Obviously once the court has come to a decision doctors should not be entitled by virtue of our recommended general statutory authority to take any action which is inconsistent with that decision. We recommend that:

65. Where a court has made a decision relating to the medical treatment of an incapable patient, doctors should not have any authority by virtue of Recommendation 58 to take any action that would be inconsistent with the court's decision. Pending the determination of an application to the court in relation to medical treatment doctors should have authority to give treatment necessary to save the patient's life or prevent a serious deterioration in his or her health, unless the court orders otherwise.

Clause 37(3)(b), (6) and (7)

Role of guardians and welfare attorneys in medical treatment decisions

5.34   Under our recommendations guardians and welfare attorneys could be appointed with powers in relation to personal welfare including medical treatment[1]. The question then arises as to what effect a decision by a guardian or attorney should have on treatments, other than those which require authorisation by the court or fall within Part X of the 1984 Act[2]. In practice it is the effect of a refusal of consent or a withholding of consent to treatment that is of greater legal significance. Neither a guardian nor an attorney can demand treatment that doctors are unwilling to provide on clinical grounds. The general statutory authority which we recommend would authorise doctors to give reasonable treatment in the circumstances and in arriving at a decision on treatment the doctors would be obliged under the general principles where reasonably practicable to consult any guardian or attorney.

5.35   We considered two options in relation to guardians[3] and attorneys[4] in our discussion paper.

(1) Doctors should be required to consult the guardian or attorney if aware of his or her existence in so far as it is reasonably practicable to do so. The views expressed should have to be taken into account.

(2) Doctors should be required to consult the guardian or attorney in so far as it is reasonably practicable to do so. If the guardian or attorney refuses to consent to the proposed treatment the doctors would be in the same position as if a competent patient had refused consent. Where the guardian or attorney could not be contacted or declined to

---

1. See Parts 6 and 3 respectively.
2. Consent by the guardian or attorney would be ineffective to authorise such treatments. They require court authority or a second opinion from an independent practitioner. See paras 5.21 to 5.30.
3. Para 3.15.
4. Paras 5.110 to 5.118 and Proposal 78(2), para 5.119.

express any view the doctors could proceed to give treatment which seemed to them clinically appropriate. Faced with a refusal to consent by the guardian or attorney doctors would have to apply to the court for authority to treat and, pending the determination of the application, should have authority to give treatment which was urgently necessary to save the patient's life or prevent serious deterioration in his or her health.

We consider the options in relation to guardians first before turning to welfare attorneys.

5.36   Consultation revealed a division of opinion. The arguments in favour of the first option are that no person should be entitled by refusing or withholding consent to veto clinically appropriate treatment proposed for an incapable adult patient, and that it enables doctors to disregard the views of an ill-informed or prejudiced guardian. It recognises the medical expertise of doctors. We were told that some of the most difficult cases are those where there is a division of opinion within the incapable patient's family as to what treatment should be provided. Giving the guardian a veto would encourage one relative to apply to become a guardian so as to impose his or her own views on the rest of the family and the doctors.

5.37   On the other hand, the guardian would have been appointed by the court after checks as to suitability and may indeed have been appointed specifically with power to take medical treatment decisions. Such a guardian ought to be more than a mere consultee - one whose views have merely to be taken into account. Strong minded or zealous doctors could simply go through the motions of consulting the guardian and taking account of the views without really doing so. The second option, which is that which applies to parents as guardians of their young children, is arguably a more suitable model for the guardians of incapable adults. However, parents have an enormous and continuing psychological and emotional interest in their children's welfare; the same will not necessarily be true of guardians of adults. Another argument against giving guardians a veto is that they are unlikely to be experienced in making difficult medical decisions in times of stress and, if the guardian was also a near relative, he or she might be too emotionally involved to make a sensible decision. Doctors, on the other hand, are more used to this and so it is arguably more appropriate for the final decision to rest with them.

5.38   The courts would be available to resolve any irreconcilable differences of opinion between doctors and guardians. Under the first option in paragraph 5.35 the guardian would have to go to court to have the doctors interdicted from treating the patient. The second option would require doctors who wish to treat despite a refusal of consent by the guardian to seek authority from the court to proceed. While litigation may have to be used for major cases, legal proceedings should not be the only or main "tie breaker" between doctors and guardians. Our preferred solution, which has evolved from discussions with representatives of some of the Royal Colleges in Scotland[1], lies between the two options outlined above, although it is somewhat closer to the first option. If no agreement can be reached between the doctors and the guardian as to the adult's treatment the doctors should have no authority to proceed until they have obtained a second opinion from an independent consultant skilled in that treatment. The consultant should have to be sought from a unit other than the one which the patient was in, should have to examine the patient, read the case notes and give the guardian an opportunity to discuss matters. Only if the independent consultant was of the opinion that the treatment was clinically appropriate and should be given considering all the circumstances should the doctors have authority to proceed. We understand that it should be possible to obtain such a second opinion within a day or so at the most, even in areas away from the main centres of population. Nevertheless, provision needs to be made for necessary treatment pending the obtaining of the second opinion. We consider that once the second opinion procedure has been initiated doctors should then be entitled to give any treatment necessary to save the patient's life or prevent any deterioration in the patient's health unless a court orders otherwise. This entitlement should last until the independent consultant's opinion is known.

5.39   Summing up the previous paragraphs we recommend that:

66. (1) The general statutory authority to give reasonable treatment in Recommendation 58 should not apply where the doctors are aware that the patient's guardian refuses to consent to the treatment in question. The doctors may proceed with treatment to which the guardian has refused consent only if they obtain an opinion from a consultant from a different unit skilled in that treatment to the effect that it is in all the circumstances (medical and non-medical) an appropriate treatment.

(2) In order to safeguard the patient's health until the opinion is obtained, doctors should have authority to give treatment necessary to save the patient's life or prevent any deterioration in his or her condition once the second opinion procedure has been initiated, unless a court has ordered otherwise.

Clause 38

---

1.   The Royal College of Physicians of Edinburgh, The Royal College of Physicians and Surgeons of Glasgow and the Scottish Division of the Royal College of Psychiatrists.

5.40 We turn now to consider the role of an attorney with powers in the field of medical treatment. The options are the same as for guardians set out in paragraph 5.35. Briefly, the attorney would either have to consent to treatment or simply have his or her views taken into account. In our opinion the arguments for requiring the attorney's consent seem less strong than those in relation to guardians. The document of appointment may have been drawn up many years previously or it may have conferred power to make medical treatment decisions without any real thought about the circumstances that the patient is now in. The person selected as attorney may no longer be appropriate to take such decisions because he or she may have ceased to be closely involved with the patient or may have acquired a material conflict of interest. A person who wished to ensure that he or she would not be subjected to certain treatments when incapable could do this by means of an advance statement[1]. However, we do not consider that an attorney's position is so much weaker than that of a guardian to justify a different regime. We would therefore adopt the second opinion provisions recommended in the previous paragraph and accordingly recommend that:

67. Recommendation 66 should apply to welfare attorneys with powers in relation to the patient's medical treatment as it applies to guardians.

Clause 38

Advance statements

5.41 We turn now to deal with advance statements made by patients while competent concerning their future treatment. An advance statement becomes effective only when the doctors consider that the patient is unable, by reason of mental disorder, to make a decision in relation to the treatment under consideration or is unable to communicate. Advance statements are sometimes referred to as "living wills", "advance directions" or "advance directives". We prefer the term "advance statement": "living will" is confusing and uninformative and "advance directions" or "advance directives" implies that a person can direct certain treatment to be given, which is not the case. Many patients will simply set out in general terms their wishes and views in relation to future treatment. An advance statement may be self-contained or form part of a document such as a welfare power of attorney. In drawing up our recommendations in this area we have derived great benefit from discussions with the Law Commission for England and Wales and from having an observer on a Working Party which has drafted a code of practice in this area[2].

5.42 As we mentioned in the previous paragraph some advance statements merely set out the patient's views or wishes as to future treatment in a general way. The general principles which we have recommended in Part 2 of this report require doctors in considering what treatment to give to have regard to the past and present wishes and feelings of the patient. No further recommendations are required to deal with such "advisory" advance statements. Advance statements which consent in advance to future treatment are also adequately dealt with by our earlier recommendations in terms of which doctors and other health care professionals are to have a general statutory authority to treat incapable patients so as to safeguard or promote their health[3]. An advance consent would add nothing to this recommended authority, although it could be helpful as an indication of the patient's wishes and feelings. We have also recommended[4] that the general statutory authority should not apply to certain specified treatments such as sterilisation, psychosurgery or abortion. However, such specified treatments would be authorised if the prior authority of a court or, in certain cases, a confirmatory second opinion from an independent specialist was obtained. The patient's advance consent should not remove the need for involving the court or the second opinion specialist. A competent patient cannot demand to be given treatment which the doctors consider to be clinically or ethically inappropriate. Patients should not be able to use advance statements to demand such treatment in the future either. The advance statements which do give rise to legal problems are those which refuse clinically and ethically appropriate treatment. This is because of the clash between the patient's refusal and the doctor's duty of care in terms of which liability to criminal and civil proceedings may arise from failure to give adequate treatment. The paradigm case is the Jehovah's Witness who refuses blood transfusions in any circumstances even if death is the result of the transfusion not being given. In the rest of this section we therefore confine the discussion to advance refusals.

5.43 We did not deal explicitly with advance statements in our discussion paper but mentioned their use in other jurisdictions in our section on welfare attorneys. Since our discussion paper was published in 1991 there have been cases in England and Wales which have considered the effect of advance refusals. *Re T (Adult: Refusal of Treatment)*[5] concerned a pregnant woman injured in a car accident. After discussion with her mother, a Jehovah's Witness, she said she did not want a blood transfusion. Subsequently she signed a form refusing to consent to a blood transfusion but it was not explained to her that a transfusion might be necessary to save her life during or after the emergency Caesarian delivery that was to take place. Her condition deteriorated so that an emergency application was made to the court for a declaration that a blood transfusion would be lawful. This was duly given and the Official Solicitor as guardian *ad litem* for the patient later appealed. The Court of Appeal decided that the refusal was made without proper appreciation of the consequences

---

1. See Recommendation 68, para 5.50.
2. See para 5.46 for further details.
3. Recommendation 58, para 5.17.
4. Recommendation 58(3), para 5.17.
5. [1993] Fam 95.

and as a result of her mother's undue influence. It could therefore be disregarded. The right of capable patients to make decisions about their future treatment was upheld, even if the effect of the decision is that the patient will die. However, as Lord Donaldson said:[1]

"If the factual situation falls outwith the scope of the refusal or if the assumption upon which it is based is falsified, the refusal ceases to be effective. The doctors are then faced with a situation in which the patient has made no decision and, he by then being unable to decide for himself, they have both the right and the duty to treat him in accordance with what in the exercise of their clinical judgment they consider to be his best interests".

Dicta in the subsequent case of *Airedale NHS Trust v Bland*[2] confirm the position regarding a patient's directions including the condition that doctors should ensure that the directions can be properly regarded as applicable in the circumstances that have occurred.

5.44   In *Re C (Adult: Refusal of Medical Treatment)*[3] a man with a gangrenous leg sought an injunction against the hospital to prevent it from amputating his leg. He refused consent when capable of doing so and wished effect to be given to that refusal should he subsequently become incapable. It was held that the High Court could rule by way of injunction or declaration that an individual is capable of refusing or consenting to medical treatment and could also determine the effect of a purported advance directive as to future medical treatment. The test of capacity is whether the patient sufficiently understands the nature, purpose and effect of the proposed treatment and the effect of an anticipatory refusal of treatment in the future. This test was satisfied in C's case and the injunction was granted.

5.45   The House of Lords Select Committee on Medical Ethics[4] commended the development of advance directives since their preparation could stimulate discussion between doctors and patients and the directives would assist the health-care team at the appropriate future date[5]. However, they concluded that legislation was unnecessary since in their view a doctor who acted in accordance with an advance direction would not be guilty of negligence or any criminal offence[6]. They recommended instead that a code of practice should be drawn up jointly by the professional organisations involved in order to assist their members[7].

5.46   The current law in England and Wales that an advance refusal is binding is qualified by the further rules that the factual situation facing the doctors must be within the scope of the refusal, the assumptions upon which it is based must not be falsified, and the patient must have been capable at the time of making the refusal. This may well also be the law in Scotland although it is not possible to state this with certainty in the absence of any authoritative statements by the courts. We consider that legislation setting out the position in Scotland regarding advance refusals would be helpful to doctors and other health-care professionals facing the difficult decision as to what, if any, treatment to give to incapable patients who have refused some or all treatment in advance. Any legislation will, however, require to be supplemented with further guidance in a code of practice or similar document. Following a recommendation from the House of Lords Select Committee on Medical Ethics a Code of Practice *Advance Statements about Medical Treatment*[8] was produced by the British Medical Association in collaboration with the Royal College of Physicians, the Royal College of Nursing and the Royal College of General Practitioners.

5.47   Should an advance refusal have to be in writing and if so should any special formalities have to be observed? In England and Wales an oral advance refusal is regarded as effective and the same is probably true in Scotland. It has to be recognised that there are dangers in relying on oral refusals. First, the doctor may not remember the precise terms of the refusal at the time when the treatment decision is being made. Second, the oral statement may well have been made to a person other than the treating doctor because of duty rotas and patients being moved to different parts of the hospital for different aspects of their treatment. Without some form of writing, even in the patient's case notes or records, it would be difficult to ensure that the treating doctors were aware of the terms of the oral advance refusal. Finally, the act of writing down an advance refusal focuses the patient's mind and helps the patient to set out the terms of the refusal in a more precise and hopefully more helpful way. However, we have come to the conclusion that there should not be undue formality in this area and that to insist on writing may deny effect to the undoubted wishes of a patient. Suppose, for example, a patient in a hospital made a clear and explicit refusal orally to a doctor in the presence of others. Clearly legal effect should be given to such a refusal in line with the patient's expectations. While we consider effect should be given

---

1. At p 114.
2. [1993] AC 789.
3. [1994] 1 All ER 819.
4. Their report was published in 1994 as HL Paper 21-I.
5. Report, para 263.
6. Report, para 264.
7. Report, para 265.
8. Published April 1995.

to clear oral refusals we would encourage patients who wish to make advance refusals to do so in writing. The task of making a written refusal could be simplified by the provision of printed forms in which blanks could be filled in or boxes ticked.

5.48   An advance refusal of appropriate treatment will involve a clash between the doctor's duty of care to the patient and the patient's own wishes. We understand that some doctors tend to treat even if the treatment will not increase the patient's quality of life. In some cases this is done for fear of being sued for negligence. Other doctors have a conscientious objection to withholding treatment, particularly life saving treatment[1]. We would reject the notion that doctors should regard advance refusals as advisory and simply take them into account in deciding how to treat incapable patients. The principle of patient autonomy requires more weight to be given to the wishes of patients. The present law in England and Wales and probably also in Scotland is that (under certain conditions and with certain exceptions) an advance refusal is binding and not merely advisory. It would be a retrograde step to recommend giving advance refusals a lesser status than they currently enjoy. We start from the accepted position that a competent patient is entitled to refuse any treatment, even if the result is death[2]. Respect for patient autonomy demands in our view that they should in general be entitled to refuse in advance treatment that may be offered to them at a future date when they are incapable, and that the refusal should have the same effect as that of a competent patient in relation to present treatment. Put another way, an advance refusal of treatment made when capable should survive any subsequent loss of capacity in much the same way as we have recommended for welfare attorneys[3]. The general authority of doctors to treat incapable patients which we have previously recommended should not apply in the face of an advance refusal. It therefore follows that a doctor should be protected from any criminal, civil or disciplinary liability if he or she withheld treatment in accordance with an advance refusal which he or she reasonably believed was valid and applicable, but should be liable if he or she gave treatment which had been validly refused in advance. Although this should be the norm there are certain conditions and certain treatments where a different approach should be taken. These are discussed further below.

5.49   Our recommendation that an advance refusal should be binding rather than merely advisory is made on the assumption that the refusal was validly made by a patient with capacity to do so. Capacity entails understanding the nature of the refusal and the likely consequences, in broad terms at least, for one's health and well-being of accepting or refusing the treatment in question. Capacity is presumed so that the onus would be on those seeking to deny effect to the refusal to rebut the presumption. Undue influence should also be an invalidating factor. If it could be established, as in *Re T (Adult: Refusal of Treatment)*[4], that the patient had been unduly influenced by others in making the advance refusal, then the refusal should not be treated as binding.

5.50   We recommend that:

68. (1)   Legislation should be introduced making it clear that, subject to certain exceptions dealt with in Recommendations 69 to 73, a valid refusal made by a competent patient of treatment that may be offered in the future when he or she is not mentally capable should have the effect that doctors have no authority to give the treatment in question.

(2)   Doctors should not be liable for withholding treatment in accordance with a refusal which they reasonably believe was validly made and is applicable in the circumstances, or for giving treatment contrary to the terms of a refusal that they reasonably believe is neither valid nor applicable.

(3)   A refusal should be effective whether it is in writing or oral. A written refusal should have to be signed by the patient but should not have to be witnessed or made in any particular form.

Clause 40

5.51   An advance refusal should have to apply to the treatment in question and to the circumstances in which the patient finds himself or herself before it is regarded as having binding effect. It will be a question of construction in each case whether these two criteria are met. In some cases, like the absolute refusal of a Jehovah's Witness to have a blood transfusion in any circumstances, the terms of the advance refusal admit no doubt. But a refusal of cardiopulmonary resuscitation "should I become severely demented" will require the patient's present condition to be assessed to see whether it amounts to severe dementia. Another problem of construction would arise where the refusal referred to specified treatments for a particular condition, but due to advances in medicine the doctors were proposing to use a somewhat different treatment. Drafting refusals in more general terms could avoid such problems.

---

1. The British Medical Association's Code, *Advance Statements about Medical Treatments*, pp 35 and 36 advises that in such circumstances doctors should hand over the treatment of the patient to colleagues. If this is not possible they must comply with a valid refusal.
2. Patients who are detained under the 1984 Act can be compulsorily treated for their mental disorder, see para 5.56.
3. See para 3.5.
4. See para 5.43 above.

Exceptions to binding nature of advance statements

5.52 **Radical change in circumstances**. Even if an advance refusal was validly made and is applicable to the circumstances that exist we consider that there are still situations where doctors should be entitled to treat notwithstanding the refusal. Doctors can discuss treatment with a competent patient so that any refusal of treatment will have been made in the knowledge of the consequences. Doctors faced with an advance refusal made by a now incompetent patient have no opportunity for dialogue. There may have been substantial advances in medical treatment since the refusal was made. An example which was cited to us is a refusal of renal dialysis by a Jehovah's Witness because this used to involve periodical blood transfusions. Now there is a drug, erythropoetin, which makes transfusions unnecessary. Patients may find themselves in vastly different circumstances from those existing when they made the advance refusal. It is not easy for individuals to foresee how they are going to think and feel about treatments when their condition may be radically different in the future. Ill people often make different treatment decisions from those who are in good health. For example, a single man who enjoys sport might make an advance refusal of antibiotics and other life-saving treatment if he were to become confined to a wheelchair by physical disability. Should doctors years later when he is indeed in that condition but married and with dependent children be bound not to treat pneumonia which has rendered him incapable of reconsidering his old refusal?

5.53 In some such cases we consider that the balancing of patient autonomy and the medical duty of care should result in doctors being allowed to treat notwithstanding a valid and applicable advance refusal. A radical change in circumstances ought to be regarded as destroying the basis on which the refusal was made. The patient's medical condition should not be regarded as such a circumstance because many advance statements are made for the very purpose of dealing with changes in medical condition. Encouraging people to review their advance refusals from time to time may help prevent such problems, but inevitably some will not have followed this advice. We would not base an exclusion on a material change of circumstances alone since what matters is the effect, or presumed effect, of such a change on the patient's intentions. We prefer to use the formula of whether there is reason to believe that the patient would have changed his or her mind in the light of the new conditions and would now accept the treatment. This formula also allows doctors to take account of indications from the patient falling short of revocation of the refusal, or statements by others of what the patient said or did while still competent which indicate a change of mind. We note that the Council of Europe's draft[1] Bioethics Convention adopts a cautious approach to this question. Article 9 provides that:

> "The previously expressed wishes relating to a medical intervention by a patient who is not, at the time of the intervention, in a state to express his wishes shall be taken into account."

The Parliamentary Assembly has since adopted an Opinion which rejected an amendment which would make previously expressed wishes "determinant"[2]. We therefore recommend that:

69. **Doctors should be entitled to disregard a valid and applicable advance refusal if, by reason of a material change of circumstances since the refusal was made (other than a change in the patient's medical condition), they reasonably believe that the patient if competent would now accept the treatment in question.**

Clause 40(6)

5.54 **Life-saving treatment.** The public interest in preserving the life and health of citizens does not prevent a competent patient from refusing life sustaining treatment but any doubt is to be resolved in favour of the preservation of life[3]. Refusal of treatment that could save the patient's life is such a serious matter for all concerned that we think the patient should be required to make it clear that the refusal is still to apply even in such circumstances. The reference to death need not be express so long as the maker's intention is clear. A refusal of blood transfusions in any circumstances would obviously include the case where failure to give a transfusion would result in the patient's death. We recommend that:

70. **An advance refusal of treatment which if not given would endanger the patient's life should be followed only if the terms of the refusal make it clear that the patient intended the refusal to apply in such circumstances.**

Clause 40(7)(a)

5.55 **Basic care.** Some jurisdictions prevent a welfare attorney refusing basic care for the adult such as normal feeding, normal hygiene and relief of severe pain[4]. We would adopt this approach for advance refusals. It would be contrary to public policy and the interests of other patients in the hospital or other institution if doctors, nurses and other health-care professionals were obliged to neglect patients to such an extent that they were left filthy or in agony. The provision of food and drink which is available for consumption by the patient in a normal fashion is not something which could be

---

1. Draft of July 1994. The full title of the draft is the "Draft Convention for the Protection of Human Rights and Dignity of the Human Being with regard to the application of Biology and Medicine: Bioethics Convention".
2. Opinion No 184 adopted by the Assembly on 2 February 1995.
3. *Re T (Adult: Refusal of Treatment)* [1993] Fam 95 at p 112.
4. Uniform Rights of the Terminally Ill Act (America): Durable Power of Attorney Health Care Act 1983 (California).

refused by an advance statement because it is not a medical treatment. The question of withholding nutrition and hydration by naso-gastric tubes or other artificial means from patients will be dealt with later[1]. We recommend that:

71. An advance refusal should be ineffective to the extent that it refuses normal hygiene or the relief of severe pain.

Clause 40(7)(b)

5.56 **Detained patients and treatment of mental disorder.** Patients who are detained under the 1984 Act may be treated for their mental disorder against their will. Section 103 permits treatment for mental disorder to be given without a patient's consent provided the treatment is given by or under the direction of the responsible medical officer. Section 98 authorises electro-convulsive therapy and drugs for more than three months if a second opinion specialist certifies that it would be appropriate in the circumstances. It has to be accepted that detention, which can be ordered for a mentally disordered person only after certain medical and legal procedures set down in the 1984 Act have been followed, carries with it the possibility of compulsory treatment for mental disorder which cannot be refused by way of an advance refusal. We recommend that:

72. An advance refusal should be ineffective in relation to a detained patient to the extent that it refuses any treatment for mental disorder which under Part X of the Mental Health (Scotland) Act 1984 can be given to the patient notwithstanding absence of consent.

Clause 40(7)(c)

5.57 **Endangering viable foetus.** A woman with a 30 week old foetus who is in a coma following a motoring accident is being fed artificially with the intention of delivering the baby by caesarian section at the due date. There is no argument between the doctors and the husband that she should be treated in this way and no advance statement had been made[2]. In similar circumstances should a woman be entitled to refuse in advance treatment necessary to keep her and her unborn baby alive? This is a very controversial issue. It can be argued that the existence of a foetus should make no difference to the right of a competent woman to decide what treatment she will have in the future. We accept that people may decline future treatment which will endanger their own lives provided they address their minds to this issue, but it seems to us that endangering the life of another adds another dimension the effect of which ought to outweigh patient autonomy. We are fortified in our conclusion by the fact that the majority of states in America limit the effectiveness of advance refusals during pregnancy[3]. Furthermore, in the English case of *Re S (Adult: Refusal of Treatment)*[4] a refusal to consent to a caesarian section by a woman in labour who was capable of making the decision was overruled by the High Court, although it has to be said that this decision has been widely criticised.

5.58 An advance refusal should not be ineffective during the whole of the woman's pregnancy for that would be too great an interference with her autonomy and her right to choose her future treatment. But as we stated in the previous paragraph the policy considerations are different once refusal endangers the life of the foetus. This pre-supposes that the foetus is viable when the treatment is under consideration. The Abortion Act 1967[5] prohibits the abortion of a foetus aged 24 or more weeks save in exceptional circumstances. We would adopt this time limit as the test for viability since the public policy considerations in advance refusals and abortions are similar. We therefore recommend that:

73. An advance refusal of treatment by a female patient should be ineffective to the extent that it refuses treatment which if not given would endanger the life of a foetus, aged 24 weeks or more, which she is carrying.

Clause 40(7)(d)

Revocation of advance statements

5.59 An advance statement once made should be capable of being revoked subsequently by the adult concerned. A revocation would be valid if capacity existed at the time of revocation. We recommended earlier[6] that it should be competent to make an advance statement either orally or in writing signed by the adult. We would adopt the same approach for revocations. The arguments in favour of giving effect to oral revocations seem to be stronger than those for advance statements. A revocation may be made in circumstances where there is little opportunity for writing and there is not the same danger of its terms being misunderstood or mistransmitted to other doctors. We also think it should be competent to empower a welfare attorney to revoke the adult's advance statement. This power should, however, have to be conferred expressly: a welfare attorney with general powers should not be able to override an advance statement. We do not think

---

1. See paras 5.77 to 5.86.
2. These were the facts of a case reported in The Times, 6 April 1995. Under our recommendations the provision of artificial nutrition and other life-sustaining treatment in such a case would be covered by the general authority already recommended. See Clause 38(1) of the draft Bill. We are assuming that the treatments and procedures adopted would be regarded as "reasonable in the circumstances to safeguard ... the physical .... health" of the woman.
3. T Klosterman, *Analysis of Health Care Directive Legislation in the United States* (1992) p 12.
4. [1993] Fam 123.
5. S 1(1) as amended by s 37(1) of the Human Fertilisation and Embryology Act 1990.
6. Recommendation 68, para 5.50.

that a guardian should be entitled to revoke an advance statement since capable adults ought to be secure in the knowledge that their statements will not be overridden by persons they have not expressly authorised to take such a step. For similar reasons the court should not have power to override by way of an intervention order. We recommend that:

74. An advance refusal should be capable of being revoked by the adult concerned and his or her welfare attorney (if expressly empowered to do so). The revocation may be oral or in writing signed by the person making the revocation.

Clause 40(2), (3)

Organ donation

5.60   Transplantation of a non-regenerative organ (a kidney for example) from a living incapable adult is not treatment to safeguard and promote the health of that adult. Accordingly, it would not fall under the general statutory authority of doctors to provide medical treatment that we have recommended in Recommendation 58 above. As we pointed out in our discussion paper the legality of transplants where the donor is incapable of consenting is not clear[1]. The power of a tutor-dative to consent on behalf of the incapable adult may well be limited to procedures that carry only a minimal risk to the donor such as a skin graft or a blood donation. Suggestions have been made in recent English cases that organ donation from living incapable individuals should require the prior authority of the court[2].

5.61   In our discussion paper[3] we set out the arguments for and against allowing transplantation of non-regenerative tissue from a living adult mentally incapable of giving consent and asked for views as to whether such transplantation should be permitted and, if so, under what conditions. Transplantation to a close relative arguably confers an indirect benefit on the incapable donor. The donor may be distressed by the critical illness of the recipient and the death or serious illness of the recipient may deprive the donor of a carer. Transplantation can also be justified on public interest grounds in alleviating pain and suffering where this can be done without causing substantial harm to others. On the other hand, a mentally disabled person's health and wellbeing is no less worthy of consideration than that of any other person. The temptation to regard incapable people merely as a source of spare parts must be firmly resisted.

5.62   A sizeable minority of those responding to our request for views thought that such transplants should be prohibited altogether. The majority view was that the procedure should be allowable in exceptional cases. Among the conditions suggested were prior approval by the court, the unavailability of a suitable organ from any other source, the unavailability of any alternative suitable treatment, and that the death or continued serious ill-health of the recipient would severely diminish the quality of the donor's life. We have had further discussions with those involved with transplants in practice. We understand that recent advances in surgery and drug therapy to prevent rejection enable successful transplants to be achieved with organs from dead bodies and that transplants from living donors now form only a small proportion of all those undertaken. The British Medical Association's view is that it is not appropriate for "live, non-autonomous individuals to donate non-regenerative tissue or organs"[4]. This prohibition does not seem to result in patients being left untreated. Finally, as far as kidney donation is concerned, transplantation cannot be regarded as involving a minimal or low risk to the donor. We have come to the view that no changes are required in this area.

Medical research

5.63   We turn now to consider medical research using people who are incapable of consenting to take part in it. Our previous recommendation[5] giving doctors and other health care professionals a statutory authority to act to safeguard and promote the health of incapable patients applies only to treatment and not to research. The distinction between medical research and medical practice is not an easy one to make. The distinguishing feature of research is the intention of the doctor. We would adopt the analysis in the report of the Royal College of Physicians of London *Guidelines on the Practice of Ethics Committees in Medical Research involving Human Subjects*, which states[6]:

"The distinction derives from the intent. In medical practice the sole intention is to benefit the individual patient consulting the clinician, not to gain knowledge of general benefit, though such knowledge may incidentally emerge from the clinical experience gained. In medical research the primary intention is to advance knowledge so that patients in general may benefit; the individual patient may or may not benefit directly".

5.64   The above definition of research includes observational research - seeing how people behave in certain situations, and research using patients' medical or other records. Such research raises issues of confidentiality and privacy and

---

1. Para 3.60.
2. *Re F (Mental Patient: Sterilisation)* [1990] 2 AC 1 at pp 33 and 52; *Re W (A Minor) (Medical Treatment)* [1992] 4 All ER 627 at 649 (organ donation by a child).
3. Paras 3.60 to 3.62.
4. *Medical Ethics Today*, para 1:7.1.2.
5. Recommendation 58, para 5.17.
6. Second edition (1990), para 3.1.

therefore requires approval by a local research ethics committee, but because no consent is required from the patients concerned there are no special issues arising in connection with incapable patients. We are therefore content to leave the regulation of such research to the existing regime and exclude it from the ambit of this report.

5.65   There is virtually no authority in Scotland as to the legality of research on people incapable of consenting to their participation. A tutor-dative with appropriate powers could give consent but only a handful of people in Scotland have had tutors-dative appointed to them. The case of *Re F (Mental Patient: Sterilisation)*[1] which justifies treatment of mentally incapable patients without their consent in England and Wales, and which would probably be followed by Scottish Courts, is limited to treatments carried out to save the patients' lives or ensure improvement or prevent deterioration in their physical or mental health, and so could not be used to justify research. We consider that there should be legislative authority and regulation of research on mentally incapable people in place of the present legal near-vacuum.

5.66   In our discussion paper we put forward the ethical case for allowing research to be carried out on people incapable of consenting to their participation[2]. Research adds to medical knowledge and leads to improved treatments or ways of preventing illnesses or diseases or enables the care of the incapable to be improved. Provided the risks to a non-consenting participant are minimal there is a public interest in allowing research to be carried out. Indeed it has been stated that it is unethical to fail to do research since otherwise present and future patients would be deprived of the possibility of better treatment[3]. One or two bodies and a couple of individual respondents were opposed to any research being done on those incapable of consenting, but most agreed with our proposal that research should be allowed provided there were proper safeguards in place to protect participants. We would adhere in principle to our original proposal. Knowledge of the causes or treatment of incapacity may be obtainable only by research on those affected by it and such knowledge, while it may be of little or no direct benefit to the participants concerned, might be of benefit to the incapacitated in general. We note that many bodies connected with medical research support the inclusion of incapacitated subjects in projects[4].

5.67   We proposed in our discussion paper that research on the incapacitated should be lawful providing it was rigorously controlled and subject to strict conditions. Proposal 26 required **all** of the following conditions to be satisfied:

(a) The research was into incapacity of the kind suffered by the subject.

(b) The research entailed only an insubstantial foreseeable risk to the subject's physical or mental health. Views were invited on what should constitute an insubstantial risk.

(c) The research had been approved by the appropriate local research ethics committee.

(d) Written consent had been given by the subject's nearest relative unless the subject had a tutor-dative or personal guardian. The nearest relative should be the first relative reasonably available out of the following list:

   (i)   husband, wife or cohabiting partner.

   (ii) an adult child.

   (iii) a parent.

   (iv) a brother or sister.

(e) Where the subject had a tutor-dative or personal guardian whose terms of appointment include power to consent to medical research, written consent had been given by the tutor-dative or personal guardian.

(f) Before seeking consent from a relative, tutor-dative or personal guardian the researchers had explained to him or her the purpose of the research, the procedures to be used and the foreseeable risks to participants.

(g) The subject did not object to participating in the research.

We implicitly assumed that any proposed research would have to be both medically useful and scientifically valid.

5.68   The first condition - that any research should be into incapacity of the kind suffered by the subject - was generally agreed by those responding to our proposal. Sense Scotland, an organisation for the deaf blind, suggested research should

1. [1990] 2 AC 1.
2. Paras 3.37-3.59 and Proposal 26, para 3.59.
3. Royal College of Psychiatrists Guidelines 1990, p 48.
4. British Medical Association, *Medical Ethics Today* 1993 pp 214-5; Medical Research Council, *The Ethical Conduct of Research on the Mentally Incapacitated* 1991 pp 12-15; Royal College of Physicians of London, *Research Involving Patients* 1990 Recommendations 27 and 32; Royal College of Psychiatrists Guidelines, Psychiatric Bulletin (1990) 14 pp 48-61; Council of Europe, Recommendation of the Committee of Ministers No R(90) 3 of 3 February 1990; The Medicines (Application for Grant of Product Licences - Products for Human Use) Regulations 1993, SI 1993/2538, implements a European Directive (91/507/EEC) which requires compliance with "good clinical practice" in testing medicinal products on people. Earlier guidelines by the European Commission which led to the regulations required the consent in writing of subjects in non-therapeutic studies.

also be allowed into the subject's physical condition. We would not be in favour of medical research being carried out on incapable subjects which could just as well be carried out on those capable of consenting and indeed we now recommend that this should be built into the conditions for research[1]. However, in the case of deaf blind people research into the causes of deaf blindness and ways of communicating with the deaf blind ought to be allowed. The extended meaning of incapacity adopted in this report which includes inability to communicate should meet the concerns of organisations like Sense Scotland, while maintaining the basic condition as to the purpose of the research. One medical organisation considered that the proposed condition was too strict since it would exclude research into Hepatitis B among residents of institutions or research into thyroid diseases in Downs Syndrome people. We do not find the first example a compelling one as there should be plenty of institutions where inmates are capable of consenting which could be used for Hepatitis B research. If there was an outbreak of disease in an institution where there were incapable residents then any investigation would be a public health matter rather than medical research. The second example suggests that a slightly wider formula should be adopted than that we used in our original proposal. We consider that physical symptoms or disorders which may be associated with the potential subject's mental disorder should also be capable of being researched. Medical researchers in subsequent discussions with us indicated that some further categories would be needed to allow much useful research to continue. For example, patients who have undergone major surgery are temporarily incapacitated either as a result of the surgery or drugs for relief of pain. Research into their bodily functions or methods of caring for them in this state is arguably neither research into their incapacity nor into an associated physical disorder. We accept this and consider that research into the care of incapable people should also be permitted. This would allow research into nursing or other methods of looking after the permanently incapacitated as well as temporary unconscious patients.

5.69   The second condition proposed was that the research entailed only an insubstantial foreseeable risk to the subject's physical or mental health. Views were invited on what should constitute an insubstantial risk. We rejected the notion of balancing the risks and discomfort against the likely benefits since that could authorise very harmful experiments where the research was likely to produce substantial advances in knowledge. Our condition was generally agreed and several definitions of insubstantial risk offered. The National Board for Nursing, Midwifery and Health Visiting for Scotland thought that it was inappropriate to further define what constitutes an insubstantial risk as it depended on the research being done and the condition of the potential participants. We agree but would substitute "minimal risk" for "insubstantial risk" as the former seems to be a well understood concept amongst health-care professionals. Minimal risk is regarded as covering a small chance of a trivial reaction or distress and a very remote chance of serious injury or death, comparable to flying as a passenger in a scheduled aircraft[2]. Moreover, our recommendation that any research involving incapable subjects has to be approved by a Scottish Ethics Committee would enable that committee to decide whether in any particular research project the procedures posed more than a minimal foreseeable risk to the participants. The Council of Europe's draft Bioethics Convention[3] refers to medical research where there is a negligible risk and minimal burden for the individual concerned. We think that the reference to minimal burden is useful. Research may involve no foreseeable risk but if it is very uncomfortable for the adult concerned, as it would be if, for example, it involved attaching him or her to measuring apparatus in a restrictive way for long periods, then it ought not to be allowed.

5.70   Our third condition was that the research should have to be approved by the appropriate local research ethics committee. This was agreed by all those who were in favour of research being carried out at all on the incapacitated. We now think it would be better to have a Scottish Committee to look at all research on incapable people. Such research raises more ethical issues than comparable research on those able to consent and should be considered by a prestigious national committee. Furthermore, it is often difficult to obtain sufficient incapable people within the area of a local committee, especially as some committees are now constituted on a hospital trust basis rather than a health board basis. Applications may have to be made to many different local ethics committees which may take different views and impose different requirements. A Scottish Committee would assist in promoting a uniform response. We do not see the Scottish Committee as being a complete substitute for the local committees, but it should be the first stage in acquiring ethical approval. The Scottish Committee should consider the research proposal in principle. It may thereafter be necessary to approach local committees for approval of detailed aspects, such as the content of information sheets to be given to those consenting on behalf of the incapable participants. In order to avoid delay in gaining approval of small scale single hospital studies the Scottish Committee should be able to delegate some matters to local committees and issue guidelines. Provided the proposed project was within the area dealt with by the guidelines it would be regarded as having the Scottish Committee's approval and therefore should only require submission to the appropriate local committee.

5.71   The Scottish Committee should be set up by the Secretary of State for Scotland. To that end the Secretary of State should have power to make regulations dealing with the composition of the Committee and its procedures. Members of the Committee would be appointed by the Secretary of State. We do not make any detailed recommendations about the composition of the Committee or its procedures as we think that these should be decided by the Secretary of State after

---

1. Article 6 of the Council of Europe's draft Bioethics Convention (see para 5.53) includes a proviso that "equally effective research may not be carried out on subjects with full capacity".
2. Report of the Royal College of Physicians of London, *Research Involving Patients*, (1990), para 5.11.
3. Article 6. See para 5.53 above.

further consultation. However, we do consider that the Committee should have a substantial lay element in order to allay public concern about research being carried out on a very vulnerable section of the community.

5.72   In our discussion paper we proposed that consent to an incapable person's participation in the research should have to be obtained from his or her tutor-dative, personal guardian or close relative. Where the person had a tutor-dative or personal guardian with powers to consent to research then consent should have to be obtained from that person rather than a close relative. Close relative was defined as being spouse, cohabiting partner, adult child, parent, brother or sister. While all those respondents in favour of allowing research on incapable people were in favour of consent having to be obtained, there was some division of opinion as to the proper source of that consent. Several medical respondents made the point that most potential participants would not have a guardian with power to consent to participation and many do not have close relatives either. Our proposal, it was said, would unduly hamper research particularly into chronic mental disorders. The availability of relatives would be enhanced if the longer list of relatives used in the 1984 Act[1] were to be adopted, as we now think it should, but even so potentially suitable participants would have to be excluded. Among the suggestions made by respondents were that consent should be capable of being given by "an independent other" or a senior nurse or social worker who had known the person for some time and had no involvement with the research. We consider this to be a useful notion. Although "an independent individual who has known the incapable person for some time" is somewhat vague we do not think, given the variety of environments in which potential subjects could be living, specifying holders of posts would be useful. The independence is of vital importance and the individual should be of sufficient standing to be in a position to refuse consent. The Scottish Committee could monitor the types of people who are asked to give consent and could issue guidelines. In deciding whether or not to give consent the independent individual should take account of the past and present wishes and feelings of the incapacitated person in so far as they can be ascertained. Welfare attorneys[2] with suitable powers should also be able to give consent. It should also be competent for capable adults to consent in advance to research being carried out on them when they are incapable.

5.73   Before seeking consent from a proxy (guardian, welfare attorney, relative or independent individual) those conducting the research should be required to explain in readily understandable terms the purpose of the research, the procedures to be used and the foreseeable risks to participants. Once given the consent should be capable of being withdrawn at any time.

5.74   The final condition we proposed for an incapable person's inclusion in a research project was that he or she does not object to participating in the research. This was generally approved but some respondents considered that it suggested that the person was capable of deciding whether to participate. We accept this criticism and would adopt a formula based on unwillingness to participate instead. This would cover those who resisted as well as those who by words or gestures showed that they did not wish to participate.

5.75   In response to our proposal three commentators suggested that research involving incapacitated people should also require prior authorisation from a court in addition to fulfilment of all the other conditions proposed. We disagree; use of the courts is in our view inappropriate and impracticable. Courts are not the appropriate forum to decide on whether a particular research project should be carried out. Such a matter raises issues of medical ethics and the likely advancement of medical knowledge, neither of which the courts have expertise in. Furthermore, the courts would largely duplicate the work of the proposed Scottish Committee. Finally, there would be likely to be a considerable number of applications increasing the workload of already hard-pressed courts.

5.76   Summing up this section we recommend that:

75. It should be lawful to carry out research on an adult who is incapable of consenting to participate only if all of the following conditions are satisfied:

   (a) the research is into the causes, treatment or care of the adult's incapacity or associated physical symptoms or disease,

   (b) the research entails only a minimal foreseeable risk and minimal discomfort to the adult,

   (c) the research could not be carried out equally effectively on subjects capable of consenting,

   (d) the research project has been approved by a Scottish Committee set up by the Secretary of State for Scotland in accordance with regulations made by the Secretary of State,

   (e) written consent has been obtained from the adult while capable or from the adult's guardian or welfare attorney. Where the adult has no guardian or welfare attorney with appropriate powers written consent should be obtained from the adult's nearest relative as defined in sections 53 to 57 of the Mental Health (Scotland) Act 1984. If the nearest relative is not readily available then written

---

1. See paras 2.68 to 2.73 for a further discussion of "nearest relative".
2. See Part 3.

consent should be sought from an independent individual who knows the adult well and is not involved with the research. The person from whom consent is sought should be given an explanation of what is involved in the proposed research, and

(f) the adult does not appear unwilling to participate in the research.

Clause 39

Withholding or withdrawing medical treatment

5.77   Advances in medical science have made it possible to keep patients alive by means of various life support systems or treatments although such measures do not improve their underlying condition. The measures may indeed be seen in some cases as only making the process of dying undignified and prolonged[1]. One situation which has been highlighted in recent years is that involving patients in a persistent vegetative state (PVS). PVS patients have an irrecoverably functionless cerebral cortex. They have no consciousness and are unable to think, feel or respond in a meaningful (as distinct from a reflex) way to their surroundings. Although they can breathe and digest naturally they generally have to be fed artificially (by means of a naso-gastric tube or other device) because they lack the swallowing reflex required for normal eating and drinking. With artificial feeding and other appropriate measures PVS patients may live in an insentient state for many years without any hope of recovery.

5.78   We have had the benefit of discussions with Professor Bryan Jennett, an acknowledged expert on PVS and with representatives of some of the Scottish Royal Colleges[2]. It has been made clear to us that PVS patients form only a small fraction of those for whom treatment-limiting decisions have to be made. A treatment-limiting decision may take the form of withholding treatment, for example not giving cardio-pulmonary resuscitation to a patient whose death from cancer is imminent and inevitable; or withdrawing treatment such as ventilation from an accident victim in intensive care where it is clear that no recovery is possible. In *Airedale NHS Trust v Bland*[3] the House of Lords held that there was no absolute obligation on doctors to prolong an incapable patient's life regardless of the circumstances or quality of life. Medical treatment, including artificial nutrition and hydration or antibiotics, could be lawfully withheld from an incapable patient even though the result would be the patient's death, provided responsible and competent medical opinion was of the view that continuing provision was futile and would not confer any benefit on the patient. We fully agree with these statements. However, it is not certain that they represent Scottish law, although it is very probable that Scottish courts would follow the House of Lords since no peculiarity of English law was involved and the case was decided on public policy grounds.

5.79   We have come to the conclusion that it would be helpful to have a new statutory provision which made it clear that under the law of Scotland the doctor's duty of care does not extend to providing treatment to incapable patients which is likely to be of no benefit to them, and that it is not necessarily of benefit to patients to keep them alive as long as possible. Other considerations, such as the quality of life and the peacefulness and dignity of the dying process should also be taken into account, in accordance with current good medical practice. Current good medical practice also involves the doctors consulting with colleagues and the patient's family in so far as it is practicable to do so and taking account of their views. This should continue to be a requirement.

5.80   The general principle that there should be no intervention unless it is unlikely to provide a benefit to the patient may give rise to doubts where withdrawal or discontinuance of treatment is under consideration. If the intervention is taken to be the discontinuance then a discontinuance which results in the patient's death might not be regarded as something that is likely to benefit the patient. We consider that for the purposes of the operation of the principle the intervention in such circumstances is the continuance of treatment so that if continuing the treatment is futile or unlikely to benefit the patient then it would be in accordance with the general principles to discontinue or withdraw it.

5.81   We recommend that:

76. In order to clarify the position regarding withholding or withdrawing medical treatment from incapable patients in Scotland there should be new statutory provisions to the effect that it should be lawful to withhold or withdraw treatment that in the reasonable opinion of the doctors concerned would be unlikely to benefit the patient. Prolongation of an incapable patient's life regardless of the circumstances should not necessarily be regarded as benefitting that patient.

Clause 41(1), (4) and (5)

---

1. In Recommendation 779 (1976) on the rights of the sick and dying the Parliamentary Assembly of the Council of Europe referred (in para 10, II) to the legal dangers for members of the medical profession when they have refrained from effecting artificial measures to prolong the death process in the case of terminal patients whose lives cannot be saved by present-day medicine".
2. The Royal College of Physicians of Edinburgh, The Royal College of Physicians and Surgeons of Glasgow and the Scottish Division of the Royal College of Psychiatrists.
3. [1993] AC 789.

It would follow from the fact that any withholding or withdrawal of treatment in accordance with the new statutory provisions would be lawful that doctors and others making and participating in such decisions would not thereby incur any liability. We think that this clear statutory immunity from criminal, civil or disciplinary proceedings would encourage doctors not to provide futile treatment defensively and would enhance the quality of life for terminally ill patients.

5.82   We would again stress that the general principles which under our recommendations would apply to any intervention under the Act would require regard to be paid to the past wishes of the adult so far as they could be ascertained and to the views of the nearest relative and primary carer in so far as it is reasonable and practicable to do so. The views of any guardian or welfare attorney with relevant powers would also have to be taken into account, in so far as it is reasonable and practicable to do so[1]. We realise that there are situations where it is not possible to obtain any of these views but we believe the draft Bill takes that fully into account. We should add that an advance statement by the adult might apply and might make resort to the statutory authority to withhold or withdraw treatment unnecessary.

5.83   Should the withdrawal of certain life supporting treatments or measures require prior authority from a court? Such a requirement exists, at least as a matter of recommended practice, in England and Wales in relation to PVS patients. The House of Lords in the *Bland* case decided that doctors should for the time being as a matter of practice apply to the High Court for a declaration that withholding nutrition and hydration supplied by artificial means would be lawful[2]. The Official Solicitor has issued a practice note on applications[3]. There should be at least two neurological reports on the patient submitted with the application, one of which will have been commissioned by the Official Solicitor, who is to be invited to act as guardian *ad litem*. The views of the next of kin and the patient's previously expressed views, if any, are very important. The views of a relative opposing withholding treatment are however not determinative[4]. The Law Commission has recommended that this practice should continue but that the Secretary of State should be given power to make regulations in the future which would enable authority to withdraw to be obtained from a duly appointed independent medical practitioner[5]. After careful and prolonged deliberation we have decided against imposing such a requirement.

5.84   The advantage of involving the court is that the decision is being made in an open forum rather than by the doctors and the patient's family in private. There is a public interest in monitoring treatment-limiting decisions which may have fatal consequences and in protecting incapable patients who are unable to protect themselves. Moreover, a declarator that a proposed withholding or withdrawing was lawful would offer complete advance immunity to the doctors and others involved[6].

5.85   On the other hand legal proceedings bring unwelcome publicity and additional stresses to the patient's family and involve much expense. Legal proceedings may be necessary if there is a dispute but if there is no dispute the court will not hear any opposing views and unless it takes a pro-active role will have to proceed on the basis of statements and reports submitted to it in connection with the application. In these cases the courts will have a purely formal role. Another factor that has weighed with us is that the Master of the Rolls in the Court of Appeal[7] and four out of the five judges in the House of Lords[8] suggested in the *Bland* case that applications to the court in every case in England and Wales might be a temporary measure. Once a body of experience and practice had built up, they thought that guidelines could be issued limiting applications to those cases where there was some special need. As we have already noted the Law Commission has recommended that the Secretary of State be given power to introduce an alternative system of authorising withdrawing of artificial nutrition and hydration from PVS patients. It would be a pity for Scotland to follow the present practice in England and Wales only to have to change yet again a few years later. Finally, requiring every treatment withholding or withdrawing decision to have to be ratified by the courts would add considerably to their work load. It seems to us unprincipled to single out PVS patients or other cases which have attracted great publicity as requiring court proceedings, while allowing other equally difficult and harrowing treatment-limiting decisions to be made by doctors and the families of patients and exposing those who make such difficult decisions to the possibility of criminal or other proceedings.

5.86   In exceptional cases, for example, where there is a dispute as to whether treatment should be withheld or withdrawn, or where there is a particularly delicate situation in which the medical team involved feel that an authoritative decision on the legal position is needed before irreversible action is taken, the courts may have to be asked for a declarator. In

---

1.   See Clause 1(4) of the draft Bill.
2.   See for example *Frenchay Healthcare NHS Trust v S* [1994] 1 WLR 601; *Swindon and Marlborough NHS Trust v S*, The Guardian 10 December 1994 and Current Law December 1994, 590.
3.   The latest version was issued in March 1994.
4.   *Re G*, 22 November 1994 (Family Division, unreported). Patient's wife and doctors in favour of withholding, mother against; declaration granted that withholding would be lawful.
5.   *Report on Medical Incapacity*, para 6.21. If the patient had a guardian or welfare attorney consent to withholding could be given by them.
6.   We understand that an application to the Court of Session in connection with withholding artificial life support measures from a PVS patient in a Scottish hospital has recently been made.
7.   [1993] AC 789, 815.
8.   Lords Keith of Kinkel, Goff of Chievley, Lowry and Browne-Wilkinson at pp 859, 873, 875 and 885 respectively.

such cases the Court of Session rather than the sheriff courts would be an appropriate forum. The application should have to be intimated to the Lord Advocate who would then have an opportunity to appear representing the public interest. We recommend that:

77. (1) **In difficult and exceptional cases resort to the Court of Session should be possible for a declarator whether a withholding or withdrawing of medical treatment from an incapable adult was or would be lawful or unlawful.**

(2) **Any person claiming an interest in the incapable adult's welfare should be entitled to apply for a declarator and the application should have to be intimated to the Lord Advocate for the public interest.**

Clause 41(3), (6)

Part 6   Intervention Orders and Guardianship

Introduction

6.1   Scottish law at present has various kinds of guardianship; guardianship under the 1984 Act, tutors-dative, curators bonis and tutors-at-law. Each of these guardians is appointed by the court after the court has been satisfied by way of reports or other evidence that the grounds for appointment have been established. In this introductory section we give a brief description of these types of guardianship and the criticisms that have been made of them. We also consider the proposals for reform of guardianship that we made in our discussion paper and conclude by recommending the introduction of a new flexible statutory system of guardianship capable of dealing with all aspects (personal welfare, medical treatment, property and financial affairs) of an incapable adult's life.

6.2   A guardian under the 1984 Act (a "mental health guardian"), may be appointed to an adult by the sheriff on application by a mental health officer (or occasionally a relative of the adult) for the local authority in which the adult lives. The application is supported by two medical reports specifying the form of mental disorder the adult is suffering from and stating that the disorder is such as to warrant guardianship, and a recommendation from the mental health officer that guardianship is necessary in the interests of the welfare of the adult[1]. The mental health guardian may be the local authority or any person chosen, or accepted as suitable, by the local authority[2]. In practice most guardians are the local authority or the Director of Social Work. The powers of a mental health guardian are statutory and three in number; power to require the adult to reside at a specified place, power to require the adult to attend for treatment or training, and power to require access to be given to doctors, mental health officers and others[3]. The local authority and the Mental Welfare Commission visit adults subject to guardianship on a regular basis.

6.3   In our discussion paper we set out the defects of mental health guardianship[4]. The powers of a mental health guardian are fixed by statute and cannot be added to or varied to suit the needs and capabilities of the adult under guardianship. The procedure for appointing a mental health guardian takes some time but there is no power to make an interim appointment to deal with an urgent situation. Where the guardian is the local authority or Director of Social Work the functions have to be delegated but it is often unclear which person concerned with the care of the adult under guardianship is actually exercising the powers[5]. Other criticisms of mental health guardianship are that because the application must include a recommendation from the mental health officer that local authority official has an effective veto on guardianship; the welfare ground for appointment "necessary in the interests of the welfare of the patient" that he or she should be subject to guardianship is vague and "necessary" sets too high a standard, and that there is no effective way guardians can enforce their powers.

6.4   Tutors-dative have been recently revived in order to provide a more personal type of guardianship[6]. They are appointed by the Court of Session after consideration of two medical certificates of incapacity. Centuries ago tutors-dative were appointed to act on behalf of incapable adults in all aspects of their lives. In modern practice tutors-dative are granted personal welfare powers only, tailored to the needs of the individual adult[7]. The appointment of a tutor-dative is not intimated to the Mental Welfare Commission or local authority and these bodies have no statutory duties to visit those subject to tutory. Tutors-at-law are also appointed by the Court of Session using a similar procedure to that used for tutors-dative. Tutors-at-law, like tutors-dative, were common centuries ago but became obsolescent. Recently, after a gap of over 100 years, a tutor-at-law has been appointed[8]. The tutor-at-law has full power over the personal welfare and financial affairs of the adult. The tutor-at-law can only be the nearest male relative. He is entitled to be appointed by virtue of his

---

1. 1984 Act, ss 36 and 37.
2. 1984 Act, s 37(2).
3. 1984 Act, s 41.
4. Paras 2.23 to 2.40.
5. This has been a concern of the Mental Welfare Commission for some time. See *Annual Report 1987*, para 8.2 and *Annual Report 1989*, paras 12.5 and 12.19.
6. See Adrian Ward's articles in 1987 SLT (News) 69 and 1992 SLT (News) 325. None of the recent tutor-dative cases have been reported except *Chapman Petrs* 1993 SLT 955.
7. *Chapman Petrs* 1993 SLT 955, but see *Queen Petr* 1992 mentioned in Adrian Ward's article *Tutors to Adults: Developments* 1992 SLT (News) 325.
8. *Britton v Britton's CB* 1992 SCLR 947.

relationship unless his unsuitability is established. A tutor-at-law supersedes any tutor-dative or curator bonis who has previously been appointed. It is understood that the petition in the *Britton* case was brought in order to replace a curator the family could not get on with.

6.5   The defects of tutory-dative are that the powers and duties of tutors-dative have to be gathered from centuries-old cases and it is not clear how far they remain authoritative today in a society with a different outlook and values. The local authority and the Mental Welfare Commission do not have the same statutory duties in relation to adults subject to tutory as they do for those subject to mental health guardianship, yet the powers of a tutor may be far greater than those of a guardian. Indeed these bodies may be unaware of the existence of a tutor-dative. Finally, tutors-dative can be appointed only by the Court of Session. Tutors-at-law are also recently revived appointees whose functions are somewhat uncertain. The fact that the post may be held only by the nearest male relative is incompatible with modern notions of sexual equality. Furthermore, relationship should be only one of a number of factors that should be considered in selecting a suitable guardian.

6.6   In our discussion paper we proposed abolishing tutors-at-law[1] and put forward three options in relation to the other existing personal guardians, mental health guardians and tutors-dative. The first was to make minor amendments to the current system of mental health guardianship and tutors-dative so as to remove some of the defects and improve their usefulness[2]. The second (which we did not favour) involved making the same minor amendments to mental health guardianship but abolishing tutors-dative[3]. Non-legislative practices could be adopted to give the family and carers of incapable adults a recognised role in their welfare. The third option[4] was to replace tutors-dative and mental health guardians by a new statutory scheme of personal guardianship. The abolition of tutors-at-law was agreed by all those who responded, although some respondents' support was conditional upon new statutory guardianship being introduced. There was unanimous support for the third option from the large number of persons commenting on these options. Many of those consulted were of the opinion that the existing law was so patchy and inadequate that a radical reform was the only solution. The advantages of new up-to-date statutory provisions dealing with personal guardianship as a whole and including the general principles of least restriction of the adult's freedoms, consultation with the family and carers of the adult and encouragement of the adult to use existing skills and acquire new skills were also stressed. A further point in favour of new statutory personal guardianship is that it would combine the flexibility of tutory-dative where powers are tailored to the adult's needs with the social welfare assessments built into mental health guardianship.

6.7   Our discussion paper was also critical of the existing system of managing an incapable adult's property and finances through the appointment of a curator bonis. In brief the criticisms we listed[5] were:-

(a) Curatory is "all or nothing". The curator takes over the management of the whole estate and the curator's powers are not tailored to the needs and abilities of the adult.

(b) The family of an incapable adult sometimes resent the imposition of an impersonal professional curator who does not liaise with them.

(c) Curatory is expensive. The problem of high costs is particularly acute with small estates.

(d) There is uncertainty as to the correct balance between conserving the estate and spending it for the adult's benefit. Many curators take a conservative approach.

(e) There is no periodic review of the curator's appointment to check that it is still needed.

(f) The ground of appointment - that the adult is incapable of managing his or her own affairs or giving instructions for their management - does not require consideration of the need for a curator or whether the adult could manage his or her finances with reorganisation and extra help.

(g) The law relating to curators is a combination of common law and statute, most of which is fairly old, and requires to be overhauled to bring it into line with modern conditions.

In view of these criticisms we proposed[6] that curatory should be replaced by a new statutory scheme involving single issue property orders and financial managers with flexible powers. There was strong support on consultation for this approach.

6.8   It is a recurring criticism of the existing law that, with the exception of tutors-at-law, each type of guardian is

---

1. Proposal 1, para 2.28.
2. Proposals 2 and 3, paras 2.33 and 2.42.
3. Paras 2.43 to 2.48 and Proposal 4.
4. Paras 2.49 to 2.53 and Proposal 5.
5. Paras 4.7 to 4.14.
6. Proposal 29, para 4.40.

responsible for either only personal welfare or only financial affairs although these two areas are intimately connected and decisions in one area may have repercussions in the other. Our discussion paper followed this division by proposing new personal guardians to replace mental health guardians and tutors-dative and new financial managers to take over from curators bonis. We also proposed single issue orders for each of the separate fields of activity which we termed personal orders and property orders. We considered that it was better to retain two separate posts - a personal guardian and a financial manager - on the ground of flexibility. One person could hold both posts, so becoming an "overall guardian" or each post could be held by a separate person. The latter solution enables people with different areas of expertise to be appointed to the area they are best suited to. We went on to propose that where the two posts were held by different people each should be obliged to consult the other[1]. We recognised that personal guardianship and financial management would have many factors in common such as the procedure for appointment, the powers of the court to vary or recall the appointment later, and the principles which should guide appointees in the exercise of their powers. Such provisions could apply to both posts leaving a small number of special provisions applicable only to one post or the other.

6.9   Although there was general agreement with our proposal for separate posts we have come to the conclusion that it would be simpler, conceptually and legislatively, to have a single post of guardian. According to the circumstances and the needs of the incapable adult, the guardian could be appointed with powers in the personal welfare field or powers in the financial field or in both fields. Combining financial and welfare guardianship would be a return to the historical roots of guardianship in Scotland. Originally the tutor-at-law or tutor-dative (or curator-at-law and curator-dative as they were termed at an even earlier stage) held full powers over all aspects of an incapable adult's life. However, if the tutor was also the adult's heir, custody of the adult was given to some other person to lessen the opportunities to accelerate the succession. Curators bonis, managing incapable adults' finances only, were introduced as a temporary appointment because it took so long to get a tutor appointed. This temporary office became a permanent one during the 18th and 19th centuries and curators ousted tutors until their recent revival[2]. But in their revived form the powers of tutors-dative have been almost exclusively confined to personal welfare aspects and the view has been taken that financial affairs are best managed by a curator bonis[3].

6.10   Some people, relatives or friends for example, may be willing to act in the personal welfare field but feel unable to cope with the financial aspects. Others, such as solicitors or accountants, would handle the financial aspects but are reluctant to deal with the personal welfare side. Combined guardianship has to be able to take account of this. Under our new scheme one or more people could be appointed guardians. They could be appointed joint guardians with the same powers and could allocate their spheres of responsibility informally amongst themselves, or such an allocation could be made more formal by the court appointing each guardian with powers restricted to particular areas of the adult's life.

6.11   We have followed the concept of combined guardianship through by merging our proposed personal and property orders. These we now term intervention orders. Each intervention order may effect an intervention in the personal welfare of the incapable adult or his or her financial affairs or in both. One advantage of the merger is that it becomes possible to grant a single order to deal with an intervention that has effects in both the personal welfare and the financial fields. The other advantage is legislative simplicity; instead of having two sets of very similar provisions, a single set suffices.

6.12   We recommend that:

78.   Legislation should be enacted to introduce a new flexible system of personal and financial guardianship for incapable adults based on the principles of least restriction, consultation with the adult and others involved and encouraging the adult to use and develop skills. This new guardianship should replace guardianship under the Mental Health (Scotland) Act 1984, tutors-at-law, tutors-dative and curators bonis.

Clauses 42-63

INTERVENTION ORDERS

6.13   In our discussion paper we put forward the idea of empowering the court to grant orders dealing with one or more particular matters in the personal welfare[4] or financial field[5]. We conceived these orders as a less restrictive alternative to guardianship in line with the principle of minimum necessary intervention. It is a criticism of curatory that long term total management of a mentally incapable adult's affairs has to be used when all that might be wanted is a simple order to deal with a specific problem[6]. This criticism does not arise to the same extent in the personal welfare field since the

---

1. Proposal 32, para 4.50.
2. See Adrian Ward, *The Power to Act*, (published by SSMH 1990). Chapter 4 gives an excellent historical account of guardianship in Scotland.
3. *Chapman Petrs* 1993 SLT 955.
4. Proposal 8(1)(a), para 2.80.
5. Proposal 34(a), para 4.63.
6. See para 6.7.

statutory powers available to a mental health guardian are only three in number, and the powers of a tutor-dative are in current practice tailored to the needs of the incapable adult[1].

6.14   Our discussion paper gave examples of situations where a single limited order might be sufficient to overcome a difficulty without having to impose continuing management on the incapable adult. On the personal welfare side these included sanctioning a major operation where potential risks and benefits were fairly evenly balanced or getting elderly persons who can no longer manage in their own homes into residential care. Financial examples included negotiating and signing a lease for the adult's accommodation or bringing a damages action in which only a small award is likely to be made. All those who responded agreed that intervention orders would be useful and approved of the notion that the court should first have to consider whether intervention orders would suffice before appointing a guardian. Other situations which have been mentioned to us by those responding included signing a receipt for the proceeds of an insurance policy, executing a deed of family arrangement to deal with a legacy due to the adult[2], or obtaining the consent of an incapable wife to her husband buying from the local authority their home of which he is the tenant[3]. Some of the examples we gave in our discussion paper were criticised. It was said that most personal welfare problems arose out of long term needs and were usually not amenable to a quick solution using a personal order. Again, a local authority housing manager at one of our public meetings said that preparing and signing a lease was only a small part of tenancy. Problems would be likely to arise later if the tenant failed to fulfil the obligations in the lease due to inability to understand them.

6.15   Many of the examples of intervention orders we had in mind or were suggested to us would involve some person being appointed to carry out the transaction. Settling a claim for legal rights and receiving payment for example would involve action over a certain period of time, as would selling property belonging to the adult and investing the proceeds so that the adult could manage thereafter without further legal intervention. It might be argued that this type of intervention order is unnecessary in that a guardian could be appointed for a limited time to carry out the specified transaction. However guardians would be subject to the supervision of the Public Guardian. They would be required to find caution, provide an inventory of property under their charge, agree a management plan, produce annual accounts for audit and their appointment would last for a period of years unless recalled earlier. We think it is simpler to have a separate entity - an intervention order - rather than a species of guardianship with most or all of the attributes of guardianship disapplied.

6.16   Some intervention orders might take a different form - directing that something be done or that somebody, the sheriff clerk for example, signs a document or gives consent on behalf of the incapable adult. Signing a receipt for money due to the adult or consenting to a spouse's purchase of the home rented from the local authority are good examples.

6.17   The Law Society in response to our proposal for financial intervention orders suggested that the sheriff should have power to declare whether or not a particular transaction which an adult of doubtful capacity had carried out was valid. It instanced a will as a document whose validity could be established in this way whilst the adult was still alive. We are not attracted by this suggestion. It would be very difficult or impossible to ensure that all those with an interest in the document when it became effective at a future date would be called as parties to the present proceedings. If they were not so called it would be wrong to make the sheriff's finding conclusive against them in future proceedings. On the other hand, unless the sheriff's finding of validity or invalidity was binding it would not prevent future litigation. Moreover, the courts do not answer hypothetical questions. The question of the validity of a document should be left to be dealt with when there are live issues arising from the document to be determined. Earlier in this report we rejected a similar suggestion that the sheriff should be empowered to declare that an adult has capacity to grant a continuing power of attorney and that such a declaration should create a presumption of capacity in other proceedings[4].

6.18   We recommend that:

79.   The court should have power to grant one or more orders relating to an incapable adult's personal welfare or financial affairs called intervention orders. It should be possible for an intervention order to take the form of:

(a)   directing some specific act to be done or consent to be given, or

(b)   appointing some person to carry out a specified transaction.

Clause 42(1), (4)

6.19   The court in granting an intervention order should have power to make ancillary orders. Thus, for example, the court might order that the person nominated to sell property belonging to the incapable adult obtains the consent of the Public Guardian to the price offered, or it might order the person to report back to the court at the conclusion of the transaction. Another useful power would be the power to give directions as to how the transaction was to be carried out.

---

1.   See paras 6.2 and 6.4.
2.   A tutor-dative was appointed for this sole purpose; *Queen Petr* (1992) mentioned in Adrian Ward's article *Tutors to Adults: Developments* 1992 SLT (News) 325.
3.   Housing (Scotland) Act 1987, s 61(5).
4.   Para 3.18.

One body commented that there was sometimes an urgent need to prevent some action to be taken on the personal welfare front in connection with an incapable adult and interdict was not always competent. We consider that this need could be met by empowering the sheriff to grant interim orders pending the determination of an application for an intervention order. We therefore recommend that:

80. The court should have power to grant an interim order pending the determination of an application for an intervention order. On granting an intervention order the court should have power to grant ancillary orders or give directions.

Clause 3

Grounds for application and those entitled to apply

6.20   We have already discussed in general terms the grounds for various applications in Part 2. The adult must be either unable to communicate or be mentally disordered and by reason of such inability or disorder unable to take the decision, perform the act or carry out the transaction in question. In short he or she must be incapable of taking the decision or doing what is required. The court would require to be satisfied as to this by means of reports as in guardianship[1]. Title to apply was also considered in general terms in Part 2. We see no reason to depart from the recommended general formula of any person claiming an interest. As we pointed out there this expression is intended to include public bodies like the Mental Welfare Commission, the local authority and the Public Guardian, as well as voluntary societies involved with the incapacitated, and carers, family or friends of incapable adults. We recommend that:

81. (1) Any person (including the adult) claiming an interest in the welfare or financial affairs of an incapable adult should be entitled to apply to the court for an intervention order.

(2) The court should be empowered to grant such an application if satisfied (by means of reports as in Recommendation 87) that the adult is incapable of taking the decision or performing the transaction in respect of which the application is made.

Clause 42(1)

Variation and recall of intervention orders

6.21   An intervention order authorises the carrying out of a specified transaction. When the transaction has been carried out, the order has been implemented and needs no formal recall. However, circumstances may arise where either the order itself or an associated direction or ancillary order needs to be recalled or varied before the order is implemented. We consider that the court should have such powers although they are unlikely to be exercised frequently because of the relatively short timescale of intervention orders. We recommend that:

82. The court which made an intervention order should have power, on application, to vary or recall it or any of the associated ancillary orders or directions on cause shown.

Clause 42(6)

The role of the local authority

6.22   One criticism of tutors-dative is that they can be appointed without the local authority being aware of the proceedings. In most cases where an incapable adult's personal welfare is in issue the local authority social work department would have a useful input as to the appropriateness of the order sought, whether the benefit expected from the order could be obtained by other means and the suitability of the person nominated to carry out the welfare intervention order. In the later section on guardianship we recommend that the local authority should be under a duty to apply for a guardian to be appointed or an intervention order to be made if satisfied that grounds exist and no-one else is applying provided such an appointment or order would be in accordance with the general principles[2]. Here we confine ourselves to recommending that:

83. Rules of Court should be made requiring an application for an intervention order relating to the personal welfare of an incapable adult to be notified to the local authority so that it has the opportunity to make representations.

Registration of intervention orders

6.23   Under our recommendations the Public Guardian is to maintain a public register of guardians and attorneys appointed and subsequent orders relating to them. The Public Guardian will also register authorisations to withdraw money from an incapable adult's bank account. We consider that intervention orders should be registered as well so that any interested organisation or individual can find out what intervention has been authorised and who is authorised to carry it out. Some will be of only transitory importance but it is the view of the present Accountant of Court, with which we

---

1. See para 6.36.
2. Recommendation 86(2), para 6.33.

G

agree, that it would be easier and more administratively efficient to register all orders than to expend resources on deciding which ones should be registered. We recommend that:

84. Intervention orders should be registered by the Public Guardian in a register open to public inspection on payment of the appropriate fee.

Clauses 4(2)(c)(v) and 42(8)

GUARDIANSHIP

Grounds for appointment of guardian

6.24   In Part 2 of this report we considered the grounds for intervention in the personal welfare or financial affairs of adults and concluded that in general the adult must either be unable to communicate or be mentally disordered and by reason of such inability or disorder unable to take the decision or do the act in question[1]. We mentioned that slightly different grounds would be required for guardianship because of the continuing nature of the appointment and the need to cater for those whose limited incapacity makes them vulnerable to exploitation or abuse[2]. Some respondents were concerned lest under grounds based on lack of cognitive capacity, as proposed in our discussion paper, personal guardianship would not be available to those who required protection and who can at present be protected using guardianship under the 1984 Act. Concern was also expressed at the lack of protection in the financial field for those whose disabilities were not such as to render them incapable but nevertheless left them open to exploitation.

6.25   We have discussed the criteria for our merged personal and financial guardianship with some of those involved with the mentally disabled and are grateful to them for their help. Guardianship should clearly be available to those who are unable to communicate. Leaving aside this small and fairly well-defined category the formula which we now put forward contains three elements in addition to the threshold requirement of mental disorder. Firstly, inability by reason of mental disorder to make decisions in relation to personal welfare or financial affairs. This deals with those who lack cognitive capacity. Secondly, inability by reason of mental disorder to act to promote or safeguard their interests in relation to personal welfare or financial affairs. This part is intended to make protective guardianship available to those who are vulnerable by reason of their mental disorder and hence liable to exploitation and abuse. It is an alternative to the first element rather than an additional requirement. The third element flows from the long-term nature of guardianship and would require either of the previous mental inabilities to be likely to continue for such a period as to justify guardianship in the interests of the adult. Where there is a likelihood of improvement as a result of proposed drug or other treatment within a reasonable timescale the court could make appropriate intervention orders[3] or continue the application and make such interim orders as seemed appropriate until the prognosis became clearer.

6.26   The new grounds set out in the previous paragraph would, in our opinion, enable a guardian to be appointed to any adult to whom a mental health guardian could currently be appointed under the 1984 Act. We illustrate this by looking at some of the particular cases mentioned in recent reports of the Mental Welfare Commission.

(i)   "Paul is a 19 year old young man with a mental handicap. He cannot manage money (although likes to spend what he has quickly) and is unable to read or write. He lives with his father who is unemployed and who "manages" Paul's income from welfare benefits. Paul made little progress in the Special School system and was offered a place at an Adult Training Centre. His preferred day time activity was to wander to the local town and play fruit machines.

His peer groups included more able, better off and sexually aware young men and Paul's emerging sexual awareness and sense of being constrained at home resulted in an assault with clear sexual intent on an adult woman neighbour. Paul could express no sense of shame concerning the incident and after appearance at the Sheriff Court was placed on guardianship under the local authority in preference to probation"[4].

(ii)   "Stephanie is a 21-year-old woman subject to guardianship with a mental handicap and speech impediment who lives with her father in a large peripheral housing estate in a city. The domestic environment is poor to the point of being deficient for the adequate care of Stephanie. She is unable to read, write or manage money, but can wash and dress herself and is an open and warm person, although sometimes withdrawn and moody. Past allegations of sexual abuse by other visiting family members had been a significant welfare ground in seeking guardianship"[5].

(iii)   "Ms X, aged 82 years, lived alone in a small country town occupying a District Council tenancy. Her only surviving relative lived abroad and Ms X had become isolated, was prone to wandering at night often in a half-dressed state, was known to eat only bread and jam, was refusing access to the home-help and was generally thought to be at unacceptable risk because of memory impairment and hypothermia. Efforts over two years had been made to

---

1. Recommendation 2, para 2.15.
2. Para 2.16.
3. See paras 6.13 to 6.18.
4. *Annual Report 1989*, p 30.
5. *Annual Report 1989*, p 31.

maintain Ms X at home in the community but professional views were increasingly confirming that she required 24 hour nursing care. Ms X adamantly refused and her daughter returned from abroad to be part of the decision-making. The latter's wishes influenced the application for guardianship"[1].

All of these adults mentioned above were mentally disordered to the extent necessary for guardianship under the 1984 Act and would also be so disordered for the purposes of our new guardianship. Furthermore, they were all unable to safeguard or promote some of their interests in relation to personal welfare or financial affairs. Finally, these inabilities were likely to continue for such a period as would justify guardianship rather than short-term intervention orders.

6.27   All the measures and services that can be provided under mental health guardianship could also be provided under our new guardianship. If the local authority needed to be formally involved then the chief social work officer could seek appointment as guardian[2]. However, we are firmly of the view that our new guardianship would be significantly better in that it would be more flexible and enable the guardianship powers to be extended beyond the three statutory powers presently conferred on mental health guardians (choosing the place of residence, taking the adult for training, treatment etc, and giving various people access to the adult)[3]. Under our new guardianship further welfare powers could be conferred on a guardian in addition to those currently enjoyed by a mental health guardian. Equally importantly, it would be possible under our new scheme to give a mainly welfare guardian some financial powers. As the Mental Welfare Commission stated in its 1989 *Annual Report* [4] -

"The protection of a person's property is undoubtedly seen as an aspect of Guardianship, but is subject to the prohibition in Section 41(3) which prevents a Guardian from "intromitting" with a patient's property. Guardianship is, therefore, not an enabling provision which can assist in making decisions about the property of an elderly person suffering from dementia or in the management of funds for a mentally handicapped person. For individuals in the community who are not capable of making decisions about property or funds and who are not subject to Curator Bonis, Guardianship offers no assistance. This can be viewed as a weakness in the Guardianship provision or simply as a gap in statutory and civil legislation."

Our new guardianship scheme would remedy this perceived weakness in mental health guardianship and fill the gap in the legislation. In the three examples of Paul, Stephanie and Ms X mentioned in the previous paragraph money and financial difficulties were also present[5]. Guardianship, by the local authority chief social work officer or another person, which combined personal welfare and financial powers would enable these difficulties to be addressed in a far simpler and more effective way than under the existing law.

6.28   The three elements set out in paragraph 6.25 comprise the necessary requirements for the appointment of a guardian, but are not in themselves sufficient. We note that some mental health guardianship is presently of short duration[6]. The general principles which we recommended in Part 2, particularly the principle of least restriction, requires that the court must also be satisfied that the lesser alternative of one or more intervention orders would not suffice. If the court is not so satisfied we consider that it should be empowered to treat the application for a guardian as an application for such intervention order or orders as the court may think fit and grant what seems to be the appropriate intervention order or orders. This procedure avoids having to dismiss the application for guardianship and requiring a new application for an intervention order to be made with the attendant delay and expense.

6.29   We recommend that:

85. (1) The court should be empowered to appoint a guardian to an adult if satisfied that:

   (a) the adult is unable to communicate or is mentally disordered, and by reason of such inability or disorder, unable to make decisions or act to protect or safeguard his or her personal welfare or financial affairs, and

   (b) that such inability is likely to continue for such a period as to justify guardianship in the interests of the adult.

   (2) Even where the above criteria are met the court should appoint a guardian only if satisfied that one or more intervention orders would not be sufficient in the circumstances to meet the needs of the adult. Where the court considers that an intervention order or orders will suffice it may treat the application for the appointment of a guardian as an application for such intervention orders and ancillary orders as the court thinks fit and grant such orders accordingly.

Clause 44(1), (2)

---

1. *Annual Report 1993/94*, p 16.
2. Recommendation 94, para 6.60.
3. 1984 Act, s 41.
4. Para 12.3.
5. In Ms X's cases the issue was how her tenancy could be terminated when she refused to give her house up.
6. Mental Welfare Commission, *Annual Report 1991*, p 25. Out of the 25 guardianships terminated in 1991, 15 had lasted for less than a year and one for as little as 3 months.

6.30 Section 29 of the 1984 Act provides for the transfer into guardianship of patients who are detained under the Act in a hospital for treatment for their mental disorder. The managers of the hospital may transfer the patient either into the guardianship of the local authority with the consent of the authority or into the guardianship of a person approved by the local authority with that person's consent. This automatic transfer would no longer be possible under our new system of guardianship. Instead an application would have to be made to the sheriff court for the appointment of a guardian with appropriate powers or for an intervention order or orders. We see this as a positive advantage. First, it would enable the intervention orders or the guardian's powers to be tailored to the adult's disabilities and requirements. Under the present system the guardian has three statutory powers which cannot be added to or subtracted from[1]. Extra powers might be useful, especially powers in the financial field, when the adult moves out of hospital into the community. Secondly, a court hearing would allow representations to be made by or on behalf of the adult and others with an interest in his or her welfare as to the appropriate order. The present transfer arrangements are automatic and give no such opportunity. Thirdly, such a change would be in line with the Mental Health (Patients in the Community) Bill [H.L.] currently before Parliament. Clause 4 of this Bill introduces community care orders for patients who leave hospital after detention there. The sheriff, on application by the responsible medical officer, is empowered to grant an order which will contain conditions with a view to ensuring that the patient receives appropriate medical treatment and after-care services.

Title to apply

6.31 We would adopt the general formula for title to apply we recommended earlier in Part 2 whereby any person claiming an interest in the welfare, property or financial affairs of the incapable adult has a title[2]. That general formula is intended to include public bodies such as the Mental Welfare Commission, the local authority and the Public Guardian, voluntary societies involved with the mentally disabled and carers, friends and family of the adult. We have already recommended use of this formula in connection with intervention orders[3].

6.32 Should any public body be under a duty to apply for the appointment of a guardian if guardianship appears to be needed and no-one else is applying? Section 92 of the 1984 Act lays such a duty on the local authority to apply for a curator bonis. Where the local authority does apply it usually nominates some official in its finance department as curator. The local authority has a similar duty in relation to mental health guardianship under the 1984 Act. In terms of section 38(4) a mental health officer (a specially trained social worker with the local authority) must make a guardianship application if satisfied that it is necessary and proper for an application to be made after taking into account the relatives' wishes and other circumstances. In Proposal 7 of our discussion paper we suggested that the local authority should be under a duty in appropriate circumstances to apply for a personal guardian and in Proposal 30(2) we made the same suggestion in relation to the appointment of a financial manager.

6.33 Most of those who responded to these proposals agreed. Some respondents commented that local authorities are reluctant to apply for a curator to be appointed because of the expense involved in making the application and because the commission allowed to curators for their services in managing modest estates does not meet the cost of providing the service. Our later recommendation for public financial guardianship at modest cost should help to reduce this disincentive to apply under the present system. The local authority would be able to nominate the Public Guardian instead of one of its own finance department officials. The Law Society considered that a local authority should apply only if guardianship was needed "in the interests of the adult". There were concerns that some local authorities might apply for a curator simply to claim legal rights or other funds due to the adults so as to meet the cost of providing care for them in a local authority home. We think this point would be met by the first of our recommended general principles, that any person proposing to intervene in the affairs of an incapable adult must be satisfied that the intervention will benefit that adult and that the benefit cannot be reasonably achieved without the intervention. There is clearly a need for some public body to act as last resort applicant where the appointment of a guardian seems necessary but no-one else is prepared to apply. The local authority is more likely than other bodies to be aware of the adult's needs and situation and to possess the resources to evaluate the situation and put forward an application. We consider that the duty on the local authority to apply for the appointment of a guardian should be extended to intervention orders as well. We recommend that:

86. (1) Any person claiming an interest in the welfare, property or financial affairs of the adult (including the Public Guardian, the Mental Welfare Commission, the local authority and the adult himself or herself) should be entitled to apply for the appointment of a guardian.

(2) The local authority should be under a duty to apply for an intervention order or the appointment of a guardian if it is satisfied that grounds for such an application exist, that an intervention order or a guardian is necessary in the interests of the adult, and that no-one else is applying or is likely to apply.

Clauses 42(2) and 43(1), (2)

---

1. 1984 Act, s 41.
2. Recommendation 7, para 2.39.
3. Recommendation 81, para 6.20.

Procedure for appointment of guardians

6.34   Earlier in this report we recommend that guardianship and other proceedings involving incapable adults should be heard by specially trained nominated sheriffs in chambers or other suitable premises using an informal procedure[1]. We turn now to consider other procedural aspects of guardianship applications.

6.35   **Reports**. Mental health guardianship applications and curatory petitions require the adult in question to be examined by at least two medical practitioners and reports of the examinations to accompany the application or petition. The same procedure has been adopted for the appointment of a tutor-dative and a tutor-at-law in recent years. In the case of mental health guardians one of the medical recommendations must be given by a practitioner approved by the health board as having special expertise in the diagnosis or treatment of mental disorder and the other, if possible, should be by the adult's general practitioner or another medical practitioner previously acquainted with the adult[2]. The medical certificates for mental health guardianship and curatory generally simply echo the rather vague grounds of appointment; suffering from mental disorder to a degree that warrants guardianship or unable to manage his or her affairs or give instructions for their management respectively. Sketchy curatory certificates have been judicially criticised in a recent case[3]. Tutor-dative petitions have much fuller certificates because the powers sought are related to the adult's needs and disabilities.

6.36   The more detailed ground of appointment that we recommend for guardianship and the application of the general principle of least restriction will require greater detail which will not be confined simply to medical reports. Reports will be required to establish that the adult is incapable, that his or her inability to take decisions or act to promote and safeguard his or her welfare or finances stems from that incapacity, and that the incapacity and consequent inability is likely to continue for such a period as to justify guardianship in the interests of the adult. Reports or statements will also be needed as to the extent of the adult's inability in these areas. Because the court has to be satisfied that the appointment of a guardian will benefit the adult and that guardianship is the only reasonable way of providing such benefit and is in the least restrictive form to achieve its purpose, evidence of these matters will also have to be presented. Finally, evidence will have to be presented as to the guardian's suitability for the post[4]. We consider that there should be at least two reports to the adult's incapacity and consequential inability. At least one of them should be given by a medical practitioner approved by the health board as being experienced in the diagnosis or treatment of mental disorder[5]. The restrictions on liberty as a result of the appointment of a guardian are at least as heavy as those for mental health guardianship, where an approved practitioner must give at least one of the reports. We would not wish to impose too great a restriction on the other report. It could be from another approved expert or from a medical practitioner who knows the adult well or a psychologist with experience in the field of mental incapacity. Evidence of the extent of the adult's inability to take decisions or safeguard or promote his or her welfare or financial affairs could appropriately come from non-medical sources as could evidence of the benefits expected from guardianship. Family, carers, nurses or neighbours who know the adult well would all be able to give useful information on these aspects. A mental health officer should be required to report on these matters where personal welfare powers were being sought. A mental health officer's report might also be submitted in connection with a purely financial guardianship application but should not be required. The sheriff might however call for it to be lodged later. All these reports or statements should require to be lodged in court along with the application. After considering these reports the sheriff may wish to obtain further reports or make further inquiries. These would be useful powers in relation to proceedings generally[6]. We recommend that:-

87.   **(1)   There should be required to be lodged in court along with the application for guardianship the following:**

      (a)   At least two reports relating to the incapacity of the adult. At least one of the reports should be given by a practitioner approved by the health board under section 20 of the Mental Health (Scotland) Act 1984 as having special expertise in the diagnosis and treatment of mental disorder and the other report(s) by a medical practitioner or other person suitably qualified in the assessment of mental disorder.

      (b)   Where powers in relation to the adult's personal welfare are applied for, a report by the local authority mental health officer as to the general appropriateness of the powers sought. Where the application relates only to powers in relation to the adult's property or financial affairs the report may be by any person with sufficient knowledge.

    (2)   The sheriff should have to be satisfied by means of reports or otherwise that the appointment of a guardian will benefit the adult and that the benefit cannot be reasonably obtained otherwise.

Clause 43(3)

---

1.   Recommendation 3, para 2.31.
2.   1984 Act, s 39.
3.   *Fraser v Paterson* 1987 SLT 562.
4.   See later, paras 6.61 to 6.70.
5.   Under s 20 of the 1984 Act.
6.   See 1984 Act, ss 21(2) and 40(2) in relation to detention and guardianship applications respectively.

6.37   In curatory the medical practitioners concerned must have personally examined the incapable adult not more than 30 days before the petition is lodged[1]. Mental health guardianship imposes a tighter timetable, only seven days are allowed between the later of the two required medical examinations and the submission of the application to the sheriff for approval[2]. We prefer the longer period used in curatory petitions for all the reports and statements accompanying the guardianship application. Those giving the reports should be asked to inform the applicant should any substantial change in the incapable adult's condition or circumstances subsequently occur. We recommend that:

> **88. The medical practitioners or others assessing incapacity under Recommendation 87 and any mental health officer should be required to have personally examined or interviewed the adult within 30 days of the date of lodging the report in court. Others giving reports or information should be required to have seen the adult within the same period.**
>
> Clause 43(3)

6.38   **Intimation of application**. The application should require to be intimated to the incapable adult unless the medical certificates state that intimation would result in substantial harm to the adult's health and the sheriff considering the application dispenses with such intimation. Since under the general principles the court has to take the views of the adult's nearest relative and primary carer into account in so far as is reasonably practicable it follows that the application has to be intimated to them if their whereabouts are known. Intimation ought also to be made to the local authority in those cases where a mental health officer's report has been lodged. The sheriff should have a discretionary power to order intimation to others depending on the circumstances of the particular case. Petitions for the appointment of a curator bonis are served on all those with an interest in the estate[3]. This is sometimes taken to mean all those who would succeed on intestacy, although in extended families a complete list is not necessary. For guardianship we envisage that all the near relatives not just the nearest would be notified. It would be for Rules of Court to identify the class of relatives who would be entitled to intimation. There should be a power to dispense with intimation to a relative. Dispensation might be necessary if, for example, a relative within the defined class was untraceable. We recommend that:

> **89. (1) Rules of Court should be made providing for intimation of the guardianship application to the incapable adult, his or her primary carer or nearest relatives and, where a report by a mental health officer accompanies the application, to the local authority. The sheriff should be empowered to order intimation to others and to dispense with intimation to the adult or others.**
>
> **(2) Intimation to the adult should be dispensed with only if the medical certificates state that it would cause substantial harm to the adult's health.**

6.39   **Interim powers**. We consider it essential that the court dealing with an application for guardianship should have power to appoint an interim guardian or make other appropriate interim orders pending the determination of the application. The inability to appoint an interim mental health guardian was noted in our discussion paper[4] as one of the disadvantages of mental health guardianship. Situations may well arise where some urgent action is necessary. The Association of Directors of Social Work in response to Proposal 8 in our discussion paper (court granting personal orders or conferring powers on personal guardian) commented that there was a need for emergency orders in the personal welfare field which could be obtained in a matters of hours rather than days. It is competent to appoint an interim curator bonis. The Accountant of Court informed us that interim curatories which last for many months or even years cause problems. We consider that interim guardianship should be limited to three months and that the court should attach a condition requiring an interim guardian to report every month to the Public Guardian or, where welfare powers are concerned to the local authority. We recommend that:

> **90. The court dealing with a guardianship application should have power to appoint an interim guardian for no more than three months or make other interim orders pending the determination of the guardianship application.**
>
> Clauses 3(2)(d) and 43(4), (5)

6.40   **Intimation of result of application**. The Accountant of Court at present receives all interlocutors appointing curators bonis. Later we recommend that guardians with financial powers should, like curators, be supervised by the Accountant of Court as Public Guardian[5]. We consider that the Public Guardian should act as registration authority, maintaining an open public register of guardians appointed by the court with a note of the powers conferred. Third parties with an interest in the adult's welfare or financial affairs may need to know whether a guardian has been appointed and if so what powers have been conferred. Although the Public Guardian would have no supervisory role in relation to guardians with only personal welfare powers we think that the Public Guardian should also act as a registration authority in respect of them. Purely welfare guardians are likely to be relatively uncommon and it would be expensive to create a

---

1. McBryde and Dowie, *Petition Procedure in the Court of Session*, (2nd edn) p 62.
2. 1984 Act, s 40(1).
3. McBryde and Dowie, p 63.
4. Para 2.37.
5. Recommendation 108, para 6.124.

separate register for them held by another authority. As far as purely personal welfare guardians are concerned the Public Guardian's role would be wholly administrative and would not involve any supervision of their functions. The responsibility for intimating the appointment of a guardian to the Public Guardian should rest on the guardian appointed. The guardian's authority to act should commence once the appointment has been registered with the Public Guardian, caution found[1] and a certificate of appointment issued. The Public Guardian should notify the incapable adult of the guardianship order. We recommend that:

91. Every guardian should intimate his or her appointment to the Public Guardian who should enter prescribed particulars of the guardian and the powers conferred in a register open to public inspection. The Public Guardian should issue the guardian with a certificate of appointment and notify the incapable adult of the guardianship.

Clauses 4(2)(c)(iv) and 44(5)

6.41 **Caution**. At present curators are required to find caution - that is, security for the due performance of their duties. Each curator must arrange a bond of caution for a sum fixed by the Accountant of Court or the court with one of the insurance companies approved for this purpose by the Lord President. The object of caution is that the insurance company will meet any claims against the curator arising out of his or her failure to discharge his duties properly. The present system involves considerable work obtaining and checking over 2,000 individual bonds of caution and ensuring that they are kept in force by the curator paying the appropriate premium. In our discussion paper we proposed that guardians (or financial managers as we then called them), like curators, be required to find caution and asked for views on a master policy scheme to be administered by the Accountant of Court[2]. All those responding agreed that caution was essential to protect the adults subject to guardianship and we would extend this to persons acting under an intervention order where the court thought there was a risk of default which would involve the adult in losses. The master policy scheme was also welcomed in principle. Some commentators took the point that the existence of a master policy scheme would enable more lay guardians to be appointed. We think there is some force in this. Executors dative who are appointed by the court to administer intestate estates and propose to act without employing a solicitor can find it very difficult to find an insurance company willing to provide caution and even if caution is available the premium may be very high in relation to the size of the estate. We understand from the present Accountant of Court that the cost of individual bonds of caution has increased because insurance companies have set a substantial minimum premium applicable to every case. We are in favour of a master policy scheme in principle but recognise that there may be practical difficulties involved in setting up such a scheme. We therefore only recommend that:

92. All guardians with financial powers should have to find caution. The sheriff in appointing someone to act under an intervention order may require him or her to find caution. Consideration should be given to the setting up of a master policy scheme to be administered by the Public Guardian.

Clauses 42(5) and 44(5)(b)

Duration of guardian's appointment

6.42 Mental health guardianship lasts for six months initially but can be renewed for a further six months and thereafter for periods of a year at a time. Curators are appointed for an indefinite period. Tutors-dative are also capable of being appointed for an indefinite period, although some of the modern appointments have been made for a limited period at the petitioner's request. In our discussion paper we proposed that both personal guardians[3] and financial managers[4] should be appointed initially for a five year period but that the court be empowered to substitute a shorter period. At the end of the initial period it would be competent to renew the appointment if it was still appropriate. Mandatory periodical review can be seen as an important safeguard, as there could be a danger that the adult might remain subject to powers that were no longer appropriate. The adult may not be capable of initiating recall proceedings and others may not be willing to take the initiative or have the necessary interest. However, it is also necessary to take into account the cost and inconvenience of reviews which, in certain cases of permanent incapacity, may be obviously unnecessary.

6.43 Nearly all of those who commented on these proposals were in favour. The former Accountant of Court however considered that the expense of court proceedings to renew the appointment of a financial manager was unjustifiable. He proposed a simpler procedure involving submission of a medical report to him. While we have considerable sympathy with the need to keep expenses of guardianship down we think that something more is needed before guardianship is renewed. Guardianship involves a substantial restriction of the adult's rights and the European Convention on Human Rights requires a fair and public hearing by an independent and impartial tribunal. Guardianship should in our opinion have to be renewed by the courts, although a simpler and less expensive procedure could be adopted than is used for the initial application.

---

1. See para 6.41.
2. Proposal 46, para 4.129.
3. Proposal 14, para 2.95.
4. Proposal 47, para 4.131.

6.44   Some commentators agreed with the initial five year period we proposed. Most, however, thought that the period was too long and suggested two or three years instead. The present Accountant of Court suggested that in some cases of irreversible incapacity the most sensible course would be an appointment of indefinite duration, that is an appointment which would last until recalled. As we mentioned in our discussion paper, a balance has to be struck between the extra work and expense of frequent mandatory reviews and allowing guardianship to continue when it is no longer necessary or appropriate. Any period is bound to be somewhat arbitrary. We suggest that the norm should be an initial period of three years as favoured by most respondents but that the sheriff should have a discretion to substitute another period. On the first and subsequent renewal a longer norm of five years seems more appropriate. In relation to both the initial appointment and a renewal the other period could be shorter or longer than the norm. In certain cases the court should be able to appoint or renew a guardian for an indefinite period, ie until recall, rather than for a specified term. We recommend that:

93. **Guardians should be appointed initially for a period of three years or, on cause shown, for such other period (specified or indefinite) as the court thinks appropriate. The appointment should be subsequently renewable, on one or more occasions, for a period of five years or, on cause shown, for such other period (specified or indefinite) as the court thinks appropriate.**

Clauses 44(3) and 47(5)

Who may be appointed as guardian?

6.45   Our discussion paper proposed[1] that personal guardianship should be open only to individuals and that it should not be competent to appoint a partnership, company or local authority. Most adults subject to guardianship under the 1984 Act have local authority guardians. A survey of guardianship cases in 1989 showed that 68 out of the 81 current cases had local authority guardians[2]. We suggested in our discussion paper[3] that where "local authority" guardianship was required a named social worker employed by that authority should be appointed rather than the authority itself or the social work department. Those responding were generally in favour of appointing only individuals but there was concern about appointing named social workers as personal guardians.

6.46   The 1984 Act does not clearly define the local authority's role when appointed as guardian. This is perhaps because earlier legislation was based on the concept of the guardian being either a relative or some other individual with whom the adult lived. At present guardianship is often used because the adult has no close relatives or they are unsuitable. In these circumstances mental health guardianship has a protective function and most guardians are the local authority or the social work department. Our new recommended form of guardianship will be sufficiently flexible to offer such protective guardianship in the cases where it is needed but the question arises who then should be appointed guardian. In matters relating to property and finance we recommend later[4] that it should be possible for the Public Guardian to be appointed guardian. However, it would not be suitable for the Public Guardian to act as guardian in personal welfare cases. That would, for one thing, require a considerable expansion of his office and would duplicate, at great cost, a role which could be better performed, as at present, by local authorities under the general supervision of the Mental Welfare Commission. The other great advantage of preserving the role of local authorities in this area is that they are local. It would not be appropriate for a central authority or official to act as a guardian in personal welfare matters and it would be unrealistic to expect the Public Guardian to establish offices in every local authority area in Scotland. We have therefore built on the existing system in which local authorities act as "public guardians" in personal welfare matters and the Mental Welfare Commission has a supervisory and monitoring role.

6.47   As many respondents pointed out, there are difficulties in appointing a named social worker as guardian. Their statutory duties and responsibilities in acting as guardian might, at least in theory, clash with their status as employees subject to conflicting directions by their superiors. This may not be an insuperable objection. Mental health officers are appointed by local authorities and yet exercise important statutory duties under the 1984 Act independently. Where guardianship was initiated by the local authority it seems inappropriate that some individual employee should be made personally liable for carrying out the duties. There are also practical disadvantages in that the named social worker may leave the local authority or be allocated to another area of work. In a recent study it was found that the person effectively exercising the guardianship functions had changed at least once, and in some cases as many as three times, in 15 out of the 22 cases of guardianship studied[5].

6.48   Alzheimer Scotland - Action on Dementia and Enable suggested using volunteers who would be trained and supported by the local authority social work department in those cases where "local authority" guardianship was

---

1. Proposal 6(b), para 2.69.
2. Richards and McGregor, *Guardianship in Scotland*, HMSO 1992, p 69.
3. Proposal 6(d).
4. Recommendation 94(2), para 6.60.
5. *The Hidden Safety Net? Mental Health Guardianship: Achievements and Limitations*, Scottish Office Central Research Unit Papers 1992, pp 34 and 35.

appropriate. These volunteers would also be available to act as guardians in other cases as well. The local authority would put forward a suitable volunteer for appointment rather than itself or one of its social workers. We are attracted by this suggestion as a trained and supported volunteer might well have a longer term relationship with the adult under guardianship than a social worker liable to be moved for management reasons. Having the local authority or any of its employees as guardians may give rise to conflicts of interest. Guardians may need to press for extra services from the local authority or complain about the services provided by it. Volunteers would not have the same conflict of interest as employees of a local authority would have. However, we have some doubts as to how easy it would be to recruit and retain sufficient volunteers. These volunteers would not simply be befrienders or advocates. They would also be decision-makers with statutory duties to perform and would be personally liable if they failed to act with reasonable care and in good faith and in accordance with the general principles. We approve of the setting up of volunteer schemes but we are reluctant to rely on an untried system for all "local authority" guardianship cases.

6.49   The Association of Directors of Social Work disagreed with our proposal to have named social workers as guardians. In its view local authorities should continue to be the guardian since they carry the legal authority and responsibility. Suitable individual employees should continue to be delegated to carry out the functions and would remain answerable to their employing authority for the exercise of their delegated powers. It has been found that there is often a lack of clear guidance within the local authority leading to uncertainty as to which employees should exercise the guardianship functions[1]. Better guidance would help to make the position clearer. The other disadvantage of having a local authority as guardian lies in its corporate nature. There is no individual who can be called to account. Some degree of individual accountability could be achieved by appointing the local authority chief social work officer (as the Director of Social Work will be called) as guardian. The chief social work officer should be appointed as an office holder so that when he or she leaves the successor would automatically become guardian. Obviously the chief social work officer could not be expected to exercise the guardianship functions personally but would have to delegate them to suitable individuals. These individuals would probably be employees in the social work department but other people, such as community nurses, might also be considered. The chief social work officer should remain liable for the way in which guardianship was exercised and would have to ensure adequate monitoring and supervision.

6.50   So far we have considered the welfare side of guardianship. We now turn to look at the financial aspects. In our discussion paper we proposed that it should be competent to appoint a suitable individual as financial manager for an incapable adult and asked for views as to the desirability of having banks, buildings societies, insurance companies or other bodies as financial managers[2]. We pointed out that corporations such as banks are often confirmed as executors. Reaction to corporate or institutional financial management was mixed. Many saw no objection to such appointments provided the institution was capable of providing an adequate level of service. Institutions such as banks have a number of advantages in that they do not die, become ill or go on holiday. Individual managers retire or resign and further procedure is needed to provide a replacement. Change of management with institutions should be much rarer. Other respondents, however, thought that institutions would provide a remote impersonal service. There was also the question of personal responsibility. With institutions there would be no individual that could be called to account unless there was a very clear system of delegation to a specific individual within the organisation. We consider that the better solution is to require guardians to be appointed as individuals, although they may hold positions within a corporation or institution.

6.51   The National Board for Nursing, Midwifery and Health Visiting for Scotland suggested that it should be competent to appoint the holder of an office so that if he or she moved the successor would automatically take over. We have decided however not to recommend this. Our later recommendation for a simple method of appointing a replacement guardian[3] lessens the need for the appointment of office holders. It is very important that the guardian is someone who can competently perform the functions and is suitable in other respects. He or she will have to have regular contact with the adult and the adult's nearest relative and primary carer. It could not be assumed that the successors in an office would always share their predecessors' attributes. We would however make two exceptions to this general rule. The chief social work officer of a local authority and the Accountant of Court as Public Guardian should be appointed as office holders rather than as individuals. Such appointments are in reality the appointment of their organisations rather than themselves as individuals. Accordingly the court should not have to be satisfied as to their personal suitability as guardians, but it might still have to consider whether an individual guardian would serve the adult better if faced with opposing nominations.

6.52   Our discussion paper also proposed a scheme of public financial management[4]. This was to be available where those seeking financial management wished it to be undertaken by a public official or where no other suitable financial manager could be found. Impartial financial management can be obtained by the appointment of a solicitor or accountant, but we thought that the main advantages of public management lay in the administration of small or modest estates. For

---

1. *The Hidden Safety Net*, pp 33 and 34 and *Guardianship in Scotland*, pp 71 and 72.
2. Proposal 31, para 4.49.
3. Recommendation 137, para 6.202.
4. Proposal 33, para 4.59.

such estates the fees for professional management are a great burden[1] and even so often fail to cover the cost of providing the service. We did not propose the establishment of a new public body to act as financial manager. Instead we looked at three existing institutions currently involved with financial management on behalf of incapacitated people and asked for views as to whether any of these or some other body should undertake public management of the financial affairs of adults lacking capacity. The three existing institutions were the Accountant of Court, local authority finance departments and sheriff clerks.

6.53   The Accountant of Court and his staff are familiar with curatories and investment of funds, albeit in a supervisory and auditing capacity. We considered that the Accountant could readily take on the additional role of public management. Administration by the Accountant's office would be impartial. The other advantages of using the Accountant's office would be that it could built up expertise in this area through dealing with a number of cases and that there would be one body with an overall view as to how the new system of public management was developing. The main disadvantage that we saw was that the Accountant's office is situated in Edinburgh so that it would not be easy for those outwith the central belt of Scotland wishing to discuss matters with the official concerned with their case to do so. There is a danger that management by the Accountant's office might be regarded as management by a remote bureaucracy.

6.54   The arguments in favour of local authorities are that they do occasionally act as curators where no one else is willing to be appointed, that officials in the finance department would be competent to deal with the administration of estates, and that the nominated official or colleagues would be reasonably accessible for consultation by the incapable adult's family and others interested in the management of the adult's estate. On the other hand there is a danger of concentrating too many functions in the hands of local authorities. For some adults the authority would already be the supplier of accommodation and the provider of social work and other services.

6.55   Our third option was for sheriff clerks to be public managers acting under the direction of sheriffs. They could also offer an impartial service. The spread of sheriff courts throughout Scotland means that a local court would be readily accessible. We noted that sheriff courts do at present carry out some administration of incapacitated persons' estates. Rules 36.14 to 36.17 of the Ordinary Cause Rules 1993 empower the sheriff to order court management of damages payable to or for the benefit of "a person under legal disability". At present the system applies mainly to children under 16 since virtually all older "legally disabled" persons involved in damages actions will have curators appointed to whom payment will be ordered[2]. We noted that the system of sheriff court administration appears to work well. On the other hand financial management of incapable adults' estates would only be a "fringe activity" for the sheriff courts. It would be difficult for each court to build up expertise in this area or retain trained staff. Furthermore, there would be no one body with an overall view of the new system of public management.

6.56   Nearly all of those responding considered that public management should be introduced. From comments made in response to our discussion paper and subsequently we conclude that a simple and cheap system of administering modest estates is urgently required. There was support for all the three options we put forward - local authorities, sheriff clerks and the Accountant of Court, with the last being the most favoured. But there was concern expressed about using local authorities. First, some felt that for them to have financial management as well as being a service provider might give rise to too great a concentration of power. Secondly, the local authority would be faced with conflicts of interest where it was providing care or services which were then charged to the adult's estate. We share these concerns. Even if internal safeguards were put in place to prevent individual officials having too much power or conflicting interests we doubt whether the system would be perceived as independent or impartial. Independence and impartiality are in our view essential elements in any scheme of public management. Another suggestion made to us was that the Lord Advocate should be the Public Manager. This would combine a centralised administration at the Crown Office with a local presence by the Procurators Fiscal. We have given this suggestion careful consideration but have decided against it. Procurators Fiscal are almost exclusively concerned with criminal proceedings. Taking on civil matters with a large element of financial management expertise would be an entirely new role which would require considerable training of existing staff or recruiting specially trained additional staff.

6.57   Public financial management by sheriffs and sheriff clerks also enjoyed some support on consultation. It offers local administration but suffers from the disadvantage of having no existing central office co-ordinating and controlling the management in individual courts. We do not think that sheriff court administration of adults' finances is the best way forward. It would constitute a fringe activity and distract the courts and their staff from their primary function.

6.58   In our view the existing expertise of the Accountant of Court's office in supervising and monitoring curators and other judicial factors forms a good foundation for building a public management scheme. As already mentioned this was

---

1. The Scottish Office Central Research Unit Survey *Financial Management of Mentally Incapacitated Adults: Characteristics of Curatories*, Fiona Rutherdale (1992), showed that the annual administration costs were often more than one third of the annual income.
2. Macphail, *Sheriff Court Practice*, p 697.

the preferred option of the majority of those responding. A central organisation offers economy of scale and continuity of approach. It also enables expertise to be built up. However, many respondents supported use of the Accountant of Court only if adequate staff were provided who had received training in the needs of the mentally incapacitated and the office had a local and accessible presence in most areas of Scotland. We would support all these points, although it is necessary to be realistic about the last. It is unlikely that there would be sufficient work to justify opening offices for every area in Scotland. Staff at present do travel to see people in connection with curatories and would no doubt also do so in their capacity as public financial managers. Some matters could be dealt with by letter or telephone. Another possible solution would be for the Accountant of Court to appoint a local solicitor, accountant or other suitably qualified person to act as a local agent. The Accountant in Bankruptcy has set up an agency scheme whereby he delegates to appointed private insolvency practitioners effectively the entire work of certain sequestrations where he is trustee[1].

6.59   Public management, as mentioned above, is required to solve the problem of managing modest estates without imposing too great a financial burden on them. In our discussion paper we suggested that such estates should either be managed free of charge or that the fees should be considerably less than the present commission allowable to curators. Large estates should, we thought, be charged the full economic cost of providing the service. The responses to our invitation for views as to what constituted a modest estate were very varied and ranged from £5,000 to £20,000. Other respondents favoured fees being set as a fixed percentage of the income, whatever the value of the estate. We do not make any detailed recommendations as to fee structure as much will depend on the volume of work and the type of estates put under public management.

6.60   Summing up we recommend that:

94. (1) It should be competent to appoint only an individual as guardian to an incapable adult. Where the guardian is appointed with personal welfare powers the chief social work officer of the local authority in which the adult is resident may be appointed. The chief social work officer should be appointed as an officeholder so that any successor would automatically take over the guardianship functions.

(2) A scheme of public financial management of the estates of incapable adults should be introduced. The fees charged should be modest in order not to impose a financial burden on small to medium estates. The Accountant of Court as holder of the office of Public Guardian should carry out such management. It should be competent to appoint the Public Guardian as guardian provided only financial powers are involved.

Clauses 4(1), (2)(a), and 45(1)

Selection of guardians

6.61   Guardians will have considerable powers conferred on them so that it is important that only suitable people are appointed. The decisions made by guardians may not be respected and followed unless third parties, particularly local authorities and others with responsibilities towards the incapacitated, are satisfied that a proper selection procedure has been used to ensure the suitability of the guardians appointed. Under section 37(2) of the 1984 Act a guardian (other than the local authority itself) must be either chosen or accepted as suitable by the local authority. The Notes on the Act[2] state that in practice the mental health officer or other social worker concerned with the welfare of patients under guardianship will carry out this task. By contrast solicitors, accountants and other financial professionals are assumed to be suitable as curators and will be appointed unless evidence to the contrary is produced. With lay curators the courts require to be satisfied that they are able to carry out their duties satisfactorily[3].

6.62   The local authority should, we think, continue to play a major part in assessing the suitability of proposed guardians, especially where welfare powers are concerned. Others may also have views that should be taken into account. We have already recommended that a report from the local authority mental health officer as to the appropriateness of guardianship should accompany any application where welfare powers are sought and this report should also give views and information regarding the suitability of the proposed applicant. In guardianship applications involving only financial powers a report by another sufficiently knowledgeable person could be used instead[4]. The sheriff is also to be empowered to require other reports or assessments to be lodged as to the proposed guardian's suitability. We do not make detailed recommendations as to the procedures the local authority should adopt in assessing suitability. Much would depend on the relationship between the proposed guardian and the adult and the powers sought. Sometimes a full assessment similar to that carried out on prospective adoptive or foster parents would be appropriate; in other cases less exhaustive checks should suffice. It was suggested to us that the parents of the adult should be regarded as suitable unless objections were taken to their appointment. We would not favour any special exceptions. We think that in every case the court should have to be positively satisfied by reports or other evidence that the proposed appointee was indeed suitable.

---

1.   J D Anderson, *The Bankruptcy (Scotland) Act 1993 in Operation*, 1994 JLSS 363, 365.
2.   Para 203. The Notes were published by the Scottish Office Home and Health Department in 1986.
3.   *B's CB* 1990 SCLR 538.
4.   Recommendation 87, para 6.36.

6.63   In our discussion paper we proposed that in appointing a personal guardian the court should have to be satisfied that the proposed appointee was suitable and that the views of the adult were taken into account in so far as it was reasonable and practicable to do so[1]. A similar proposal was made in relation to financial managers but additional criteria were also suggested[2]. These were -

(1) no material conflict of interest between guardian and adult,

(2) capability of carrying out the duties satisfactorily, and

(3) a satisfactory relationship between the guardian and the adult.

We suggested that lay management (ie by individuals other than solicitors or accountants) ought to be encouraged for modest estates. These proposals were generally agreed, although many respondents considered that further guidance was required as to suitability.

6.64   We have given further thought to criteria for suitability. The most important seems to us to be the ability to carry out the duties to a satisfactory standard. Our suggestion that non-professional financial managers should be encouraged where the estate was modest was welcomed by many of those responding. Financial management by relatives or friends could lead to a more personal, responsive service than one provided by professionals. Lay financial management was also seen as a way of reducing the costs of administration since lay managers would generally not seek remuneration, but only reimbursement of outlays. Professional management fees form a substantial burden on modest estates, even though they are often below the cost to the professional of providing the service. If lay guardians are to provide a satisfactory service they will usually need to obtain assistance from time to time. It would of course be self defeating for lay guardians to hand over the whole management to solicitors or accountants (as lay executors generally do), although certain transactions like selling property or settling complex tax claims would need professional help. The Accountant of Court's staff at present help lay curators and we would hope that the Public Guardian would continue providing such assistance. Voluntary societies could also be another useful source of help. A proposed guardian, especially a lay guardian, should have to satisfy the sheriff that he or she was aware of the duties and was able to carry them out with appropriate assistance.

6.65   Another aspect of ability is knowledge of the adult's incapacity, circumstances and his or her needs arising out of the incapacity. A near relative or friend or carer is more likely to possess such knowledge than a person who is less close to the adult. The latter would have to obtain the necessary information by consulting the adult and others knowledgeable about the adult's welfare and situation.

6.66   The accessibility of the proposed guardian to the adult and his or her primary carer is another consideration. Guardianship, particularly where welfare powers are concerned, ought to involve a fairly close relationship between the parties involved. Guardians have a duty to consult the adult, nearest relative and primary carer when making major decisions and may take the views of others into account. All this will be more difficult if the guardian is far away and there is a danger that physical remoteness will lead to an impersonal service. However, we do not think it appropriate to create artificial limitations such as residence in Scotland or even in the United Kingdom. Modern communications and ease of travel make it possible for guardians to fulfil their functions even though they live hundreds or even thousands of miles away. Some degree of personal contact is highly desirable, but a son living in New York and visiting his mother from time to time might be a better choice of guardian than say a solicitor who lived in the same town.

6.67   The Law Society drew our attention to the *Declaration of General and Special Rights of the Mentally Retarded* issued by the International League of Societies for Persons with Mental Handicap which includes a statement that "no person rendering direct services to the mentally retarded should also serve as his guardian". We think that this is an important factor to be borne in mind but is not one that should be elevated into an absolute prohibition. The person in charge of a small hostel or home may be the most suitable person to act as guardian to an adult who has no available relatives. Moreover, the declaration would rule out local authority guardianship which we have already recommended should continue to be available. The League's statement encapsulates two factors, conflict of interest and concentration of power. We think that it is these underlying factors which should be before the court in deciding who is suitable as guardian. Direct provision of services as guardian will usually involve conflicting interests and accrual of undue power, but conflicts of interest or undue concentration of power may arise outwith direct service provision. Close relatives or those living with incapable adults will inevitably have conflicts of interest and making them guardians will increase their powers. For example, a son who succeeds under his mother's will faces conflicts of interest in deciding how much to pay for care for her. Again, a wife looking after her dementing husband at home would acquire considerable extra powers by being appointed his guardian with full welfare and financial powers. But in many cases close relatives or those living with the adult would be the best guardians on grounds of knowledge of the adult's disability and needs, and accessibility.

---

1. Proposal 6(a), para 2.69.
2. Proposal 31(1) and (2), para 4.49.

Lay guardianship, which we are anxious to promote in appropriate cases, would be stifled at birth if relatives and carers were to be ruled out on grounds of conflict of interest or undue concentration of power arising simply out of relationship or living together.

6.68   The factors we have already mentioned are not intended to form an exhaustive list. The court should also be able to take into account any other relevant matter. Being an undischarged bankrupt or having been convicted of an offence involving dishonesty, for example, would be highly relevant in considering whether to appoint someone as guardian with financial powers.

6.69   We recommend earlier[1] that the court should be empowered to appoint the chief social work officer of the local authority or the Public Guardian as guardian. These officer holders are not being appointed personally, in reality it is their staff who will act as guardian. Accordingly, it should not be necessary for the court to have to be satisfied as to their suitability. Suitability should be a necessary but not a sufficient condition for appointment. The court should be able to appoint a suitable individual rather than the Public Guardian or the chief social work officer if having regard to the general principles that seemed the better course.

6.70   We recommend that:

95. (1) A proposed guardian (other than the Public Guardian or the local authority chief social work officer) should be appointed only if the court is satisfied by means of reports or otherwise that he or she is suitable. In assessing suitability the court should have regard to the following factors and any other relevant matters:

   (a) the ability of the individual to carry out the guardianship duties;

   (b) the accessibility of the individual to the adult and the ease with which he or she can consult the primary carer and others interested in the adult's welfare;

   (c) the individual's awareness of the adult's circumstances and needs;

   (d) any conflict of interest between the individual and the adult and whether guardianship would increase the powers of the individual over the adult to too great an extent.

(2) In order to promote the appointment of non-professional guardians the court should in assessing ability take account of any free assistance that would be available from official and other sources. Conflicts of interest or undue concentration of power arising out of the individual being related to or living with the adult should be taken into account but should not by themselves prevent the individual becoming a guardian.

Clause 45(2)-(4)

Joint guardianship

6.71   By joint guardianship we mean two or more guardians being appointed with the same powers to act jointly. Two or more guardians each of whom has been appointed with different and non-overlapping powers would not constitute joint guardianship because each guardian would be solely responsible for exercising the powers conferred on him or her. In our discussion paper we proposed that it should be competent to appoint joint personal guardians[2] and joint financial managers[3]. Guardians under the 1984 Act are invariably a single individual, but it is common to appoint joint tutors-dative. Joint curators, while not incompetent[4], are unknown in current practice.

6.72   All but two of those responding were in favour of joint appointees. The Accountant of Court considered that joint financial managers would lead to delays in decision-making and difficulties in accountability. It would also defeat the purpose of bringing the financial manager into a close relationship with the incapable adult. However, the Accountant thought that a joint appointment might be acceptable in the case of the parents of an incapable adult. The other respondent, a solicitor who frequently acts as curator, gave no reasons for her opposition to joint appointments. We accept that joint guardianship might lead to difficulties in accountability in that each guardian might tend to blame the other for any failure. We discuss the liability of joint guardians later. We are not sure that delays in decision-making would be significant since if the other guardian were not a joint guardian he or she would probably have to be consulted or would wish to offer views to the guardian anyway. Moreover, we recommend later[5] that joint guardians should be able to agree between themselves that consulting each other would be unnecessary in relation to certain matters. We do not think that the existence of another joint guardian who is less close to the adult would lessen the first guardian's relationship with the adult. We

---

1. Recommendation 94, para 6.60.
2. Proposal 6(b), para 2.69.
3. Proposal 31(3), para 4.49.
4. *Kirk* (1836) 14 S 814.
5. Recommendation 99, para 6.78.

imagine that in many cases the joint guardians will be equally close such as two children for an aged parent or both parents for their grown up child.

6.73   We do not consider that joint guardianship should be the norm in the same way as it is customary to appoint more than one executor. Later in this report we recommend the introduction of a simple procedure whereby the court may replace a guardian who has died or wishes to resign. The existence of this procedure would make it less necessary to appoint joint guardians to guard against death or resignation. We consider that joint guardianship should generally be confined to close relatives; parents, children or siblings. The sheriff should also be able to appoint joint guardians in other cases but should have to be satisfied that there was a need for such an appointment. We therefore recommend that:

96.   It should be competent to appoint two or more individuals to act as joint guardians. Except in the case of the parents, siblings or children of the adult the sheriff should have to be satisfied there was a need for joint guardianship.

Clause 47(1)(a), (2)

6.74   Where a single guardian was appointed by the court but joint guardianship is desired at a later stage we consider that it should be possible to appoint an additional guardian. We think this should be done by the court using a simple procedure. The application for appointment of an additional guardian would have to be notified to those concerned such as the adult, the existing guardian, the primary carer and the nearest relative and those people would have to be given an opportunity to object. The sheriff would also have to be satisfied that the additional guardian was suitable using the same criteria that we have recommended[1] for appointing a guardian initially. We recommend that:

97.   The sheriff should be empowered to appoint a suitable individual to be an additional guardian to act jointly along with an existing guardian or guardians.

Clause 47(1)(b), (2), (4)

6.75   If two or more guardians are appointed to act jointly should all of them have to participate in every decision and sign every document, or should each guardian have power to act independently? As we pointed out in our discussion paper there are analogies for either approach. Where there are two trustees or executors both must join in any transaction[2], but parents who are exercising parental rights in relation to their children may act independently unless the court orders otherwise[3]. Provisionally in our discussion paper we favoured each personal guardian or financial manager being entitled to act independently and proposed that any third party should be entitled to rely on a consent, approval or decision by any one appointee[4]. There was general agreement on consultation and we would adhere to our proposals. Requiring all guardians to join in any transaction creates difficulties where prompt action is required. The Keeper of the Registers of Scotland commented that our proposal did not go far enough. A provision was required entitling any third party including the Keeper to rely on the actings of any one or more of the joint guardians. We recommend that:

98.   Each joint guardian should be entitled to act independently and there should not be a requirement that any action has to be taken by all the joint guardians. A third party in good faith should be entitled to rely on an act or decision by one joint guardian.

Clause 47(6), (8)

6.76   In our discussion paper we suggested that joint guardians should be required to consult amongst themselves except in an emergency[5]. The Sheriffs' Association commented that some definition of emergency was required as otherwise one guardian might act unilaterally so abusing the rights of the other. We remain in favour of consultation generally but there will be circumstances where consultation is not possible. We have reconsidered the concept of emergency. Emergency connotes a situation where a decision is required immediately. But there may be decisions that while not immediate are still needed quickly, but consultation is not practicable within the time available. Also "emergency" strikes the wrong note in relation to financial matters. Shares might have to be sold quickly but that would not be regarded as an emergency by many people. We prefer to use the notion of impracticable in the circumstances.

6.77   We consider that joint guardians should be able to agree between themselves that consultation is not necessary. For example, a son and a daughter who are joint guardians of their mother might agree that the daughter would be responsible for all routine financial matters while the son who lived near his mother would take routine decisions relating to her personal welfare.

6.78   We recommend that:

---

1. Recommendation 95, para 6.70.
2. Trusts (Scotland) Act 1921, s 3.
3. Law Reform (Parent and Child) (Scotland) Act 1986, s 2(4); to be replaced by s 2(2) of the Children (Scotland) Act 1995.
4   Proposals 6(b) and 31(3), paras 2.69 and 4.49 respectively.
5. Proposal 6(b), para 2.69 (personal guardian); Proposal 31(3), para 4.49 (financial manager).

99. One joint guardian should be under a duty to consult the other(s) before exercising any guardianship powers, except where they agree that consultation should not take place. Consultation should also not have to take place if it is impracticable in the circumstances.

Clause 47(7)

Substitute guardianship

6.79   In our discussion paper[1] we put forward the idea of an alternate guardian - a guardian who would take over on the death or resignation of the primary guardian without the need for any further application to the court. Alternate guardianship exists in Alberta and Victoria. Joint guardians could also be used to achieve a succession since the remaining joint guardian acts on the death or resignation of the other guardian[2], but the primary guardian may not wish to share the duties while he or she is capable of performing them. We now prefer the term substitute guardian as alternate suggests that guardianship may switch to and fro between the original guardian and the other. Substitute guardianship deals with the problem of succession by enabling the court to appoint a successor in advance of the event. We proposed that on the death, incapacity, removal or resignation of the guardian the substitute should become personal guardian without further procedure. The powers enjoyed by the substitute guardian would be exactly the same as those conferred on the primary guardian. We also proposed substitute financial managers in the same terms[3].

6.80   All those responding to these proposals were in favour of substitute guardianship, but some practical concerns were raised. The Accountant of Court queried how any third party would know that the event which triggers the replacement of the primary guardian by the substitute had occurred. The answer lies in the register of guardians to be kept by the Public Guardian. On the occurrence of the triggering event the substitute guardian should present to the Public Guardian documentary evidence of it, such as a certificate of the death of the primary guardian. The Public Guardian would thereafter amend the register to show that the substitute guardian was now the guardian and would issue him or her with a certificate of authority. The procedure would be an entirely administrative one.

6.81   The Law Society thought that careful definition was necessary of the "triggering" events which would lead to the substitute becoming guardian. Death or removal of the primary guardian by the court require no further definition. We deal with the procedure for resignation of guardians at paragraph 6.205. Provided resignation was in accordance with the procedure it should be effective to trigger substitute guardianship. Incapacity of the primary guardian should also be a triggering event, the substitute having to present a medical certificate of incapacity. A somewhat analogous procedure exists at present whereby a curator may be discharged by the Accountant of Court on presentation of medical evidence of the ward's recovery[4].

6.82   Alzheimer Scotland - Action on Dementia and Enable both suggested that a substitute guardian should be able to act during the temporary absence of the primary guardian. We are not in favour of this as it would involve issuing and cancelling certificates of authority and amending the register of guardians twice. It would be simpler for the primary guardian to delegate his or her powers to the substitute as an individual during any temporary absence. A signed statement of delegation would be all that was necessary should documentation be required.

6.83   One respondent suggested that the substitute guardian should be entitled to act if an emergency arose and the primary guardian was unavailable. While we see the usefulness of such provision we think it would be difficult to define what constituted an emergency and to demonstrate to third parties that there was an emergency which enabled them to accept the authority of the substitute. In our opinion emergencies are best dealt with by way of joint guardianship since any one joint guardian's authority may be relied on by a third party[5].

6.84   Two helpful observations came from the Association of Directors of Social Work which we are happy to accept. First, that the court before appointing an individual as substitute guardian should have to be satisfied that he or she is suitable. We agree since there is no subsequent procedure at which suitability could appropriately be considered. Secondly, that the local authority could be the substitute guardian. We have previously recommended[6] that "local authority" guardianship should be entrusted to the chief social work officer as an office holder and would adopt the same approach for substitutes. We would also extend this idea to allowing the Public Guardian to be appointed substitute guardian where only financial powers were involved.

6.85   We see no reason to confine the appointment of substitute guardians to the initial consideration of guardianship

---

1.   Proposal 6(c), para 2.69.
2..   Joint tutory has been used for this purpose. In *Buchanan Petr* 1989 a much younger family friend was appointed along with the adult's mother.
3.   Proposal 31(4), para 4.49.
4.   Judicial Factors Rules 1992, rule 19.
5.   See Recommendation 98, para 6.75.
6.   Recommendation 94, para 6.60.

by the court. It should be competent to apply at any time afterwards to add a substitute. Suppose, for example, the initial guardian died and the substitute took over. It could be useful to appoint yet another substitute to guard against the death or resignation of the first substitute who was now guardian.

6.86   Being appointed substitute guardian would not bind the person to take up the duties when the triggering event occurred. Circumstances may have changed or the substitute may no longer feel up to the task. The substitute guardian should simply notify the Public Guardian in writing that he or she is not willing to take up the appointment when the triggering event occurs.

6.87   Summing up this section on substitute guardianship we recommend that:

100. (1)   In order to provide for the continuation of guardianship without having to re-apply to the court should the acting guardian die, resign, became mentally incapable or be removed it should be competent for the court at any time to appoint a substitute guardian who would become guardian (if willing) when such an event occurred.

(2)   The substitute guardian may be an individual, the chief social work officer of a local authority if the guardianship powers include powers in the personal welfare field or the Public Guardian if purely financial powers are involved. Before appointing an individual as substitute the court would have to be satisfied that he or she was suitable in terms of Recommendation 95.

(3)   On the acting guardian's death, resignation, removal or mental incapacity the Public Guardian, after receiving documentary evidence of its occurrence, should amend the register of guardians and issue the substitute guardian with a certificate of authority.

Clause 48

Powers conferrable on guardians

6.88   In our discussion paper we proposed that it should be competent for personal guardians[1] and financial managers[2] to be appointed with powers limited in some way. This partial guardianship would represent the least restrictive option where the incapable adult was able to make some welfare or financial decisions. As we noted in our discussion paper it is a criticism of the current curatory system that it is all or nothing and that there is no possibility of partial management. Our proposed partial guardianship was welcomed in both the welfare and financial field. The Accountant of Court and a Glasgow solicitor experienced in curatories considered that partial guardianship could give rise to more legal proceedings if the adult's situation worsened or something unforeseen arose which was not within the scope of the powers conferred. The Accountant suggested that he should be given power to vary the powers previously conferred on the guardian by the court. We disagree; increasing the powers of a guardian ought to be a judicial act, not one that should be dealt with administratively. Article 6 of the European Convention on Human Rights requires that any determination of civil rights and obligations be carried out by an independent and impartial tribunal established by law with a fair and public hearing. We consider that an application for the increase in the powers of an already appointed guardian could be dealt with expeditiously in the courts by way of a minute in the existing process. Where it is clear that the adult's mental faculties are declining the court in setting the powers could anticipate the decline by granting the guardian powers needed then and in the near future.

6.89   The Committee of Scottish Clearing Bankers supported partial guardianship provided that third parties dealing with partial guardians could be certain as to the boundaries of their authority. It would have to be made clear whether any particular asset or account could be dealt with by the adult or whether the guardian had to be involved. The certificate of authority which we recommend that the Public Guardian should issue to guardians would detail the powers as set out in the court's interlocutor. Those applying for guardianship powers should frame them in such a way that third parties are certain of the scope of the guardian's authority.

6.90   In our discussion paper we considered how the powers that might be conferred on personal guardians[3] or financial managers[4] should be expressed. One approach is to have a statutory list of powers from which the court would select those which are required in a particular case. Another approach is to empower the court to confer whatever powers are appropriate without any statutory formulation of them. The existing legislation in Australia, Canada and New Zealand contains examples of both approaches. We pointed out that a statutory list helps applicants and the courts draw up appropriate orders, avoids diversity in the wording of powers and inadvertent omission of necessary powers. On the other hand it is virtually impossible to list all the powers that might be required, particularly in the financial field. A statutory list would be rigid and difficult to vary in the light of experience. Courts would also be reluctant to grant powers outwith

---

1.   Proposal 8, para 2.80.
2.   Proposal 34, para 4.63.
3.   Paras 2.72 to 2.80.
4.   Paras 4.92 to 4.94.

the statutory list unless they were expressly empowered to do so. For these reasons we preferred the second approach of simply empowering the courts to grant appropriate powers to guardians. However, we considered it would be helpful if styles of powers likely to be frequently used were to be drawn up by the appropriate authorities after consultation with the courts, lawyers and others interested in the welfare of the incapacitated. The styles would be for guidance only and their use would not be obligatory. Nevertheless the existence of the styles would achieve some measure of uniformity.

6.91   The Law Society, Alzheimer Scotland - Action on Dementia and the Scottish Association for Mental Health supported our "styles for guidance" approach. The Law Society commented that the powers currently being sought for tutors-dative are derived from the list in the Albertan legislation but that they are being modified and developed in the light of experience. This comment reinforces our view that a statutory list of powers would not be a sensible approach in what will be a new and probably fast developing field. One respondent thought that practitioners might use styles unthinkingly. We agree that such a danger exists but it is less likely to occur with styles in a guidance document than with styles set out in primary or subordinate legislation. The styles might, we think, be set out in a code of practice to be prepared by the Secretary of State and published after consultation with interested organisations.

6.92   Partial guardianship may take the form of specific powers to deal with particular matters or items of property such as deciding where the adult is to live or managing the upkeep and repairs of the adult's dwelling-house. Another form of partial guardianship might focus on a particular area specified in the order of appointment and grant general powers to deal with everything within that area. Thus a guardian could be given powers to manage the adult's investments, leaving the adult free to manage his or her own income.

6.93   We recommend that:

101. (1)   The court should be empowered to grant a guardian such powers as are appropriate in the circumstances and consistent with the least restrictive approach. The powers conferred may be powers in relation to specified matters or a general power to deal with or manage specified aspects of the adult's personal welfare or financial affairs.

(2)   A code of practice should be issued by the Secretary of State containing styles of powers in the welfare and financial fields that might be conferred on guardians. The styles should be for guidance only and their use should not be mandatory.

Clauses 10(1)(c) and 49(1)

6.94   In our discussion paper we suggested that a full personal guardian should have the same powers over an incapable adult as parents have in respect of their pupil children[1]. Use of such a formula was not found attractive by those responding as it perpetuates the notion that the incapable are the same as children and should be treated in the same way. Furthermore, expressing guardianship powers by reference to parental powers over pupils is no longer possible because the status of pupillarity has been abolished since our discussion paper was published. The capacity of children under 16 and consequently parental rights in relation to them now depend to a large extent on the child's level of understanding and what transactions are currently entered into by children of similar age and in similar circumstances[2]. Some of those responding favoured full guardians being appointed with all the powers on a list of powers, but we do not think it is possible to draw up such a list. Any list of powers, however extensive, would always be incomplete in that powers that might be needed in some cases would have been omitted. In our view the only sensible approach, where limited or partial guardianship is not sufficient, is to empower the courts to confer power on guardians to deal with or manage all aspects of the adult's personal welfare or financial affairs. Existing statute common law and the specific limitations that we recommend later would limit such apparently all embracing authority. We recommend that:

102.   The court in appointing a guardian should be empowered to confer a general power to deal with all aspects of the incapable adult's personal welfare or to manage all aspects of the adult's financial affairs. This power would be subject to the limitations contained in any enactment or rule of law or set out in Recommendation 103.

Clause 49(1)

6.95   In our discussion paper we considered that guardians should not have certain powers. We proposed[3] that it should not be competent for a personal guardian to be granted power to make any decision relating to the adult's marriage or adoption of his or her children or to inflict corporal punishment upon the adult. In the financial field we proposed[4] that a financial manager should not have power to make or alter the adult's will, create a trust on his or her behalf or exercise any powers the adult possessed as executor or trustee.

---

1.   Proposal 8(1)(c), para 2.80.
2.   Age of Legal Capacity (Scotland) Act 1991.
3.   Proposal 8(3), para 2.80.
4.   Proposal 40(4), para 4.96.

H

6.96   All but one of those responding agreed with our proposed restrictions on the powers of personal guardians. Some respondents suggested additional restrictions which we deal with in paragraph 6.97 below. One respondent mentioned the case of his son who had received severe brain injuries. The son's wife had left him and was living with another man. The parents who were looking after the son thought that it should be possible for a guardian or some other person to bring divorce proceedings on the son's behalf. The purpose of the divorce would be to prevent the wife continuing to enjoy that status and also to cut off her succession rights to the son's estate which might by the time of his death have been augmented by his parents' estates. At present a divorce action cannot be brought on an incapacitated adult's behalf by a curator bonis nor will the court appoint a curator *ad litem* to act. It is possible that a tutor-dative could bring an action since tutors have powers over the personal affairs[1]. Where a defender is suffering from mental disorder the court will appoint a curator *ad litem* and the curator may defend or let the action proceed as undefended[2]. It could be argued that marriage is so personal a matter that actions by representatives should not be allowed, but it seems somewhat odd that representatives can defend but perhaps not pursue. Cases can be imagined where it would benefit an incapable disabled adult for a divorce action to be brought on his or her behalf, for example, where money which would be awarded by way of financial provision on divorce was needed to improve the adult's standard of living. On the other hand there will be cases where, from the point of view of the adult, there is no justification for bringing a divorce action. In our opinion the range of possible circumstances points to the court having a discretion rather than having an absolute rule either forbidding or allowing guardians to institute divorce actions. We consider that the power to bring an action of divorce should have to be expressly applied for and granted and should not be implied from some other general power.

6.97   Consent to marriage must be given personally and cannot be given by a representative. There should be no change in this respect, but we do not think it necessary for the legislation to contain an express prohibition as the principle of personal consent is firmly embedded in the existing law. Parental agreement to the adoption of children and dispensing with such agreement in appropriate circumstances is regulated by the Adoption (Scotland) Act 1978. Section 16(2)(a) empowers the court to dispense with the agreement of a parent who is incapable of giving agreement. In the light of this specific provision we see no need to expressly prohibit a guardian from obtaining powers in relation to adoption. It was suggested to us by some respondents that the guardian should not be able to vote on behalf of an incapable adult. The Representation of the People Acts contain distinct provisions about voting by persons of doubtful mental capacity so that provisions prohibiting guardians from voting on behalf of incapable adults are unnecessary. Our decision not to describe the powers of a full guardian by reference to the powers of the parents over their pupil children[3] makes it unnecessary to have an express prohibition relating to corporal punishment by guardians.

6.98   For certain treatments for mental disorder set out in Part X of the Mental Health (Scotland) Act 1984 the consent of a detained patient is required. These treatments are psychosurgery, implantation of hormones to reduce male sex drive, electro-convulsive therapy (ECT) and medication after it has been given for three months. For the last two treatments the patient's lack of consent can be overridden if a second opinion is obtained that the treatment should be given. We do not consider that these protective provisions should be circumvented by obtaining a consent from the guardian. In Part 5 of this report we recommend that psychosurgery[4] and hormone implantation[5] for incapable patients should require prior approval from the sheriff and that ECT and medication for more than three months[6] should require a second opinion whether or not the patient was detained. We also recommend that certain other medical treatments such as sterilisation of incapable adults should require prior authorisation by the sheriff[7] and others (abortion for example) should require an independent second opinion in favour of the treatment[8]. While guardians should be permitted to make representations about such treatments to the court or to the second opinion doctors concerned we consider that they should not have power to authorise them by giving their consent. We also recommend that doctors should not be authorised to use force against their patients except if it is urgently necessary for the avoidance of serious harm to the patient[9]. Again this protective measure should not be side-stepped by the guardian consenting. For other "ordinary" treatments a guardian would be required to consent on behalf of the adult if relevant powers had been conferred. A refusal to consent should be capable of being overridden by obtaining a second opinion that the treatment is appropriate and should be given[10].

6.99   A guardian who has been granted power to decide where an incapable adult is to live could use it to place the adult in a mental hospital. Guardianship under the 1984 Act has been used for such a purpose, but this has been adversely

---

1. Fraser, *Husband and Wife*, p 1145 leaves this open and in *Thomson* (1887) 14R 634 counsel for pursuer and defender in an action of separation brought on behalf of an insane wife both agreed that a tutor-dative could competently have brought the action.
2. Ordinary Cause Rules 1993, rule 33.16.
3. See para 6.94.
4. Recommendation 62, para 5.28.
5. Recommendation 63, para 5.30.
6. Recommendation 60, para 5.25.
7. Recommendation 59, para 5.24.
8. Recommendation 61, para 5.26.
9. Recommendation 64, para 5.32.
10. Recommendation 66, para 5.39.

commented upon by the Mental Welfare Commission[1]. We recommend earlier that an attorney should not be entitled to exercise any welfare powers so as to place the granter in hospital for treatment of mental disorder against his or her will[2]. Where some measure of compulsion is needed we consider that the detention provisions in the 1984 Act should be used and the welfare attorney should have the same powers as the nearest relative has in relation to detention. We would adopt the same approach for guardians. Thus a guardian with appropriate powers could apply for the adult's admission to and detention in hospital, require a mental health officer to consider the case for admission, consent to an emergency admission and initiate discharge proceedings. We would stress that any action by the guardian would not in itself result in detention. Further action by doctors, mental health officers or the courts would also be required. Our prohibition against removal of the adult to hospital against his or her will should apply only to removal for the purpose of treating mental disorder. Guardians should be entitled to place adults under their guardianship in hospital for assessment and treatment of physical disorders and also in emergencies. Temporary placement in order to give their carers a break ("respite care") also seems an appropriate use of the power to decide where the adult is to live.

6.100   We recommend that:

103. (1) The existing legislation or common law whereby entering into a marriage, agreeing to the adoption of one's children, or consenting to any of the treatments in Part X of the Mental Health (Scotland) Act 1984 can be done only by the individual in question should be retained. Accordingly it should not be competent for a guardian to consent or agree on behalf of an incapable adult in any of these matters.

(2) It should be competent for a guardian to be granted power to bring or defend an action of divorce or separation on behalf of the adult but such power should have to be expressly conferred.

(3) A guardian should not be entitled to place the adult in a hospital for treatment of mental disorder against his or her will. However, a guardian should, if appropriate powers have been conferred, have the same rights in relation to detention as the adult's nearest relative has under the Mental Health (Scotland) Act 1984.

(4) Guardians should not be entitled to use their powers to consent to medical treatment so as to circumvent the protective provisions we recommend in Part 5, whereby certain treatments require prior authorisation from the court or a second opinion and doctors should not be entitled to use force except to protect patients from serious harm.

Clause 49(1)(c) and (2) and Schedule 4, paragraph 15

6.101   Some of those responding to our proposals for personal guardianship mentioned that volunteers advocating for or representing incapable adults would be in a stronger position if they had formal powers. Third parties, particularly professionals, it was said, tended not to take informal arrangements seriously. There was also felt to be a need for people who would be representatives and advisers rather than decision-makers. We have given these suggestions careful consideration, but have come to the conclusion that guardianship should not be used simply to appoint representatives or people to speak on behalf of incapable adults. Guardianship applications involve medical and other reports and a certain amount of court time and require too complex a procedure for this limited purpose. If guardianship were available for this purpose the effect might be to force all informal advocates and representatives to take formal legal proceedings. There would be a danger that third parties would take even less notice than they do now of those advocates or representatives who had no formal powers if machinery for obtaining formal powers came into existence. However, where a guardian has been appointed to deal with or manage certain aspects of the adult's welfare or finances the guardian will under our recommendations also enjoy powers to represent the adult in relation to matters within the scope of his or her authority[3].

6.102   Enable pointed out that where people have partial capacity it is unrealistic to expect that they will be able to take full responsibility for certain decisions but no responsibility for others. In fact their ability to take all decisions will be impaired to a greater or lesser extent. The organisation suggested that it should be possible to appoint a guardian to assist such people to make decisions, rather than the guardian making them. Quebec has a similar system of people called advisers[4]. They are appointed to adults who are generally able to manage their finances but require advice and assistance in the administration of their property. The adviser may be appointed on a temporary basis or in relation to certain transactions. The court in appointing an adviser may specify which transactions require assistance by the adviser. Otherwise all transactions beyond simple administration require assistance. Transactions where the adviser should have been involved but was not may be annulled "if the acts entail lesion".

6.103   We were initially attracted by Enable's suggestion as it seemed to fit in with our principle that any action should be the least restrictive of an adult's rights and freedoms. An adviser would be more of a partner to the adult than a guardian.

1. *Annual Report* 1986, para 9.5.
2. Recommendation 23, para 3.48.
3. Recommendation 112, para 6.136.
4. An Act respecting the Public Curator and amending the Civil Code and other legislative provisions, S.Q. 1989 c 54.

Although he or she could veto actions of the adult he or she could not act independently and take decisions overruling those of the adult. Consideration of the possible grounds for appointing an adviser have led us to think that advisers should not be introduced as well as intervention orders and guardianship.

6.104   The guardianship and intervention orders we recommend assume that the adult in question lacks capacity, this lack of capacity justifying some decision being made or action carried out by the court or some other person on the adult's behalf. In contrast the assumption behind advisership is that the adult has capacity albeit impaired capacity. The least restrictive option principle suggests that no intervention should occur so that the adult remains free, like others who find some aspects of their finances beyond them, to seek informal advice or assistance or to appoint someone else to act on a more formal and permanent basis. Legislation is not needed to enable advice and assistance to be provided. Legislation would be needed to provide a form of veto but such provisions would be restrictive rather than enabling. Moreover, we think it would be difficult in practice to distinguish between those who have sufficient capacity for any intervention to be unwarranted, those who had impaired capacity justifying the appointment of an adviser and those who had sufficient incapacity to justify the making of an intervention order or the appointment of a guardian. Finally, instituting a third category of advisers would lead to yet more complicated legislation. We therefore do not recommend any statutory system of advisers.

6.105   Returning to the financial aspects of guardianship, we proposed in our discussion paper[1] that financial managers should not have power to make or vary a will on behalf of incapable adults, to create trusts on their behalf or to exercise any functions the adult might have as a trustee or executor. Those responding were generally in agreement with our proposals. One organisation involved with the mentally handicapped thought that giving the court power to make a will should not be ruled out as there would be potential benefits. There are, however, objections in principle to allowing one person to make a will for another and, in the absence of any widespread support for change[2], we think the law should remain as it is. At present neither a curator nor a court can make or vary a will for an incapable adult.

6.106   One organisation thought that there might be cases where it should be competent for the court or guardian to create a trust on behalf of the adult. Our prohibition was intended to strike at a trust containing testamentary provisions or a trust where the guardian handed over responsibility for the funds under his or her management to trustees. The first type of trust would be tantamount to a will and should be prohibited for the reasons set out in the previous paragraph. Under the present law a curator or other judicial factor appointed by the court is not permitted to divest himself or herself of the responsibility by handing over the funds to trustees and we think the same approach should be adopted for guardians. Where the guardian transferred part of the adult's estate to trustees to hold for the benefit of a third party this would be a donation which we discuss in paragraph 6.109 below.

6.107   Two solicitors pointed out that our proposal to prohibit the guardian exercising any functions the adult possessed as trustee or executor might leave no-one to act in the trust or executory. We have considered whether the guardian or the court appointing the guardian should be given power to nominate a replacement but have decided against it. The role of guardians is to manage the adults' financial affairs and they should not get involved with the administration of third parties' affairs. Replacement of the adult by a new trustee or executor is best left to existing procedures which should be pursued separately from guardianship applications. It would be difficult to combine an application for the appointment of a guardian with an application for a replacement trustee or executor as the parties would not be the same and the purpose of the applications would be different.

6.108   We therefore make no recommendation on the matters covered in the three preceding paragraphs. We do not consider that express provisions are required in our guardianship legislation to achieve the required results. Exercising testamentary powers or acting as trustee or executor are matters that are personal to the individual in question. They are functions which, under the general law, could not be exercised by a legal representative.

Gifts by guardian

6.109   The making of gifts out of an incapable adult's estate involves the curator seeking special powers from the court. It is not part of the usual administration powers of a curator nor has the Accountant of Court authority to consent to it using the procedure in section 2 of the Trusts (Scotland) Act 1961[3]. Special powers have been granted to authorise continued donations to charities the adult supported in the past[4] and payments for the maintenance of relatives whom the adult is not legally obliged to support[5]. The starting point should be that a guardian has no implied power to make any gift out of the adult's estate but may be authorised to do so. Comments have been made to us that curators cannot make birthday or Christmas gifts to members of the family and that an application for special powers is not worthwhile in view

---

1. Proposal 40(4), para 4.96.
2. See also our *Report on Succession*, Scot Law Com No 124 (1990), paras 4.78 to 4.80.
3. Added by the Law Reform (Miscellaneous Provisions) (Scotland) Act 1980, s 8.
4. *M's CB* (1904) 12 SLT 30.
5. *Hamilton's Tutors* 1924 SC 364 (a case involving tutors of a pupil but the principle applies to curators).

of the modest sums involved. The continuance of family gifts may be seen as benefiting the incapable adult by maintaining the family good will. We consider that authorisation of gifts is something that could safely be delegated to the Public Guardian. This power should be restricted to modest gifts. Large gifts for such purposes as avoiding inheritance tax that would otherwise be payable on the adult's death could not be regarded as for the benefit of the adult and should not be allowed. Such large gifts could materially alter the succession to the adult's estate. In our *Report on Succession* we recommended against allowing the court or the curator to make a will on behalf of an incapable adult since those consulted were overwhelmingly opposed[1].

6.110   The guardian should have to apply to the Public Guardian for authority to make a gift. The Public Guardian should then intimate the application to the incapable adult and his or her nearest relative and primary carer giving them an opportunity to object and make representations. The Public Guardian should not refuse the application without giving the guardian an opportunity to make representations nor should the application be granted without affording similar facilities to any objectors. The Public Guardian should be able to remit difficult cases to the sheriff either on his or her own initiative or on request by an objector. In considering whether to authorise a gift the Public Guardian would be bound by the general principles already recommended. He or she would be bound to consider whether the gift would benefit the adult indirectly (for example, by giving the adult a feeling of pleasure or by helping to maintain family goodwill). The benefit criterion would also require consideration to be given to the value of the gift, the size of the incapable adult's estate or income and the needs of the adult. The other general principles would require the Public Guardian to take account of the present and past wishes of the adult so far as they can be ascertained and, so far as reasonable and practicable, of the views of the guardian, primary carer, nearest relative and certain others[2]. We recommend that:

> **104.   The Public Guardian should, on application by the guardian, be empowered to authorise the guardian to make gifts out of the incapable adult's estate. The Public Guardian should give the adult and his or her nearest relative and primary carer an opportunity to object, but should be entitled to grant the application after considering objections and further representations by the guardian or objectors or to remit the application to the sheriff.**
>
> Clause 50(1) to (5)

Giving effect to a guardian's welfare decisions

6.111   Where a guardian has welfare powers in relation to an incapable adult the adult may refuse to comply with a decision of the guardian. For example, the adult may abscond from the place of residence selected by the guardian or refuse to go there. Some procedure is necessary to ensure that effect is given to the guardian's decisions where it is appropriate to do so. In the above example, the guardian (or some person authorised by the guardian) should be entitled to take or return the adult to the place where he or she is supposed to be. However, we consider that neither the guardian nor the authorised person should be entitled to use or threaten to use force. Such a substantial encroachment on personal autonomy should require a warrant from the sheriff granted only after the guardian has satisfied the sheriff that in all the circumstances a warrant is necessary. The warrant should authorise a police officer to take the adult to a place as directed by the guardian and to enter premises in order to carry out this duty. Reasonable force may be used to achieve entry or removal and conveyance of the adult. Section 117 of the 1984 Act sets out a somewhat similar procedure for removal to a place of safety of a mentally disordered adult who is being ill-treated or is unable to care for himself or herself.

6.112   Third parties may also refuse to give effect to a guardian's decision in welfare matters. We consider that in such circumstances the guardian should be entitled to apply to the sheriff for an order directing the third party to implement or comply with the guardian's decision. An opportunity should be given to the third party to make representations before the order is granted. In terms of the general principles the sheriff would have to be satisfied that to do so would benefit the adult and was the only reasonable way of achieving that benefit. The sheriff should also have to be satisfied that compliance by the third party was both possible and appropriate. Failure to obey the sheriff's order would be contempt of court.

6.113   We recommend that:

> **105. (1) Where the adult under guardianship refuses to go to or return to a place of residence selected by the guardian the guardian should be entitled to apply to the sheriff for a warrant authorising a police officer to apprehend and convey the adult to that place. The police officer should have power under the warrant to enter premises and to use reasonable force in executing the warrant.**
>
> **(2) Where any person refuses to comply with or implement a lawful decision of the guardian in relation to the adult's personal welfare the guardian should be entitled to apply to the sheriff for an order directing that person to do so. Rules of Court should be made giving the person an opportunity to make representations before the order is granted.**
>
> Clause 55

---

1.   Scot Law Com No 124 (1990), para 4.80.
2.   Recommendation 14, para 2.73.

Supervision of guardians

6.114   In our discussion paper we looked at whether personal guardians and financial managers should be supervised and if so which was the appropriate body to carry out the task. We proposed that personal guardians should be supervised by the Mental Welfare Commission[1] and financial managers by the Accountant of Court[2].

6.115   Mental health guardians (but not tutors-dative) are monitored by the Mental Welfare Commission. Appointments of mental health guardians are reported to the Commission which arranges for the person subject to guardianship to be visited by someone from the Commission. The local authority also exercises general supervision via its social work department. It is under a duty to visit those subject to guardianship at least once every three months and where the guardian is not the local authority or one of its officials may call for reports and request information from the guardian[3]. We proposed the Mental Welfare Commission as the single supervisory authority because a local authority would have a conflict of interest in supervising its own officials when they acted as guardians.

6.116   All those who responded were in favour of personal guardians being supervised. Supervision is we think essential because those subject to guardianship are unlikely to be capable of taking the necessary action to deal with their guardians' deficiencies themselves. Supervision also has a vital role to play in reassuring the public that statutory powers to intervene in other people's lives are being used properly. While some respondents agreed with our proposal that the Mental Welfare Commission should be the supervisory authority others preferred that the present system of dual supervision by the Commission and local authorities in relation to guardians under the 1984 Act should continue. Making the Commission the sole authority might, depending on the number of guardians with welfare powers appointed, involve a large increase in staff to carry out the supervisory functions. Doubts were expressed as to whether adequate resources would be provided for the Commission's expanded role. Others saw positive benefit in guardians being supervised locally by people from the local authority social work department as well as by the Mental Welfare Commission. On reconsideration we think that the existing "dual control" system should be retained as it appears to work satisfactorily. Although there is an inherent conflict of interest where the local authority supervises its own guardians, in practice the guardianship functions are entrusted to a social worker who is supervised by senior people in the social work department.

6.117   The Secretary of State has power under section 43 of the 1984 Act to make regulations relating to the exercise of their functions by guardians and imposing duties on guardians and local authorities. The current regulations, the Mental Health (Specified Treatments, Guardianship Duties etc.) (Scotland) Regulations 1984[4], require the local authority among other things to visit persons subject to guardianship at least once every three months. A similar rule-making power is necessary in relation to our recommended new guardians who possess personal welfare powers. These rules should also be complemented by a Code of Practice dealing with the functions of guardians and local authorities respectively. The Mental Welfare Commission has a duty under section 3(2)(b) of the 1984 Act to visit those subject to guardianship under that Act. This should continue in relation to our new guardianship but only where the guardian had welfare powers in relation to the adult.

6.118   We recommend that:

106. Guardians should be supervised in the exercise of their welfare powers by the local authority in accordance with regulations made by the Secretary of State. The Mental Welfare Commission should have a monitoring role similar to that which it has in relation to guardians appointed under the Mental Health (Scotland) Act 1984. A Code of Practice giving guidance to local authorities and guardians should also be prepared and published.

Clauses 8(1)(a), (2)(a), 10(1)(a), (c) and Schedule 4, paragraph 15(1), (2)

6.119   A guardian should be under a duty to comply with any order or demand made by the local authority in the exercise of its supervisory functions. Sanctions are needed for failure to comply. The local authority could, under our recommendations, be entitled to apply to the court for removal of the guardian. This may be too drastic a remedy and we consider that it would be useful if the local authority could obtain judicial backing for its demands by applying to the court for an order addressed to the guardian in the same terms as the local authority's order. Failure to obey the court order would lay the guardian open to the penalties for contempt of court. We recommend that:

107. Guardians should be under a statutory duty to comply with any order made by the local authority in the exercise of its supervisory powers. Where the guardian fails to obey the local authority order then, without prejudice to any other course of action, the local authority should be entitled to apply to the court for an order in similar terms.

Clause 49(7)(a)

---

1. Proposal 12, para 2.90.
2. Proposal 43, para 4.119.
3. See para 6.117 below.
4. SI 1984/1494.

6.120   There was general agreement with our proposal[1] that financial managers should be supervised by the Accountant of Court, now to be the Public Guardian. This is the current position under the Judicial Factors Act 1849 in relation to curators bonis, tutors with financial powers and other judicial factors. It seems sensible to build on the existing expertise in the Accountant's office. Supervision is no doubt irksome and increases the cost of administration, but it is necessary for maintaining confidence in a system of involuntary management of the estates of the incapacitated. Some of those responding saw a role for the Mental Welfare Commission. Our proposal was not intended to deprive the Commission of its existing functions in this area which are of an investigative and general nature. However we do not think that the Mental Welfare Commission should become involved with detailed supervision of guardians in the exercise of their financial powers. The Accountant and the Commission liaise with each other at present and we recommend later[2] that they should continue to do so.

6.121   In our discussion paper we also asked for views as to how supervision by the Accountant of Court could be more flexible or less burdensome especially in relation to small or modest estates. Many of those responding suggested that the Accountant should be concerned only with the general way in which an adults' affairs were managed and that the present annual accounting requirement should be relaxed, with simpler or less frequent accounts in appropriate cases. The former Accountant himself suggested that a management scheme be agreed in the light of the guardian's financial powers and the adult's needs and estate soon after the appointment of the guardian by the court. The Accountant or the court would then need to be approached only for truly exceptional expenditure. We have found all of these suggestions, especially the management scheme, very helpful and have adopted them. We discuss the "management scheme" or, as we term it, the "management plan" in paragraph 6.161 below.

6.122   The National Schizophrenia Fellowship said that making all managers subject to the supervision of the Accountant of Court would seem to embrace many of the disadvantages of a curatory. It suggested that supervision should be by independent professionals such as solicitors or accountants. In our opinion supervision in the public interest ought to be carried out by some accountable public official or body. Moreover, we think it is possible that solicitors or accountants would charge considerably more than the Public Guardian for carrying out the supervisory functions. However, the Public Guardian might consider appointing some solicitors or accountants as local agents and delegating to them some of the supervisory functions. This would be a simple way of establishing a "local presence", particularly in the less populated areas of Scotland[3].

6.123   When discussing supervision of guardians with welfare powers we recommended[4] that the guardians should be under a duty to obey any order or demand by the supervising local authority. Failure to obey should entitle the local authority to apply to the court for an order in similar terms. We would extend this recommendation to orders or demands made by the Public Guardian when supervising guardians in the exercise of their financial powers.

6.124   We recommend that:

108. Guardians should be supervised by the Public Guardian in the exercise of their financial powers. Guardians should be under a statutory duty to comply with any order or demand made by the Public Guardian. Should the guardian fail to obey such an order or demand the Public Guardian should be entitled to apply to the court for an order in similar terms.

Clauses 4(2)(b) and 49(7)(b)

6.125   Our recommendations will result in guardians with both financial and welfare powers being supervised by three different bodies. The Public Guardian will supervise the exercise by guardians of their financial powers, while the Mental Welfare Commission and the local authority will supervise and monitor the welfare side of guardianship. Ideally there should perhaps be a single central supervisory body, but we think it better to build on the expertise of existing organisations. The Mental Welfare Commission and the Accountant of Court consult each other on matters of mutual concern at present and we hope that this will continue. There will be a need for closer links in the future since the Public Guardian is to act as registration authority for all guardians and intervention orders whatever the nature of the powers conferred. The Public Guardian should have to pass on details of any welfare powers conferred on guardians, and on any intervention orders with welfare aspects, to the Mental Welfare Commission and the local authority. The local authority should likewise pass on information of interest to the Public Guardian. We recommend that:

109. In order to improve the supervisory regimes we have recommended, the Mental Welfare Commission, the Public Guardian and the local authority should each be under a duty to consult about matters of mutual concern in relation to guardians and generally, and to exchange relevant information.

Clauses 4(2)(h), 7(1)(b) and 8(1)(b)

---

1. Proposal 43, para 4.119.
2. Recommendations 109 and 111, paras 6.125 and 6.129.
3. See para 6.58.
4. Recommendation 107, para 6.119.

6.126   Earlier in Part 3 we recommend[1] that the court should have power to give directions to a continuing or welfare attorney as to the exercise of his or her functions. We think this power would also be useful in guardianship since it would enable persons other than the Public Guardian, the Mental Welfare Commission or the local authority to challenge actions or proposed actions by the guardian. A guardian might also seek directions when unsure what action to take. We therefore recommend that:

110.   Any person claiming an interest in the welfare, property or financial affairs of an adult under guardianship should be entitled to apply to the court for an order giving directions to the guardian as to the exercise of the functions conferred.

Clause 3(3)

Investigating complaints about guardians

6.127   The Mental Welfare Commission frequently receive complaints about mismanagement of the welfare or finances of the mentally disordered. It is under a duty to make enquiry[2] -

"into any case where it appears to them that there may be ill-treatment, deficiency in care or treatment, or improper detention of any person who may be suffering from mental disorder, or where the property of any such person may, by reason of his mental disorder, be exposed to loss or damage".

We consider that it would be useful to confer investigative powers on the Public Guardian and the local authority in relation to guardianship. Detention and treatment should however be excluded as these are matters where they would have no expertise. With many bodies having a similar power there is a danger of duplication of effort. The Mental Welfare Commission, the Public Guardian and the local authority should be able to agree between themselves as to who is to carry out an investigation or whether each should investigate different aspects. For example, the Public Guardian may discover after initial enquiries that a complaint is really about the welfare aspects of guardianship. The Public Guardian should therefore inform the Mental Welfare Commission and suggest that it takes over the investigation with the Public Guardian supplying information relating to any financial aspects. Similarly the Mental Welfare Commission or the local authority may find out that a complaint about the finances of an adult under guardianship reveals such deficiencies that the investigation warrants the expertise of the Public Guardian's office. It could then inform the Public Guardian, who could take over the investigation. We make recommendations in Part 2 to deal with these points[3].

6.128   Merely receiving complaints and investigating them does not in our opinion go far enough. The Public Guardian, the Mental Welfare Commission and the local authority should not simply report the results of their investigations to the complainers and leave them to take such actions as they think fit. These supervisory organisations ought to take a more active role in appropriate cases. Administrative steps may be sufficient to deal with the problem, but in other cases legal proceedings (for example an application to the court for an order giving directions to the guardian or replacing the guardian) may be required. We are not suggesting that all litigation about guardianship should be carried out by one of the supervisory bodies. That would be a very time consuming task and one that would involve considerable public expenditure. However, if a supervisory body is satisfied that legal proceedings are needed to safeguard the welfare or finances of adults subject to guardianship and that no-one else is applying to the court then it should apply for the appropriate remedy.

6.129   We recommend that:

111.   (1)   The Mental Welfare Commission should retain its existing investigative role under the Mental Health (Scotland) Act 1984 in relation to the welfare and finances of the mentally disordered. The Public Guardian should have a similar role in relation to the finances of adults subject to guardianship and the local authority in relation to their welfare.

(2)   The Mental Welfare Commission, the local authority or the Public Guardian may, as a result of investigations, make any application to the court that seems to be required in order to safeguard the welfare or finances of an adult under guardianship.

Clauses 4(2)(d)(iv), 7(1)(c)(ii), 8(1)(c)(ii) and 9(1)

Effect of appointment of guardian

6.130   The effect of the appointment of a guardian will obviously depend on the powers conferred by the court. Any decision made or transaction entered into by the guardian on behalf of the incapable adult within the scope of the authority conferred should generally be regarded as having the same legal effect as if it had been made or entered into by the adult himself or herself and the adult had had full capacity to do so. In short the guardian should be the adult's legal representative

---

1.   Recommendation 30, para 3.68.
2.   1984 Act, s 3(2)(a).
3.   Recommendation 9, para 2.45.

for matters within the scope of his or her authority. Some less obvious aspects of this representational power would be attending meetings which the adult could attend or obtaining information that would be given to the adult[1]. Mr Adrian Ward, a solicitor with great experience in connection with tutors-dative, suggested to us that power to open and read correspondence addressed to the adult would be useful. The Code of Practice relating to guardianship could draw attention to the scope of a guardian's representational powers and perhaps give some of the powers just mentioned as examples. While in general the guardian should be regarded as standing in place of the adult we consider that there should be an exclusion in relation to refusal of consent to medical treatment because of the special risk involved in allowing a non-medical person to veto treatment of another person which is considered appropriate by those with a professional duty to provide appropriate treatment for patients. We recommend earlier in this report[2] that doctors should be entitled to give reasonable treatment to safeguard or promote the health of the adult in spite of a refusal or withholding of consent by the guardian, but only if they obtained an opinion from an independent consultant that in all the circumstances the treatment should be given despite the guardian's opposition.

6.131   Like curators bonis, guardians should be managers of any property belonging to the incapable adult (if the property is within the scope of their powers) and should not seek to have the adult's property transferred to their own name. The guardian's authority to manage should (unless limited in the appointment) as a matter of Scottish law apply to property wherever it is situated, although other jurisdictions may require the guardian to take further legal or administrative steps in respect of property situated there. Where money or some other obligation becomes due to the adult payment should have to be made, or performance tendered, to the guardian, if the guardian's powers encompass such matters.

6.132   The present law relating to the liability of curators is not clear although Gloag expresses the view that a curator incurs no personal liability on ordinary contracts[3]. We proposed in our discussion paper that in entering into transactions on behalf of the adult a financial manager should have to make it clear that he or she was indeed acting in a representative capacity in order to escape personal liability[4]. A similar proposal was made in relation to personal guardians[5], for even in the area of personal welfare transactions might have financial consequences. Most of those responding agreed with our proposals. One organisation and one individual considered that financial managers and personal guardians should be personally liable even when acting in a representative capacity. We do not agree with this dissenting view. Appointment to act in a representative capacity necessarily carries with it freedom from personal liability provided the representative acts within the scope of his or her authority. Moreover, it would be very hard to find guardians willing to act if they were always personally liable. Sense in Scotland expressed concerns about personal guardians entering into transactions which were not in the interests of the adults and personal guardians obtaining material benefits for themselves as a result of transactions on behalf of adults. The first concern of Sense in Scotland would be met by our previous recommendation[6] that any decision by a guardian (or other person exercising functions under our recommendations) should be governed by the general principle which states that any action must be for the benefit of the incapable adult. Guardians who obtained material benefits from their position would be in breach of their fiduciary duty[7].

6.133   Looking at the other side, what should be the effect of the appointment of a guardian on the adult's capacity in relation to transactions? The present position as regards curators is not absolutely clear. The appointment of a tutor-dative to a person following cognition as insane was said to reduce his or her status to that of a pupil child so that the person could not validly enter into any further transaction[8]. Bell, however, was of the view that cognition raised a rebuttable presumption of insanity, but it was open to lead evidence to show that the transaction was done in a lucid interval[9]. As far as the appointment of a curator is concerned there is authority for the proposition that the appointment renders the adult legally incapable of managing his or her affairs or disposing of property[10].

6.134   In our discussion paper we proposed[11] that the adult should be deemed to be lacking any capacity to transact in relation to any estate or matters within the authority of the financial manager. We also proposed that the adult should not be presumed to be incapable of entering into a transaction in areas outwith the manager's authority[12]. Nearly all those

---

1. Under the Access to Health Records Act 1990, for example.
2. Recommendation 66, para 5.39.
3. *Contract*, (2nd edn) p 135, followed in *Scottish Brewers Ltd v J Douglas Pearson & Co* 1995 GWD 20-1111 (Sheriff Lothian, Edinburgh).
4. Proposal 37, para 4.71.
5. Proposal 10, para 2.85.
6. Recommendation 11, para 2.54.
7. Recommendation 15, para 2.79.
8. Fraser, *Parent and Child*, pp 684-5.
9. Principles, 2111.
10. *Mitchell and Baxter v Cheyne* (1891) 19R 324 (no action allowed on cheques granted by adult after curator appointed - adult "superseded in the management of his affairs"). See also Gloag, *Contract* (2nd edn) 1929, p 94; Walker, *Judicial Factors*, p 26. Contrast McBryde, *Contract*, p 143.
11. Proposal 92, para 7.30.
12. Proposal 96, para 7.40.

who responded agreed. One organisation favoured the notion of people with dementia being deemed capable of making some decisions. Our recommended scheme of guardianship gives effect to this notion. A guardian would be appointed only in relation to those areas where the adult was regarded incapable of taking decisions in relation to or safeguarding his or her finances or welfare[1]. This deemed lack of capacity means that as far as the legal effect of any transaction within the scope of the guardian's authority was concerned an adult should be regarded as being without capacity, and that it should not be allowable to lead evidence to show that in fact he or she did have capacity[2]. If the adult turns out to have capacity in an area covered by the guardian's authority then the scope of that authority should be varied by way of application to the court.

6.135   We have considered other possible solutions including -

(a) a rule that the appointment of a guardian has no effect on capacity;

(b) a rule that the appointment of a guardian has no effect on capacity, unless the court expressly removes capacity, and

(c) a rebuttable presumption of incapacity in those areas covered by the guardian's appointment.

We can see advantages in these approaches, which could be said to be more consistent with the principle of minimum necessary intervention. However, given that guardians have a protective function and given that their powers ought in any event to be the minimum required in the interests of the adult, we remain in favour of the rule supported by our consultees that there should be legal incapacity in those areas, but only in those areas, covered by the guardian's powers. The other solutions mentioned above would open up the possibility that third parties might, for example, prevail upon the adult to enter into transactions or sign cheques in their favour[3] even although a guardian had been appointed precisely to guard against these dangers. It might be difficult, or impossible, to have these transactions set aside by reference to the general law on vices of consent. A clear rule of legal incapacity would also ease the position of third parties, such as banks[4]. Guardianship would be a matter of public record and in important transactions, where there was any cause for doubt, reference to the register of guardianships to be kept by the Public Guardian would produce a clear answer in relation to matters within the guardian's powers.

6.136   We recommend that:

112. (1) A guardian acting within the scope of the powers conferred by the court should generally be regarded as the legal representative of the incapable adult concerned. Any decision made or transaction entered into by a guardian within the scope of his or her powers should accordingly have the same effect as if it were made or entered into by the adult concerned and as if the adult had capacity to make the decision or enter into the transaction.

(2) A guardian should be entitled to manage and deal with the adult's estate in so far as it falls within the scope of his or her powers. This entitlement should include the right to demand that sums due to the adult be paid to the guardian.

(3) Any decision made or transaction entered into by the guardian within the scope of the powers conferred by the court should bind the adult's estate and the guardian should not be personally liable provided the guardian made it clear that he or she was acting in a representative capacity.

(4) In order to maximise protection and avoid any conflict of competence between an adult under guardianship and the guardian, the adult should be deemed to have no capacity to enter into transactions in those areas where the guardian has authority.

Clause 49(3) and 51(1), (2), (4)

6.137   In order to more effectively prevent incapable adults from dealing with their homes and other heritable property where a guardian has been appointed, we asked for views as to whether a notice should be registerable in the Register of Inhibitions and Adjudications. This register is searched as a matter of course by those intending to buy heritage so that a notice there would alert people to the appointment of a guardian and prevent them entering into an invalid transaction with the adult. Some of those consulted were in favour, others saw problems with the permanency of notices in the register. The Keeper of the Registers of Scotland considered that notification of the appointment of a guardian would be a novel departure as at present entries in the Register of Inhibitions and Adjudications are made only where there is some form of debtor/creditor relationship. He also expressed concern that there could be a large number of notices which would swamp the register and so reduce its effectiveness in other areas. No notice of a curator's appointment is registered at present and this seems not to have given rise to problems. Our recommended register of guardians which would be held

---

1. See also para 6.138 dealing with testamentary capacity.
2. Proposal 93, para 7.31.
3. As happened in *Mitchell and Baxter v Cheyne*, (1891) 19 R 324.
4. This is also illustrated by *Mitchell and Baxter v Cheyne*, where the bank refused to pay the cheques.

by the Public Guardian and be open to public inspection would be of assistance to those proposing to transact with the adult in respect of heritable and other property. The Keeper noted that it would also be open to the guardian to have his or her appointment noted on the title sheet of land belonging to the adult where the title was registered in the Land Register of Scotland[1]. This would be as effective a notice to third parties as a notice in the Register of Inhibitions and Adjudications. In coming years more and more titles will be registered in the Land Register as the system is progressively extended to the whole of Scotland. We recommend that:

113. It should not be competent to register the appointment of a guardian to an adult in the Register of Inhibitions and Adjudications. Public notification of the appointment of guardians should be achieved by the open public register maintained by the Public Guardian in accordance with Recommendation 91.

6.138   The adult's testamentary capacity would be unaffected by our earlier recommendation of legal incapacity in those areas where the guardian had been authorised to act. This is because the guardian would not, under our scheme, have any functions in relation to the making of wills[2]. In our discussion paper we proposed[3] that only the appointment of a financial manager with full powers should give rise to a rebuttable presumption of testamentary incapacity. The appointment of a personal guardian or limited financial manager should not give rise to any presumption. Most respondents agreed, but Enable pointed out that the presumption of incapacity would be difficult to rebut after the adult's death. They suggested that there should be some procedure for enabling the presumption to be rebutted at the time of making the will. The Law Society and Alzheimer Scotland - Action on Dementia were also in favour of some such procedure. We have already considered and rejected this suggestion in our discussion of intervention orders[4], but it has led us to reconsider our proposal. We now think that the better approach would be to have no presumption arising from the appointment of a guardian so that testamentary capacity would be a question of fact in each case. It seems somewhat artificial to draw a distinction between a "limited" guardian with powers over almost all the adult's financial affairs and a guardian with "full" powers. If there was any doubt as to the adult's testamentary capacity we envisage that, as is done in current practice, the adult would be examined by a psychiatrist or other specialist in order to elucidate whether such capacity exists. A report stating that testamentary capacity exists would not be conclusive, nor should it be, but it would present a formidable obstacle to those seeking to challenge the will after the death of an adult to whom a guardian had been appointed. We therefore recommend that:

114. There should be no presumption of incapacity to make a will arising out of the appointment of a guardian. Testamentary capacity would therefore be a question of fact in each case.

Clause 51(1)

6.139   In Scotland a marriage is valid provided each person involved was at the time of celebration mentally capable of understanding the nature of marriage and of consenting to it. Marriage is a fairly simple concept whose broad effects are widely known. Participants therefore require only limited mental capacity in order to enter into a valid marriage[5]. The appointment of a curator or mental health guardian to an adult does not necessarily mean that the adult is incapable of entering into a valid marriage. We recommend earlier in this report that a guardian should not be able to consent to marriage on behalf of the adult[6]. We proposed in our discussion paper that an adult should be neither deemed nor presumed incapable of entering into a valid marriage solely on the ground that a personal guardian or financial manager had been appointed[7]. This was agreed by all those who commented and we would adhere to our proposal. Capacity for marriage should be a question of fact in each case. We therefore recommend that:

115. The appointment of a guardian should not result in the adult in question being deemed or presumed to lack the capacity to enter into a valid marriage.

Clause 51(1)

6.140   The guardian, like any other person, could object to a proposed marriage. Section 5 of the Marriage (Scotland) Act 1977 provides that an objection can be submitted in writing to the district registrar to whom notice of intention to marry has been given. Where the objection is on the ground that "one or both of the parties is or are incapable of understanding the nature of a marriage ceremony or of consenting to marriage" a medical certificate has to accompany the objection. The matter is then referred to the Registrar General for decision and an appeal lies against the Registrar General's decision to the courts. A guardian with financial powers would also be regarded as having sufficient title and interest to bring an action for declarator of nullity as the marriage would have financial consequences for the adult's estate[8]. We proposed no change in the law in these areas[9] and all those who commented agreed. We remain of the view

---

1. Land Registration (Scotland) Act 1979, s 2(4)(c).
2. See para 6.105.
3. Proposal 100, para 7.63.
4. Para 6.17.
5. *Long v Long* 1950 SLT (Notes) 32.
6. Recommendation 103, para 6.100.
7. Proposal 98, para 7.48.
8. Clive, *Husband and Wife*, (3rd edn) p 111.
9. Proposal 99, para 7.54.

that the guardian should be entitled to object to a proposed marriage or bring nullity proceedings if he or she has been granted powers over the adult's estate. Even if the guardian is so entitled it would not follow that he or she would be obliged to take action. The decision to act would be governed by our recommended general principles in which the likely benefit to the incapable adult and his or her wishes and feelings feature prominently.

Duty to act and delictual liability of guardians

6.141   In our discussion paper we dealt with the related questions of whether a personal guardian or financial manager should have a statutory responsibility to look after or manage the incapable adult's affairs and whether liability should arise for failure to act where necessary. Tutors-dative and curators are liable in damages under the existing law if the adult's estate suffers loss as a result of their acts or omissions[1]. We expressed the view that a statutory duty to look after the adult's welfare and estate would be too onerous, particularly if it were to be interpreted as requiring the adult and his or her affairs to be kept under constant review[2]. It might prove difficult to obtain guardians willing to undertake such heavy duties. We proposed instead that personal guardians should have a responsibility to safeguard and promote the welfare of the adult within the areas covered by their powers of appointment[3]. Financial managers were to have a responsibility to manage the adult's affairs and estate within the scope of powers conferred on appointment[4]. These proposals were supported by almost all those who commented. One regional council official considered that the responsibility to promote the adult's welfare was an onerous one, particularly for guardians who were not social workers or other professionals. Another respondent was not in favour of our proposal in relation to personal guardians but no reason was given. The Scottish Association for Mental Health and Enable both stated that encouraging the adults to do as much as possible themselves ought to be included as a statutory duty, as should the duty to consult. These last points are incorporated into our recommended general principles set out in Part 2 of this report.

6.142   We have now come to the view that it is unnecessary to place an express statutory responsibility on guardians. Powers are to be conferred on guardians by the court and under the common law guardians would in certain circumstances be liable for failing to exercise them. Any statutory responsibility or duty would not add anything to these rules.

6.143   In our discussion paper we took the view that the relation of personal guardian or financial manager and incapable adult was such that a duty of care would be held to exist. The result would be that the existing law of delict would apply to such appointees as it already applies to curators and tutors-dative. We asked for views as to whether a guardian's liability in relation to the exercise or non-exercise of powers conferred should be governed by the existing law of delict or new statutory provisions imposing liability for acting without reasonable care or for failing to act when it would have been reasonable to have acted[5]. Most of those responding preferred the proposed new statutory provisions although a sizeable minority favoured the existing law of delict. The Law Society said that professional financial managers should be required to show the expertise and skill of their profession. We agree, but think that this would be implied in any formula based on a reasonable standard of care. Higher standards in both welfare and financial areas would be expected of those guardians who had been appointed because of their professional skills. The existing law provides for liability for breach of the duty of care and there seems little point in having a statutory provision to this effect. We think it would be helpful however to have a statutory provision restricting liability in certain situations.

6.144   The Scottish Association for Mental Health drew our attention to section 122 of the 1984 Act as a possible model for limiting the liability of personal guardians. Section 122(1) provides that no person shall be liable in respect of any act purporting to be done under the Act unless the act was done in bad faith or without reasonable care. Enable, on the other hand, took the view that this provision may have allowed some staff to avoid responsibility for ill-treatment of mentally disordered patients. In *Skinner v Robertson*[6] a charge nurse was acquitted of several charges of assaulting mentally disturbed young patients on the grounds that the physical force used was the minimum reasonably necessary in the circumstances to fulfil the nurse's responsibility to care for and control the patient or patients involved. Clearly there must be some restriction of liability and we think that it should be framed partly with reference to reasonable care. What is regarded as reasonable will depend on the circumstances, the individuals involved and the prevailing attitudes in relation to the mentally disabled. However, reasonableness by itself is not enough. Section 122(1) of the 1984 Act adds the requirement of good faith which we would adopt. Good faith implies that a person knew or ought to have known a particular fact. In *B v Forsey* Lord Davidson in the Outer House[7] commented that the defenders could not rely on the good faith exemption in section 122(1) since they were clearly aware that their actings were in breach of statutory

---

1. Fraser, *Parent and Child*, p 392 (Tutors-dative); *Semple v Tennent* (1888) 15R 810 and *Crabbe v Whyte* (1891) 18R 1065 (Curators).
2. See *G's CB v Grampian Health Board* 1995 SLT 652. Mental hospital staff liable for not following close observation regime for suicidal patient.
3. Proposal 9, para 2.84.
4. Proposal 35, para 4.67.
5. Proposal 9(2), para 2.84 (personal guardians) and Proposal 35(2), para 4.67 (financial managers).
6. 1980 SLT (Sh Ct) 43 on the same provision in the Mental Health (Scotland) Act 1960.
7. 1988 SC (HL) 28 at p 38.

provisions in the 1984 Act. Whether the guardian acted in accordance with the general principles is another factor that should be taken into account in assessing liability. We make a similar recommendation in connection with liability for breach of fiduciary duty[1]. We therefore recommend that:

116. New statutory provisions should provide that a guardian is not to be liable for any loss or damage to the adult if the guardian acted reasonably, in good faith and in accordance with the general principles.

Clause 64

6.145   We have recommended[2] that a guardian should not be personally liable in respect of transactions entered into with third parties as long as the guardian made it clear that he or she was acting in a representative capacity on behalf of the adult. Where the guardian failed to disclose his or her representative capacity the third party might have a claim against the guardian rather than the adult's estate. Although guardians should be personally liable in the first instance we think that they should not have to bear the cost from their own pockets where they acted in accordance with their powers and observed all other requirements imposed on them. They should in these circumstances be entitled to be reimbursed from the estate, provided the estate has funds to do so. We therefore recommend that:

117. Where the guardian becomes personally liable due to failure to disclose that he or she acted in a representative capacity, the guardian should be entitled to be reimbursed from the adult's estate provided the guardian acted within the scope of his or her authority and observed all other requirements.

Clause 51(4)

6.146   So far it has been assumed that the guardian is acting within the scope of his or her authority. We now consider the situation where the guardian acts outwith that authority, as for example where the guardian sells the adult's home, having been given power to sell only some investments. The first question is whether the transaction should be valid or void. We think it should be valid in the sense that it should not be challengeable by reason only of the guardian's lack of authority. Third parties would be exposed to considerable risks if transactions outwith the guardian's authority were void and they might have to resort to complex enquiries or even litigation to satisfy themselves that the guardian had indeed authority. The Keeper of the Registers of Scotland noted his concerns in relation to property registered in the Land Register of Scotland. In order to avoid compensation claims he stated that he would have to investigate the circumstances fully or rely on comprehensive certification from the applicant for registration that the transaction was in order. This would increase costs and delay the process of registration. We note that a similar approach is taken in section 2 of the Trust (Scotland) Act 1961 in relation to trustees who are defined to include judicial factors such as curators bonis[3]. Section 2 provides that certain transactions shall not be challengeable on the ground that the act in question is at variance with the terms and purposes of the trust. There is, however, a proviso that the protection does not apply where the transaction requires the consent of the Accountant of Court and the trustee or judicial factor has failed to obtain it. We would adopt this basic approach but consider that a third party's title from a guardian should be unchallengeable even if the guardian failed to obtain the required consent of the Public Guardian[4]. It would complicate conveyancing and other business transactions if a potential purchaser had to seek assurances that the Public Guardian's consent was not required. This protection against challenge should apply only in relation to transactions for value and where the third party is in good faith. For example, gifts out of the adult's estate by a guardian to the adult's relatives, friends or even charities should be reclaimable unless the guardian was authorised to make such gifts.

6.147   Given that the transaction is unchallengeable on ground of lack of authority the next question is whether any liability arising out of it should be that of the guardian personally or the adult's estate. One approach would be to hold the adult's estate liable even if the guardian exceeded his or her authority. We reject this as imposing too great a liability on adults' estates. It also renders somewhat pointless the concept of limited guardianship if a guardian acting as such can always bind the adult's estate. We prefer the approach whereby any acting of the guardian as such should bind the adult's estate only if the guardian acted within the scope of his or her authority. Acting outwith such scope would entail personal liability. If third parties wish to ensure that the adult's estate would be liable in respect of any transaction then they should have to satisfy themselves, by examining the document setting out the powers conferred or otherwise, that the guardian was acting within the scope of his or her authority. Accordingly we recommend that:

118. (1) A transaction for value between the guardian and a good faith third party should not be challengeable solely on the ground that the guardian was acting outwith his or her authority or that any other requirement under our recommendations was not observed.

(2) A guardian who acts outwith his or her authority should be personally liable in respect of the transaction.

Clause 51(4)(b), (7)

---

1. Para 2.78.
2. Recommendation 112(3) at para 6.136.
3. Trusts (Scotland) Act 1961, s 6(1) and Trusts (Scotland) Act 1921, s 2; *Barclay Petr* 1962 SC 594.
4. Consent is to be required to the sale of the adult's dwellinghouse (Recommendation 127, para 6.164) and the sheriff could impose the requirement of consent in other cases.

Liability of joint guardians

6.148   Where there are two or more joint guardians appointed to an adult should the guardians be jointly and severally liable or should some other rule apply? Joint curators are unknown in current practice so that the question of liability between two or more curators does not arise. We are not in favour of joint and several liability for it would impose too great a liability on a guardian who was not consulted about the particular act which gave rise to liability. We prefer the rule that applies to trustees. Trustees are liable only for their own acts and intromissions and not for the acts or intromissions of co-trustees and are not liable for omissions, unless the trust deed provides otherwise[1]. This statutory formula, declaratory of the common law, is regarded as making trustees liable for a failure to act where to act would be reasonable and for holding one trustee liable for his or her co-trustee's acts or omissions if he or she adopted or ratified them or acquiesced in them[2]. We consider it would be better to express the liability for co-guardians' actions and omissions in a statutory provision rather than rely on the current law on trustees' liability being held to be applicable to guardians. Except in cases of emergency, joint guardians are expected to act as a body so that each is under a duty to oversee the actions of the others and to take steps to prevent any breach of duty. Accordingly we recommend that:

119.   **Each joint guardian should be liable for his or her own acts or failure to act. A joint guardian should also be liable for any act or failure to act of another joint guardian but only if he or she did not take reasonable care to prevent such act or failure to act.**

Clause 47(6)

Penalty for inadequate performance by guardian

6.149   Section 6 of the Judicial Factors Act 1849 empowers the court where there is misconduct or failure to discharge the duties on the part of a curator to impose a fine on the curator, to order the forfeiture of his or her commission in whole or in part, to suspend or remove the curator from office and to find the curator liable in expenses for such proceedings. In our discussion paper we took the view that criminal penalties should not be used as sanctions in civil matters and proposed[3] that the sheriff should be empowered to remove a financial manager or reduce or cancel the manager's entitlement to remuneration on grounds of failure to carry out the duties properly. We also proposed[4] that the Accountant of Court in fixing remuneration should be empowered to reduce the manager's remuneration for performance which fell below the accepted standard.

6.150   All those who commented were in favour of our proposals. The Law Society drew our attention to the inadequate professional services provision set out in section 42A of the Solicitors (Scotland) Act 1980[5] whereby the Council of the Society can reduce or cancel the solicitor's right to fees or order the solicitor to pay compensation or rectify any errors at his or her own expense. The Scottish Association for Mental Health suggested the introduction of a compensation order as being a more accessible remedy than a claim for damages. We do not think that such complex provisions as are contained in the Solicitors (Scotland) Act 1980 are necessary in relation to guardians and we are not in favour of compensation orders in this context. Where a guardian's action or inaction has caused loss to the adult's estate a claim for damages could be made and this claim could be incorporated in the application for removal of the guardian or forfeiture of remuneration. We have reconsidered our proposal that the Accountant of Court should be entitled to reduce the guardian's remuneration for poor performance even, if as many respondents suggested, the Accountant's decision should be appealable to the sheriff. Reduction of remuneration is a serious step which should be reserved to the sheriff. We deal with the replacement of an unsatisfactory guardian later at paragraph 6.197. We recommend that:

120.   **The sheriff should have power, on application, to order a guardian who fails to carry out the duties to an acceptable standard to forfeit (wholly or partly) the right to remuneration that would otherwise be due.**

Clause 53

Delegation by guardian

6.151   The Law Society commented in relation to the appointment of financial managers that a manager should have power to delegate subject to careful definition and limitation. We consider that this would be useful also in the personal welfare field. For example, a guardian going abroad might delegate to a solicitor the sale of property or a guardian living some distance away might give the proprietor of a nursing home authority to make day-to-day treatment and welfare decisions.

6.152   In our *Report on Family Law* we recommended[6] that a person with parental responsibilities or rights in relation to a child should not be able to surrender or transfer any part of those responsibilities or rights to another but should be

---

1. Trusts (Scotland) Act 1921, s 3(d).
2. Norrie and Scobbie, *Trusts*, p 146.
3. Proposal 36(1) at para 4.70.
4. Proposal 36(2) at para 4.70.
5. Inserted by Solicitors (Scotland) Act 1988, s 1.
6. Scot Law Com No 135 (1992), Recommendation 8.

able to arrange for some or all of them to be met or exercised by one or more persons acting on his or her behalf. The Children (Scotland) Act 1995 modifies this slightly by using the word "abdicate"[1] instead of "surrender or transfer". We would adopt our earlier formula for guardianship and accordingly recommend that:

121. A guardian should not be entitled to surrender or transfer any of his or her powers to anyone else but may arrange for some or all of them to be exercised by another individual or individuals on the guardian's behalf.

Clause 49(6)

Guardian allowing adult to handle affairs

6.153   One of our recommended general principles is that a guardian should encourage the adult to use existing skills and develop new skills in so far as it is reasonable and practicable to do so[2]. In our discussion paper we proposed[3] that a financial manager should be entitled to allow the adult to deal with any of the matters under management. We saw this as particularly useful in relation to young mentally handicapped adults who need to be encouraged to make the best use of their abilities. There was no dissent on consultation in principle but some respondents asked how any third party would know that the adult had been authorised. We envisage that the guardian would sign a document of authorisation which the adult could show to the third party. This authority could extend to buying food or clothes, paying for accommodation or even operating a bank account into which the guardian would put a modest amount of money. The former Accountant of Court suggested that any authorisation should require the Accountant's prior approval. This is a sensible idea in line with current practice whereby the Accountant may permit a curator to let the adult handle some financial matters. We think approval by the Public Guardian is necessary since guardians having unfettered powers would make the Public Guardian's proposed supervisory and monitoring role very difficult.

6.154   A transaction by an adult which fell within the scope of the guardian's powers would, under our earlier recommendation[4], be void since the adult would lack legal capacity to enter into it. Clearly this rule has to be disapplied where an adult transacts with the guardian's authority as otherwise nobody would be willing to enter into any transaction with the adult, so defeating our purpose of encouraging the adult to exercise and develop skills. In our discussion paper we proposed[5] that any transaction by an adult which had been authorised by the guardian should not be challengeable on the grounds that the adult lacked capacity. The Law Society and Enable both considered that an authorised transaction should remain capable of being set aside on grounds of facility and circumvention, where the third party had exerted pressure which the adult was unable to withstand because of mental disability. We agree and consider that all the grounds apart from lack of capacity for setting aside a transaction, such as essential error, would remain available. We recommend that:

122. (1)   In order to encourage an adult under guardianship to use existing skills and acquire new skills where this is practicable and reasonable the guardian should be entitled to authorise the adult to enter into a financial transaction within the scope of the guardian's powers.

(2)   Such authority should only be granted with the consent of the Public Guardian.

(3)   Where a third party is aware that the adult has authority from the guardian to carry out the transaction in question, the third party should not be entitled to challenge the transaction on the ground that the adult lacked capacity.

Clause 51(5), (6)

Changes of address

6.155   In order that people with an interest in the incapable adults and their guardianship can keep track of them, a guardian should be obliged to inform the Public Guardian of any change (other than a temporary one) in his or her own address and that of the adult. The Public Guardian should then amend the register and notify any other organisations (such as the Mental Welfare Commission and the local authority where the guardian had welfare powers) that might be required to be informed. We recommend that:

123. (1)   A guardian should be under a duty to inform the Public Guardian of any permanent change in his or her own or the adult's address within seven days of such change.

(2)   The Public Guardian should amend the register and notify the Mental Welfare Commission and the local authority where the guardian has welfare powers.

Clause 49(4)

---

1.   S 3(5).
2.   See para 2.59.
3.   Proposal 39, para 4.77.
4.   Recommendation 112(4), para 6.136.
5.   Proposal 39, para 4.77.

Financial aspects of guardianship

6.156   **Lodging an inventory.** Earlier in this Part we recommend that, like curators at present, guardians with financial powers should act under the supervision of the Public Guardian (the successor to the Accountant of Court)[1]. We turn now to look at the duties imposed on the guardian by this supervisory function. One of a curator's first tasks is to investigate the adult's estate and submit an inventory to the Accountant of Court. This inventory is then checked and once approved forms the basis for subsequent accounts. We consider that this should in general continue but that the Public Guardian should be empowered to waive the requirement to submit an inventory and should be able to substitute some other document or procedure if an inventory seems unnecessary. Any inventory or substitute should be in a form prescribed by the Public Guardian. The Public Guardian should be entitled to require the guardian to provide adequate documentation for entries in the inventory and to make such further enquiries as seem necessary. At present curators must lodge an inventory as soon as possible and at least within six months of their bond of caution being received[2]. We consider that in most cases a shorter period would be sufficient as the adult's estate will have been investigated to some extent before applying for guardianship. A period of three months seems in general sufficient but to cater for complex estates the Public Guardian should have power to extend the time. The time limit should run from the date of registration of the guardian's appointment by the Public Guardian. We recommend that:

124. (1) **A guardian having financial powers should be under a duty to submit to the Public Guardian a full inventory of the adult's estate falling within the scope of his or her authority within three months of the date of registration of the guardian's appointment.**

(2) **The Public Guardian should have power to dispense with the need for an inventory or to allow further time for the submission of an inventory, and to prescribe the forms for inventories.**

Schedule 2, paragraph 3

6.157   **Plan for managing the estate.** The interlocutor appointing a curator confers upon him or her "the usual powers". The extent of such powers has to be gathered from Acts of Sederunt made between 1690 and 1730, later legislation and case law. Because curatory was originally conceived as a temporary expedient the usual powers are regarded as those necessary for protecting and conserving the estate. Writing in 1881 Thoms stated that curators are appointed "with a view to doing no acts but those of necessary administration"[3]. The usual powers include ingathering and taking possession of the estate, realising it where appropriate or necessary, investing the proceeds and making payments for the support of the adult under curatory and his or her dependents.

6.158   A curator who seeks to do anything which is outwith the usual powers may apply to the Court of Session for special powers under section 7 of the Judicial Factors Act 1849[4]. In order to cut down the number of applications to the Court of Session a new procedure was introduced in 1980. Now a curator (among others) can, instead of applying to the court, obtain authority from the Accountant of Court to do an act mentioned in paragraphs (a) to (ee) of section 4(1) of the Trusts (Scotland) Act 1921 provided the act is not expressly prohibited by the terms of the appointment. These acts consist of selling any part of the estate, granting feus or leases, borrowing money, excambing land and acquiring a residence for the adult. The curator's application has to be intimated to various people including the cautioner and those on whom the petition for the curator's appointment was served[5]. If there are no objections the Accountant of Court is empowered to consent if he or she considers that the proposed act is in the best interests of the adult or any other individual whom the adult has a duty to support. The main use of the Accountant of Court's consent procedure has been for the sale of the adult's residence. In *Broadfoot's CB* 1989 SLT 566 it was held that subject to certain limited exceptions encroachment on capital required a grant of special powers from the court. Following that case the Court of Session made a new rule of court whereby authority to encroach on capital for the adult's maintenance could be obtained from the Accountant by a similar procedure[6]. Special powers are still needed for matters such as other encroachments on capital or electing between legal rights and testamentary provisions[7].

6.159   In our discussion paper we were not in favour of the present rules relating to curators' powers being used for financial managers[8]. Financial managers should not we felt be given only administrative powers so forcing them back to the Accountant of Court or the courts for anything beyond these. Managers should be given greater freedom within the

---

1.   Recommendation 108, para 6.124.
2.   Judicial Factors Act 1849, s 3.
3.   *Judicial Factors*, (2nd ed), p 105.
4.   S 5 of the Trusts (Scotland) Act 1921 provides an alternative route but it is not commonly used.
5.   Trusts (Scotland) Act 1961, s 2(3)-(6) added by Law Reform (Miscellaneous Provisions) (Scotland) Act 1980, s 8; Rules of Court, rule 61.4. Judicial Factors Rules 1992, rule 16.
6.   Now rule 61.13 of the 1994 Rules of Court (Court of Session) or rule 15 of the Judicial Factors Rules 1992 (sheriff court).
7.   *Allan's Exs v Allan's Trs* 1975 SLT 227
8.   Para 4.91.

scope of the powers conferred by the court on appointment and we asked for views as to how this might be achieved within the framework of the Accountant of Court's supervision[1].

6.160   The former Accountant suggested a "management agreement" whereby some time after the guardian's appointment the Accountant of Court and the guardian could agree, in the light of the powers conferred on the guardian by the court, a realistic management package to suit the individual circumstances of the adult. This would be designed to give the guardian as much freedom as possible, so that the Accountant would only have to be approached for truly exceptional expenditure and any encroachment on capital. We think this is an excellent suggestion and have adopted it, but have changed the wording to a "management plan". The Law Society put forward an almost identical suggestion in response to our proposals about the investment powers of financial managers.

6.161   A management plan should not be obligatory in every case. Where the guardian has only limited financial powers or the estate is very simple the sheriff should be able to dispense with the need for a management plan. The management plan would cover the investment and realisation of the adult's estate in so far as it fell within the guardian's powers and the application of both income and capital to meeting the adult's present needs and likely future needs. The guardian should be required to submit a draft plan to the Public Guardian within three months of appointment along with or after the inventory. The Public Guardian should be able to allow more time if necessary. In drawing up the draft the guardian should, in accordance with our recommended general principles, have consulted, in so far as reasonable and practicable, the adult, the adult's nearest relative and carer and any guardian with welfare powers. The Public Guardian should thereafter adjust the draft with the guardian and once a version is agreed the Public Guardian would approve it. Any irreconcilable differences of opinion between the guardian and the Public Guardian should have to be resolved by the sheriff. Until the management plan is approved the guardian should be entitled to exercise only management functions of a routine nature, such as taking control of the adult's assets and paying for the adult's daily needs. In some cases greater powers will be required in the interval between appointment and the approval of the management plan. If these were anticipated the sheriff could authorise the exercise of such powers. If not, the Public Guardian should have a similar authorising power. The management plan should not be rigid, but should be kept under review and varied whenever it seems appropriate.

6.162   We recommend that:

125.   The way in which a guardian manages the adult's estate falling within the scope of the powers conferred by the court should be governed by a management plan drawn up by the guardian and approved by the Public Guardian. The guardian should be entitled to appeal to the sheriff against the Public Guardian's refusal to approve.

Schedule 2, paragraphs 1 and 2

6.163   **Running the adult's business.** At present it is doubtful whether a curator can be authorised to run the adult's business, except on a temporary basis until disposal. In *Gilray* the Lord President said[2] that the court "cannot sanction his carrying on the manufactory with the funds of the estate under his charge". In *Drew* the court in refusing an application for special powers to run an incapable adult's business doubted whether it was ever competent to grant such powers[3] but commented that it was open to the curator to run the business at his or her own risk or enter into a suitable indemnity arrangement with the family who were maintained from the profits. In our opinion there are situations where the adult's business should be kept going by the guardian in his or her official capacity and not on a personal basis. Examples include a business or farm in which other members of the family were involved or where there was some chance of the adult recovering capacity in the not too distant future. The guardian should be able to continue an existing business if it falls within the scope of the authority conferred by the court on appointment. The Public Guardian should however be entitled to give directions to the guardian including a direction to dispose of the business. Starting up a new business using the adult's funds, however, should not be competent as that would put the estate at too great a risk. We recommend that:

126.   (1)   A guardian should be entitled to carry on any business of the adult in existence at the date of appointment provided the business falls within the scope of his or her authority. A guardian should not however be entitled to start a new business using funds from the adult's estate.

(2)   The Public Guardian should be empowered to give directions to the guardian as to the running of the business and may require the guardian to dispose of it.

Schedule 2, paragraph 5(7)

6.164   **Sale or purchase of dwelling-house**. The sale of an incapable adult's dwelling-house or the purchase of residential accommodation for the adult can be carried out by a curator at present. The Accountant of Court's consent is however required using the procedure set out in section 2(3) of the Trusts (Scotland) Act 1961 and associated rules of court. The

---

1.   Proposal 43, para 4.119.
2.   (1872) 10M 715 at p 717.
3.   1938 SLT 435.

rules provide for notification of the application for consent to the incapable adult, the cautioner, the applicant for the appointment of the curator and those to whom that application was intimated and all others with an interest in the estate[1]. We think that this should remain the position for guardians. These transactions raise quite different issues from sales or purchases of other assets and it is right that those affected should be expressly consulted about them. But we consider that the Public Guardian should be able to grant consent even if objections were made provided that an opportunity was given to make representations and difficult cases could be remitted to the sheriff. We make similar recommendations in relation to the Public Guardian's powers to authorise individuals to withdraw from incapable adults' accounts[2] or guardians to make gifts out of an incapable adult's estate[3]. We recommend that:

> **127. Any disposal of an incapable adult's dwelling-house or acquisition of residential accommodation for the adult by the guardian should be competent only if the Public Guardian consents. An application by the guardian to the Public Guardian for consent should be notified to the adult, the adult's nearest relative and primary carer and any other individual whom the Public Guardian thinks ought to be notified. Those notified should be given an opportunity to object. The Public Guardian should have power to grant consent after considering any objections and any further representations by the applicant and any objectors, or to remit the matter to the sheriff.**
>
> Schedule 2, paragraph 6

6.165   **Investment powers.** The investment powers of curators are regulated by the Trustee Investments Act 1961. This Act enables curators to invest in bank and building society deposit and share accounts, National Savings products, a wide range of central and local government bonds and also in unit trusts and ordinary shares of United Kingdom companies which have a paid up capital of £1m or more and have paid a dividend in each of the last five years.

6.166   If a curator wishes to invest in unit trusts and ordinary shares the funds available for investment must be divided into two. One half has to be placed in narrow range investments (bank deposits, government securities and UK company debentures, loans secured on property, building society deposits etc), and the other in the wider range investments[4]. Gains and losses on realisation accrue to the range from which the investment came[5]. Surplus revenue has to be equally divided between the ranges,[6] but capital to meet a deficit in income may be taken from either range at the discretion of the curator[7]. Investing in wider-range investments is generally considered to be not worthwhile for modest estates (under £20,000) because of the extra administration involved in coping with the Act.

6.167   Curators must also consider whether a particular investment is suitable for the estate and keep in mind the need to diversify so that the whole estate is not invested in one or two particular securities or sectors of the market[8]. A proposed investment must also be prudent. Advice from a stockbroker or other person qualified to give financial advice should be obtained. The Accountant of Court has a duty to consider the investments made and their suitability and may require a curator to sell unsuitable investments[9].

6.168   The court may grant a curator special power to retain an investment previously held by the adult which is not authorised under the Trustee Investments Act 1961[10]. The 1961 Act does not prevent the court authorising new investment in a non-Trustee Act investment, but such authority is rarely given[11].

6.169   In our discussion paper we rejected the option of giving financial managers unfettered discretion regarding investments, as being incompatible with judicial protection of the estate and the supervisory role of the Accountant of Court. Although most private trusts allow trustees very wide investment powers we thought somewhat stricter standards ought to apply to involuntary management. We proposed that a financial manager should have authority to invest in any Trustee Act investments without having to divide the estate into two and that the court should continue to be empowered to approve non-Trustee Act investments[12]. We also proposed that the financial manager should be entitled to retain any of the adult's existing non-Trustee Act investments unless the court ordered disposal[12].

6.170   There was overall agreement with our proposals. The Accountant of Court, however, thought that the financial manager should have to satisfy the court that existing non-Trustee Act investments should be retained rather than having

---

1. Rules of Court, rule 61.14 (Court of Session curators); Judicial Factors Rules 1992, rule 16 (sheriff court curators).
2. Recommendation 39, para 4.15.
3. Recommendation 104, para 6.110.
4. Trustee Investments Act 1961, s 2(1).
5. S 2(3)(a).
6. S 2(3)(b).
7. S 2(4).
8. S 6.
9. Judicial Factors Act 1849, s 13.
10. *Fraser v Paterson (No 2)* 1988 SLT 124 (shares in family company).
11. S 15, see *Henderson Petr* 1981 SLT (Notes) 40.
12. Proposal 41, para 4.107.

statutory authority to retain them unless the court ordered otherwise. The Law Society suggested that investments should be dealt with by means of a management plan. Subject to any directions from the court on appointing the guardian, the guardian and the Public Guardian should agree an investment strategy based on the size of the estate and the adult's current and likely future needs. We find this suggestion appealing in principle but consider that some further guidance is needed to assist the guardian and Public Guardian. First, the guardian should be entitled to retain any existing non-Trustee Act investments held by the adult provided independent advice is obtained recommending retention, although the Public Guardian should have power to direct their disposal should circumstances change. Secondly, investment via personal equity plans should be available to guardians. At present curators cannot invest in this way because the Accountant of Court requires all investments to be in the name of the adult or the curator while the personal equity plan rules require them to be held by the plan managers. Adults under guardianship should not be deprived of the advantages of this method of investment. Thirdly, in considering the investment strategy, either when drawing up the management plan or later, the guardian and Public Guardian should have regard to the current general investment principles: that an investment should be prudent and suitable for the adult's estate, and that there should be a diversity of investments. Except for investments like bank or building society accounts and National Savings products the guardian should be required to obtain independent advice in writing from a stockbroker or other qualified person. Finally, the Public Guardian should be able to authorise the guardian to invest part of the adult's estate in non-Trustee Act investments and to direct the guardian to dispose of any investments. We consider that this kind of investment decision does not require to be dealt with by the court, although the court would have to be involved if the Public Guardian and the guardian were unable to agree on the investment strategy. We recommend that:

128. **(1) The management plan set out in Recommendation 125 above should be used for deciding how the estate of an adult under guardianship should be invested.**

   (2) Unless the court orders otherwise, the guardian should have authority to retain investments held by the adult immediately prior to the guardian's appointment.

   (3) The rules relating to investment in a personal equity plan should be changed so as to allow a guardian to invest in this way on behalf of the adult.

   (4) New investments made by the guardian should normally be limited to those items specified in Schedule 1 to the Trustee Investments Act 1961, but the Public Guardian should have power to authorise other investments.

Schedule 2, paragraph 5

6.171   **Lodging money belonging to adult**. A curator must, at present, lodge money belonging to the incapable adult in a bank or building account in his own name as curator. A curator who keeps money in excess of £500 unbanked for more than 10 days is charged penal interest and is to be dismissed from office without commission unless the money was retained from "innocent causes"[1]. We consider that several changes should be made to this provision in relation to guardianship. First, any account ought to be in the name of the adult with the guardian authorised to operate the account. This would emphasise that the guardian is merely a manager not a trustee. Secondly, all money received by the guardian on behalf of the adult should be banked forthwith. The type of account should depend on the amount of money, the number of likely withdrawals and the need for access. For modest estates with few disbursements a building society account may be the best, larger estates may require a current account plus one or two deposit accounts. Fixed rules would be difficult to frame because the circumstances of estates vary so much. Selection of a suitable account or accounts should be left to the guardian with advice from the Public Guardian as necessary. The guardian should however be required to place in an interest bearing account any sum over £500. Failure to bank money forthwith should be regarded as a serious breach of duty, especially if the guardian uses it for his or her own purposes. If the Public Guardian becomes aware of such a breach he or she should be entitled to apply for the guardian's replacement, but we do not think it should form an express statutory ground for removal. A guardian who left large sums of money in a non-interest bearing account for a substantial period would not have been acting with reasonable care and could therefore be held liable for damages for the loss of interest. We recommend that:

129. **(1) A guardian should be under a duty to lodge all money received on behalf of the adult under guardianship in a bank or building society account forthwith. The account should be in the name of the adult. The type of account should be selected by the guardian so as to provide the best return, bearing in mind the amount of money likely to be involved, the need for access and the likely number of withdrawals.**

   (2) A guardian should be required to place so as to earn interest any balance over £500 (or such other sum as may be prescribed).

Schedule 2, paragraph 4

6.172   **Accounting and auditing of accounts**. Curators at present are required to submit an account of their dealings

---

1. Judicial Factors Act 1849, s 5.

with the adult's estate to the Accountant of Court annually for audit[1]. The accounts are required to be in the form of an account of charge and discharge. They must be submitted within one month of the due date but the Accountant may give up to two months extra time[2].

6.173   In our discussion paper[3] we thought that financial managers should generally be required to submit accounts for auditing by the Accountant of Court but that the system could be made more flexible in a number of ways. We proposed that the court or the Accountant of Court should be empowered to waive the requirement for accounts or allow accounts at intervals greater than a year, for example where the estate is modest and there is little change from year to year. We also asked for views as to whether the form of account should be prescribed and whether accounts should be capable of being certified by a solicitor or accountant rather than audited by the Accountant of Court.

6.174   There was general support from respondents for our proposals for waiving or extending the accounting requirements. It was suggested that the Accountant should prescribe a series of forms of account so that an appropriate one could be selected for a particular estate. We think this is a useful suggestion and would adopt it. Some respondents were in favour of allowing certification by solicitors or accountants as an alternative to audit by the Accountant of Court. The majority, however, considered that the present practice of audit by the Accountant of Court should continue. They saw virtue in having accounts audited by a single central body adopting consistent standards. The Accountant of Court pointed out that the audit also gave the Accountant an opportunity to monitor the actings of the curator and to review investments and the curatory generally. However, he considered that independent certification might be useful where, for example, the estate included a business. The external accountant's certificate would relate to the business part and could be accepted by the Accountant, although the Accountant would have to audit the rest of the accounts. We recommend that:

> **130. (1) Guardians should generally be required to submit annual accounts to the Public Guardian for audit.**
>
> **(2) The Public Guardian should be empowered to substitute a period longer than a year for the normal accounting period or even waive the need for accounts altogether and substitute some other documentation.**
>
> **(3) The Public Guardian should be empowered to prescribe suitable styles of accounts and to direct the guardian as to which style should be used.**
>
> Schedule 2, paragraph 7

6.175   On receiving a curator's accounts the Accountant of Court audits them, fixes the curator's commission and states the result of the audit in a short report. The Accountant may raise queries and ask for further information[4]. The curator has 20 days from intimation of the audit and report to lodge written objections. In the absence of written objections the audit and report are conclusive against the factor, but others interested in the incapable adult's estate may open up the accounts subsequently. Objections that cannot be resolved between the Accountant and the curator may be sent to the court for a ruling[5].

6.176   We assumed in our discussion paper that these audit provisions would by and large be applicable to financial managers. In order to prevent a disproportionate amount of effort being expended in relation to small sums of money, we proposed that an account containing minor discrepancies (including the absence of receipts for minor items) should be capable of being approved provided the Accountant was satisfied that the financial manager had acted in good faith and approval was in the best interests of the adult[6]. There was no dissent on consultation.

6.177   Section 13 of the Judicial Factors Act 1849 provides that a curator's accounts are to be examined and audited by the Accountant. This task will generally be done on the Accountant's behalf by a member of the office. We understand that some of the more complex accounts are occasionally sent to external auditors for audit and that it would be helpful for the Accountant to have express statutory authority to do this. We see no reason why this should not be authorised in relation to guardianship accounts provided the estate remains liable only for such fee as the Public Guardian would have charged if the external accountant's charges are greater.

6.178   We recommend that:

---

1. The first account is submitted in respect of a period starting with the date of the curator's bond of caution being received and ending with the date selected by the Accountant of Court not less than 6 months nor more than 18 months from the starting date; Judicial Factors Act 1849, s 11.
2. Judicial Factors Act 1849, s 4.
3. Proposal 42, para 4.110.
4. Judicial Factors Act 1849, s 13.
5. Judicial Factors Act 1849, s 15.
6. Proposal 42, para 4.110.

131. **(1) The current rules relating to the audit of curatory accounts by the Accountant of Court should generally be adopted for the audit of guardianship accounts by the Public Guardian. The Public Guardian should be entitled to approve accounts containing minor discrepancies (including the absence of receipts for modest disbursements) provided he or she is satisfied that the guardian had acted reasonably and in good faith.**

(2) The Public Guardian should be entitled to delegate the auditing of guardianship accounts to external auditors. Audit by external auditors should not lead to the audit fee being greater than would have been charged for an audit carried out by the Public Guardian.

Schedule 2, paragraphs 7(6) and 8

Variation of guardianship orders

6.179   In our discussion paper[1] we proposed that the court should be empowered to vary a personal guardianship order at any time on application by any person having an interest. There was no dissent from this proposal on consultation. The discussion paper contained no express proposals for the variation of powers conferred on a financial manager. Clearly a change of circumstances may give rise to the need to vary the guardian's financial powers as well. The applicant for variation would, we imagine, normally be made by the guardian, but any other person with an interest in the adult's welfare or estate should be entitled to apply. The documentation that should be presented in support of the application for variation would depend on the variation being sought. Under our recommendations dealing with the appointment of a guardian the sheriff has power to make interim orders[2]. Interim orders would also be useful pending the determination of an application for variation. The court's interlocutor varying the guardian's powers should be sent to the Public Guardian who should amend the guardianship register accordingly. Where welfare powers were varied the Public Guardian would also need to inform the Mental Welfare Commission and the local authority. We recommend that:

132. **(1) The sheriff should have power to vary the powers conferred on a guardian if there has been a material change in circumstances since the guardian was appointed.**

(2) The guardian or any other person claiming an interest in the incapable adult's welfare or estate should be entitled to apply for a variation.

(3) The sheriff should have power to grant an interim variation or make any other interim order pending the determination of the application for variation.

Clauses 3(2)(d) and 59

Renewal of guardianship

6.180   Guardianship under the 1984 Act lasts for six months initially. The guardianship may be renewed for a further six months. After that further renewals are possible for periods of a year at a time[3]. Tutors-dative and curators are appointed until further order of the court, although most of the modern petitions for tutors-dative have sought appointment for a limited period only[4]. In our discussion paper we pointed out that most of the systems of personal guardianship enacted over the last few years in Commonwealth countries incorporate mandatory periodic reviews of the need for guardianship to continue. Without mandatory review it is considered that there is a danger of adults remaining subject to guardianship when it is no longer needed because no-one applies for recall[5].

6.181   We recommend earlier[6] that guardians should normally be appointed for three years initially, but that the court should have power to appoint for a shorter or longer period or, in appropriate cases, for an indefinite period. The recommendation also provides that fixed term appointments should be renewable on one or more occasions. It remains to be considered how renewal should be effected.

6.182   We consider that the sheriff should have to renew a guardianship order. We do not regard a renewal as something that should be decided by an administrative body like the Public Guardian, the Mental Welfare Commission or the local authority, even if there were to be a right of appeal to the sheriff. Our preference for the courts is however based on a simple and inexpensive application procedure being used. Applications could be made using printed forms. A medical report and a "social circumstances" report should be required to satisfy the court that guardianship is still necessary. One medical report should be sufficient as it would be required only to confirm that there was no substantial improvement in the adult's condition. The "social circumstances" report could be provided by someone who knows the adult well, a social

---

1. Proposal 14(c), para 2.95.
2. Recommendation 90, para 6.39.
3. 1984 Act, s 47.
4. *Morris Petr* 1989, 5 years; *Henderson Petr* 1989, 5 years.
5. In *Winterwerp v Netherlands* 24 October 1979 the European Court of Human Rights decided that a mentally ill detainee had a right to periodic and meaningful reviews of his condition.
6. Recommendation 93, para 6.44.

worker, the primary carer or even a close relative or friend for example. If the guardian had welfare powers a report should be required from the local authority mental health officer. The application should be intimated to the adult, his or her nearest relatives and primary carer who should be given an opportunity to object. Such procedure would we think be fairly rapid and inexpensive and could be operated without legal representation at least in unopposed cases. Provided guardianship did not have to be renewed too frequently such a procedure should not impose too heavy a burden on the adult's estate.

6.183   We recommend earlier[1] that renewal should normally be for five years, but that the court should be able to specify a shorter or longer period, or renew until further order. The Law Society suggested that any renewal should be capable of lasting up to 10 years in order to avoid too many renewals for those who have a mental disability which is life-long and static. Others favoured a shorter period, such as two or three years. The Scottish Association for Mental Health suggested that the review dates should be flexible so that the sheriff could select an appropriate period. We are attracted by this suggestion but think it would be helpful to indicate a norm of five years for each renewal. A longer period on renewal is justifiable since adults whose condition remains the same for the first three years are unlikely to change much thereafter. The sheriff should be able to fix a period longer or shorter than five years or even renew guardianship until further order. Indefinite renewal of guardianship would be appropriate for those cases, such as the severely head-injured or Alzheimer's sufferers, where there is no foreseeable hope of recovery.

6.184   We recommend that:

133. On the expiry of any initial period specified in the guardianship order, the order should lapse but should be capable of being renewed by the sheriff on application by any person claiming an interest in the adult's welfare or estate, using a simple and inexpensive procedure.

Clause 46

6.185   The simplified procedure for renewal set out above should apply only if the application is made while the guardianship order remains in force. If it terminates by the expiry of its specified period then a new application for guardianship should have to be made. Once an application has been made, however, this should have the effect of extending the life of the guardianship order at least until the determination of the application. We recommend that:

134. The effect of an application to renew guardianship should be that the existing guardianship order should continue to have effect until the determination of the application.

Clause 46(1)

Termination of guardianship

6.186   It is clear that a guardianship order must come to an end on the death of the adult under guardianship. Consideration needs to be given to the effect this has on the guardian and third parties who transact with the guardian in ignorance of the adult's death. The Keeper of the Registers of Scotland and the Committee of Scottish Clearing Bankers were concerned that third parties involved with the guardian might be unaware that the guardian's authority had come to an end on the lapse of the guardianship order. The common law in relation to attorneys is that an attorney may continue to exercise the powers as long as he or she acts in good faith and without knowledge of the granter's death (or any other event terminating the powers)[2]. A similar rule applies to third parties who transact with an attorney; they are protected if they are unaware of the termination of the attorney's authority and act in good faith[3]. We would adopt a similar approach for guardianship and accordingly recommend that:

135. (1) A guardian should continue to be entitled to act after the adult's death or other event terminates the guardianship order, provided he or she acted in good faith and was unaware of the death or other terminating event.

(2) A third party should be entitled to rely on a guardian's authority which had terminated provided the third party acted in good faith and was unaware of the termination.

Clause 62

Recall of guardianship

6.187   Occasionally a curatory is terminated because the adult recovers, or is found in a later examination to have sufficient capacity to take over the management of his or her financial affairs. In our discussion paper we pointed out several defects in the existing procedure for recall of curatory on the ground of the adult's recovery which we considered should not be incorporated into the new system of financial management. First, the onus rests on the applicant for recall to show that capacity has been recovered. The court assumes that the original order was correctly made. But this can lead

---

1.   Recommendation 93, para 6.44.
2.   *Campbell v Anderson* (1829) 3 W&S 384.
3.   *Pollok v Paterson* Dec 10 1811 FC.

to a curatory being continued in circumstances where no curator would be appointed. Secondly, recall is based on the medical issue of recovery of capacity. Circumstances may have changed however, so that even with little or no change in capacity the adult can manage his or her affairs. Thirdly, the title to apply for recall is not clear and it would be unsatisfactory to confine it to the adult. We therefore proposed[1] that recall should be available if the grounds for appointment of a financial manager (a mixture of medical and benefit grounds) were no longer satisfied, that there should be no presumption of capacity or incapacity of the adult and that an application should be able to be made by any person interested in the adult's estate.

6.188   A person subject to guardianship under the 1984 Act may be discharged in a number of ways. These are by:

(a) the responsible medical officer if he or she is satisfied that the adult is not "suffering from mental disorder of a nature or degree which warrants his remaining under guardianship"[2] (the medical ground);

(b) the local authority if satisfied that it is not "necessary in the interests of the welfare of the patient that he should remain under guardianship"[3] (the welfare ground);

(c) the Mental Welfare Commission if satisfied that either the medical ground or the welfare ground or both is not applicable[4];

(d) the person's nearest relative[5];

(e) the sheriff on an appeal by the nearest relative under paragraph (d) above[6] or on an appeal by the adult under guardianship against renewal of guardianship[7].

In our discussion paper we proposed[8] that the court should have power to recall a personal guardianship order at any time on application by any person having an interest.

6.189   Those responding to our proposals relating to recall of a financial manager's appointment (set out in paragraph 6.187) were generally in favour. The Law Society suggested that the grounds for recall should be widened to include that either the estate or the management needs had changed so as to render management by a financial manager no longer necessary. Enable made a somewhat similar suggestion that a recall should be granted where it would produce a substantial benefit to the adult. These proposals and suggestions were made against the background of guardianship being available to an adult who lacked the capacity wholly or partly to understand the nature of and to foresee the possible implications of financial decisions and where financial management would produce a substantial benefit to them. Under our recommendations guardianship would be available to those who are incapable and by reason of such incapacity, unable to make decisions or act to promote or safeguard their interests in relation to their property, financial affairs or personal welfare. Although the focus has shifted from capacity to ability to cope with an existing state of affairs, we consider that it would still be helpful to have an express provision whereby guardianship could be recalled if the estate had become simpler or alternative measures, advisory or management, were available so that the adult's affairs could be managed by the adult or other person without guardianship.

6.190   Respondents were in favour of the category of people with title to apply for recall being widely drawn, but the Sheriffs' Association suggested safeguards to prevent frivolous or malicious applications. We think that the cost of making an application and the likelihood of being found liable for the whole expenses of the application (including the guardian's expenses in opposing it) should be a sufficient deterrent. In addition legal aid would not be made available to those who could not demonstrate a reasonable case for making the application. The Scottish Association for Mental Health suggested that if the local authority had been involved in the guardian's appointment it should be under a duty to investigate if it suspected guardianship was no longer necessary and be under a duty to apply for recall if it seemed no longer necessary. The principle of least restriction, which is one of our recommended general principles that is to apply to all decision-makers including guardians, should encourage guardians to consider from time to time whether guardianship is still necessary and make an application for recall if it is not. In our view it is unnecessary to place a statutory duty to apply for recall on guardians and it would be invidious to select the local authority as the only category of guardian under such a statutory duty.

---

1. Proposal 49, para 4.137.
2. S 50(3).
3. S 50(4).
4. S 50(3) and (4).
5. S 51. The nearest relative may notify the local authority of his or her intention to order the adult's discharge. The mental health officer of the local authority then first considers whether the welfare ground for guardianship continues to apply. If so the responsible medical officer is then asked whether the medical ground of guardianship continues to apply. If either ground (or both) is considered not to continue to apply the nearest relative's order for discharge will stand. But where both grounds are considered to continue to apply the local authority so informs the nearest relative and the effect is to render any order for discharge by the nearest relative ineffective.
6. S 47(6). The sheriff will order discharge unless the grounds for guardianship are regarded as still continuing to apply.
7. S 51(2).
8. Proposal 14(c), para 2.95.

6.191   Most of those responding agreed with our proposal that the court should have power to recall the appointment of a personal guardian at any time on the application of any person having an interest. The Scottish Association for Mental Health pointed out that our proposal implied that the other ways of discharging a patient from guardianship under the 1984 Act (set out in paragraph 6.188) would not be applicable to the new personal guardianship. The Mental Welfare Commission, local authority, responsible medical officer and nearest relative would, of course, be entitled to apply to the court for recall of guardianship under our proposals. But the first three would not be under a duty, as they are at present, to recall guardianship if satisfied that the grounds no longer applied nor would they have the power to recall. The same point was made subsequently at several seminars and meetings.

6.192   There would be a certain symmetry in making recall a judicial function only. Since only a court can appoint a guardian, it might be argued that only a court should be empowered to recall the appointment. On reconsideration, in the light of the responses and other representations made to us, we now think that where a guardian has welfare powers the Mental Welfare Commission and the local authority should be able to recall these powers[1]. Where the guardian was appointed with financial and welfare powers the result of the Mental Welfare Commission or local authority exercising their powers to recall would be to leave the guardian with only financial powers. The Mental Welfare Commission and the local authority would under our recommendations have statutory duties in relation to guardianship, supervising and monitoring the guardian or in the case of the local authority perhaps with the chief social work officer acting as guardian. The Commission and the local authority will make the same visits to those under new style guardianship with welfare powers as they do at present in relation to those under mental health guardianship. This would give them an opportunity to see whether the welfare powers are still required and to assess the adult's reactions to the past use of welfare powers and possible future use. Recall by the local authority or the Mental Welfare Commission would not involve the guardian or the adult's estate in expense which an application to the court would involve. Both the local authority and the Mental Welfare Commission contain specialists who will be able to judge whether or not the welfare powers of a guardian should be recalled. None of these considerations necessarily apply to the adult's responsible medical officer or nearest relative. In our view if they consider that the welfare powers should be recalled they should either notify the Mental Welfare Commission or local authority so that one of these bodies could consider exercising their powers to recall or they should apply for recall to the Commission or the local authority or the court. We considered requiring the Mental Welfare Commission or the local authority to apply to the court for recall of welfare powers once they were satisfied that they should be recalled, instead of recalling the powers themselves. While this would preserve the legal symmetry mentioned above it would give the court a merely formal role in those cases (the vast majority probably) which were unopposed.

6.193   The grounds for recall of welfare powers should be along the same lines as those we suggested for recall of financial guardianship by the court. Accordingly, welfare powers should be recalled if the grounds for granting them are no longer applicable or methods other than guardianship can now be used to achieve the same welfare purposes. All bodies with power to recall (the sheriff, the Mental Welfare Commission and the local authority) should be required to use the same grounds so as to achieve consistency. In a court-based procedure the guardian and the adult would, as a matter of course, be given notice of the application to recall welfare powers and given an opportunity to make representations. Earlier in the report we recommended a procedure which the Public Guardian should follow in granting authority to a person to withdraw money from an incapable adult's account[2]. This involves intimation to various people and considering objections. A similar procedure should be adopted by the Mental Welfare Commission and local authority in recalling guardianship powers.

6.194   We now turn to look at recall of the financial powers of a guardian otherwise than by the sheriff. A few curatories are brought to an end because there is no longer estate to be managed (the estate is said to be exhausted) or the estate becomes small enough to be handed over to hospital managers to manage on behalf of the adult under section 94 of the 1984 Act[3]. In order to avoid the expense of a formal petition for discharge the Accountant of Court informally "writes off" the curatory. In our discussion paper we suggested that this sensible practice should be adopted for financial managers and extended[4]. We saw this procedure being mainly used for small estates which no longer needed management by a financial manager. The estate, could in terms of our other proposals, either be handed over to the managers of a hospital, nursing home or other residential establishment or put in a bank account from which carers or relatives could be authorised to withdraw money for the adult's benefit.

6.195   Those responding to the proposals in the discussion paper were generally in favour of them. Some bodies considered that impersonal institutional management was not preferable to financial management by a relative. Others pointed out that the adult's income might still need to be managed even though the estate had a very small capital value.

---

1. See para 6.188 for the grounds of recall.
2. Para 4.15. The same procedure would apply to the discharge of a former guardian, see para 6.217
3. Scottish Office Central Research Unit Paper, *Financial Management of Incapacitated Adults: Characteristics of Curatories*, Fiona Rutherdale (1992), para 5.5.
4. Proposal 48, para 4.133.

Since our discussion paper was published new rules of court have been made[1]. Rule 19 of the Judicial Factors Rules 1992 gives the Accountant of Court power, on application by a curator appointed in the sheriff court, to grant a discharge where the adult has recovered capacity or died or where the estate is exhausted. A similar rule exists in relation to Court of Session curatories[2]. A curatory can now be terminated administratively by the Accountant of Court if two medical certificates are produced stating that the adult has recovered and can now manage his or her own affairs. It would be a retrograde step not to give similar power to the Public Guardian in relation to recall of the financial powers of a guardian. In "recovery" cases the test for recall should be whether the grounds for appointing a guardian are no longer fulfilled rather than that the adult has recovered capacity for managing his or her own affairs. We also consider that the Public Guardian should have power to recall the guardian's financial powers where the adult's estate can be satisfactorily managed otherwise than by guardianship. The procedure should be similar to that we have already recommended for recall of welfare powers by the Mental Welfare Commission or the local authority[3].

6.196   Summing up this section we recommend that:

136. (1) Where the condition of the adult under guardianship has improved so that the grounds for guardianship (set out in Recommendation 85) are no longer satisfied in relation to the adult's welfare or financial affairs or the circumstances are now such that the adult's welfare or financial affairs could be satisfactorily dealt with otherwise than by guardianship, the sheriff should be empowered, on application by any person claiming an interest in the adult's welfare or estate, to recall the welfare and financial powers of the guardian.

(2) The Mental Welfare Commission and the local authority should have powers similar to those of the sheriff in paragraph (1) above but in relation to welfare powers only. The Public Guardian should have similar powers in relation to financial powers only. The Mental Welfare Commission, the local authority or the Public Guardian should be entitled to act on application by any person claiming an interest or at their own instance. In either case the guardian, the adult and the adult's nearest relative and primary carer and any other interested persons should be notified, giving them an opportunity to object and make representations before a decision is taken. The Mental Welfare Commission, local authority or Public Guardian should be entitled to remit the matter to the sheriff on their own initiative or on request by any objector.

Clauses 56(1)(c) and 58(1)-(8)

Resignation and replacement of guardians

6.197   We turn now to deal with a change of guardian. A change may be necessary because the existing guardian wishes to resign, has died or has become unsuitable. At present the grounds for replacement of a curator include his or her bankruptcy, acquisition of an adverse interest, becoming mentally incapable or otherwise unfit or unable to carry out the duties[4]. In our discussion paper we proposed[5] that in addition to the presently recognised grounds it should be competent to replace a financial manager whose relationship with the incapable adult or the adult's family and carers was such that it would be in the adult's best interests that someone else took over as curator. This proposal was supported on consultation but the Accountant of Court and the Sheriffs' Association were concerned lest suitable people were replaced for frivolous or malicious reasons. The likelihood of being found liable for the expenses of an unfounded application should we think be a sufficient deterrent. The Law Society thought it important that replacement on grounds of incompatibility did not imply criticism of the existing manager, the adult or others involved. Guardians will be expected to work more closely with the adults under guardianship and their carers than curators are expected to at present and the relationship may not work through no fault of either party. To stigmatise the guardian as unsuitable, or to use some similar phrase, could in some circumstances lead to bitter and contested litigation. We prefer not to set out express grounds for replacement. The court's decision would therefore be made on the basis of the general principles in which the benefit to the adult from a change of guardian would be assessed, taking into account the views of the adult, the adult's nearest relative and carer and others with an interest such as the guardian.

6.198   Guardians will also be required to be replaced where the existing guardian wishes to be released from the post or has died. In these circumstances appointment of a new guardian should generally be uncontentious. At present a petition for the appointment of a new curator has to be presented and this gives rise to considerable expenditure. In our discussion paper we put forward a simple procedure for the replacement of a financial manager who wished to resign[6]. We did not consider that a financial manager should simply be allowed to resign[7]. Financial managers would be appointed to look

---

1. Under s 34A of the Judicial Factors Act 1849 added by s 67 of the Law Reform (Miscellaneous Provisions) (Scotland) Act 1990.
2. Court of Session Rules 1993, rule 61.31.
3. Para 6.193.
4. Irons, *The Law and Practice in Scotland relative to Judicial Factors*, p 343.
5. Proposal 50, para 4.139.
6. Proposal 51, para 4.143.
7. The position is different with joint appointees or where a substitute has been appointed, see para 6.205.

after the adult's financial affairs so that resignation without replacement would leave the adult unprotected. Our proposed procedure involved a written application by the proposed new financial manager in which the applicant would be required to state that he or she had no substantial adverse interest, the Accountant of Court would be required to state that the retiring financial manager's administration had so far been correct and that the adult, the family and others with an interest would be given an opportunity to object. In the absence of any objection the application for replacement of the existing manager would be granted. Views were invited as to whether this procedure should be limited to solicitors or accountants applying to be replacement financial managers.

6.199   Those responding were generally in favour of our proposed procedure. The Accountant of Court observed that a replacement financial manager would also be required where the existing manager had died and drew our attention to section 10 of the Judicial Factors (Scotland) Act 1889. This provision lays a duty on the Accountant of Court to seek a replacement for a deceased judicial factor where no other person is applying to be appointed. We would agree that a simple administrative procedure should be available to provide a replacement to a deceased guardian. The application should be capable of being made by any interested person, including the Public Guardian who may nominate a suitable individual or nominate himself or herself as Public Guardian. Another situation where a simple administrative procedure would be appropriate would be where the existing guardian became mentally incapable of performing the duties. In this case the application should have to be accompanied by a medical certificate of the existing guardian's incapacity.

6.200   The Law Society and some other respondents considered that further provisions were required where the existing financial manager's administration had not been correct. On reflection we think that the discharge or exoneration of an existing guardian is a separate matter from his or her replacement although it should be capable of being dealt with in the same application. The protection of the adult by a replacement guardian should not be held up pending the resolution of disputes as to the correctness of the former guardian's or a deceased guardian's administration.

6.201   Respondents were not in favour of restricting the proposed simple procedure to cases where the replacement was a solicitor or accountant. All applicants should in our view be required to satisfy the court as to their suitability using the criteria we recommend for the initial appointment of a guardian[1]. "Professional" guardians especially those whose functions are confined to the financial field, should be able to satisfy the court as to their suitability relatively easily. Others might have to submit statements by the local authority or some other person or organisation as to their suitability. The Public Guardian or the chief social work officer should automatically be regarded as suitable and should not be required to submit any evidence of this. The appointment of either of these officials could still be objected to on the ground that a relative or friend would be a more suitable guardian in the circumstances.

6.202   We recommend that:

137. **(1) The sheriff should be empowered to replace an existing guardian with another suitable guardian on the application of any person with an interest in the incapable adult's welfare or finances.**

(2) **Rules of Court should be made to allow a simple procedure to be used where the existing guardian wishes to relinquish the post, or has died or has become mentally incapable of acting as guardian. A hearing should be necessary only if objections were made.**

Clause 56(1)(a)

6.203   The court should also have power to remove a guardian without appointing a replacement where there were joint guardians or a substitute guardian willing to act. Removal of an "unsatisfactory" guardian would enable the remaining joint guardian or guardians to act alone or the substitute to take over the guardianship. We recommend that:

138. **The court should have power to remove a guardian where the guardian sought to be removed was a joint guardian or where a substitute had already been appointed.**

Clause 56(1)(b)

6.204   We recommend earlier that where a chief social work officer or the Public Guardian is appointed as guardian that official is appointed by virtue of his or her position and not as an individual[2]. It follows that where the office holder ceases to hold that position his or her successor will automatically take over the guardianship functions. Where the chief social work officer has been appointed guardian to an adult and that adult subsequently becomes habitually resident in another local authority area the guardian ought to be changed. The chief social work officer of the local authority where the adult used to live ought not to continue to act as guardian because of the lack of legal and operational authority between that officer and the officials of the new local authority who would in practice have to carry out the guardianship functions. This transfer of guardianship should not require any application to the court. The chief social work officer of the former authority should notify the equivalent in the new local authority who would in turn notify the Public Guardian. The Public

---

1. Recommendation 95, para 6.70.
2. Recommendation 94, para 6.60.

Guardian would then amend the guardianship register, issue the new guardian with a certificate of authority and inform the adult of the change of guardian. We recommend that:

139. Where an adult has as guardian the chief social work officer of a local authority and subsequently becomes habitually resident in another local authority area, the chief social work officer of the new local authority should become guardian automatically without any application to the court having to be made. The change of residence should be notified to the chief social work officer of the new local authority who should in turn notify the Public Guardian who should amend the guardianship register accordingly, issue a certificate of authority to the new guardian and inform the incapable adult.

Clause 61

6.205   Guardians, like curators or executors-dative, who are appointed by the court to carry out specified functions, should not be permitted simply to resign leaving no-one to look after the welfare or financial affairs of the incapable adult. We recommend earlier that generally they should have to apply to the court for a replacement to be appointed[1]. However, where joint guardians or a substitute guardian have been appointed resignation should be permitted since the adult would still be left with at least one guardian in post as long as the remaining joint guardian or guardians or the substitute are willing to act. The notice of resignation should have to be given to the Public Guardian who would then amend the register and notify the adult accordingly. To be effective the notice should have to be accompanied by evidence of the other joint guardian's willingness to continue to act or the substitute guardian's willingness to take up guardianship. A substitute guardian who has not become a guardian but is merely waiting "in the wings" should be able to resign by notifying the Public Guardian. The adult will continue to be protected by the acting guardian. We recommend that:

140. (1) A joint guardian should be permitted to resign by giving notice to the Public Guardian. The resignation should be effective only if accompanied by a statement from the remaining joint guardian or guardians that they are willing to continue to act.

(2) A guardian should also be permitted to resign if a substitute guardian has been appointed and is willing to act as guardian.

(3) A substitute guardian who is not an acting guardian should be entitled to resign by giving notice to the Public Guardian.

(4) The Public Guardian on receiving an effective resignation should amend the register of guardians and notify the incapable adult.

Clause 60

Remuneration of guardians

6.206   At present tutors-dative and guardians under the 1984 Act are not entitled to remuneration for their services. In our discussion paper we proposed[2] that this should be the position for personal guardians. Relatives and friends would, we thought, normally undertake the duties on a basis of affection or concern rather than gain, while the local authority social work department would be acting in pursuance of its statutory duties. Nearly all of those who responded agreed with our proposal. It was suggested, however, that the court should be given a discretion to allow fees to be charged since the adult might need a professional personal guardian, such as a non-local authority social worker. We think that this should be allowed in exceptional circumstances for non-local authority guardians.

6.207   Curators are remunerated by way of commission fixed by the Accountant of Court. The amount awarded is what is fair, bearing in mind the size and nature of the income and capital transactions over the accounting period. The commission covers all normal administration. Fees and accounts payable by the curator to others for business or professional services are outlays chargeable directly against the estate. If the curator is a partner in a firm of solicitors the firm cannot charge the curator a fee for legal work done[3]. Solicitors, accountants and others acting as curators in a professional capacity expect to be paid; lay curators often waive wholly or partly the commission to which they are entitled.

6.208   In our discussion paper we proposed[4] that financial managers who act as such as part of their professional business should be entitled to receive remuneration as fixed by the Accountant of Court. Other financial managers were not to be so entitled. Consultation revealed a difference of views. The Senators of the College of Justice considered that officials or members of voluntary agencies concerned with the incapacitated could act as financial managers but they would be

---

1. Recommendation 137, para 6.202.
2. Proposal 13(1), para 2.93.
3. *Mitchell v Burness* (1878) 5 R 1124, but legal fees for work done up to the appointment are a proper charge. *Watt v Watt and others* 1909 1 SLT 103.
4. Proposal 44(1), para 4.123.

discouraged by a lack of remuneration. The present Accountant of Court has indicated to us that in his view even lay guardians exercising financial powers ought to be paid a small fee because administration of someone else's financial affairs is an onerous and responsible task. The Law Society and Alzheimer Scotland - Action on Dementia were in favour of a system of properly trained financial managers who would require to be approved by the Public Guardian and whose performance of their duties would be monitored by that official. In their view only approved financial managers should be entitled to fees. We fully support these respondents' objectives of ensuring that guardians should be aware of the needs arising from incapacity and the importance of having a good working relationship with adults under guardianship, their family and carers. But we are of the opinion that a statutory licensing system for guardians is too bureaucratic. It would entail a considerable increase in the staff of the Public Guardian's office in order to approve the training, license individual applicants and monitor their performance.

6.209   We have reconsidered this matter and now think that guardians should normally be entitled to remuneration in respect of their financial functions but that the sheriff should be able to order otherwise. Factors that would be relevant to the sheriff's decision include the value of the adult's estate and the likely difficulty of managing it. The Public Guardian should fix the remuneration in the light of what the guardian has actually done in the period in question.

6.210   At present the curator's commission is fixed when auditing the accounts. This can cause problems for professional curators who may have to wait for 15 months or more for commission to cover work done early in the accounting period. In our discussion paper we proposed[1] that the Accountant of Court should have authority to allow a payment to account of remuneration. This was agreed by all those who responded. The need for interim remuneration would be greater if, as we recommend earlier[2], the Public Guardian could lengthen the accounting period. Some guardians, such as those with only welfare powers, would not have to submit accounts. They should be entitled to apply to the Public Guardian at appropriate intervals for their remuneration to be fixed.

6.211   We recommend that:

141. (1) Guardians should not generally be entitled to remuneration in relation to the exercise of their welfare functions but the sheriff should have power to award remuneration in exceptional cases to guardians other than the chief social work officer.

(2) Guardians should generally be entitled to remuneration in relation to the exercise of their financial functions. In deciding whether to allow remuneration the sheriff should have regard to the value of the estate and likely difficulty in managing it.

(3) The Public Guardian should fix any remuneration payable to the guardian having regard to the amount of work done when auditing the guardian's accounts or at another time on application by the guardian. The Public Guardian should be able to authorise payment of interim remuneration.

Clause 52(4)-(7)

Reimbursement of guardians

6.212   In a curatory the expenses of the petition for appointment and outlays incurred by the curator during the curatory are chargeable against the adult's estate. In our discussion paper we proposed[3] that all outlays incurred by financial managers in connection with their administration of the estate should be met out of the estate. A similar proposal was made in relation to personal guardians[4]. Our proposal in relation to financial managers was agreed by all those who responded. The Law Society commented that only outlays which were reasonable having regard to the value of the estate and its management needs should be allowed. We accept this suggestion and consider that the Public Guardian should be empowered to disallow unreasonable outlays incurred by guardians in the exercise of their functions. Disallowed outlays would not be chargeable against the estate but would have to be met by the guardian personally. We understand that some lay curators at present hand over most, if not all the work, to solicitors or others with the result that the estate is burdened with substantial fees in addition to the curator's commission. Guardians should be expected to perform personally tasks that lie within their competence.

6.213   Although most of those who responded thought that personal guardians should be entitled to recover outlays reasonably incurred in the exercise of their functions, two bodies were not in favour of this proposal. The Mental Welfare Commission considered that no reimbursement should be allowed as the incapacitated should not have to meet the costs of guardianship which had been imposed on them. The Law Society thought that reimbursement should be competent only if specifically authorised in the appointment of the guardian and if it was reasonable in all the circumstances, including the means of the adult. We think different rules for guardians with financial powers and those with welfare powers cannot

---

1. Proposal 45, para 4.124.
2. Recommendation 130(2), para 6.174.
3. Proposal 44(2), para 4.123.
4. Proposal 13(2), para 2.93.

be justified. If an outlay is reasonably incurred in the exercise of a guardian's functions then it should be chargeable against the adult's estate. Non-recovery of outlays could constitute a disincentive to lay guardianship which we are anxious to encourage, for modest estates at least.

6.214   In our discussion paper we asked for views as to whether a local authority should be entitled to recover out of the adult's estate the expenses of its application for personal guardianship or the running costs of such guardianship[1]. At present expenditure by local authorities in connection with guardianship under the 1984 Act is not charged against the estates of those subject to guardianship. All those who responded considered that the current position should apply to the new personal guardianship. A different rule from that applicable to private guardians can be justified because the local authority in becoming guardian is acting in pursuance of its statutory social work functions. Adoption of a unified system of guardianship, instead of separate financial managers and personal guardians, has led us to reconsider the question of local authority outlays. A local authority official exercising financial powers ought to be entitled to recover reasonable outlays incurred. This is the position at present if he or she acts as curator. Where the chief social work officer has been appointed with purely welfare powers then the cost of the application to the court and any administrative costs should not be chargeable to the adult's estate. The local authority should however be entitled to charge for goods and services delivered if a person in similar circumstances but without a guardian would have been charged. For example, the guardian may decide that the adult would benefit from the home help service. Those who can afford to pay are charged for this service and we see no reason to waive payment simply because the chief social work officer rather than some private individual is the guardian. Where the chief social work officer or some other local authority official was guardian with financial and welfare powers, the court should be empowered to allow a proportion of the expenses of the application for appointment against the adult's estate. As far as the running and administrative costs of such a local authority guardianship are concerned the Public Guardian could allow outlays incurred in the exercise of the financial powers. Outlays incurred in the exercise of welfare powers should be allowed only if the Public Guardian is satisfied that the local authority would have charged a person without a guardian for the goods or services supplied.

6.215   We therefore recommend that:

142. (1) Guardians (other than the chief social work officer of a local authority) should be entitled to reimbursement from the adult's estate for outlays they have reasonably incurred in the exercise of their functions. Guardians should not however be reimbursed for outlays in relation to services which they are expected to perform personally. The Public Guardian should have power to disallow outlays that have not been reasonably incurred.

(2) Where the chief social work officer of a local authority is the guardian he or she should not be entitled to reimbursement from the adult's estate for outlays incurred in the exercise of any welfare functions, unless an adult in similar circumstances but without a guardian would be charged.

Clause 52(1)-(3)

Discharge of guardian

6.216   Section 34 of the Judicial Factors Act 1849 provides a judicial procedure whereby a curator may obtain a discharge and exoneration from the court. Intimation of the application is made to all persons interested in the estate and the Accountant is asked by the court to provide a report. All the curator's previous accounts may be re-examined. A decree discharging the curator is conclusive against all parties concerned, subject to certain provisos. The Law Reform (Miscellaneous Provisions) (Scotland) Act 1990[2] empowered the Court of Session to make rules for an administrative discharge by the Accountant of Court where a curatory terminates by reason of the death or recovery of the adult or the exhaustion of the estate[3]. The Accountant's discharge is thought to be conclusive in the same way as a judicial discharge. There is also the practice of "writing off" curatories. If the curator is willing to dispense with a judicial discharge the Accountant may, on being satisfied that the estate has been fully accounted for, report the case to the court with a view to writing the case off. Under this procedure the curator's actings remain open to later challenge by any interested person.

6.217   We consider that the system of administrative discharges should be extended to guardianship and should be available whatever the reason for the termination of the guardian's appointment or the guardianship. Widening the administrative discharge should preclude the need for informal "write offs" for guardianship. The Public Guardian should be required to follow a similar procedure to that we have recommended for authority to withdraw from an incapable adult's bank account[4]. The application should be intimated, objections considered and difficult cases should be remitted to the sheriff. There should also be a right of appeal to the sheriff against the Public Guardian's decision to grant or refuse

---

1. Proposal 13(2), para 2.93.
2. S 67.
3. This power has been implemented by rule 19 of the Judicial Factors Rules 1992 (sheriff court) and rule 61.31 of the Rules of Court 1993 (Court of Session).
4. Recommendation 40, para 4.15.

a discharge or to remit. In these circumstances we do not see any need for a parallel judicial discharge procedure. We recommend accordingly that:

143. (1) The Public Guardian, on application by a former guardian or the executors of a deceased guardian, should be empowered to grant a discharge to the guardian in respect of his or her dealings with the incapable adult's estate.

(2) The Public Guardian should give the incapable adult and his or her nearest relative and primary carer an opportunity to object to the application. The Public Guardian should have power to grant the application after considering any objections and any further representations by the applicant and any objector, or to remit the application to the sheriff.

Clause 57(1) to (5)

Private international law aspects

6.218   We turn now to consider some United Kingdom and international aspects of guardianship, but by and large confine ourselves to looking at the existing law and pointing out some areas where reform might be considered appropriate. This area of law contains many difficult issues to which there are no obvious answers and about which we have not consulted. These issues include, for example, the law which should govern the conditions which have to be fulfilled before a guardian can be appointed[1]; the question of when and to what extent a guardian appointed or acting by operation of law in one country should be recognised as guardian in another country; the question of the extent to which a guardian appointed by a court in one country, or entitled to act by operation of law under the law of one country,[2] should become subject to the laws of another country when the adult under guardianship becomes habitually resident in that country; and the question whether the supervisory bodies of a country should register "foreign" guardians and monitor their actings within that country. The drawing up of a coherent and comprehensive scheme on these and related issues would be best done by agreement between all the jurisdictions involved. The private international law relating to the protection of incapable adults is on the agenda of the Hague Conference on Private International Law[3], so that it is possible that there may be an international convention on this subject within the foreseeable future. This, in our view, would be a very useful development.

6.219   **Financial powers**. Scottish common law recognises the position of certain non-Scottish guardians, by which we mean guardians not appointed by a Scottish court. As Anton puts it:

"The Scottish court will recognise the title of a foreign guardian, whether appointed to the office by the courts of the ward's domicile or recognised as holding the office by the ward's domiciliary law, to sue for personal debts and otherwise deal in the ward's moveable property in Scotland[4]."

There are also statutory provisions dealing with recognition within the United Kingdom. The 1984 Act[5] contains provisions for reciprocal arrangements in relation to powers of curators, tutors and judicial factors and their Northern Irish equivalents. Thus a curator bonis, tutor or judicial factor appointed under Scottish law may exercise powers over the adult's property and affairs in Northern Ireland unless a committee, receiver or guardian has been appointed for that adult in Northern Ireland. Similarly the Northern Irish committee, receiver or guardian can exercise powers over property and affairs in Scotland unless a curator, tutor or judicial factor has been appointed in Scotland. Land and interests in land (other than rent or income arising from land) are excluded[6] so that a Scottish curator or a Northern Irish committee has to be appointed to deal with such matters in Scotland or Northern Ireland respectively. The reciprocal arrangements between Scotland and England and Wales are in identical terms apart from changes in terminology[7].

6.220   We have no doubt that there are aspects of the existing private international law on the guardianship of incapable adults which are in need of reform. For example, the rules on recognition of foreign guardians currently refer to the law of the adult's domicile. It would be more consistent with developments elsewhere in the law, and more sensible, to refer to the law of the adult's habitual residence. Again, there are special exemptions for immoveable property and land and interests in land in the existing common and statute law. The powers of a foreign guardian are not generally recognised in relation to such assets.[8] This, however, reflects an old-fashioned view that such assets are somehow different from

---

1. Different countries, for example, may have different definitions of the type of incapacity which justifies the appointment of a guardian. If an application is made to a Scottish court for the appointment of a guardian to a person who is domiciled or habitually resident in a country outside Scotland, but who has property in Scotland, should a Scottish court apply Scottish law or the foreign law?
2. In some countries a parent or spouse of an incapable adult may be entitled to act as guardian without any court appointment.
3. See the Final Act of the 16th session of the conference, part B(3)(c).
4. Anton, *Private International Law*, (2nd edn), p 569; *Sawyer v Sloan* (1875) 3 R 271; *Forsyth* 1932 SLT 462.
5. S 95.
6. S 95(3).
7. Mental Health Act 1983, s 110.
8. *The Public Trustee of New Zealand Petr* 1921 2 SLT 240; *Waring Petr* 1933 SLT 190.

other kinds of property. It is also more expensive and inconvenient to have an extra guardian appointed by the courts of the country where the immoveables are situated simply to deal with those assets. It is certainly arguable that if a non-Scottish guardian, whose appointment as such is recognised in Scotland, has authority in terms of his or her appointment to deal with immoveable property wherever situated then such powers ought to be recognised in Scotland. We expressed similar views in our *Report on Family Law*[1] in relation to foreign guardians of children domiciled abroad who at present are also prohibited from dealing with Scottish heritage[2]. However, we have not consulted on any of these issues and we think it better not to make recommendations on them in this report. We do consider that, as a matter of Scottish law, the powers of a guardian appointed by a Scottish court should extend to property wherever situated and of whatever kind[3]. It would, of course, be a matter for the law of the country where the property was situated whether to recognise a Scottish guardian's powers. We therefore recommend that:

144. The powers of a Scottish guardian in relation to the property of the incapable adult should extend to property wherever situated, whether moveable or immoveable.

Clause 52(2)(a)

6.221   **Welfare powers**. There is virtually no common law authority as to the exercise of welfare powers by foreign guardians in Scotland or the exercise abroad of welfare powers by Scottish guardians. Section 83 of the 1984 Act empowers the Secretary of State to authorise the removal of a patient who is neither a British citizen nor a Commonwealth citizen with a right of abode in the United Kingdom to another country where proper arrangements will be made for the patient's care. The 1984 Act and the equivalent legislation for England and Wales, the Mental Health Act 1983, contain provisions for the transfer of adults liable to be detained or subject to guardianship under this legislation from one part of the United Kingdom to another. Thus, section 77(1) of the 1984 Act empowers the Secretary of State to authorise the removal of an adult subject to guardianship in Scotland to England and Wales for reception into guardianship there if removal appears to be in the interests of the adult. The adult on removal is to be treated as if he or she had been received on the date of arrival into guardianship under the 1983 Act. Almost identical powers exist in relation to transfers from England and Wales or Northern Ireland to Scotland and from Scotland to Northern Ireland.

6.222   The above statutory provisions should be retained for persons liable to be detained in a hospital, but we do not think they are suitable for the new type of guardianship which we recommend or for the managers with personal welfare powers recommended by the Law Commission of England and Wales in their *Report on Mental Incapacity*[4]. First, the authority of the Secretary of State should not be necessary to enable an adult to go from Scotland to another part of the United Kingdom. The guardian of a Scottish adult should be entitled, if appropriate powers have been conferred by the court, to move the adult from a residence in Scotland to another in England without reference to the Secretary of State. Again, the parents who are looking after, and who are guardians of, their grown-up mentally handicapped daughter should be able to move to live in Wales taking their daughter with them should they wish to do so. Secondly, the provisions predicate, perhaps because they are primarily concerned with detention in hospital of mentally disordered patients or prisoners, a controlling or coercive view of guardianship and one that is exercised by public authorities.

6.223   A guardian who is validly appointed in Scotland should, as a matter of Scottish law, be entitled to exercise the welfare powers conferred whether the adult is within or outwith Scotland. This would, for example, enable the guardian to consent to medical treatment abroad if the adult went there on a holiday. It would, of course, be a matter for the law of the country where the adult was whether the Scottish guardian's powers would be recognised. We therefore recommend that:

145. The powers of a Scottish guardian in relation to the personal welfare of the incapable adult should, as a matter of Scottish law, be exercisable even if the adult is outside Scotland.

Clause 51(3)

6.224   Problems may arise when incapable adults move or are taken from one country to another. For example, should it be necessary to apply for a new guardianship order in the country of the new habitual residence? At the very least in such cases there will often be a need for information and co-operation between the supervising authorities in the respective countries. In some cases it may be appropriate to have some mechanisms in place to enable the return of the adult to be arranged. In others there may be a need to prohibit by way of interdict and other measures the removal of incapable adults

---

1. Scot Law Com No 135 (1992), para 6.5.
2. *Ogilvy v Ogilvy's Trs* 1927 SLT 83.
3. The current reciprocal arrangements within the United Kingdom noted in the preceding paragraph extend a Scottish curator's powers to moveables in all the constituent jurisdictions. See also section 13 of the Judicial Factors (Scotland) Act 1889 which gives the title of any judicial factor (which term includes curators) "the full force and effect of an assignment or transfer...of all funds, property, and effects situated or invested in any part of the British dominions".
4. Law Com No 231 (March 1995), Part VIII.

from Scotland to another country where objections are made to this action[1]. These are issues that we can only raise in this report but we hope that the appropriate authorities will take steps to consider them at least on a United Kingdom basis and preferably on a wider international basis.

6.225 **Scope of Bill's provisions.** Although we have not, in the absence of consultation on the issue, thought it right to make recommendations on questions of private international law generally, we have had to consider whether the provisions on guardians in the draft Bill appended to this report should apply only to guardians appointed by a Scottish court or also to other guardians[2]. The answer varies according to the nature of the provision. For example, where there is an obligation to consult a guardian who is known to exist, that obligation should extend to a guardian appointed in England and recognised in Scotland just as it extends to a guardian appointed in Scotland. However, the system of registration, supervision and regulation by the Public Guardian and, in the case of personal welfare matters, the specific supervisory obligations of the Mental Welfare Commission and the local authorities, are intended, at least for the time being, to apply only to guardians appointed by a Scottish court. It is only in the case of such guardians that there will be a mechanism for bringing the guardianship to the attention of the relevant supervisory authorities. That does not apply to the investigation of complaints. There is no reason why only incapable adults with a guardian appointed in Scotland should have the protection of official investigations into allegations of abuse or malpractice. This protection should, in our view, be available to any incapable adult habitually resident in Scotland or, if the complaint relates to property, to any incapable adult having property in Scotland. Similarly, the sheriff's powers to make protective orders ought to apply generally where the incapable adult is habitually resident in Scotland or has property in Scotland (or, in cases of urgency, is present in Scotland), no matter where the guardian may have been appointed. It may be useful in such cases, for example, for the sheriff to be able to replace a foreign guardian by a local guardian who would be subject to supervision. And the rules on the liability of guardians and on the validity of transactions entered into by guardians ought not to be confined to guardians appointed in Scotland. These are the principles on which the applicability of particular provisions in the draft Bill has been determined on a clause by clause basis. The question of whether a particular guardian appointed or acting under the law of another country is recognised in Scotland is left to the general rules on private international law on this subject. It will be for consideration at a later date, possibly in the light of reciprocal international agreements, whether any of the supervisory and regulatory functions which at present are applicable only to guardians appointed in Scotland should be made applicable to foreign guardians where the adult in question becomes habitually resident in Scotland.

---

1. See *Re S (Hospital Patient: Court's Jurisdiction)* [1995] 1 All ER 449.
2. Similar questions arise in relation to continuing and welfare attorneys and our general approach has been the same as in the case of guardians, see para 3.83.

Part 7 Miscellaneous

Introduction

7.1   In this Part we discuss some miscellaneous questions relating to procedure, appeals, transitional provisions and consequential amendments and repeals. We also refer to three matters which were raised in the discussion paper but which we have decided not to pursue.

Procedure

7.2   The draft Bill provides for various applications to the sheriff. Some of these would replace applications for guardianship under the 1984 Act and applications for the appointment of a curator bonis under the Judicial Factors Acts. Others would be new types of application. At present section 40(6) of the 1984 Act (guardianship applications) provides that:

> "The sheriff in the exercise of the functions conferred on him by this section shall have the like jurisdiction, and the like powers as regards the summoning and examination of witnesses, the administration of oaths, the awarding of expenses, and otherwise, as if he were acting in the exercise of his civil jurisdiction."

This implies that the functions in question are not part of the sheriff's civil jurisdiction. We think that proceedings under the new legislation which we are recommending are clearly civil proceedings for the purposes of the Sheriff Courts (Scotland) Act 1907, thus attracting not only the ordinary powers of the sheriff in civil cases but also the rule-making power of the Court of Session[1].

Appeals

7.3   The draft Bill gives the Public Guardian certain decision-making powers. For example, the Public Guardian may authorise an individual to withdraw money from an incapable adult's bank account in order to use it for the adult's benefit[2], allow a guardian to make gifts from the adult's estate[3] or recall a financial guardianship when the adult's estate can be managed satisfactorily otherwise[4]. The Mental Welfare Commission or the local authority also have power to recall the personal welfare powers conferred on a guardian if the powers are no longer needed[5]. We think that all these decision-making powers are justified in the interests of efficiency. We have no desire to force people into unnecessary court proceedings. However, because such decisions could affect, or at least reflect adversely on, individuals we think it is important in the interests of justice that an appeal should lie to the sheriff. We therefore recommend that:

146. An appeal should lie from any decision of the Public Guardian, the Mental Welfare Commission or the local authority in the exercise of their functions to the sheriff.

Clauses generally

7.4   Generally the result of an appeal to the sheriff should be that the Public Guardian's decision should not be put into effect pending the determination of the appeal. Where the Public Guardian decides to suspend or terminate a withdrawer's authority we consider that the decision should remain in effect until it is reversed on appeal. The adult's affairs may be in need of immediate protection and this may be achievable only if the authority is suspended with immediate effect. We recommend that:

147. The Public Guardian's decision to suspend or terminate the authority granted to a person to withdraw funds from the account of an incapable adult should remain in effect notwithstanding any appeal to the sheriff until it is reversed on appeal.

Clause 24(4)

---

1. The Court of Session has power under s 32 of the Sheriff Courts (Scotland) Act 1971 to regulate and prescribe the procedure and practice to be followed in any civil proceedings in the sheriff court.
2. Recommendation 37, para 4.12.
3. Recommendation 102, para 6.109.
4. Recommendation 134, para 6.192.
5. Recommendation 134, para 6.192.

K

7.5   Appeals from the sheriff are presently governed by sections 7 and 27 to 29 of the Sheriff Courts (Scotland) Act 1907. Briefly, any final judgment and a few specified interlocutors may be appealed either to the sheriff principal and thence to the Inner House of the Court of Session or directly to the Inner House. Other interlocutors are appealable only with the leave of the sheriff. Where the value of the claim does not exceed £1,500 an appeal to the Inner House is incompetent. We see no reason to depart from this scheme for most of the matters that would be decided by the sheriff under our recommendations. A few judgments, particularly some of those decided on appeal from the Public Guardian, however, are matters of management and do not involve any infringement of civil liberties or substantial sums of money. The smooth administration of an incapable adult's affairs could be jeopardised by a series of appeals. We consider that the sheriff's decision should be final in such cases. Examples of finality include the sheriff's decision in relation to the guardianship management plan[1], the sheriff's determination on appeal from a refusal by the Public Guardian to authorise an increase in the amount the managers of an establishment are entitled to manage[2] or a refusal by the Public Guardian to allow the guardian interim payments of remuneration to account[3]. We recommend that:

148.   The existing rules relating to appeals from a determination by a sheriff should apply to all determinations by a sheriff under our recommendations except in relation to the following determinations which should be final and not subject to appeal.

(a)   The sheriff's determination of an appeal from a decision of the Public Guardian:

   (i)   refusing to accept that the attorney is accepting the appointment (Recommendation 20),

   (ii)   refusing to accept that an event has occurred which allows registration of a continuing power of attorney (Recommendation 22),

   (iii) in relation to an application for authority to withdraw from a bank or building society account or to remit the application to the sheriff (Recommendation 40),

   (iv)   granting an extension of authority to a withdrawer (Recommendation 41(2)),

   (v)   suspending or terminating the authority of a withdrawer (Recommendation 44(2)),

   (vi)   refusing to allow the managers of an approved establishment to manage money or property in excess of the prescribed value (Recommendation 54(2)),

   (vii) refusing to authorise the making of a gift by the guardian or to remit the application to the sheriff (Recommendation 104),

   (viii) refusing to consent to the incapable adult entering into a transaction which falls within the scope of the guardian's authority (Recommendation 122(2)),

   (ix)   giving directions to the guardian as to the running or disposal of the adult's business (Recommendation 126),

   (x)   in relation to purchase or disposal of accommodation for the incapable adult or to remit the application to the sheriff (Recommendation 127),

   (xi)   in relation to investments of the incapable adult's estate (Recommendation 128(4)),

   (xii) refusing to remit an application or proposal for recall of a guardian's financial powers to the sheriff (Recommendation 136(2)),

   (xiii) refusing to allow interim remuneration to the guardian (Recommendation 141(3)),

   (xiv) refusing to remit an application for discharge of a former guardian to the sheriff (Recommendation 143(2));

(b)   An order by the sheriff requiring a continuing or welfare attorney to submit accounts or reports or be subject to supervision by the Public Guardian or local authority (Recommendations 27 to 30);

(c)   The sheriff's determination of an application by the guardian in relation to the management plan (Recommendation 125);

(d)   The sheriff's determination of an appeal from a refusal by the Mental Welfare Commission or the local authority to remit an application or proposal for recall of a guardian's welfare powers to the sheriff (Recommendation 143(2)).

Clauses and Schedules generally

Transitional provisions

7.6   **General.** The draft Bill attached to this report provides a new regime for continuing attorneys, hospital managers managing incapable patients' funds and for guardians of incapable adults. However, when the new legislation comes into force there will already be some attorneys acting under powers of attorney which continue in force after the incapacity of the granters, there will already be hospital managers holding funds for patients under the existing law and there will

---

1. Recommendation 30, para 3.68.
2. Recommendation 53, para 4.64.
3. Recommendation 138, para 6.207.

already be "guardians" of various kinds - guardians under the 1984 Act, curators bonis, tutors-dative and possibly the occasional tutor-at-law. It is necessary to decide how these various office-holders should be fitted in to the new legislation. One possibility would be to provide that the new Act simply did not apply to them so that they would continue to operate under the old law. This would, however, lead to a long period when two systems of law were in operation simultaneously, with some potential for confusion and inefficiency. Certainly, there should be no need for the various office-holders we have mentioned to have to apply for re-appointment or seek a new basis for their powers. Their powers should continue. However, we think that it would be in their interests and in the interests of the incapable adults if in other respects they came under the new regime. In particular it would seem to be right that the general principles in Part 2 of this report should apply to them and that they should be under the general supervisory and investigative jurisdiction of the Public Guardian, the Mental Welfare Commission or the local authority depending on whether the matter was one relating to finance and property or personal welfare. This is the general approach which we have adopted. We now consider the different applications of it in more detail.

7.7   **Attorneys.** Attorneys appointed under powers of attorney granted on or after 1 January 1991 can continue to act even after the granter has become incapable of managing his property and affairs by reason of mental disorder[1]. Attorneys appointed under powers granted before that date are in an uncertain legal position[2] but the prevailing view in practice was that their powers lapsed when the granter became incapable. There can be no doubt that attorneys who, under the law in force at the time of their appointment, could continue to act after the granter's incapacity should continue to be able to do so. Any other solution would frustrate arrangements legitimately made under the law in force at the time. We think, however, that it would be reasonable to require such attorneys, when acting on behalf of incapable granters, to observe the general principles we recommend earlier in Part 2 and to place them under the general supervisory and investigative jurisdiction of the Public Guardian. Such attorneys would not be registered with the Public Guardian and therefore the supervisory and investigative jurisdiction would in practice come into operation only if a complaint was made or if the case were otherwise brought to the Public Guardian's attention. A pre-commencement attorney should also be subject to the recommended increased jurisdiction of the courts and the attorney's authority should terminate on his or her divorce from the granter (unless the power of attorney provides otherwise). We recommend that:

149. **Where an attorney has been appointed prior to the date of commencement of the new legislation under a power of attorney which, under the law in force on the date when the power was granted, continues to have effect after the granter has become incapable of managing his or her property and affairs:**

   (a) **nothing in the new legislation should affect the powers of the attorney, and in particular his or her authority to act should not depend on registration with the Public Guardian, but**

   (b) **when acting for a granter who has become so incapable, the attorney should in other respects be treated as a continuing attorney under the new legislation.**

Schedule 3, paragraph 6

7.8   **Hospital managers.** A similar transitional problem arises in the case of hospital managers who, at the date of commencement, are managing the funds of a patient under section 94 of the 1984 Act. Clearly, there should be no question of their having to have patients whose funds are already being managed re-certified under the provisions of the new Act. Their powers to act should continue. However, we think that it would be reasonable to place them in other respects under the new regime recommended for post-commencement management. This would mean, in particular, that the recommended general principles would apply and that the managers would be under the supervisory and investigative jurisdiction of the Public Guardian. At present the Mental Welfare Commission has the supervisory role and it would be inconvenient to have two systems of supervision in operation in relation to different patients. We therefore recommend that:

150. **Where a person's money or valuables are at the date of commencement of the new legislation held by the managers of a hospital under section 94 of the Mental Health (Scotland) Act 1984:**

   (a) **nothing in the new legislation should affect their powers to continue to hold and apply the money or valuables, and in particular they should not require to have the person re-certified, but**

   (b) **they should be treated in other respects as the managers of an approved establishment under the new legislation.**

Schedule 3, paragraph 7

7.9   **Curators, tutors and guardians.** The new legislation will provide for one type of guardian. The new type of guardian will replace (a) "mental health guardians" appointed under the 1984 Act, (b) curators bonis, (c) tutors-dative and (d) tutors-at-law. After the commencement of the new legislation it will not be possible to apply for appointments in

---

1. Law Reform (Miscellaneous Provisions) (Scotland) Act 1990, s 71.
2. Contrast *Pollok v Paterson* Dec 10 1811 FC and *Wink v Mortimer* (1849) 11D 995 and see Bell, *Commentaries*, I 525.

any of these four categories. However, some people will have been already appointed, and will be exercising functions, when the new Act comes into force. There can be no question of requiring them to seek appointment afresh under the new legislation. Nor can there be any question of altering the essential nature of the powers conferred on them. Curators bonis would continue to be concerned with financial affairs and property. Guardians under the 1984 Act would continue to have their existing limited powers. However, it would seem to be reasonable to bring them under the new regime in other respects and in particular to require them to observe the general principles and to place them under the supervisory and investigative jurisdiction of the Public Guardian in so far as their powers relate to financial matters and under the similar jurisdiction of the Mental Welfare Commission and the local authority in so far as their powers relate to personal welfare. In effect this would mean that the Accountant of Court's office would continue to supervise curators bonis and the Mental Welfare Commission and the local authority would continue to supervise "mental health guardians". Tutors-dative have generally been appointed for personal welfare purposes and would come under the supervision of the Mental Welfare Commission and the local authority. Tutors-at-law form a very small category indeed and, as they have powers over both the estate and the person, would come under the jurisdiction of both bodies.

7.10   A further transitional problem arises in relation to applications for appointment as curator bonis, tutor or mental health guardian to an adult which are pending at the date of commencement. It would be possible to regard all such applications pending at the date of commencement as applications for appointment as guardian under the new legislation. However, this would give rise to procedural problems relating to notifications and would require the sheriff to be given a broad discretionary power. This might well involve unnecessary difficulties and delays while, for example, it was decided whether or not to apply some of the new procedures to the existing applications. In general it is better to avoid changing procedural rules half way through a court process and we therefore think that it would be better to allow the applications to proceed under the existing law and to modify the transitional measures to cover people appointed in this way as well as those already appointed when the new legislation comes into force. We therefore recommend that:

151. (1) Nothing in the new legislation should restrict the powers of:

(i) guardians appointed under the Mental Health (Scotland) Act 1984

(ii) curators bonis

(iii) tutors-dative or

(iv) tutors-at-law

if already appointed at the date of commencement of the new legislation but in other respects they should be treated for all purposes (including the purposes of enactments amended by the new legislation to substitute "guardian" for "tutor or curator") as guardians appointed with equivalent powers under the new legislation and accordingly

(a) guardians appointed under the Mental Health (Scotland) Act 1984 would be treated as guardians with the statutory powers which they had immediately prior to commencement

(b) curators bonis would be treated as guardians with full powers over the adult's property and financial affairs

(c) tutors-dative would be treated as guardians with the powers which they had immediately prior to commencement, and

(d) tutors-at-law would be treated as guardians with full powers over the adult's property and financial affairs and personal welfare.

(2) Where an application for appointment as guardian under the 1984 Act, curator bonis or tutor is pending before a court at the date of commencement it should continue to be dealt with under the law in force immediately prior to the date of commencement and any person so appointed should be treated in the same way as if already appointed at the date of commencement.

Schedule 3, paragraphs 1 to 4, 8 and 9

7.11   **Existing statutory references** Another transitional problem is that there are references in existing statutes, and may be references in private documents, to tutors and curators in the context of incapable adults. Some enactments can be amended to update the language, and this is done in Schedule 4 to the draft Bill, but some are United Kingdom enactments which it would not be appropriate to change for Scotland only or by an Act applying to Scotland only[1]. There

---

1. See eg the Taxes Management Act 1970 ss 42, 72 and 78. If this Act were being amended on a United Kingdom basis after the legislation to implement this report were in force we suggest that consideration should be given to the following amendments:
    In s 42, repeal "guardian, tutor or curator" and substitute "or guardian or by any person entitled as his legal representative".
    In s 72, repeal "tutor, curator" and substitute "legal representative".
    In s 78 repeal "tutor, curator" and substitute "legal representative".

is also a danger that there may be statutory references to tutors or curators of incapable adults which we have failed to identify. There is, of course, no way of knowing how many references to tutors or curators of such adults there may be in private deeds. What is needed is a general translation of these terms. We recommend that:

152. (1) **References in existing enactments or documents to tutors in relation to adults under mental disability or incapacitated should be construed as including references to guardians appointed under the new legislation with powers relating to the personal welfare of the adult.**

   (2) **References in existing enactments or documents to curators, or curators bonis, in relation to adults under mental disability or incapacitated should be construed as including references to guardians appointed under the new legislation with powers relating to the property and financial affairs of the adult.**

Schedule 4, paragraph 1

Consequential amendments and repeals

7.12   The schedules to the draft Bill contain many consequential amendments and repeals. Most of these are self explanatory, but the changes to the Judicial Factors Acts and the 1984 Act are sufficiently important to warrant comment. We also refer here to the Sale of Goods Act 1979.

7.13   **The Judicial Factors Acts.** The Judicial Factors Acts 1849 to 1889 currently apply to tutors and curators of those suffering from mental disorder. The Acts subject such tutors and curators to a fairly demanding accounting regime. One of the main objectives of the recommendations in this report on the management of the financial affairs of incapable adults has been to replace this regime with a more flexible regime, more carefully tailored to the needs of each adult. The scheme which we have recommended would be under the supervision of the Public Guardian in so far as guardians appointed under it had powers over finance and property. It would be self-contained and would not simply apply provisions from the Judicial Factors Acts. It follows that references in those Acts to tutors and curators of those suffering from mental disorder can now be repealed without any replacement in those Acts. This accounts for a substantial number of the minor and consequential amendments and repeals in the schedules to the draft Bill. These amendments and repeals were included at a time when the Children (Scotland) Bill was still before Parliament. Some of them may require to be changed slightly now that the Bill has been enacted.

7.14   **The Mental Health (Scotland) Act 1984.** The main change here is the repeal of the provisions relating to guardianship. Guardians under the Act will be replaced by the new generic type of guardian under the new legislation. The protective and supervisory roles of the Mental Welfare Commission and of local authorities in relation to guardianship under the 1984 Act will be replaced by similar roles in relation to guardians with personal welfare powers under the new legislation. These changes have as their consequence the repeal of the main provisions on guardianship in sections 36 to 52 of the 1984 Act and also of many other references to guardianship in that Act.

7.15   Another major consequential change in the 1984 Act is the repeal of the provisions on the protection of the property of patients in sections 92 to 94 of the Act[1]. These will be replaced by corresponding, but in some respects wider, provisions in the new legislation.

7.16   **The Criminal Procedure (Scotland) Act 1975.** Section 175 of the Criminal Procedure (Scotland) Act 1975 allows the High Court or the sheriff court, on convicting a person of an offence punishable by imprisonment, to place that person under the guardianship of a local authority or of a person approved by a local authority. This option is available if the person is suffering from mental disorder of a nature or degree which warrants his reception into guardianship. It is not available if the offence is one, such as murder, for which the sentence is fixed by law. Before placing the person under guardianship, the court must be of the opinion, having regard to all the circumstances including the nature of the offence and the character and antecedents of the offender, and to the other available methods of dealing with him, that guardianship is the most suitable method of disposing of the case. The court must also be satisfied, after taking into consideration the evidence of a mental health officer, that it is necessary in the interests of the welfare of the person that he should be placed under guardianship. Section 175 relates to solemn procedure. Section 376 of the 1975 Act makes similar provisions in relation to summary procedure. Section 61 of the 1984 Act provides that a guardianship order under these provisions confers on the authority or person named as guardian the same powers as a guardian appointed in the normal way under the 1984 Act.

7.17   The provisions on guardianship in the 1984 Act would be repealed under our recommendations and replaced by the new provisions on guardianship in the draft Bill. It will therefore be necessary to adapt the provisions in the Criminal Procedure (Scotland) Act 1975 to the new situation. We do not set out the detailed changes that will be needed because the Criminal Justice (Scotland) Bill, currently before Parliament, amends some of the existing guardianship provisions in the 1975 Act. At this stage we confine ourselves to recommending that:

---

1.   Section 92(2) is not, however, repealed. It amends s 48 of the National Assistance Act 1948 and is still needed.

153. The provisions in the Criminal Procedure (Scotland) Act 1975 on the making of guardianship orders should be amended to allow the court to make the new type of guardianship orders recommended in this report.

7.18   **The Sale of Goods Act 1979.** The Sale of Goods Act 1979 provides in section 3(2) (as it applies in Scotland) that:

"Where necessaries are sold and delivered to a person who by reason of mental incapacity or drunkenness is incompetent to contract, he must pay a reasonable price for them."

Section 3(3) defines "necessaries" as:

"goods suitable to the condition in life of the person concerned and to his actual requirements at the time of the sale and delivery".

In our discussion paper we criticised the above definition of necessaries because it required the supplier to make enquiries as to the person's actual requirements. Other criticisms of practical importance are that it does not apply to contracts for the supply of goods other than by sale - for example, contracts of hire-purchase or barter - and that it does not apply to contracts for the supply of services to the incapacitated person. We are considering the consequences of void contracts in our examination of the law of unjustified enrichment and intend to make proposals that would apply to contracts in general and not merely to those where mental incapacity was present. In view of this we have decided to make no recommendation at present for changes to section 3 of the 1979 Act.

Matters not pursued

7.19   We now turn to three matters on which we consulted in the discussion paper but on which we have decided to make no recommendation.

7.20   **Leave of absence.** In our discussion paper we considered the provisions of section 27 of the 1984 Act whereby patients liable to be detained may be granted leave of absence and we asked whether these provisions required to be amended[1]. The results of consultation were mixed and, in any event, the question of leave of absence has since been the subject of a special consultation by the Scottish Office Home and Health Department[2]. Following this consultation a Bill was introduced which is currently before Parliament[3]. It goes beyond the main subject of this report which is incapacity for decision-making rather than mental illness or disorder as such. In these circumstances we make no recommendation on this subject.

7.21   **Sexual offences.** Sections 106 and 107 of the 1984 Act contain provisions making sexual intercourse with mentally disabled women illegal in a wide range of situations. We reviewed these provisions in our discussion paper and expressed the tentative view that arguably they were too restrictive[4]. We invited views on the question whether these provisions should be replaced by provisions which concentrated more on whether there was any element of exploitation or abuse in the conduct. The results of consultation suggest that there would be some support for some revision of these provisions. However, we did not give this matter any particular prominence in the discussion paper, which was largely concerned with less potentially controversial matters. We are not sure that our consultation elicited the full range of views likely to be held on a matter which is, in any event, a matter of criminal law which goes beyond the scope of this report. We consider that it would be appropriate for those responsible for the review and updating of the criminal law of Scotland to examine sections 106 and 107 with a view to reform but make no recommendation ourselves.

7.22   **Administrative trusts.** In our discussion paper we examined the notion of administering the property and financial affairs of an incapable adult by means of an administrative trust[5]. The basic idea was that the court would appoint two or more trustees, one of which would usually be a solicitor and the other a relative or friend of the adult. These trustees would administer the estate for the benefit of the adult and would have the same powers and duties as normal trustees unless other powers were conferred by the legislation or the court. The trustees would not be supervised by the Accountant of Court as Public Guardian although an investigation could be carried out on receipt of a complaint. The trust purposes would be set out in a statute but could be modified by the court. Briefly the income and where appropriate the capital of the estate would be available to meet the needs of the adult. Alternatively, the trustees could submit a management plan with appropriate purposes, powers and duties to the court for approval.

7.23   The idea of administrative trusts found little favour on consultation. Most of those responding saw it as an unnecessary addition, in that a flexible system of guardianship could achieve much the same results. Another argument

---

1. Paras 2.111 to 2.113.
2. *Review of Legal Powers on Care of Mentally Disordered People in the Community - A Consultation Paper* November 1993.
3. Mental Health (Patients in the Community) Bill [HL].
4. Para 2.110.
5. Paras 4.144 to 4.153.

against was that a trust was a more restrictive option than guardianship. It is an essential feature of a trust that the trust assets are held by the trustees. The incapable adult's property would therefore have to be transferred to the trustees. Under our recommended scheme of guardianship, on the other hand, the guardian only manages the estate which remains in the ownership of the adult. One of the main distinguishing features of the proposed administrative trust as against guardianship is the lack of supervision of the trustees by the Public Guardian with a consequential small saving in fees. This should not be seen as an advantage. We think such supervision is a necessary feature of the management of an incapable adult's estate by court appointees. In view of the responses we decided not to proceed further with administrative trusts.

Part 8   List of Recommendations

1.   The recommendations in this report should apply only in relation to individuals aged 16 and over.

Paragraph 2.2; Clause 67(1)

2.   (1) An intervention should be capable of being made under our recommendations if the adult is:

      (a) mentally disordered, or

      (b) unable to communicate due to physical or other disability
         and by reason of such mental disorder or inability to communicate unable to take the decision or carry out the act in question.

    (2) Mental disorder should mean mental illness or mental handicap however caused or manifested, but a person should not be regarded as mentally disordered by reason solely of promiscuity or other immoral conduct, sexual deviancy, dependence on alcohol or drugs or acting as no prudent person would act.

Paragraph 2.15; Clause 67(2)

3.   (1) Applications and other proceedings under legislation implementing our recommendations should be dealt with in the sheriff courts. These proceedings as well as proceedings under the Mental Health (Scotland) Act 1984 should be heard, so far as possible, by nominated sheriffs who have received special training.

    (2) Rules of Court should be made providing that the hearings should take place in chambers, or in another place considered appropriate by the sheriff, rather than in a public court room and should be conducted, so far as practicable, in an informal manner.

Paragraph 2.31; Clause 2(5), Schedule 4, paragraph 15(18) and Bill generally

4.   A sheriff court should have jurisdiction to deal with any application under our recommendations if:

      (a) the incapable adult in question is then habitually resident in the sheriffdom, or

      (b) the application relates to property belonging to the adult which is situated in the sheriffdom.

In addition a sheriff should have jurisdiction to make an order which is immediately necessary for the protection of the adult if the adult is present within the sheriffdom at the date of application.

Paragraph 2.34; Clause 2(2), (3)

5.   The sheriff court which made a guardianship order or an intervention order should have jurisdiction to deal with an application relating to that order if no other court (Scottish or non-Scottish) has jurisdiction to deal with such an application or if it is unreasonable to expect the applicant to make the application to another court with jurisdiction.

Paragraph 2.35; Clause 2(4)

6.   The sheriff should consider whether to appoint a safeguarder to an incapable adult in respect of whom an application has been made. The safeguarder should have similar powers and duties to one appointed under section 18A of the Social Work (Scotland) Act 1968 (safeguarders to children involved in proceedings relating to the assumption of parental rights by local authorities).

Paragraph 2.36; Clause 3(4), (5)

7.   The Public Guardian, Mental Welfare Commission, local authority and any individual (including the adult himself or herself) or organisation claiming an interest in the welfare or financial affairs of an incapable adult should be entitled to apply to the court under our recommendations, except in relation to matters where a more restricted title is recommended.

Paragraph 2.39; Clause 67(1) and Clauses generally

8.   The court should have a discretionary power to award expenses to the Public Guardian if he or she has initiated or entered proceedings in order to protect an incapable adult's property or to represent the public interest.

Paragraph 2.42; Clause 6

9.   The Public Guardian, the Mental Welfare Commission and the local authority should be under a duty to collaborate and liaise with each other in relation to investigations.

Paragraph 2.45; Clause 9(2)

10.   The Public Guardian should be required to provide advice and information, on request, to those exercising functions under our recommendations relating to incapable adults' property and financial affairs. The Mental Welfare Commission and the local authority should be under a similar obligation in relation to personal welfare functions.

Paragraph 2.46; Clauses 4(2)(g), 7(1)(e) and 8(1)(e)

11.   Any intervention in the welfare or financial affairs of an incapable adult under or in pursuance of the proposed new legislation should be required to produce a benefit for that adult. Any person proposing to intervene should have to be satisfied that the intended benefit cannot be reasonably achieved otherwise than by the intervention.

Paragraph 2.54; Clause 1(2)

12.   Any proposed intervention in the welfare or finances of an incapable adult under or in pursuance of the proposed new legislation should be that which is least restrictive of the adult's freedom having regard to the purpose of the intervention.

Paragraph 2.58; Clause 1(3)

13.   Any guardian, continuing or welfare attorney or the managers of an establishment managing an adult's finances under our recommendations should be required to encourage the adult to use existing financial and welfare skills and acquire new skills, but only in so far as it is reasonable and practicable to do so.

Paragraph 2.59; Clause 1(5)

14.   (1) A person proposing to make an intervention in the welfare or financial affairs of an incapable adult under or in pursuance of the proposed new legislation should be required to take account of the present and past wishes of the adult.

(2) An intervener should also be required to consult with the incapable adult's nearest relative, primary carer, any guardian or continuing attorney or welfare attorney with relevant powers, but only in so far as it is reasonable and practicable to do so. The intervener should take account of the views expressed.

(3) An intervener should also be required to take into account the views of any other person appearing to have an interest in the incapable adult's welfare or the proposed intervention, but should not be under a duty to seek out such views.

(4) The sheriff should, on application, have power to direct that a specified person should have to be consulted and their views taken into account in relation to every or any particular intervention (under consideration or in the future) relating to the incapable adult.

(5) An adult's nearest relative should be determined by the provisions of sections 53 to 57 of the Mental Health (Scotland) Act 1984.

Paragraph 2.73; Clauses 1(4) and 67(1)

15.   (1) A guardian, continuing or welfare attorney, person authorised to withdraw funds from accounts under Recommendation 37, managers of an establishment authorised to manage residents' affairs under Recommendation 47 and a person carrying out an intervention order who has acted reasonably, in good faith and in accordance with the general principles should not be liable for any breach of fiduciary duty to the incapable adult in question.

(2) Codes of Practice and other publications should make guardians and others aware of their fiduciary duties and the need to avoid acting in breach of them.

Paragraph 2.79; Clause 64(1)

16.   Any person exercising welfare powers under our recommendations who ill-treats or wilfully neglects an incapable adult should be guilty of an offence and liable to imprisonment and/or payment of a fine.

Paragraph 2.80; Clause 65

17.   (1) A person having a power of attorney granted after the commencement date of legislation implementing our recommendations should have power to act after the granter's incapacity only if the contract of mandate or agency conferring the power of attorney clearly shows that that was the granter's intention.

(2) There should be no style prescribed for conferring a power of attorney which is to have effect after the granter's incapacity.

(3) Section 71 of the Law Reform (Miscellaneous Provisions) (Scotland) Act 1990 should be repealed with respect to powers of attorney granted on or after the commencement date of legislation implementing our recommendations.

Paragraph 3.10; Clauses 11(1), (3)(b) and 12(1), (3)(b) and Schedule 5

18.   A contract of mandate or agency conferring a continuing or welfare power of attorney should be required to be in a written document and subscribed by the granter in order to be formally valid.

Paragraph 3.12; Clauses 11(3)(a) and 12(3)(a)

19.   In order to be formally valid a document conferring a continuing or welfare power of attorney should:

   (a) contain a certificate by a solicitor (or a member of some other class of persons to be prescribed by the Secretary of State) that, after interviewing the granter and obtaining any necessary reports, he or she is satisfied that the granter understood the nature and effect of the document, and

   (b) contain a certificate by a solicitor or other certifying person that he or she has no reason to believe that the document was being signed as a result of anything which would vitiate the granting of the power.

Paragraph 3.19; Clauses 11(3)(c) and 12(3)(c)

20.   (1) A welfare attorney should be permitted to exercise welfare powers notwithstanding his or her bankruptcy or the bankruptcy of the granter.

   (2) Welfare powers under a welfare power of attorney should be exercisable only by individuals.

Paragraph 3.26; Clause 12(4), (6)

21.   (1) The Public Guardian should set up and maintain a register of documents conferring continuing or welfare powers of attorney.

   (2) The Public Guardian should not be required to register a document conferring continuing or welfare powers of attorney unless the document appears to comply with the requirements of Recommendations 18 and 19 (signature by granter and certification of granter's understanding and absence of vitiating factors) and he or she is satisfied that the attorney accepts the appointment.

   (3) The register should be open to inspection by any member of the public. On registration the Public Guardian should give a copy of the document to the attorney or other ingiver with a certificate of registration and also send a copy to the granter and, if the document requests this to be done, to up to two other specified individuals.

   (4) A continuing or welfare attorney should have no authority by virtue of the power of attorney until the document conferring such a power is registered with the Public Guardian.

   (5) Once the document conferring the power has been registered the Public Guardian should be notified of any permanent change of address of the granter or continuing or welfare attorney or the death of the granter.

   (6) The Public Guardian should be required to investigate complaints made about the actings of continuing attorneys and alert the competent authorities in order to prevent further abuse. The Mental Welfare Commission and the local authority should have similar functions in relation to welfare attorneys.

   (7) A power of attorney conferred after the commencement of the new legislation otherwise than in accordance with our recommendations should lapse on the granter's incapacity.

Paragraph 3.36; Clauses 4(2)(c), 4(2)(d), 7(1)(c), 8(1)(c), 13, 14(1), (2), (5), and 16

22.   Where the terms of a document conferring a continuing or welfare power of attorney prohibit registration until the occurrence of a specified event, the Public Guardian should not register it unless satisfied that the event has occurred.

Paragraph 3.40; Clause 14(3)

23.   A welfare attorney should not be entitled to exercise a welfare power contained in the document conferring the power of attorney unless the granter is incapable of making a decision regarding the welfare matter in question, or the attorney reasonably believes the granter to be incapable.

Paragraph 3.42; Clause 12(4)

24.   (1) A welfare attorney should not be entitled to place the granter in a hospital for treatment of mental disorder against the granter's will. However, the welfare attorney should, if the power of attorney confers such powers, have the same rights in relation to detention as the granter's nearest relative has under the Mental Health (Scotland) Act 1984.

   (2) A welfare attorney should not be entitled to authorise any of the prescribed treatments in Recommendations 59 to 64 or consent to the adult being restrained.

Paragraph 3.48; Clause 12(5) and Schedule 4, paragraph 15

25.   (1) Continuing and welfare attorneys should not be monitored or supervised either by the Public Guardian, Mental Welfare Commission or local authority except where a court order is made to this effect under Recommendation 26. This should be without prejudice to the existing and recommended investigative and protective functions of the Public Guardian, Mental Welfare Commission and local authority.

(2) The Secretary of State should prepare and publish a Code of Practice containing guidance to continuing and welfare attorneys as to the exercise of their functions.

Paragraph 3.56; Clause 10(1)(b)

26. In order to better protect granters of continuing or welfare powers of attorney, the court should have power, on application by any person claiming an interest in the granter's welfare or finances, to make various orders relating to the attorney. The power should be exercisable only if the court is satisfied that the granter is incapable of giving directions to the attorney or of safeguarding his or her own interests in relation to the matters covered by the power of attorney and that the making of the order is necessary to safeguard the granter.

Paragraph 3.60; Clause 15(1), (2)

27. The court should have power under Recommendation 26 to order a continuing attorney to produce accounts of his or her transactions with the granter's estate. Accounts should be ordered in respect of all or any of the period from the date of registration of the document conferring the continuing power to the date of the order. The accounts should be audited by the Public Guardian and the accounts and audit report thereafter lodged in court.

Paragraph 3.65; Clause 15(2)(b)

28. The court should have power under Recommendation 26 to order that a continuing attorney should in future be subject to such supervision by the Public Guardian as it thinks fit.

Paragraph 3.66; Clause 15(2)(a)

29. (1) The court should have power under Recommendation 26 to order a welfare attorney to produce a report as to how any welfare powers have been exercised in all or any of the period between registration of the document conferring the welfare power and the date of the order.

(2) As a result of the report or otherwise the court should have power to order the welfare attorney to be subject in future to such supervision by the local authority in respect of any welfare powers as it thinks fit.

Paragraph 3.67; Clause 15(2)(c), (d)

30. The court should have power under Recommendation 26 to give directions to a continuing or welfare attorney as to the exercise of his or her functions.

Paragraph 3.68; Clause 3(3)

31. The court should have power under Recommendation 26 to revoke a continuing or welfare attorney's appointment (including one or more joint attorneys or a substitute attorney) and to revoke in whole or in part the continuing or welfare power of attorney. The revocation should be notified to the Public Guardian.

Paragraph 3.72; Clauses 15(2)(e), (3)

32. The court should not have power to vary the terms of a contract of mandate or agency conferring a continuing or welfare power of attorney.

Paragraph 3.74

33. (1) In order to prevent a lapse in arrangements made for the safeguarding of the granter's welfare and financial affairs a continuing or welfare attorney acting under a registered power of attorney should have to give notice of his or her intention to resign to the granter, the Public Guardian, the granter's primary carer, and, if the local authority was supervising the attorney or a guardian had been appointed, also to the local authority or guardian.

(2) The resignation should become effective 28 days after notification to the Public Guardian. But where the attorney's resignation would still leave at least one continuing or welfare attorney (joint or substitute) in post the resignation should be effective as soon as the Public Guardian is satisfied that the remaining joint attorney(s) will continue to act or the substitute attorney is willing to act.

Paragraph 3.77; Clause 17

34. (1) The appointment by the granter of his or her spouse as continuing or welfare attorney should be revoked automatically by a decree of separation, divorce or nullity relating to the granter and his or her spouse, unless the granter provides otherwise in the contract of mandate or agency conferring the continuing or welfare power of attorney.

(2) Where a guardian is appointed with certain powers the authority of a continuing or welfare attorney in relation to matters within the scope of those powers should automatically terminate.

Paragraph 3.79; Clause 18(1), (2)

35.   Subject to Recommendation 36 the effect during the granter's incapacity in Scotland of a mandate or agency conferring a continuing or welfare power of attorney (however expressed) should be determined according to the proper law of the mandate or agency.

Paragraph 3.82; Clause 19

36.   The following recommendations in Part 3 relating to Scottish continuing or welfare attorneys should apply to their equivalents appointed under the law of any other country:

(a) Recommendation 23 (welfare powers exerciseable only during granter's incapacity),

(b) Recommendation 24 (welfare attorney not to place granter in hospital for treatment of mental disorder against granter's will),

(c) Recommendations 26-31 (various court orders relating to continuing or welfare attorneys), and

(d) Recommendation 34(2) (appointment of guardian terminates attorney's authority in so far as powers coincide).

Paragraph 3.83; Clauses 12(7), 15(5) and 18(3)

37.   (1) The Public Guardian, on application, should be empowered to authorise the applicant to withdraw money, or arrange for payments to be made, from a specified bank account held at a branch situated in Scotland of an adult who is incapable of operating the account and habitually resident in Scotland.

(2) The Public Guardian should keep a public register of individuals authorised to withdraw.

Paragraph 4.12; Clauses 4(2)(c)(iii) and 20(1), (2)(a), (3)

38.   (1) The withdrawal scheme recommended in Recommendation 37 should not apply if the incapable adult's bank account was subject to an existing intervention order or powers granted to a guardian or continuing attorney or similar appointee under the law of any other country.

(2) No liability should be incurred by any person who acts in good faith and in ignorance of any grant or appointment.

Paragraph 4.13; Clause 26

39.   (1) An applicant for authority to withdraw should have to apply on a prescribed form. The form should require details of the applicant, the incapable adult and the bank account to be provided. It should also contain a declaration by a member of a prescribed class of persons that to the best of his or her knowledge and belief the applicant was a fit and proper person to be granted authority to withdraw.

(2) The application should be accompanied by a certificate from a medical practitioner or other person qualified to assess incapacity that the adult was incapable of operating his or her bank account.

Paragraph 4.14; Clause 21(1)

40.   The Public Guardian should give the incapable adult and his or her nearest relative and primary carer an opportunity to object to the application. The Public Guardian should have power to grant the application after considering any objections and any further representations by the applicant and any objector, or to remit the matter to the sheriff.

Paragraph 4.15; Clause 22(3)-(6)

41.   (1) The Public Guardian's authorisation should entitle (but not oblige) the bank to allow the applicant to:

(a) withdraw £50 per week (or such other sum as may be prescribed by the Secretary of State) in cash, and

(b) authorise the bank to pay by direct debit or standing order for fuel, accommodation, clothing, sustenance and related goods and services;

in order to meet the living expenses of the incapable account holder. The authorisation should not entitle the withdrawer to overdraw the account.

(2) The Public Guardian should be empowered, if satisfied that an extension of authority is needed, to authorise:

(a) payment otherwise than by direct debit, standing order or cash to specified suppliers of goods and services, or

(b) payment for specified goods and services outwith those listed in paragraph (1)(b) above.

Paragraph 4.18; Clause 22(1), (2), (7)

42.   (1) The withdrawer should use money withdrawn under the scheme only for the benefit of the incapable account holder except in so far as otherwise authorised by the Public Guardian. If money is used otherwise the withdrawer should be obliged to repay it with interest at 5% above the rate from time to time applicable to a sheriff court decree in the absence of any rate specified in the decree.

148

(2) The Public Guardian should be entitled to receive and investigate complaints and carry out checks on individual withdrawers even in the absence of complaints.

(3) The Secretary of State should issue a Code of Practice containing guidance to withdrawers and banks as to how they should exercise their functions.

(4) The Secretary of State should have power to make regulations requiring withdrawers to keep records of their expenditure under the scheme and to produce them to the Public Guardian on demand.

Paragraph 4.20; Clauses 4(2)(d)(ii), 10(1)(d), (e), 22(4)-(6), and 23

43. (1) The bank should be liable for allowing cash withdrawals over the weekly limit but on restoring the money to the incapable adult's account it should be entitled to claim against the withdrawer.

(2) The bank should not be liable for making payments for goods and services that were outwith the ambit of the withdrawer's authority.

Paragraph 4.21; Clause 22(3)(a)

44. (1) A withdrawer's authority should cease two years after the date of its grant, but the withdrawer should be able thereafter to make a fresh application to the Public Guardian.

(2) The Public Guardian should be empowered at his or her sole discretion to suspend or terminate the authority. The authority should automatically terminate on the appointment of a guardian or continuing attorney or the making of an intervention order in relation to the account.

(3) Notification of suspension or termination should be given by the Public Guardian to the withdrawer and the branch of the bank at which the account is held. The withdrawer and bank should not be liable for withdrawals made in good faith and in ignorance of the suspension or termination.

Paragraph 4.25; Clauses 22(3)(b) and 24(1)-(3), (5)

45. The scheme set out in Recommendations 37 to 44 should be applicable to building society accounts in the same way as it applies to bank accounts. The Secretary of State should have power by regulations to extend the scheme to other organisations similar to banks or building societies.

Paragraph 4.27; Clause 20(2)(b), (c)

46. (1) If two or more individuals are holders of a joint bank or building society account at a branch situated in Scotland whose terms allow any one individual to operate it and one individual becomes incapable of operating the account, then the other account holder or holders should continue to have authority to operate the account.

(2) The continued authority to operate should not apply if the account holders have agreed, or the court has ordered, otherwise, or a guardian or continuing attorney has been appointed or an intervention order made in relation to the account.

Paragraph 4.32; Clauses 25 and 26

47. (1) The management of patients' finances by the managers of hospitals under section 94 of the Mental Health (Scotland) Act 1984 should be replaced by a new scheme as set out in Recommendations 48 to 57.

(2) The new scheme should apply to NHS hospitals in Scotland (including NHS trust hospitals and the State hospital), unless the sheriff terminates their authority to manage.

(3) The new scheme should also apply to residential establishments in Scotland run by, or registered with, the local authority under the Social Work (Scotland) Act 1968, private hospitals and nursing homes in Scotland registered under the Nursing Homes Registration (Scotland) Act 1938; but only if the Public Guardian so permits after an application for approval made by the managers of the establishment. The managers of one or more establishments seeking approval for them should be entitled to submit a single application in respect of all of them.

(4) The Secretary of State should have power to make regulations amending the list of establishments in paragraphs (2) and (3) above.

Paragraph 4.45; Clauses 4(2)(f), 27(1)-(4) and 28(1) and Schedule 5

48. The management scheme should be available for managing the financial affairs of:

(a) persons who are liable to be detained in a hospital under the provisions of the Mental Health (Scotland) Act 1984 or who are receiving treatment for mental disorder as resident patients in a hospital, and

(b) persons who are resident patients in an NHS hospital, an NHS Trust hospital or the State Hospital.

(c) persons who have as their main residence an establishment approved by the Public Guardian under Recommendation 47.

Paragraph 4.47; Clause 27(5)

49. (1) The managers of an approved establishment should have authority to manage the financial affairs specified in Recommendation 53 of a resident who has been certified as incapable of managing them by a doctor suitably qualified to assess capacity who does not possess a financial interest in the establishment.

(2) Where a certificate has been issued under paragraph (1) above an application may be made to the sheriff, by any person claiming an interest in the resident's welfare or finances, for a determination of the resident's mental capacity to manage his or her financial affairs.

(3) The managers should cease to have authority when the resident is certified as capable of managing them by a suitably qualified doctor or declared to be so capable by the sheriff.

(4) In deciding whether a resident is incapable of managing his or her own affairs account should be taken of assistance that is available or that could reasonably be made available.

Paragraph 4.53; Clauses 29 and 35

50. The authority of the managers of an establishment should be subject to any existing intervention order or to the existing authority of a previously appointed guardian or continuing attorney (or their equivalents under other legal systems), a DSS appointee or an individual authorised to withdraw from the resident's bank or building society account.

Paragraph 4.54; Clause 36

51. The authority of the managers of an establishment should be subordinated to the authority of a guardian or continuing attorney (or their equivalents under other legal systems) appointed or registered after the managers have commenced to act, but the guardian or continuing attorney may appoint the managers to act as his or her agent.

Paragraph 4.55; Clause 31

52. The managers of an establishment should be entitled, but not bound, to continue managing the financial affairs of a former resident if no other adequate arrangements appear to have been made.

Paragraph 4.57; Clause 32(6)

53. The managers of an establishment should be entitled to:

(a) claim and receive any pension or benefit due to the resident while certified and any sums falling due to the resident while certified and to hold them along with any other money brought by the resident into the establishment.

(b) spend any money so held by them on behalf of the resident in order to enhance his or her quality of life in accordance with the provisions of the Code of Practice recommended in Recommendation 56.

(c) hold or dispose of items which the resident brought into the establishment or which have been acquired by or on behalf of the resident subsequently.

(d) withdraw money from an existing bank or building society account in the name of the resident.

Paragraph 4.61; Clauses 30 and 32(3)

54. (1) The managers of an establishment should be entitled to manage money and items up to £5,000 in total value, or such other sum as may be prescribed, for each individual certified resident.

(2) The power to permit the management of money and items in excess of the above limit should be transferred from the Mental Welfare Commission to the Public Guardian. The Public Guardian should be empowered to grant approval subject to conditions.

(3) The Secretary of State should be empowered to make regulations prescribing a limit or limits other than £5,000 for establishments other than NHS hospitals and altering the £5,000 limit and other limits from time to time.

Paragraph 4.64; Clause 32(1), (2) and (7)

55. The Public Guardian should be under a duty to receive and investigate complaints about the management of certified residents' funds by managers of approved establishments and be entitled to question the managers regarding their transactions with funds of specified residents, and require them to produce accounts and records even in the absence of complaints.

Paragraph 4.65; Clauses 4(2)(d)(iii) and 33

56. (1) The managers of an approved establishment should be under a statutory duty to:

    (a) keep certified residents' funds separate from those of the establishment.

    (b) if the funds are not in separate bank or building society accounts for each individual resident, maintain records enabling the balance due to each resident at any time to be ascertained.

    (c) place sums over £50 (or such other amount as may be prescribed by the Secretary of State) in an interest-bearing account.

    (d) spend a resident's money only on goods and services that are of benefit to that resident, not including items which should be provided by the establishment as part of the normal service to residents.

    (e) adhere to a Code of Practice drawn up and published by the Secretary of State.

(2) The managers should be liable for any loss to a resident's funds arising from a breach of the duty of care or any misuse of funds, only if they fail to act reasonably, in good faith and in accordance with the general principles set out in Recommendations 11 to 14, and should be under a duty to make proper provision for indemnification for losses for which they are liable.

Paragraph 4.70; Clauses 10(1)(f), 32(4) and 64

57. (1) The sheriff should have power, on application by the Public Guardian, to withdraw approval from an establishment or to impose conditions on its continued approval. The sheriff should have to be satisfied that the managers had failed to carry out any statutory requirements relating to the management of certified residents' funds or that the managers or the establishment were otherwise no longer suitable.

(2) Any conditions imposed should be capable of being subsequently removed, varied or added to.

(3) On withdrawing approval the sheriff should have power to appoint the Public Guardian as interim guardian of the funds of the certified residents of that establishment with the same powers that the managers had.

(4) The sheriff should have power to make any appropriate interim order (including the suspension of approval) pending the determination of the application by the Public Guardian.

Paragraph 4.74; Clauses 3(2)(d) and 34

58. (1) A doctor should have authority to give treatment which is reasonable in the circumstances in order to safeguard or promote the health of a patient who, in the doctor's opinion, is incapable of making a decision relating to it.

(2) Treatment should include any surgical, medical, nursing, psychiatric, psychological, optical or dental treatment, procedure, examination or assessment. Treatment for mental disorder of incapable patients liable to be detained under the Mental Health (Scotland) Act 1984 should continue to be governed by Part X of that Act with the exception of psychosurgery which could be authorised by the sheriff under Recommendation 62.

(3) The general authority in paragraph (1) above should not apply to those matters more specifically dealt with in Recommendations 59 to 68.

Paragraph 5.17; Clause 37(1), (2)

59. Sterilisation of an adult incapable of consenting to it should require prior authorisation by a sheriff, unless the procedure is to be carried out to treat an existing serious malfunction or disease of the adult's reproductive organs.

Paragraph 5.24; Clause 37(4)(c)

60. Section 98 of the Mental Health (Scotland) Act 1984, providing for an independent medical practitioner appointed by the Mental Welfare Commission to certify that electro-convulsive therapy and the giving of medicines for mental disorder for more than three months is an appropriate treatment, should be extended to incapable patients who are not liable to be detained under the Act.

Paragraph 5.25; Clause 37(5)

61. The termination of a pregnancy of a woman incapable of consenting to termination should be carried out only if it would be lawful under the Abortion Act 1967 in the case of a consenting patient and an independent medical practitioner appointed by the Mental Welfare Commission certifies that termination is appropriate.

Paragraph 5.26; Clause 37(5)(b)

62. Psychosurgery should be able to be carried out on a patient incapable of consenting to it (whether or not detained under the Mental Health (Scotland) Act 1984) but only if the court authorises it and the patient does not resist it.

Paragraph 5.28; Clause 37(4)(b)

63. (1) Hormonal treatment for the patient's libido by means of an implant should be carried out on an incapable patient only if a court authorises it and the patient does not resist it.

(2) The Secretary of State should have power to make regulations prescribing other treatments which should require court approval or a second opinion.

Paragraph 5.30; Clause 37(4)(a), (5)(b)

64.   The general authority to treat so as to safeguard and promote health in Recommendation 58 should not authorise restraint or detention of an incapable patient, except where urgently necessary to prevent serious harm to that patient.

Paragraph 5.32; Clause 37(3)(a)

65.   Where a court has made a decision relating to the medical treatment of an incapable patient, doctors should not have any authority by virtue of Recommendation 58 to take any action that would be inconsistent with the court's decision. Pending the determination of an application to the court in relation to medical treatment doctors should have authority to give treatment necessary to save the patient's life or prevent a serious deterioration in his or her health, unless the court orders otherwise.

Paragraph 5.33; Clause 37(3)(b), (6) and (7)

66.   (1) The general statutory authority to give reasonable treatment in Recommendation 58 should not apply where the doctors are aware that the patient's guardian refuses to consent to the treatment in question. The doctors may proceed with treatment to which the guardian has refused consent only if they obtain an opinion from a consultant from a different unit skilled in that treatment to the effect that it is in all the circumstances (medical and non-medical) an appropriate treatment.

(2) In order to safeguard the patient's health until the opinion is obtained, doctors should have authority to give treatment necessary to save the patient's life or prevent any deterioration in his or her condition once the second opinion procedure has been initiated, unless a court has ordered otherwise.

Paragraph 5.39; Clause 38

67.   Recommendation 66 should apply to welfare attorneys with powers in relation to the patient's medical treatment as it applies to guardians.

Paragraph 5.40; Clause 38

68.   (1) Legislation should be introduced making it clear that, subject to certain exceptions dealt with in Recommendations 69 to 73, a valid refusal made by a competent patient of treatment that may be offered in the future when he or she is not mentally capable should have the effect that doctors have no authority to give the treatment in question.

(2) Doctors should not be liable for withholding treatment in accordance with a refusal which they reasonably believe was validly made and is applicable in the circumstances, or for giving treatment contrary to the terms of a refusal that they reasonably believe is neither valid nor applicable.

(3) A refusal should be effective whether it is in writing or oral. A written refusal should have to be signed by the patient but should not have to be witnessed or made in any particular form.

Paragraph 5.50; Clause 40

69.   Doctors should be entitled to disregard a valid and applicable advance refusal if, by reason of a material change of circumstances since the refusal was made (other than a change in the patient's medical condition), they reasonably believe that the patient if competent would now accept the treatment in question.

Paragraph 5.53; Clause 40(6)

70.   An advance refusal of treatment which if not given would endanger the patient's life should be followed only if the terms of the refusal make it clear that the patient intended the refusal to apply in such circumstances.

Paragraph 5.54; Clause 40(7)(a)

71.   An advance refusal should be ineffective to the extent that it refuses normal hygiene or the relief of severe pain.

Paragraph 5.55; Clause 40(7)(b)

72.   An advance refusal should be ineffective in relation to a detained patient to the extent that it refuses any treatment for mental disorder which under Part X of the Mental Health (Scotland) Act 1984 can be given to the patient notwithstanding absence of consent.

Paragraph 5.56; Clause 40(7)(c)

73.   An advance refusal of treatment by a female patient should be ineffective to the extent that it refuses treatment which if not given would endanger the life of a foetus, aged 24 weeks or more, which she is carrying.

Paragraph 5.58; Clause 40(7)(d)

74.   An advance refusal should be capable of being revoked by the adult concerned and his or her welfare attorney (if expressly empowered to do so). The revocation may be oral or in writing signed by the person making the revocation.

Paragraph 5.59; Clause 40(2), (3)

75.   It should be lawful to carry out research on an adult who is incapable of consenting to participate only if all of the following conditions are satisfied:

   (a) the research is into the causes, treatment or care of the adult's incapacity or associated physical symptoms or disease,

   (b) the research entails only a minimal foreseeable risk and minimal discomfort to the adult,

   (c) the research could not be carried out equally effectively on subjects capable of consenting,

   (d) the research project has been approved by a Scottish Committee set up by the Secretary of State for Scotland in accordance with regulations made by the Secretary of State,

   (e) written consent has been obtained from the adult while capable or from the adult's guardian or welfare attorney. Where the adult has no guardian or welfare attorney with appropriate powers written consent should be obtained from the adult's nearest relative as defined in sections 53 to 57 of the Mental Health (Scotland) Act 1984. If the nearest relative is not readily available then written consent should be sought from an independent individual who knows the adult well and is not involved with the research. The person from whom consent is sought should be given an explanation of what is involved in the proposed research, and

   (f) the adult does not appear unwilling to participate in the research.

Paragraph 5.76; Clause 39

76.   In order to clarify the position regarding withholding or withdrawing medical treatment from incapable patients in Scotland there should be new statutory provisions to the effect that it should be lawful to withhold or withdraw treatment that in the reasonable opinion of the doctors concerned would be unlikely to benefit the patient. Prolongation of an incapable patient's life regardless of the circumstances should not necessarily be regarded as benefitting that patient.

Paragraph 5.81; Clause 41(1), (4) and (5)

77.   (1) In difficult and exceptional cases resort to the Court of Session should be possible for a declarator whether a withholding or withdrawing of medical treatment from an incapable adult was or would be lawful or unlawful.

   (2) Any person claiming an interest in the incapable adult's welfare should be entitled to apply for a declarator and the application should have to be intimated to the Lord Advocate for the public interest.

Paragraph 5.86; Clause 41(3), (6)

78.   Legislation should be enacted to introduce a new flexible system of personal and financial guardianship for incapable adults based on the principles of least restriction, consultation with the adult and others involved and encouraging the adult to use and develop skills. This new guardianship should replace guardianship under the Mental Health (Scotland) Act 1984, tutors-at-law, tutors-dative and curators bonis.

Paragraph 6.12; Clauses 42-63

79.   The court should have power to grant one or more orders relating to an incapable adult's personal welfare or financial affairs called intervention orders. It should be possible for an intervention order to take the form of:

   (a) directing some specific act to be done or consent to be given, or

   (b) appointing some person to carry out a specified transaction.

Paragraph 6.18; Clause 42(1), (4)

80.   The court should have power to grant an interim order pending the determination of an application for an intervention order. On granting an intervention order the court should have power to grant ancillary orders or give directions.

Paragraph 6.19; Clause 3

81.   (1) Any person (including the adult) claiming an interest in the welfare or financial affairs of an incapable adult should be entitled to apply to the court for an intervention order.

   (2) The court should be empowered to grant such an application if satisfied (by means of reports as in Recommendation 87) that the adult is incapable of taking the decision or performing the transaction in respect of which the application is made.

Paragraph 6.20; Clause 42(1)

82.   The court which made an intervention order should have power, on application, to vary or recall it or any of the associated ancillary orders or directions on cause shown.

Paragraph 6.21; Clause 42(6)

83.   Rules of Court should be made requiring an application for an intervention order relating to the personal welfare of an incapable adult to be notified to the local authority so that it has the opportunity to make representations.

Paragraph 6.22

84.   Intervention orders should be registered by the Public Guardian in a register open to public inspection on payment of the appropriate fee.

Paragraph 6.23; Clauses 4(2)(c)(v) and 42(8)

85.   (1) The court should be empowered to appoint a guardian to an adult if satisfied that:

(a) the adult is unable to communicate or is mentally disordered, and by reason of such inability or disorder, unable to make decisions or act to protect or safeguard his or her personal welfare or financial affairs, and

(b) that such inability is likely to continue for such a period as to justify guardianship in the interests of the adult.

(2) Even where the above criteria are met the court should appoint a guardian only if satisfied that one or more intervention orders would not be sufficient in the circumstances to meet the needs of the adult. Where the court considers that an intervention order or orders will suffice it may treat the application for the appointment of a guardian as an application for such intervention orders and ancillary orders as the court thinks fit and grant such orders accordingly.

Paragraph 6.29; Clause 44(1), (2)

86.   (1) Any person claiming an interest in the welfare, property or financial affairs of the adult (including the Public Guardian, the Mental Welfare Commission, the local authority and the adult himself or herself) should be entitled to apply for the appointment of a guardian.

(2) The local authority should be under a duty to apply for an intervention order or the appointment of a guardian if it is satisfied that grounds for such an application exist, that an intervention order or a guardian is necessary in the interests of the adult, and that no-one else is applying or is likely to apply.

Paragraph 6.33; Clauses 42(2) and 43(1), (2)

87.   (1) There should be required to be lodged in court along with the application for guardianship the following:

(a) At least two reports relating to the incapacity of the adult. At least one of the reports should be given by a practitioner approved by the health board under section 20 of the Mental Health (Scotland) Act 1984 as having special expertise in the diagnosis and treatment of mental disorder and the other report(s) by a medical practitioner or other person suitably qualified in the assessment of mental disorder.

(b) Where powers in relation to the adult's personal welfare are applied for, a report by the local authority mental health officer as to the general appropriateness of the powers sought. Where the application relates only to powers in relation to the adult's property or financial affairs the report may be by any person with sufficient knowledge.

(2) The sheriff should have to be satisfied by means of reports or otherwise that the appointment of a guardian will benefit the adult and that the benefit cannot be reasonably obtained otherwise.

Paragraph 6.36; Clause 43(3)

88.   The medical practitioners or others assessing incapacity under Recommendation 87 and any mental health officer should be required to have personally examined or interviewed the adult within 30 days of the date of lodging the report in court. Others giving reports or information should be required to have seen the adult within the same period.

Paragraph 6.37; Clause 43(3)

89.   (1) Rules of Court should be made providing for intimation of the guardianship application to the incapable adult, his or her primary carer or nearest relatives and, where a report by a mental health officer accompanies the application, to the local authority. The sheriff should be empowered to order intimation to others and to dispense with intimation to the adult or others.

(2) Intimation to the adult should be dispensed with only if the medical certificates state that it would cause substantial harm to the adult's health.

Paragraph 6.38

90.   The court dealing with a guardianship application should have power to appoint an interim guardian for no more than three months or make other interim orders pending the determination of the guardianship application.

Paragraph 6.39; Clauses 3(2)(d) and 43(4), (5)

91.   Every guardian should intimate his or her appointment to the Public Guardian who should enter prescribed particulars of the guardian and the powers conferred in a register open to public inspection. The Public Guardian should issue the guardian with a certificate of appointment and notify the incapable adult of the guardianship.

Paragraph 6.40; Clauses 4(2)(c)(iv) and 44(5)

92.   All guardians with financial powers should have to find caution. The sheriff in appointing someone to act under an intervention order may require him or her to find caution. Consideration should be given to the setting up of a master policy scheme to be administered by the Public Guardian.

Paragraph 6.41; Clauses 42(5) and 44(5)(b)

93.   Guardians should be appointed initially for a period of three years or, on cause shown, for such other period (specified or indefinite) as the court thinks appropriate. The appointment should be subsequently renewable, on one or more occasions, for a period of five years or, on cause shown, for such other period (specified or indefinite) as the court thinks appropriate.

Paragraph 6.44; Clauses 44(3) and 47(5)

94.   (1) It should be competent to appoint only an individual as guardian to an incapable adult. Where the guardian is appointed with personal welfare powers the chief social work officer of the local authority in which the adult is resident may be appointed. The chief social work officer should be appointed as an officeholder so that any successor would automatically take over the guardianship functions.

        (2) A scheme of public financial management of the estates of incapable adults should be introduced. The fees charged should be modest in order not to impose a financial burden on small to medium estates. The Accountant of Court as holder of the office of Public Guardian should carry out such management. It should be competent to appoint the Public Guardian as guardian provided only financial powers are involved.

Paragraph 6.60; Clauses 4(1), (2)(a), and 45(1)

95.   (1) A proposed guardian (other than the Public Guardian or the local authority chief social work officer) should be appointed only if the court is satisfied by means of reports or otherwise that he or she is suitable. In assessing suitability the court should have regard to the following factors and any other relevant matters:

        (a) the ability of the individual to carry out the guardianship duties;

        (b) the accessibility of the individual to the adult and the ease with which he or she can consult the primary carer and others interested in the adult's welfare;

        (c) the individual's awareness of the adult's circumstances and needs;

        (d) any conflict of interest between the individual and the adult and whether guardianship would increase the powers of the individual over the adult to too great an extent.

        (2) In order to promote the appointment of non-professional guardians the court should in assessing ability take account of any free assistance that would be available from official and other sources. Conflicts of interest or undue concentration of power arising out of the individual being related to or living with the adult should be taken into account but should not by themselves prevent the individual becoming a guardian.

Paragraph 6.70; Clause 45(2)-(4)

96.   It should be competent to appoint two or more individuals to act as joint guardians. Except in the case of the parents, siblings or children of the adult the sheriff should have to be satisfied there was a need for joint guardianship.

Paragraph 6.73; Clause 47(1)(a), (2)

97.   The sheriff should be empowered to appoint a suitable individual to be an additional guardian to act jointly along with an existing guardian or guardians.

Paragraph 6.74; Clause 47(1)(b), (2), (4)

98.   Each joint guardian should be entitled to act independently and there should not be a requirement that any action has to be taken by all the joint guardians. A third party in good faith should be entitled to rely on an act or decision by one joint guardian.

Paragraph 6.75; Clause 47(6), (8)

99.   One joint guardian should be under a duty to consult the other(s) before exercising any guardianship powers, except where they agree that consultation should not take place. Consultation should also not have to take place if it is impracticable in the circumstances.

Paragraph 6.78; Clause 47(7)

100. (1)   In order to provide for the continuation of guardianship without having to re-apply to the court should the acting guardian die, resign, became mentally incapable or be removed it should be competent for the court at any time to appoint a substitute guardian who would become guardian (if willing) when such an event occurred.

(2)   The substitute guardian may be an individual, the chief social work officer of a local authority if the guardianship powers include powers in the personal welfare field or the Public Guardian if purely financial powers are involved. Before appointing an individual as substitute the court would have to be satisfied that he or she was suitable in terms of Recommendation 95.

(3)   On the acting guardian's death, resignation, removal or mental incapacity the Public Guardian, after receiving documentary evidence of its occurrence, should amend the register of guardians and issue the substitute guardian with a certificate of authority.

Paragraph 6.87; Clause 48

101. (1)   The court should be empowered to grant a guardian such powers as are appropriate in the circumstances and consistent with the least restrictive approach. The powers conferred may be powers in relation to specified matters or a general power to deal with or manage specified aspects of the adult's personal welfare or financial affairs.

(2)   A code of practice should be issued by the Secretary of State containing styles of powers in the welfare and financial fields that might be conferred on guardians. The styles should be for guidance only and their use should not be mandatory.

Paragraph 6.93; Clauses 10(1)(c) and 49(1)

102. The court in appointing a guardian should be empowered to confer a general power to deal with all aspects of the incapable adult's personal welfare or to manage all aspects of the adult's financial affairs. This power would be subject to the limitations contained in any enactment or rule of law or set out in Recommendation 103.

Paragraph 6.94; Clause 49(1)

103. (1)   The existing legislation or common law whereby entering into a marriage, agreeing to the adoption of one's children, or consenting to any of the treatments in Part X of the Mental Health (Scotland) Act 1984 can be done only by the individual in question should be retained. Accordingly it should not be competent for a guardian to consent or agree on behalf of an incapable adult in any of these matters.

(2)   It should be competent for a guardian to be granted power to bring or defend an action of divorce or separation on behalf of the adult but such power should have to be expressly conferred.

(3)   A guardian should not be entitled to place the adult in a hospital for treatment of mental disorder against his or her will. However, a guardian should, if appropriate powers have been conferred, have the same rights in relation to detention as the adult's nearest relative has under the Mental Health (Scotland) Act 1984.

(4)   Guardians should not be entitled to use their powers to consent to medical treatment so as to circumvent the protective provisions we recommend in Part 5, whereby certain treatments require prior authorisation from the court or a second opinion and doctors should not be entitled to use force except to protect patients from serious harm.

Paragraph 6.100; Clause 49(1)(c) and (2) and Schedule 4, paragraph 15

104. The Public Guardian should, on application by the guardian, be empowered to authorise the guardian to make gifts out of the incapable adult's estate. The Public Guardian should give the adult and his or her nearest relative and primary carer an opportunity to object, but should be entitled to grant the application after considering objections and further representations by the guardian or objectors or to remit the application to the sheriff.

Paragraph 6.110; Clause 50(1) to (5)

105. (1)   Where the adult under guardianship refuses to go to or return to a place of residence selected by the guardian the guardian should be entitled to apply to the sheriff for a warrant authorising a police officer to apprehend and convey the adult to that place. The police officer should have power under the warrant to enter premises and to use reasonable force in executing the warrant.

(2)   Where any person refuses to comply with or implement a lawful decision of the guardian in relation to the adult's personal welfare the guardian should be entitled to apply to the sheriff for an order directing that person

to do so. Rules of Court should be made giving the person an opportunity to make representations before the order is granted.

Paragraph 6.113; Clause 55

106.	Guardians should be supervised in the exercise of their welfare powers by the local authority in accordance with regulations made by the Secretary of State. The Mental Welfare Commission should have a monitoring role similar to that which it has in relation to guardians appointed under the Mental Health (Scotland) Act 1984. A Code of Practice giving guidance to local authorities and guardians should also be prepared and published.

Paragraph 6.118; Clauses 8(1)(a), (2)(a), 10(1)(a), (c) and
Schedule 4, paragraph 15(1), (2)

107.	Guardians should be under a statutory duty to comply with any order made by the local authority in the exercise of its supervisory powers. Where the guardian fails to obey the local authority order then, without prejudice to any other course of action, the local authority should be entitled to apply to the court for an order in similar terms.

Paragraph 6.119; Clause 49(7)(a)

108.	Guardians should be supervised by the Public Guardian in the exercise of their financial powers. Guardians should be under a statutory duty to comply with any order or demand made by the Public Guardian. Should the guardian fail to obey such an order or demand the Public Guardian should be entitled to apply to the court for an order in similar terms.

Paragraph 6.124; Clauses 4(2)(b) and 49(7)(b)

109.	In order to improve the supervisory regimes we have recommended, the Mental Welfare Commission, the Public Guardian and the local authority should each be under a duty to consult about matters of mutual concern in relation to guardians and generally, and to exchange relevant information.

Paragraph 6.125; Clauses 4(2)(h), 7(1)(b) and 8(1)(b)

110.	Any person claiming an interest in the welfare, property or financial affairs of an adult under guardianship should be entitled to apply to the court for an order giving directions to the guardian as to the exercise of the functions conferred.

Paragraph 6.126; Clause 3(3)

111.	(1)	The Mental Welfare Commission should retain its existing investigative role under the Mental Health (Scotland) Act 1984 in relation to the welfare and finances of the mentally disordered. The Public Guardian should have a similar role in relation to the finances of adults subject to guardianship and the local authority in relation to their welfare.

(2)	The Mental Welfare Commission, the local authority or the Public Guardian may, as a result of investigations, make any application to the court that seems to be required in order to safeguard the welfare or finances of an adult under guardianship.

Paragraph 6.129; Clauses 4(2)(d)(iv), 7(1)(c)(ii), 8(1)(c)(ii) and 9(1)

112.	(1)	A guardian acting within the scope of the powers conferred by the court should generally be regarded as the legal representative of the incapable adult concerned. Any decision made or transaction entered into by a guardian within the scope of his or her powers should accordingly have the same effect as if it were made or entered into by the adult concerned and as if the adult had capacity to make the decision or enter into the transaction.

(2)	A guardian should be entitled to manage and deal with the adult's estate in so far as it falls within the scope of his or her powers. This entitlement should include the right to demand that sums due to the adult be paid to the guardian.

(3)	Any decision made or transaction entered into by the guardian within the scope of the powers conferred by the court should bind the adult's estate and the guardian should not be personally liable provided the guardian made it clear that he or she was acting in a representative capacity.

(4)	In order to maximise protection and avoid any conflict of competence between an adult under guardianship and the guardian, the adult should be deemed to have no capacity to enter into transactions in those areas where the guardian has authority.

Paragraph 6.136; Clause 49(3) and 51(1), (2), (4)

113.	It should not be competent to register the appointment of a guardian to an adult in the Register of Inhibitions and Adjudications. Public notification of the appointment of guardians should be achieved by the open public register maintained by the Public Guardian in accordance with Recommendation 91.

Paragraph 6.137

114. There should be no presumption of incapacity to make a will arising out of the appointment of a guardian. Testamentary capacity would therefore be a question of fact in each case.

Paragraph 6.138; Clause 51(1)

115. The appointment of a guardian should not result in the adult in question being deemed or presumed to lack the capacity to enter into a valid marriage.

Paragraph 6.139; Clause 51(1)

116. New statutory provisions should provide that a guardian is not to be liable for any loss or damage to the adult if the guardian acted reasonably, in good faith and in accordance with the general principles.

Paragraph 6.144; Clause 64

117. Where the guardian becomes personally liable due to failure to disclose that he or she acted in a representative capacity, the guardian should be entitled to be reimbursed from the adult's estate provided the guardian acted within the scope of his or her authority and observed all other requirements.

Paragraph 6.145; Clause 51(4)

118. (1) A transaction for value between the guardian and a good faith third party should not be challengeable solely on the ground that the guardian was acting outwith his or her authority or that any other requirement under our recommendations was not observed.

(2) A guardian who acts outwith his or her authority should be personally liable in respect of the transaction.

Paragraph 6.147; Clause 51(4)(b), (7)

119. Each joint guardian should be liable for his or her own acts or failure to act. A joint guardian should also be liable for any act or failure to act of another joint guardian but only if he or she did not take reasonable care to prevent such act or failure to act.

Paragraph 6.148; Clause 47(6)

120. The sheriff should have power, on application, to order a guardian who fails to carry out the duties to an acceptable standard to forfeit (wholly or partly) the right to remuneration that would otherwise be due.

Paragraph 6.150; Clause 53

121. A guardian should not be entitled to surrender or transfer any of his or her powers to anyone else but may arrange for some or all of them to be exercised by another individual or individuals on the guardian's behalf.

Paragraph 6.152; Clause 49(6)

122. (1) In order to encourage an adult under guardianship to use existing skills and acquire new skills where this is practicable and reasonable the guardian should be entitled to authorise the adult to enter into a financial transaction within the scope of the guardian's powers.

(2) Such authority should only be granted with the consent of the Public Guardian.

(3) Where a third party is aware that the adult has authority from the guardian to carry out the transaction in question, the third party should not be entitled to challenge the transaction on the ground that the adult lacked capacity.

Paragraph 6.154; Clause 51(5), (6)

123. (1) A guardian should be under a duty to inform the Public Guardian of any permanent change in his or her own or the adult's address within seven days of such change.

(2) The Public Guardian should amend the register and notify the Mental Welfare Commission and the local authority where the guardian has welfare powers.

Paragraph 6.155; Clause 49(4)

124. (1) A guardian having financial powers should be under a duty to submit to the Public Guardian a full inventory of the adult's estate falling within the scope of his or her authority within three months of the date of registration of the guardian's appointment.

(2) The Public Guardian should have power to dispense with the need for an inventory or to allow further time for the submission of an inventory, and to prescribe the forms for inventories.

Paragraph 6.156; Schedule 2, paragraph 3

125. The way in which a guardian manages the adult's estate falling within the scope of the powers conferred by the

court should be governed by a management plan drawn up by the guardian and approved by the Public Guardian. The guardian should be entitled to appeal to the sheriff against the Public Guardian's refusal to approve.

Paragraph 6.162; Schedule 2, paragraphs 1 and 2

126. (1) A guardian should be entitled to carry on any business of the adult in existence at the date of appointment provided the business falls within the scope of his or her authority. A guardian should not however be entitled to start a new business using funds from the adult's estate.

    (2) The Public Guardian should be empowered to give directions to the guardian as to the running of the business and may require the guardian to dispose of it.

Paragraph 6.163; Schedule 2, paragraph 5(7)

127. Any disposal of an incapable adult's dwelling-house or acquisition of residential accommodation for the adult by the guardian should be competent only if the Public Guardian consents. An application by the guardian to the Public Guardian for consent should be notified to the adult, the adult's nearest relative and primary carer and any other individual whom the Public Guardian thinks ought to be notified. Those notified should be given an opportunity to object. The Public Guardian should have power to grant consent after considering any objections and any further representations by the applicant and any objectors, or to remit the matter to the sheriff.

Paragraph 6.164; Schedule 2, paragraph 6

128. (1) The management plan set out in Recommendation 125 above should be used for deciding how the estate of an adult under guardianship should be invested.

    (2) Unless the court orders otherwise, the guardian should have authority to retain investments held by the adult immediately prior to the guardian's appointment.

    (3) The rules relating to investment in a personal equity plan should be changed so as to allow a guardian to invest in this way on behalf of the adult.

    (4) New investments made by the guardian should normally be limited to those items specified in Schedule 1 to the Trustee Investments Act 1961, but the Public Guardian should have power to authorise other investments.

Paragraph 6.170; Schedule 2, paragraph 5

129. (1) A guardian should be under a duty to lodge all money received on behalf of the adult under guardianship in a bank or building society account forthwith. The account should be in the name of the adult. The type of account should be selected by the guardian so as to provide the best return, bearing in mind the amount of money likely to be involved, the need for access and the likely number of withdrawals.

    (2) A guardian should be required to place so as to earn interest any balance over £500 (or such other sum as may be prescribed).

Paragraph 6.171; Schedule 2, paragraph 4

130. (1) Guardians should generally be required to submit annual accounts to the Public Guardian for audit.

    (2) The Public Guardian should be empowered to substitute a period longer than a year for the normal accounting period or even waive the need for accounts altogether and substitute some other documentation.

    (3) The Public Guardian should be empowered to prescribe suitable styles of accounts and to direct the guardian as to which style should be used.

Paragraph 6.174; Schedule 2, paragraph 7

131. (1) The current rules relating to the audit of curatory accounts by the Accountant of Court should generally be adopted for the audit of guardianship accounts by the Public Guardian. The Public Guardian should be entitled to approve accounts containing minor discrepancies (including the absence of receipts for modest disbursements) provided he or she is satisfied that the guardian had acted reasonably and in good faith.

    (2) The Public Guardian should be entitled to delegate the auditing of guardianship accounts to external auditors. Audit by external auditors should not lead to the audit fee being greater than would have been charged for an audit carried out by the Public Guardian.

Paragraph 6.178; Schedule 2, paragraphs 7(6) and 8

132. (1) The sheriff should have power to vary the powers conferred on a guardian if there has been a material change in circumstances since the guardian was appointed.

    (2) The guardian or any other person claiming an interest in the incapable adult's welfare or estate should be entitled to apply for a variation.

(3)   The sheriff should have power to grant an interim variation or make any other interim order pending the determination of the application for variation.

Paragraph 6.179; Clauses 3(2)(d) and 59

133.   On the expiry of any initial period specified in the guardianship order, the order should lapse but should be capable of being renewed by the sheriff on application by any person claiming an interest in the adult's welfare or estate, using a simple and inexpensive procedure.

Paragraph 6.184; Clause 46

134.   The effect of an application to renew guardianship should be that the existing guardianship order should continue to have effect until the determination of the application.

Paragraph 6.185; Clause 46(1)

135.   (1)   A guardian should continue to be entitled to act after the adult's death or other event terminates the guardianship order, provided he or she acted in good faith and was unaware of the death or other terminating event.

(2)   A third party should be entitled to rely on a guardian's authority which had terminated provided the third party acted in good faith and was unaware of the termination.

Paragraph 6.186; Clause 62

136.   (1)   Where the condition of the adult under guardianship has improved so that the grounds for guardianship (set out in Recommendation 85) are no longer satisfied in relation to the adult's welfare or financial affairs or the circumstances are now such that the adult's welfare or financial affairs could be satisfactorily dealt with otherwise than by guardianship, the sheriff should be empowered, on application by any person claiming an interest in the adult's welfare or estate, to recall the welfare and financial powers of the guardian.

(2)   The Mental Welfare Commission and the local authority should have powers similar to those of the sheriff in paragraph (1) above but in relation to welfare powers only. The Public Guardian should have similar powers in relation to financial powers only. The Mental Welfare Commission, the local authority or the Public Guardian should be entitled to act on application by any person claiming an interest or at their own instance. In either case the guardian, the adult and the adult's nearest relative and primary carer and any other interested persons should be notified, giving them an opportunity to object and make representations before a decision is taken. The Mental Welfare Commission, local authority or Public Guardian should be entitled to remit the matter to the sheriff on their own initiative or on request by any objector.

Paragraph 6.196; Clauses 56(1)(c) and 58(1)-(8)

137.   (1)   The sheriff should be empowered to replace an existing guardian with another suitable guardian on the application of any person with an interest in the incapable adult's welfare or finances.

(2)   Rules of Court should be made to allow a simple procedure to be used where the existing guardian wishes to relinquish the post, or has died or has become mentally incapable of acting as guardian. A hearing should be necessary only if objections were made.

Paragraph 6.202; Clause 56(1)(a)

138.   The court should have power to remove a guardian where the guardian sought to be removed was a joint guardian or where a substitute had already been appointed.

Paragraph 6.203; Clause 56(1)(b)

139.   Where an adult has as guardian the chief social work officer of a local authority and subsequently becomes habitually resident in another local authority area, the chief social work officer of the new local authority should become guardian automatically without any application to the court having to be made. The change of residence should be notified to the chief social work officer of the new local authority who should in turn notify the Public Guardian who should amend the guardianship register accordingly, issue a certificate of authority to the new guardian and inform the incapable adult.

Paragraph 6.204; Clause 61

140.   (1)   A joint guardian should be permitted to resign by giving notice to the Public Guardian. The resignation should be effective only if accompanied by a statement from the remaining joint guardian or guardians that they are willing to continue to act.

(2)   A guardian should also be permitted to resign if a substitute guardian has been appointed and is willing to act as guardian.

(3)   A substitute guardian who is not an acting guardian should be entitled to resign by giving notice to the Public Guardian.

(4) The Public Guardian on receiving an effective resignation should amend the register of guardians and notify the incapable adult.

Paragraph 6.205; Clause 60

141. (1) Guardians should not generally be entitled to remuneration in relation to the exercise of their welfare functions but the sheriff should have power to award remuneration in exceptional cases to guardians other than the chief social work officer.

(2) Guardians should generally be entitled to remuneration in relation to the exercise of their financial functions. In deciding whether to allow remuneration the sheriff should have regard to the value of the estate and likely difficulty in managing it.

(3) The Public Guardian should fix any remuneration payable to the guardian having regard to the amount of work done when auditing the guardian's accounts or at another time on application by the guardian. The Public Guardian should be able to authorise payment of interim remuneration.

Paragraph 6.211; Clause 52(4)-(7)

142. (1) Guardians (other than the chief social work officer of a local authority) should be entitled to reimbursement from the adult's estate for outlays they have reasonably incurred in the exercise of their functions. Guardians should not however be reimbursed for outlays in relation to services which they are expected to perform personally. The Public Guardian should have power to disallow outlays that have not been reasonably incurred.

(2) Where the chief social work officer of a local authority is the guardian he or she should not be entitled to reimbursement from the adult's estate for outlays incurred in the exercise of any welfare functions, unless an adult in similar circumstances but without a guardian would be charged.

Paragraph 6.215; Clause 52(1)-(3)

143. (1) The Public Guardian, on application by a former guardian or the executors of a deceased guardian, should be empowered to grant a discharge to the guardian in respect of his or her dealings with the incapable adult's estate.

(2) The Public Guardian should give the incapable adult and his or her nearest relative and primary carer an opportunity to object to the application. The Public Guardian should have power to grant the application after considering any objections and any further representations by the applicant and any objector, or to remit the application to the sheriff.

Paragraph 6.217; Clause 57(1) to (5)

144. The powers of a Scottish guardian in relation to the property of the incapable adult should extend to property wherever situated, whether moveable or immoveable.

Paragraph 6.220; Clause 52(2)(a)

145. The powers of a Scottish guardian in relation to the personal welfare of the incapable adult should, as a matter of Scottish law, be exercisable even if the adult is outside Scotland.

Paragraph 6.223; Clause 51(3)

146. An appeal should lie from any decision of the Public Guardian, the Mental Welfare Commission or the local authority in the exercise of their functions to the sheriff.

Paragraph 7.3; Clauses generally

147. The Public Guardian's decision to suspend or terminate the authority granted to a person to withdraw funds from the account of an incapable adult should remain in effect notwithstanding any appeal to the sheriff until it is reversed on appeal.

Paragraph 7.4; Clause 24(4)

148. The existing rules relating to appeals from a determination by a sheriff should apply to all determinations by a sheriff under our recommendations except in relation to the following determinations which should be final and not subject to appeal.

(a) The sheriff's determination of an appeal from a decision of the Public Guardian:

(i) refusing to accept that the attorney is accepting the appointment (Recommendation 20),

(ii) refusing to accept that an event has occurred which allows registration of a continuing power of attorney (Recommendation 22),

(iii) in relation to an application for authority to withdraw from a bank or building society account or to remit the application to the sheriff (Recommendation 40),

(iv) granting an extension of authority to a withdrawer (Recommendation 41(2)),

(v) suspending or terminating the authority of a withdrawer (Recommendation 44(2)),

(vi) refusing to allow the managers of an approved establishment to manage money or property in excess of the prescribed value (Recommendation 54(2)),

(vii) refusing to authorise the making of a gift by the guardian or to remit the application to the sheriff (Recommendation 104),

(viii) refusing to consent to the incapable adult entering into a transaction which falls within the scope of the guardian's authority (Recommendation 122(2)),

(ix) giving directions to the guardian as to the running or disposal of the adult's business (Recommendation 126),

(x) in relation to purchase or disposal of accommodation for the incapable adult or to remit the application to the sheriff (Recommendation 127),

(xi) in relation to investments of the incapable adult's estate (Recommendation 128(4)),

(xii) refusing to remit an application or proposal for recall of a guardian's financial powers to the sheriff (Recommendation 136(2)),

(xiii) refusing to allow interim remuneration to the guardian (Recommendation 141(3)),

(xiv) refusing to remit an application for discharge of a former guardian to the sheriff (Recommendation 143(2));

(b) An order by the sheriff requiring a continuing or welfare attorney to submit accounts or reports or be subject to supervision by the Public Guardian or local authority (Recommendations 27 to 30);

(c) The sheriff's determination of an application by the guardian in relation to the management plan (Recommendation 125);

(d) The sheriff's determination of an appeal from a refusal by the Mental Welfare Commission or the local authority to remit an application or proposal for recall of a guardian's welfare powers to the sheriff (Recommendation 143(2)).

Paragraph 7.5; Clauses and Schedules generally

149.   Where an attorney has been appointed prior to the date of commencement of the new legislation under a power of attorney which, under the law in force on the date when the power was granted, continues to have effect after the granter has become incapable of managing his or her property and affairs:

(a) nothing in the new legislation should affect the powers of the attorney, and in particular his or her authority to act should not depend on registration with the Public Guardian, but

(b) when acting for a granter who has become so incapable, the attorney should in other respects be treated as a continuing attorney under the new legislation.

Paragraph 7.7; Schedule 3, paragraph 6

150.   Where a person's money or valuables are at the date of commencement of the new legislation held by the managers of a hospital under section 94 of the Mental Health (Scotland) Act 1984:

(a) nothing in the new legislation should affect their powers to continue to hold and apply the money or valuables, and in particular they should not require to have the person re-certified, but

(b) they should be treated in other respects as the managers of an approved establishment under the new legislation.

Paragraph 7.8; Schedule 3, paragraph 7

151.   (1)   Nothing in the new legislation should restrict the powers of:

(i) guardians appointed under the Mental Health (Scotland) Act 1984

(ii) curators bonis

(iii) tutors-dative or

(iv) tutors-at-law

if already appointed at the date of commencement of the new legislation but in other respects they should be treated for all purposes (including the purposes of enactments amended by the new legislation to substitute "guardian" for "tutor or curator") as guardians appointed with equivalent powers under the new legislation and accordingly

  (a) guardians appointed under the Mental Health (Scotland) Act 1984 would be treated as guardians with the statutory powers which they had immediately prior to commencement

  (b) curators bonis would be treated as guardians with full powers over the adult's property and financial affairs

  (c) tutors-dative would be treated as guardians with the powers which they had immediately prior to commencement, and

  (d) tutors-at-law would be treated as guardians with full powers over the adult's property and financial affairs and personal welfare.

(2) Where an application for appointment as guardian under the 1984 Act, curator bonis or tutor is pending before a court at the date of commencement it should continue to be dealt with under the law in force immediately prior to the date of commencement and any person so appointed should be treated in the same way as if already appointed at the date of commencement.

Paragraph 7.10; Schedule 3, paragraphs 1 to 4, 8 and 9

152. (1) References in existing enactments or documents to tutors in relation to adults under mental disability or incapacitated should be construed as including references to guardians appointed under the new legislation with powers relating to the personal welfare of the adult.

  (2) References in existing enactments or documents to curators, or curators bonis, in relation to adults under mental disability or incapacitated should be construed as including references to guardians appointed under the new legislation with powers relating to the property and financial affairs of the adult.

Paragraph 7.11; Schedule 4, paragraph 1

153. The provisions in the Criminal Procedure (Scotland) Act 1975 on the making of guardianship orders should be amended to allow the court to make the new type of guardianship orders recommended in this report.

Paragraph 7.17

Appendix A

Incapable Adults (Scotland) Bill

PART III

ACCOUNTS AND FUNDS OF INCAPABLE ADULTS

PART IV

MANAGEMENT OF RESIDENTS' FINANCES

PART V

MEDICAL TREATMENT, CARE AND RESEARCH

Authority

Advance statements

Withholding and withdrawal of medical treatment from incapable adults

PART VI

INTERVENTION ORDERS AND GUARDIANSHIP ORDERS

Intervention orders

Guardianship orders

Joint and substitute guardians

Functions etc. of guardian

Termination and variation of guardianship and replacement, removal or resignation of guardian

PART VII

MISCELLANEOUS

m

DRAFT

OF A

BILL

A.D. 1995.

TO

Make provision for Scotland as to the property, financial affairs and personal welfare of adults who are incapable by reason of mental disorder or inability to communicate; and for connected purposes.

BE IT ENACTED by the Queen's most Excellent Majesty, by and with the advice and consent of the Lords Spiritual and Temporal, and Commons, in this present Parliament assembled, and by the authority of the same, as follows:—

PART I

GENERAL

General principles

General principles.

1.—(1) The principles set out in subsections (2) to (4) below shall be given effect to in relation to any intervention in the affairs of an incapable adult under or in pursuance of this Act, including any order made in or for the purpose of any proceedings under this Act for or in connection with an incapable adult.

(2) There shall be no intervention in the affairs of an incapable adult unless the person responsible for authorising or effecting the intervention is satisfied that the intervention will benefit the adult and that such benefit cannot reasonably be achieved without the intervention.

(3) Where it is determined that an intervention as mentioned in subsection (1) above is to be made, such intervention shall be the least restrictive option in relation to the freedom of the adult, consistent with the purpose of the intervention.

(4) In determining if an intervention is to be made and, if so, what intervention is to be made, account shall be taken of—

   (a) the present and past wishes and feelings of the adult so far as they can be ascertained;

   (b) the views of the nearest relative and the primary carer of the adult in so far as it is reasonable and practicable to do so;

   (c) the views of—

      (i) any guardian, continuing attorney or welfare attorney of the adult who has powers relating to the proposed intervention; and

      (ii) any person whom the sheriff has directed to be consulted,

   in so far as it is reasonable and practicable to do so; and

   (d) the views of any other person appearing to the person responsible for authorising or effecting the intervention to have an interest in the welfare of the adult or in the proposed intervention, where these views have been made known to the person responsible, in so far as it is reasonable and practicable to do so.

(5) Any guardian, continuing attorney, welfare attorney or manager of an establishment exercising functions under this Act or under any order of the sheriff in

relation to an incapable adult shall, in so far as it is reasonable and practicable to do so, encourage the adult to exercise whatever skills he has concerning his property, financial affairs or personal welfare, as the case may be, and to develop new such skills.

(6) In subsection (4)(c)(i) above any reference to—

(a) a guardian shall include a reference to a guardian (however called) appointed under the law of any country to, or entitled under the law of any country to act for, an adult during his incapacity, if the guardianship is recognised by the law of Scotland;

(b) a continuing attorney shall include a reference to a person granted, under a contract, grant or appointment governed by the law of any country, powers (however expressed), relating to the granter's property or financial affairs and having continuing effect notwithstanding the granter's incapacity;

(c) a welfare attorney shall include a reference to a person granted, under a contract, grant or appointment governed by the law of any country, powers (however expressed) relating to the granter's personal welfare and having effect during the granter's incapacity.

The sheriff

Applications and other proceedings.

2.—(1) This section shall apply for the purposes of any application which may be made to and any other proceedings before the sheriff under this Act.

(2) Subject to subsection (3) below, the sheriff having jurisdiction to dispose of an application or other proceedings under this Act shall be the sheriff in whose sheriffdom—

(a) the adult who is the subject of the application or proceedings is habitually resident at the date the application is made or the proceedings are commenced; or

(b) any property or establishment which is the subject of the application or proceedings is situated.

(3) Notwithstanding that any other court has jurisdiction to entertain an application under this Act or, in the case of a court outwith Scotland, to entertain an application for an order having corresponding effect to an order under this Act, the sheriff shall have jurisdiction to entertain such an application if—

(a) the adult who is the subject of the application is present in the sheriffdom on the date of the application; and

(b) the sheriff considers that it is necessary, in the interests of that adult, to make such an order immediately.

(4) Without prejudice to subsection (2) above, where the adult who is the subject of the application or proceedings ceases to be habitually resident in the sheriffdom mentioned in that subsection, the sheriff of that sheriffdom shall, if he has made an intervention order or a guardianship order in relation to the adult, nevertheless continue to have jurisdiction to dispose of any application or other proceedings relating to that order if—

(a) no other court has jurisdiction; or

(b) another court has jurisdiction but it would be unreasonable to expect the applicant to invoke that jurisdiction.

(5) All applications and proceedings under this Act shall be disposed of by a sheriff nominated for the time being for that purpose by the sheriff principal, unless no such sheriff is available to do so.

Powers of sheriff.

3.—(1) In an application or any other proceedings under this Act, the sheriff may make such consequential or ancillary order, provision or direction as he considers appropriate.

M

(2) Without prejudice to the generality of subsection (1) above or to any other powers conferred by this Act, the sheriff may—

    (a) make any order granted by him subject to such conditions and restrictions as appear to him to be appropriate;

    (b) order that any reports relating to the person who is the subject of the application or proceedings be lodged with the court or that the person be assessed or interviewed and that a report of such assessment or interview be lodged;

    (c) make such further inquiry or call for such further information as appears to him to be appropriate;

    (d) make such interim order as appears to him to be appropriate pending the disposal of the application or proceedings.

(3) On an application by any person claiming an interest in the property, financial affairs or personal welfare of an incapable adult, the sheriff may give such directions to any person exercising—

    (a) functions conferred by this Act; or

    (b) functions of a like nature conferred by the law of any country,

as to the exercise of those functions and the taking of decisions or action in relation to the incapable adult as appear to him to be appropriate.

(4) In an application or any other proceedings under this Act, the sheriff—

    (a) shall consider whether it is necessary to appoint a person for the purpose of safeguarding the interests of the person who is the subject of the application or proceedings; and

    (b) without prejudice to any existing power to appoint a person to represent the interests of the person who is the subject of the application or proceedings may, if he thinks fit, appoint a person to act for the purpose specified in paragraph (a) above.

(5) The power to make rules under section 32 of the Sheriff Courts (Scotland) Act 1971 shall include power to make rules providing for the procedure relating to appointment under subsection (4) above and to the functions of a person so appointed.

The Public Guardian

4.—(1) The Accountant of Court shall be the Public Guardian.

(2) The Public Guardian shall have the following general functions under this Act—

    (a) to act as guardian if appointed to do so;

    (b) to supervise any other guardian or any person who is authorised under an intervention order in the exercise of his functions relating to the property or financial affairs of the incapable adult;

    (c) to establish, maintain and make available during normal office hours for inspection by members of the public on payment of the prescribed fee, separate registers of—

        (i) all documents relating to continuing powers of attorney;

        (ii) all documents relating to welfare powers of attorney;

        (iii) all authorisations to withdraw funds under Part III of this Act;

        (iv) all documents relating to guardianship orders under Part VI of this Act;

        (v) all documents relating to intervention orders under Part VI of this Act,

in which he shall enter any matter which he is required to enter under this Act and any other matter of which he becomes aware relating to the existence or scope of the power, authorisation or order as the case may be;

(d) to receive and investigate any complaints regarding the exercise of functions relating to the property or financial affairs of an incapable adult made—

    (i) in relation to continuing attorneys;

    (ii) concerning the withdrawal of funds under Part III of this Act;

    (iii) concerning the handling by approved establishments of the affairs of residents of such establishments under Part IV of this Act;

    (iv) in relation to guardians or persons appointed to carry out intervention orders;

(e) to investigate any circumstances made known to him in which the property or financial affairs of an incapable adult seem to him to be at risk, where the incapable adult is habitually resident, or the property is situated, in Scotland;

(f) to approve establishments under Part IV of this Act for the purpose of the management by the establishments of the financial affairs of residents therein and generally to supervise the management by establishments of the affairs of residents under that Part;

(g) to provide, when requested to do so, a guardian, a continuing attorney, a withdrawer, a manager of an establishment or a person authorised to act under an intervention order with information and advice about the performance of functions relating to property or financial affairs under this Act;

(h) to consult the Mental Welfare Commission and any local authority on cases or matters relating to the exercise of functions under this Act in which there is, or appears to be, a common interest.

(3) In paragraph (d) of subsection (2) above any reference to—

(a) a guardian shall include a reference to a guardian (however called) appointed under the law of any country to, or entitled under the law of any country to act for, an adult during his incapacity, if the guardianship is recognised by the law of Scotland;

(b) a continuing attorney shall include a reference to a person granted, under a contract, grant or appointment governed by the law of any country, powers (however expressed), relating to the granter's property or financial affairs and having continuing effect notwithstanding the granter's incapacity,

and the power conferred by that paragraph shall, in relation to such a guardian or continuing attorney, be exercisable only where the incapable adult is habitually resident, or the property in question is situated, in Scotland.

The Public Guardian: further provision.

5.—(1) The Secretary of State may prescribe—

(a) the form and content of the registers to be established and maintained under subsection (2)(c) of section 4 of this Act and the manner and medium in which they are to be established and maintained;

(b) the form and content of any certificate which the Public Guardian is empowered to issue under this Act;

(c) the forms and procedure for the purposes of any application required or permitted to be made under this Act to the Public Guardian in relation to any matter.

(2) The Public Guardian may charge the prescribed fee for anything done by him in connection with any of his functions under this Act and he shall not be obliged to act until such fee is paid.

(3) Any certificate which the Public Guardian issues under this Act shall, for the purposes of any proceedings, be conclusive evidence of the matters contained in it.

6. Where in any court proceedings the Public Guardian is a party for the purpose of—

(a) protecting the interests of an incapable adult; or

(b) representing the public interest,

the court may make an award of expenses in his favour against the estate of the incapable adult or against any person whose actings have resulted in the proceedings.

The Mental Welfare Commission

7.—(1) Without prejudice to their functions under the 1984 Act, the Mental Welfare Commission shall have the following general functions under this Act—

(a) to exercise protective functions in respect of any incapable adult in respect of whom an intervention or guardianship order has been granted, in so far as that order relates to the personal welfare of the adult;

(b) to consult the Public Guardian and any local authority on cases or matters relating to the exercise of functions under this Act in which there is, or appears to be, a common interest;

(c) to receive and investigate any complaints relating to the exercise of functions relating to the personal welfare of an incapable adult made—

(i) in relation to welfare attorneys;

(ii) in relation to guardians or persons appointed to carry out intervention orders;

(d) to investigate any circumstances made known to them in which the personal welfare of an incapable adult seems to them to be at risk, where the incapable adult is habitually resident or, where his personal welfare is immediately at risk, present in Scotland;

(e) to provide a guardian, welfare attorney or person authorised to act under an intervention order, when requested to do so, with information and advice in connection with the performance of his functions in relation to personal welfare under this Act.

(2) In paragraph (c) of subsection (1) above any reference to—

(a) a guardian shall include a reference to a guardian (however called) appointed under the law of any country to, or entitled under the law of any country to act for, an adult during his incapacity, if the guardianship is recognised by the law of Scotland;

(b) a welfare attorney shall include a reference to a person granted, under a contract, grant or appointment governed by the law of any country, powers (however expressed) relating to the granter's personal welfare and having effect during the granter's incapacity,

and the power conferred by that paragraph shall, in relation to such a guardian or person, be exercisable only where the incapable adult is habitually resident or, where his personal welfare is immediately at risk, present in Scotland.

Local authorities

8.—(1) A local authority shall have the following general functions under this Act—

(a) to supervise a guardian appointed with functions relating to the personal welfare of an incapable adult in the exercise of those functions;

  (b) to consult the Public Guardian and the Mental Welfare Commission on cases or matters in which there is, or appears to be, a common interest;

  (c) to receive and investigate any complaints relating to the exercise of functions relating to the personal welfare of an incapable adult made—

    (i) in relation to welfare attorneys;

    (ii) in relation to guardians or persons appointed to carry out intervention orders;

  (d) to investigate any circumstances made known to them in which the personal welfare of an incapable adult seems to them to be at risk, where the incapable adult is habitually resident or, where his personal welfare is immediately at risk, present in Scotland;

  (e) to provide a guardian, welfare attorney or person authorised to act under an intervention order, when requested to do so, with information and advice in connection with the performance of his functions in relation to personal welfare under this Act.

(2) The Secretary of State may make provision by regulations as regards the supervision by local authorities of the performance of their functions—

  (a) by guardians, in relation to the personal welfare of incapable adults under this Act;

  (b) where the supervision has been ordered by the sheriff—

    (i) by persons appointed to carry out intervention orders;

    (ii) by welfare attorneys.

(3) In paragraph (c) of subsection (1) above any reference to—

  (a) a guardian shall include a reference to a guardian (however called) appointed under the law of any country to, or entitled under the law of any country to act for, an adult during his incapacity, if the guardianship is recognised by the law of Scotland;

  (b) a welfare attorney shall include a reference to a person granted, under a contract, grant or appointment governed by the law of any country, powers (however expressed) relating to the granter's personal welfare and having effect during the granter's incapacity,

and the power conferred by that paragraph shall in relation to such a guardian or person be exercisable only where the incapable adult is habitually resident or, where his personal welfare is immediately at risk, present in Scotland.

Investigations

9.—(1) In consequence of any investigation carried out under—

  (a) section 4(2)(d) or (e) of this Act by the Public Guardian;

  (b) section 7(1)(c) or (d) of this Act by the Mental Welfare Commission; or

  (c) section 8(1)(c) or (d) of this Act by a local authority,

the Public Guardian, the Mental Welfare Commission or the local authority, as the case may be, may take such steps, including the making of an application to the sheriff, as seem to him or them to be necessary to safeguard the property, financial affairs or personal welfare, as the case may be, of the incapable adult.

(2) For the purposes of any investigation mentioned in subsection (1) above, the Public Guardian, Mental Welfare Commission and local authority shall provide each other with such information and assistance as may be necessary to facilitate the investigation.

Codes of practice

10.—(1) The Secretary of State shall prepare and from time to time revise codes of practice containing guidance as to—

(a) the exercise by local authorities and their chief officers of social work of their functions under this Act;

(b) the exercise by continuing and welfare attorneys of their functions under this Act;

(c) the exercise by guardians of their functions under this Act;

(d) the exercise by withdrawers of their functions under this Act;

(e) the exercise by banks and building societies of their functions under this Act;

(f) the exercise by managers of establishments of their functions under this Act;

(g) such other matters arising out of or connected with this Act as the Secretary of State considers appropriate.

(2) Before preparing any code of practice under this Act or making any alteration in it the Secretary of State shall consult such bodies as appear to him to be concerned.

(3) The Secretary of State shall lay copies of any such code and of any alteration in it before Parliament; and if either House of Parliament passes a resolution requiring the code or any alteration in it to be withdrawn the Secretary of State shall withdraw the code or alteration and, where he withdraws the code, shall prepare a code in substitution for the one withdrawn.

(4) No resolution shall be passed by either House of Parliament under subsection (3) above in respect of a code or alteration after the expiry of the period of 40 days beginning with the day on which a copy of the code or alteration was laid before that House; but for the purposes of this subsection no account shall be taken of any time during which Parliament is dissolved or prorogued or during which both Houses are adjourned for more than 4 days.

(5) The Secretary of State shall publish every code of practice made under this Act as for the time being in force.

PART II

CONTINUING POWERS OF ATTORNEY AND WELFARE POWERS OF ATTORNEY

11.—(1) Where an individual grants a power of attorney relating to his property or financial affairs in accordance with the following provisions of this section that power of attorney shall, notwithstanding any rule of law, continue to have effect in the event of the granter's becoming incapable of making or becoming incapable of communicating decisions about the matter to which the power of attorney relates.

(2) In this Act a power of attorney granted under subsection (1) above is referred to as a "continuing power of attorney" and a person on whom such power is conferred is referred to as a "continuing attorney".

(3) A continuing power of attorney shall be valid only if it is expressed in a written document which—

(a) is subscribed by the granter;

(b) incorporates a statement which clearly expresses the granter's intention that the power be a continuing power;

(c) incorporates a certificate in the prescribed form by a solicitor or by a member of another prescribed class that—

(i) he has interviewed the granter immediately before the granter subscribed the document;

   (ii) he is satisfied, either because of his own knowledge of the granter or because he has consulted other persons (whom he names in the certificate) who have knowledge of the granter, that at the time the continuing power of attorney is granted the granter understands its nature and extent;

   (iii) he has no reason to believe that the granter is acting under undue influence or that any other factor vitiates the granting of the power.

Creation and
exercise of welfare
power of attorney.

12.—(1) An individual may grant a power of attorney relating to his personal welfare in accordance with the following provisions of this section.

(2) In this Act a power of attorney granted under this section is referred to as a "welfare power of attorney" and an individual on whom such power is conferred is referred to as a "welfare attorney".

(3) A welfare power of attorney shall be valid only if it is expressed in a written document which—

   (a) is subscribed by the granter;

   (b) incorporates a statement which clearly expresses the granter's intention that the power be a welfare power to which this section of this Act applies;

   (c) incorporates a certificate in the prescribed form by a solicitor or by a member of another prescribed class that—

      (i) he has interviewed the granter immediately before the granter subscribed the document;

      (ii) he is satisfied, either because of his own knowledge of the granter or because he has consulted other persons (whom he names in the certificate) who have knowledge of the granter, that at the time the welfare power of attorney is granted the granter understands its nature and extent;

      (iii) he has no reason to believe that the granter is acting under undue influence or that any other factor vitiates the granting of the power.

(4) A welfare power of attorney—

   (a) may be granted only to an individual; and

   (b) shall not be exercisable unless—

      (i) the granter is incapable of making or is incapable of communicating decisions about the matter to which the welfare power of attorney relates; or

      (ii) the welfare attorney reasonably believes that sub-paragraph (i) above applies.

(5) A welfare attorney may not—

   (a) place the granter in a hospital for the treatment of mental disorder against the granter's will;

   (b) consent on behalf of the granter to anything mentioned in section 37(3), (4) or (5) of this Act.

(6) A welfare power of attorney shall not come to an end in the event of the bankruptcy of the granter or the welfare attorney.

(7) Any reference to a welfare attorney—

   (a) in relation to paragraph (b) of subsection (4) above in a case where the granter is habitually resident in Scotland; and

   (b) in subsection (5) above,

shall include a reference to a person granted, under a contract, grant or appointment governed by the law of any country, powers (however expressed) relating to the granter's personal welfare and having effect during the granter's incapacity.

Power of attorney not granted in accordance with this Act.

13. A power of attorney granted after the commencement of this Act which is not granted in accordance with section 11 or 12 of this Act shall have no effect during any period when the granter is incapable of making or is incapable of communicating decisions about the matter to which the power of attorney relates.

Registration of continuing or welfare power of attorney.

14.—(1) A continuing or welfare attorney shall have no authority to act until the document conferring the power of attorney has been registered under this section.

(2) For the purposes of registration, the document conferring the power of attorney shall be sent to the Public Guardian who, if he is satisfied that a person appointed to act is prepared to act, shall—

> (a) enter particulars of it in the register maintained by him under section 4(2)(c)(i) or (ii) of this Act as the case may be;

> (b) send a copy of it with a certificate of registration to the sender;

> (c) if it confers a welfare power of attorney, send a copy of it to the Mental Welfare Commission.

(3) The document conferring a continuing or welfare power of attorney may contain a condition that the Public Guardian shall not register it under this section until the occurrence of a specified event and in that case the Public Guardian shall not register it until he is satisfied that the specified event has occurred.

(4) A copy of a document conferring a continuing or welfare power of attorney authenticated by the Public Guardian shall be accepted for all purposes as sufficient evidence of the contents of the original and of any matter relating thereto appearing in the copy.

(5) The Public Guardian shall—

> (a) on the registration of a document conferring a continuing or welfare power of attorney, send a copy of it to the granter; and

> (b) where the document conferring the continuing or welfare power of attorney so requires, send a copy of it to not more than two specified individuals or holders of specified offices or positions.

(6) It shall be a sufficient compliance with subsection (5) above for the Public Guardian to send the copy by ordinary post to the individual at the address given in the document or, where this has changed, to the individual's known address.

(7) A decision of the Public Guardian under subsection (2) above as to whether or not a person is prepared to act or under subsection (3) above as to whether or not the specified event has occurred may be appealed to the sheriff, whose decision shall be final.

Powers of sheriff.

15.—(1) An application for an order under subsection (2) below may be made to the sheriff by any person claiming an interest in the property, financial affairs or personal welfare of the granter of a continuing or welfare power of attorney.

(2) Where, on an application being made under subsection (1) above, the sheriff is satisfied that the granter is incapable of making or is incapable of communicating decisions about, or is incapable of acting to safeguard or promote his interests in, his property, financial affairs or personal welfare insofar as the power of attorney relates

to them, and that it is necessary to safeguard or promote these interests, he may make an order—

    (a) ordaining that the continuing attorney shall be subject to the supervision of the Public Guardian to such extent as may be specified in the order;

    (b) ordaining the continuing attorney to submit accounts in respect of any period specified in the order for audit to the Public Guardian;

    (c) ordaining that the welfare attorney shall be subject to the supervision of the local authority to such extent as may be specified in the order;

    (d) ordaining the welfare attorney to give a report to him as to the manner in which the welfare attorney has exercised his powers during any period specified in the order;

    (e) revoking—

        (i) any of the powers granted by the continuing or welfare power of attorney; or

        (ii) the appointment of an attorney.

(3) Where the sheriff makes an order under this section the sheriff clerk shall send a copy of the interlocutor containing the order to the Public Guardian who shall—

    (a) enter prescribed particulars in the register maintained by him under section 4(2)(c)(i) or (ii) of this Act as the case may be;

    (b) notify—

        (i) the granter;

        (ii) the continuing or welfare attorney;

        (iii) where the sheriff makes an order under subsection (2)(c) above, the local authority.

(4) An order of the sheriff under paragraphs (a) to (d) of subsection (2) above, and a decision of the sheriff not to make such an order, shall be final.

(5) In this section any reference to—

    (a) a continuing power of attorney shall include a reference to a power (however expressed) under a contract, grant or appointment governed by the law of any country, relating to the granter's property or financial affairs and having continuing effect notwithstanding the granter's incapacity;

    (b) a welfare power of attorney shall include a reference to a power (however expressed) under a contract, grant or appointment governed by the law of any country, relating to the granter's personal welfare and having effect during the granter's incapacity,

and "continuing attorney" and "welfare attorney" shall be construed accordingly.

Notification of
change of address
etc.

16. After a document conferring a continuing or welfare power of attorney has been registered under section 14 of this Act, the attorney shall notify the Public Guardian—

    (a) of any change in his address;

    (b) of any change in the address of the granter of the power of attorney; or

    (c) of the death of the granter of the power of attorney,

and the Public Guardian shall enter prescribed particulars in the register maintained by him under section 4(2)(c)(i) or (ii) of this Act as the case may be.

17.—(1) A continuing or welfare attorney who wishes to resign after the document conferring the power of attorney has been registered under section 14 of this Act shall give notice in writing of his intention to do so to—

(a) the granter of the power of attorney;

(b) the Public Guardian;

(c) any guardian or, where there is no guardian, the granter's primary carer;

(d) the local authority, where they are supervising the welfare attorney.

(2) Subject to subsection (3) below, the resignation shall not have effect until the expiry of a period of 28 days commencing with the date of receipt by the Public Guardian of the notice given under subsection (1) above; and on its becoming effective the Public Guardian shall enter prescribed particulars in the register maintained by him under section 4(2)(c)(i) or (ii) of this Act as the case may be.

(3) The resignation of a joint attorney, or an attorney in respect of whom the granter has appointed a substitute attorney, shall take effect on the receipt by the Public Guardian of notice under subsection (1)(b) above if evidence that—

(a) the remaining joint attorney is willing to continue to act; or

(b) the substitute attorney is willing to act,

accompanies the notice.

18.—(1) If the granter and the continuing or welfare attorney are married to each other the power of attorney shall, unless the document conferring it provides otherwise, come to an end upon the granting of—

(a) a decree of separation to either party;

(b) a decree of divorce to either party;

(c) declarator of nullity of the marriage.

(2) The authority of a continuing or welfare attorney in relation to any matter shall come to an end on the appointment of a guardian with powers relating to that matter.

(3) In subsection (2) above any reference to—

(a) a continuing attorney shall include a reference to a person granted, under a contract, grant or appointment governed by the law of any country, powers (however expressed), relating to the granter's property or financial affairs and having continuing effect notwithstanding the granter's incapacity;

(b) a welfare attorney shall include a reference to a person granted, under a contract, grant or appointment governed by the law of any country, powers (however expressed) relating to the granter's personal welfare and having effect during the granter's incapacity.

(4) No liability shall be incurred by any person who acts in good faith in ignorance of—

(a) the coming to an end of a power of attorney under subsection (1) above; or

(b) the appointment of a guardian as mentioned in subsection (2) above.

19. Subject to the provisions of sections 12(4)(b) and (5) of this Act and to any order of the sheriff under section 15 of this Act addressed to an attorney to whom the section applies by virtue of subsection (5) thereof, any question as to the scope or effect, during any period when the granter is incapable of making or is incapable of communicating any decision about the matter to which it relates, of a power of attorney (or power of a like nature) relating to his personal welfare or moveable or immoveable property shall be determined by the proper law of the contract, grant or appointment under which the power is conferred.

PART III

ACCOUNTS AND FUNDS OF INCAPABLE ADULTS

Authority to intromit with funds of incapable adults.

20.—(1) Subject to section 26 of this Act, an individual may apply to the Public Guardian for authority under this Part of this Act to intromit with funds held by an organisation to which this Part of this Act applies on behalf of an adult habitually resident in Scotland who is—

(a) incapable of making or incapable of communicating decisions about the funds; or

(b) incapable of safeguarding his interests in the funds,

and is the sole holder of an account in his name.

(2) This Part of this Act applies to the following organisations—

(a) a bank;

(b) a building society; and

(c) any such other organisation or class of organisations as may be prescribed.

(3) An application for authority under this section shall be made in respect of a specified account at a specified branch in Scotland of the organisation and shall not be made if there is an existing authority to intromit under this Part of this Act.

Application for authority to intromit.

21.—(1) An application form for authority to intromit with funds shall—

(a) be signed by the applicant;

(b) be countersigned by a member of such class of persons as is prescribed, who shall declare in the form that—

(i) he knows the applicant and the adult;

(ii) he believes the information contained in the document to be true; and

(iii) to the best of his knowledge and belief, the applicant is a fit and proper person to intromit with the funds;

(c) contain the names and addresses of the nearest relative and primary carer of the adult, if known;

(d) specify the branch of the organisation and identify the account in relation to which the authority is sought; and

(e) be accompanied by a certificate from a medical practitioner suitably qualified in the assessment of incapacity that the adult is—

(i) incapable of making or incapable of communicating decisions about; or

(ii) incapable of safeguarding his interests in,

the funds.

(2) The applicant shall, not later than 14 days after the form has been countersigned as mentioned in subsection (1)(b) above, send the completed form to the Public Guardian.

(3) On receipt of a properly completed form sent timeously to him under subsection (2) above, the Public Guardian shall intimate the application to the incapable adult, his

nearest relative, his primary carer and any person who the Public Guardian considers has an interest in the application and advise them of the prescribed period within which they may object to the granting of the application; and he shall not grant the application without affording to any objector an opportunity of being heard.

(4) Having heard any objections as mentioned in subsection (3) above the Public Guardian may grant the application and where he does so he shall—

(a) register the name of the withdrawer in the register maintained by him under section 4(2)(c)(iii) of this Act; and

(b) issue a certificate of authority to the withdrawer.

(5) Where the Public Guardian proposes to refuse the application he shall intimate his decision to the applicant and advise him of the prescribed period within which he may object to the refusal; and he shall not refuse the application without affording to the applicant, if he objects, an opportunity of being heard.

(6) The Public Guardian may at his own instance or at the instance of the applicant or of any person who objects to the granting of the application remit the application to the sheriff for determination.

(7) A decision of the Public Guardian—

(a) to grant an application under subsection (4) above or to refuse an application; or

(b) to refuse to remit an application to the sheriff under subsection (6) above,

may be appealed to the sheriff, whose decision shall be final.

(8) In this Act an individual in respect of whom a form is registered under subsection (4) above is referred to as a "withdrawer".

Withdrawal and use of funds.

22.—(1) On presentation to it of the certificate issued under section 21(4)(b) of this Act, the branch of the organisation specified in the form may make arrangements—

(a) allowing the withdrawer to withdraw from the account up to £50 (or such sum as may be prescribed) each week in cash; and

(b) to the extent authorised by the certificate, for making payments on the instructions of the withdrawer on a regular or occasional basis by direct debit, standing order, or by any other prescribed means, from funds in the account to meet expenditure relating to—

(i) the payment of local and central government taxes for which the incapable adult is responsible; and

(ii) the provision of sustenance, accommodation, fuel, clothing and related goods and services for the incapable adult.

(2) The Public Guardian may, in any case, authorise—

(a) a method of payment other than a method mentioned in subsection (1)(b) above; and

(b) payment for the provision of items other than those mentioned in subsection (1)(b)(ii) above.

(3) The organisation concerned shall be liable to the incapable adult—

(a) for any withdrawal which it allows from the funds in his account in excess of the limit referred to in subsection (1)(a) above; and

(b) for any funds removed from such account under this section at any time when it was aware that the withdrawer's authority to withdraw funds or make other arrangements had been terminated or suspended by the Public Guardian under section 24(3) of this Act, but, on meeting such liability, the organisation shall have a right of relief against the withdrawer.

(4) Subject to subsection (5) below, any funds used under this section by the withdrawer shall be applied only for the benefit of the incapable adult.

(5) Where the withdrawer lives with the incapable adult he may, to the extent authorised by the certificate, apply any funds withdrawn towards household expenses.

(6) Where the withdrawer uses any funds under this section in contravention of subsection (4) or (5) above or after having received intimation of the suspension or termination of his registration under section 24 of this Act, he shall be liable to repay the funds so used, with interest thereon at the rate fixed by Act of Sederunt as applicable to a decree of the sheriff, to the account of the incapable adult.

(7) A certificate of authority under section 21(4)(b) of this Act shall not authorise the withdrawer to overdraw the account of the incapable adult.

(8) A decision of the Public Guardian not to authorise—

(a) a method of payment other than a method mentioned in subsection (1) above; or

(b) a payment under subsection (2)(b) above,

may be appealed to the sheriff, whose decision shall be final.

Records and inquiries.

23.—(1) The Secretary of State may by regulations provide that a withdrawer shall keep a record of his intromissions with the funds and that the Public Guardian may at any time require a withdrawer to produce such record for the Public Guardian's inspection.

(2) The Public Guardian may—

(a) make inquiries from time to time as to the manner in which a withdrawer has exercised his functions under this Part of this Act; and

(b) ask the withdrawer to produce any vouchers which he has relating to his intromissions.

Duration and termination of registration.

24.—(1) Subject to the following provisions of this section, the authority of a withdrawer to withdraw funds under section 21 of this Act shall be valid for a period of 2 years commencing with the date of issue of the certificate by the Public Guardian under section 21(4)(b) of this Act.

(2) Subsection (1) above is without prejudice to the right of the withdrawer to make subsequent applications under the said section 21 after the end of any such period.

(3) The Public Guardian may suspend or terminate the authority of a withdrawer and shall forthwith intimate such suspension or termination to—

(a) the withdrawer;

(b) the specified branch of the organisation of which details were given in the application under section 21 of this Act.

(4) A decision of the Public Guardian to suspend or terminate the authority of a withdrawer under subsection (3) above may be appealed to the sheriff, whose decision shall be final; and the suspension or termination shall remain in force until the appeal is determined.

(5) The authority of a withdrawer to withdraw funds under section 21 of this Act shall come to an end—

(a) on the appointment of a guardian with powers relating to the funds or account in question; or

(b) on the granting of an intervention order relating to the funds or account in question; or

(c) on a continuing attorney's acquiring authority to act in relation to the funds or account in question,

and no liability shall be incurred by any person who acts in good faith under this Part of this Act in ignorance of the coming to an end of a withdrawer's authority under this subsection.

(6) In subsection (5) above any reference to—

(a) a guardian shall include a reference to a guardian (however called) appointed under the law of any country to, or entitled under the law of any country to act for, an adult during his incapacity, if the guardianship is recognised by the law of Scotland;

(b) a continuing attorney shall include a reference to a person granted, under a contract, grant or appointment governed by the law of any country, powers (however expressed), relating to the granter's property or financial affairs and having continuing effect notwithstanding the granter's incapacity.

Joint accounts.

25. Where an individual who along with one or more others is the holder of a joint account at a branch in Scotland of an organisation to which this Part of this Act applies becomes incapable of making or becomes incapable of communicating decisions about, or of safeguarding his interests in, the funds in the account, any other joint account holder may continue to operate the account unless—

(a) the terms of the account provide otherwise; or

(b) he is barred by an order of any court from so doing.

Disapplication of

26.—(1) This Part of this Act shall not apply in the case of any incapable adult in relation to whom—

(a) there is a guardian or continuing attorney with powers relating to the funds or account in question; or

(b) an intervention order has been granted relating to the funds or account in question,

and no liability shall be incurred by any person who acts in good faith under this Part of this Act in ignorance of any such appointment or grant.

(2) In this section any reference to—

(a) a guardian shall include a reference to a guardian (however called) appointed under the law of any country to, or entitled under the law of any country to act for, an adult during his incapacity, if the guardianship is recognised by the law of Scotland;

(b) a continuing attorney shall include a reference to a person granted, under a contract, grant or appointment governed by the law of any country, powers (however expressed), relating to the granter's property or financial affairs and having continuing effect notwithstanding the granter's incapacity.

PART IV

MANAGEMENT OF RESIDENTS' FINANCES

27.—(1) This Part of this Act applies to the management of the matters set out in section 30 of this Act relating to any resident of an establishment—

    (a) to which subsection (2) below applies; or

    (b) of a description mentioned in subsection (3) below which has been approved by the Public Guardian under section 28 of this Act for the purposes of this Part of this Act,

in this Part of this Act referred to as an "approved establishment".

    (2) The establishments to which this subsection applies are—

    (a) a hospital vested in the Secretary of State under the National Health Service (Scotland) Act 1978;

    (b) a hospital managed by a National Health Service trust established under section 12A of the said Act of 1978;

    (c) a State hospital.

    (3) The descriptions of establishments referred to in paragraph (b) of subsection (1) above are—

    (a) a private hospital registered under Part IV of the 1984 Act;

    (b) an unregistered private hospital;

    (c) a residential establishment provided by a local authority under section 59 of the Social Work (Scotland) Act 1968;

    (d) an establishment in respect of which there is registration under section 62 or 63 of the said Act of 1968;

    (e) a nursing home in respect of which there is registration under the Nursing Homes Registration (Scotland) Act 1938.

    (4) The Secretary of State may by regulations amend the lists of establishments set out in subsections (2) and (3) above.

    (5) In this Part of this Act, "resident" in relation to an establishment means an adult whose main residence for the time being is the establishment or who is liable to be detained there under the 1984 Act.

28.—(1) The Public Guardian may, on an application by the managers of an establishment of a description mentioned in section 27(3) of this Act, approve the establishment for the purposes of this Part of this Act.

    (2) A refusal by the Public Guardian to approve an establishment under subsection (1) above may be appealed by the managers of the establishment to the sheriff.

    (3) In this Part of this Act "the managers" in relation to an establishment shall be construed in accordance with Schedule 1 to this Act.

29.—(1) Subject to sections 31 and 32 of this Act, the managers of an approved establishment shall be entitled to manage on behalf of any resident in the establishment any of the matters set out in section 30 of this Act which a medical practitioner suitably qualified in the assessment of incapacity has certified that the resident is incapable of managing.

    (2) In considering whether to issue a certificate under this section, the medical

practitioner shall take into account any assistance available or likely to be available to the resident to manage the matter.

(3) The medical practitioner who certifies under subsection (1) above shall not have any direct or indirect financial interest in the establishment.

Matters which may be managed.

30. The matters which may be managed under this Part of this Act by the managers of an establishment are—

(a) claiming, receiving, holding and spending any pension or benefit;

(b) claiming, receiving, holding and spending any money which falls due to the resident while he is certified under section 29 of this Act;

(c) holding and spending any money brought by the resident into the establishment;

(d) holding any other items brought by the resident into the establishment or acquired by him during his period of residence;

(e) disposing of any items brought by the resident into the establishment or acquired by him during his period of residence.

When establishment will cease to act on behalf of resident.

31.—(1) Where, in relation to a resident of an approved establishment—

(a) a guardian is appointed after the managers of the establishment have been authorised to manage any of the matters set out in section 30 of this Act; or

(b) a continuing attorney acquires authority to act in relation to such matters after the resident has been certified under section 29 of this Act,

he shall replace the managers in the management of the said matters to the extent that his powers as guardian or as continuing attorney, as the case may be, coincide with the powers of the managers.

(2) A guardian or a continuing attorney may authorise the managers of an approved establishment to act as his agents in respect of such of the matters set out in section 30 of this Act as fall within his powers.

(3) In this section any reference to—

(a) a guardian shall include a reference to a guardian (however called) appointed under the law of any country to, or entitled under the law of any country to act for, an adult during his incapacity, if the guardianship is recognised by the law of Scotland;

(b) a continuing attorney shall include a reference to a person granted, under a contract, grant or appointment governed by the law of any country, powers (however expressed), relating to the granter's property or financial affairs and having continuing effect notwithstanding the granter's incapacity.

Functions of managers of approved establishment.

32.—(1) Subject to subsection (2) below, the managers of an approved establishment shall be entitled to hold and manage money and other property of a resident up to an aggregate value of £5,000 or such other sum as may be prescribed.

(2) The Public Guardian may authorise the managers of an approved establishment to hold and manage money and other property in excess of the aggregate value referred to in subsection (1) above, and such authorisation may at any time be made subject to such conditions as the Public Guardian thinks fit.

(3) The managers of an approved establishment shall be entitled—

(a) to open an account with a bank or building society on behalf of a resident whose matters they are entitled to manage under section 29 of this Act;

(b) to withdraw funds from, or make arrangements for the use of funds in, an account with a bank or building society which was opened by such a resident before he was certified under the said section 29.

(4) The managers of an approved establishment shall, in relation to residents whose matters they are managing under section 29 of this Act—

(a) keep the funds of residents separate from the funds of the establishment;

(b) ensure that where, at any time, the total amount of funds held and managed on behalf of any resident exceeds £50 (or such other sum as may be prescribed) they shall be placed so as to earn interest;

(c) keep proper records of all transactions made in relation to the funds held and managed by them in respect of each resident for whose benefit the funds are held and managed and, in particular, ensure that details of the balance and any interest due to each resident can be ascertained at any time;

(d) spend money only on items or services which are of benefit to the resident on whose behalf the funds are held and managed, not being items or services which are provided by the establishment to or for such resident as part of its normal service;

(e) make proper provision for indemnifying residents against any loss attributable to any act or omission on the part of the managers of the establishment in exercising the powers conferred by this Part of this Act or of others for whom the managers are responsible or attributable to any expenditure in breach of paragraph (d) above;

(f) adhere to the code of practice drawn up by the Secretary of State under section 10 of this Act.

(5) Anything done by the managers when acting within the scope of their authority shall have the same effect as if done by the resident when he had the capacity to act.

(6) Where a person ceases to be a resident of an establishment the managers of the establishment who have been managing the matters set out in section 30 of this Act on his behalf immediately before he ceased to be a resident may continue to do so until it appears to them that adequate arrangements have been made for managing these matters.

(7) For the purposes of subsections (1) and (4)(b) above, the Secretary of State may prescribe different sums for different classes of establishment.

(8) A refusal by the Public Guardian to authorise the managers of an establishment under subsection (2) above to hold and manage money in excess of the aggregate value referred to in subsection (1) above may be appealed by them to the sheriff, whose decision shall be final.

Inquiries.

33.—(1) The Public Guardian may from time to time make inquiries as to the manner in which the managers of an approved establishment have exercised their functions under this Part of this Act.

(2) The Public Guardian may require the managers of an establishment to produce records and accounts relating to the affairs of all or any residents for the management of whose finances they are responsible under this Part of this Act.

Conditions and withdrawal of approval.

34.—(1) Where it appears to the Public Guardian that—

(a) the managers of an approved establishment have failed to comply with any requirement of this Part of this Act;

(b) it is no longer appropriate for an establishment to be approved for the purposes of this Part of this Act; or

N

(c) an establishment has ceased to be—

(i) one to which subsection (2) of section 27 of this Act applies; or, as the case may be,

(ii) one of a description of establishments mentioned in subsection (3) of that subsection,

he may apply to the sheriff for an order under this section.

(2) Where the sheriff is satisfied in considering an application under subsection (1) above that any of the matters mentioned therein is established he may make an order—

(a) attaching conditions to the approval;

(b) varying or recalling any such conditions already attached to the approval; or

(c) withdrawing the approval.

(3) Where the sheriff makes an order under subsection (2)(c) above he shall appoint the Public Guardian as interim manager of any funds held and managed under this Part of this Act by the managers of the establishment; and as interim manager the Public Guardian shall have the same powers in relation to such funds as the managers of the establishment had.

End of entitlement to manage.

35.—(1) The entitlement of the managers of an establishment to manage a matter under section 29 of this Act shall cease when—

(a) a medical practitioner as mentioned in section 29(1) of this Act certifies that the resident is no longer incapable of managing that matter; or

(b) the sheriff grants a declarator under subsection (3) below.

(2) The medical practitioner who certifies under subsection (1) above shall not have any direct or indirect financial interest in the establishment.

(3) The sheriff may, on an application by any person claiming an interest in the property, financial affairs or personal welfare of the resident grant a declarator to the effect that the resident is no longer incapable of managing the matter.

(4) In considering whether to issue a certificate under subsection (1) above or grant a declarator under subsection (3) above, the medical practitioner or, as the case may be, the sheriff shall take into account any assistance available or likely to be available to the resident to manage the matter.

Disapplication of Part IV.

36.—(1) This Part of this Act shall not apply to any of the matters which may be managed under section 30 of this Act if—

(a) there is a guardian, continuing attorney, or other person with powers relating to that matter; or

(b) an intervention order has been granted relating to that matter,

and no liability shall be incurred by any person who acts in good faith under this Part of this Act in ignorance of any guardian, continuing attorney, other person or intervention order.

(2) In this section any reference to—

(a) a guardian shall include a reference to a guardian (however called) appointed under the law of any country to, or entitled under the law of any country to act for, an adult during his incapacity, if the guardianship is recognised by the law of Scotland;

(b) a continuing attorney shall include a reference to a person granted, under a contract, grant or appointment governed by the law of any country, powers (however expressed), relating to the granter's property or financial affairs and having continuing effect notwithstanding the granter's incapacity.

PART V

MEDICAL TREATMENT, CARE AND RESEARCH

Authority

Authority of persons
responsible for
medical treatment.

37.—(1) Without prejudice to any authority conferred by any other enactment or rule of law and subject to sections 38 and 40 of this Act and to the following provisions of this section, any person who is responsible for the medical treatment of an adult who in the opinion of that person is incapable of making or is incapable of communicating a decision about the medical treatment in question shall have authority to do what is reasonable in the circumstances to safeguard or promote the physical or mental health of that adult.

(2) In subsection (1) above, "medical treatment" includes—

    (a) surgical, medical, nursing, optical or dental procedure or treatment;

    (b) ventilation, nutrition and hydration by artificial means;

    (c) any other procedure or treatment designed to safeguard or promote physical or mental health.

(3) The authority conferred by subsection (1) above shall not authorise—

    (a) the use of force or detention, unless it is immediately necessary and only for so long as it is necessary to avoid serious harm to the adult;

    (b) action which would be inconsistent with any decision by a competent court.

(4) The authority conferred by subsection (1) above shall not authorise—

    (a) medical treatment of a description prescribed as requiring the authority of the sheriff;

    (b) medical treatment of mental disorder by means of any surgical operation for destroying brain tissue or for destroying the functioning of brain tissue;

    (c) sterilisation other than as an integral part of the medical treatment of an existing serious malfunction or disease of the reproductive organs,

unless the sheriff, on an application by any person claiming an interest in the personal welfare of the incapable adult, so authorises.

(5) The authority conferred by subsection (1) above shall not authorise—

    (a) medical treatment of mental disorder by the administration of medicine by any means to an incapable adult for a period in excess of 3 months; or

    (b) medical treatment of a description prescribed as requiring a second opinion in its favour,

unless a second opinion in favour of such medical treatment is obtained from a medical practitioner appointed for the purposes of this Part of this Act by the Mental Welfare Commission, being a medical practitioner who is not otherwise involved in the medical treatment.

(6) Subject to subsection (7) below, where any question as to the authority of any person to provide medical treatment in pursuance of subsection (1) above—

    (a) is the subject of proceedings in any court (other than for the purposes of an application to the sheriff under subsection (4) above); and

    (b) has not been determined,

medical treatment authorised by the said subsection (1) may be given where it is necessary, in the opinion of the person giving the medical treatment, for the preservation of the life of the adult or the prevention of serious deterioration in his medical condition.

(7) Nothing in subsection (6) above shall authorise the provision of any medical treatment where an interdict has been granted and continues to have effect prohibiting the provision of such medical treatment.

Medical treatment where guardian or welfare attorney refuses consent.

38.—(1) Subsection (1) of section 37 of this Act shall not apply in the case of an incapable adult in respect of whom there is appointed a guardian or a welfare attorney with power in relation to any medical treatment referred to in that subsection if, to the knowledge of the person responsible for the medical treatment of the incapable adult, the guardian or welfare attorney has refused consent to the medical treatment.

(2) The person responsible for the medical treatment of an incapable adult in respect of whom a guardian or welfare attorney has been appointed as mentioned in subsection (1) above may, if the guardian or welfare attorney has refused consent to medical treatment, seek an opinion from a relevant medical practitioner as to the medical treatment proposed.

(3) Where a relevant medical practitioner certifies that in his opinion, having regard to all of the circumstances, the proposed medical treatment should be given, the person responsible for the medical treatment of the incapable adult may give the medical treatment notwithstanding that the guardian or, as the case may be, the welfare attorney had refused to consent to the medical treatment.

(4) Where an opinion has been sought as mentioned in subsection (2) above, the person responsible for the medical treatment of the incapable adult may, until the opinion is obtained, give such medical treatment as is necessary to save the life of the incapable adult or to prevent any serious deterioration in his medical condition.

(5) In this section a "relevant medical practitioner" is a medical practitioner—

(a) skilled in the medical treatment proposed to be given by the person responsible for the medical treatment of the incapable adult;

(b) not involved in the proposed medical treatment; and

(c) professionally independent of, and a member of a separate clinical unit from, the person responsible for the medical treatment.

(6) In this section any reference to—

(a) a guardian shall include a reference to a guardian (however called) appointed under the law of any country to, or entitled under the law of any country to act for, an adult during his incapacity, if the guardianship is recognised by the law of Scotland;

(b) a welfare attorney shall include a reference to a person granted, under a contract, grant or appointment governed by the law of any country, powers (however expressed) relating to the granter's personal welfare and having effect during the granter's incapacity.

Authority for research.

39.—(1) No surgical, medical, dental or psychological research shall be carried out on any adult who is incapable of making or is incapable of communicating a decision about participation in the research unless the circumstances mentioned in subsection (2) below are satisfied.

(2) The circumstances referred to in subsection (1) above are that—

(a) the purpose of the research is to obtain knowledge of—

          (i) the incapable adult's incapacity or of any treatment for it; or

          (ii) any physical disorder associated with such incapacity or of any treatment for such physical disorder;

          (iii) the effect of any care given to the adult during his incapacity; and

  (b) the research entails no foreseeable risk, or only a minimal foreseeable risk, to the incapable adult; and

  (c) the research imposes no discomfort, or only minimal discomfort, on the incapable adult; and

  (d) the research has been approved by or on behalf of the Ethics Committee; and

  (e) consent to the research was given orally or in writing by the adult before his incapacity and has not been overruled by a guardian or welfare attorney who has power to do so; or

  (f) where paragraph (e) above does not apply, consent has been obtained from any guardian or welfare attorney who has power to consent to the incapable adult's participation in research or, where there is no such guardian or welfare attorney, from—

          (i) the incapable adult's nearest relative; or

          (ii) if such a relative is not reasonably available, a person who knows the incapable adult well; and

  (g) the incapable adult does not express unwillingness to participate in the research.

(3) In seeking consent under subsection (2)(f) above, the person carrying out the research shall explain to the person whose consent is sought the procedure to be used and the foreseeable risks involved in the research.

(4) The Ethics Committee shall be constituted by regulations made by the Secretary of State and such regulations may make provision as to the composition of, appointments to and procedures of the Ethics Committee and may make such provision for the payment of such remuneration, expenses and superannuation as the Secretary of State may, with the consent of the Treasury, determine.

(5) In this section any reference to—

  (a) a guardian shall include a reference to a guardian (however called) appointed under the law of any country to, or entitled under the law of any country to act for, an adult during his incapacity, if the guardianship is recognised by the law of Scotland;

  (b) a welfare attorney shall include a reference to a person granted, under a contract, grant or appointment governed by the law of any country, powers (however expressed) relating to the granter's personal welfare and having effect during the granter's incapacity.

Advance statements

Advance statements.

40.—(1) This section applies to any statement ("advance statement") which an adult may make as to the circumstances in which medical treatment of a description specified in the statement is not to be afforded to him at any time when the statement is operative.

(2) An advance statement may be—

  (a) made or revoked orally or in writing by the adult;

  (b) revoked orally or in writing by a welfare attorney to whom the adult has given authority to do so.

(3) Where an advance statement or the revocation of an advance statement is in writing

it shall not be valid unless it is signed by the adult or, as the case may be, by the welfare attorney.

(4) An advance statement is operative during any period when—

    (a) the circumstances specified in the statement exist; and

    (b) the adult is incapable of making or is incapable of communicating a decision about such medical treatment.

(5) Subject to subsections (6) and (7) below, where an advance statement is validly made and is operative any authority to carry out medical treatment of a description specified in the statement in the circumstances mentioned in the statement shall have no effect.

(6) An advance statement may be disregarded by the person responsible for the medical treatment where he reasonably believes that—

    (a) the circumstances, other than the medical condition of the adult, have changed to a material degree since the statement was given; and

    (b) in consequence of such changed circumstances the adult, if he were capable of making and communicating a decision, would authorise the medical treatment.

(7) An advance statement shall not have effect—

    (a) where compliance with it would endanger the life of the adult, unless the terms of the statement expressly provide for such an effect;

    (b) to prohibit the provision of procedures to maintain adequate standards of hygiene and measures to relieve serious pain;

    (c) to prohibit the treatment for mental disorder by virtue of Part X of the 1984 Act of a patient liable to be detained under that Act;

    (d) in the case of a female adult, where compliance with it would endanger the development of a foetus being carried by her where the pregnancy has exceeded its twenty-fourth week.

(8) Where the advance statement was valid and operative or the person responsible for the medical treatment reasonably believed that it was valid and operative, the person responsible for the medical treatment and any person withholding it, or participating in the withholding of it, in accordance with the advance statement shall not thereby incur liability.

(9) Where—

    (a) the person responsible for the medical treatment—

        (i) did not know of the existence of an advance statement relating to the medical treatment in question; or

        (ii) reasonably believed—

            (*aa*) that such an advance statement was not valid or was not operative; or

            (*bb*) that subsection (7) above applied to the case; or

    (b) such an advance statement was disregarded by virtue of subsection (6) above,

and medical treatment was carried out contrary to the terms of the advance statement, the person responsible for the medical treatment and any person carrying it out or participating in it, shall not thereby incur liability.

(10) In this section—

"medical treatment" has the same meaning as in section 37 of this Act; and

"welfare attorney" includes a person granted, under a contract, grant or appointment governed by the law of any country, powers (however expressed) relating to the granter's personal welfare and having effect during the granter's incapacity.

Withholding and withdrawal of medical treatment from incapable adults

41.—(1) Subject to subsections (2) and (3) below, it shall be lawful for a medical practitioner to withhold or withdraw, or to authorise the withholding or withdrawal of, medical treatment from an adult who is incapable of making or is incapable of communicating a decision about the medical treatment if in his reasonable opinion the medical treatment or its continuation would not be of benefit to the adult, notwithstanding that such withholding or withdrawal would result in the death of the adult.

(2) Before withholding or withdrawing, or authorising the withholding or withdrawal of, medical treatment from the adult the medical practitioner shall carry out such consultation as accords with good medical practice.

(3) The Court of Session, on an application by any person claiming an interest in the personal welfare of the adult, may, if it is satisfied—

(a) that the adult is in Scotland at the date of the application;

(b) that the adult is incapable of making or is incapable of communicating a decision about his medical treatment; and

(c) that in all the circumstances of the case it is appropriate to do so,

grant an order declaring that the withholding or withdrawal, or that the continued withholding or withdrawal, of the medical treatment would be lawful or, as the case may be, would not be lawful.

(4) In considering whether or not the medical treatment or its continuation would be of benefit to the incapable adult, it shall not be assumed that the prolongation of the life of an adult, regardless of his circumstances, is necessarily of benefit to him.

(5) For the purposes of the application of section 1(2) to (4) of this Act to this section, the intervention referred to in that section is the giving or continuation of the medical treatment.

(6) An application under subsection (3) above shall be intimated to the Lord Advocate for the public interest.

(7) In this section "medical treatment" has the same meaning as in section 37 of this Act.

PART VI

INTERVENTION ORDERS AND GUARDIANSHIP ORDERS

Intervention orders

42.—(1) The sheriff may, on an application by any person (including the adult himself) claiming an interest in the property, financial affairs or personal welfare of an adult, if he is satisfied that the adult is incapable of taking the action, or is incapable of making or is incapable of communicating the decision about his property, financial affairs or personal welfare to which the application relates, make an order (in this Act referred to as an "intervention order").

(2) Where it appears to the local authority that—

(a) the adult is incapable as mentioned in subsection (1) above; and

(b) no application has been made or is likely to be made for an order under this section; and

(c) an intervention order is necessary for the protection of the property, financial affairs or personal welfare of the incapable adult,

they shall apply under this section for an order.

(3) Subsection (3) of section 43 of this Act shall apply to an application under this section and, for this purpose, for the reference to the individual or office holder nominated for appointment as guardian there shall be substituted a reference to a person nominated in such application.

(4) An intervention order may—

(a) direct the taking of any action specified in the order;

(b) authorise the person nominated in the application, to take such action or make such decision in relation to the property, financial affairs or personal welfare of the incapable adult as is specified in the order.

(5) In making an intervention order, the sheriff may require the person authorised under the order to find caution.

(6) The sheriff may, on an application by—

(a) the person authorised under the intervention order; or

(b) where no person has been so authorised, any person claiming an interest in the property, financial affairs or personal welfare of the incapable adult,

make an order varying the terms of, or recalling, the intervention order or any other order made for the purposes of the intervention order.

(7) Anything done under an intervention order shall have the same effect as if done by the incapable adult when he had the capacity to do so.

(8) Where an intervention order is made, the applicant shall forthwith send a copy of the interlocutor containing the order to the Public Guardian who shall—

(a) enter in the register maintained by him under section 4(2)(c)(v) of this Act such particulars of the order as may be prescribed; and

(b) notify the incapable adult.

(9) Sections 49(2) and 62 of this Act shall apply to an intervention order as they apply to a guardianship order and, for this purpose, for any reference to—

(a) a guardianship order there shall be substituted a reference to an intervention order; and

(b) a guardian there shall be substituted a reference to the person authorised to intervene.

Guardianship orders

Application for guardianship order.

43.—(1) An application may be made under this section by any person (including the adult himself) claiming an interest in the property, financial affairs or personal welfare of an incapable adult to the sheriff for an order appointing an individual or office holder as guardian in relation to the incapable adult's property, financial affairs or personal welfare.

(2) Where it appears to the local authority that—

(a) the conditions mentioned in paragraphs (a) and (b) of section 44(1) of this Act apply to the incapable adult; and

(b) no application has been made or is likely to be made for an order under this section; and

(c) a guardianship order is necessary for the protection of the property, financial affairs or personal welfare of the incapable adult, they shall apply under this section for an order.

(3) There shall be lodged in court along with an application under this section—

(a) reports of an examination and assessment of the incapable adult carried out not more than 30 days before the lodging of the application by at least two persons—

(i) both of whom are suitably qualified in the assessment of incapacity; and

(ii) one of whom, in a case where the incapacity is by reason of mental disorder, must be a medical practitioner approved for the purposes of section 20 of the 1984 Act as having special experience in the diagnosis or treatment of mental disorder;

(b) where the application relates to the personal welfare of the incapable adult, a report from the mental health officer within the meaning of the 1984 Act of the local authority containing his opinion as to—

(i) the general appropriateness of the order sought, based on an interview and assessment of the incapable adult carried out not more than 30 days before the lodging of the application; and

(ii) the suitability of the individual nominated in the application to be appointed guardian; and

(c) where the application relates only to the property or financial affairs of the incapable adult, a report, based on an interview and assessment of the incapable adult carried out not more than 30 days before the lodging of the application, by a person who has sufficient knowledge to make such a report as to the matters referred to in sub-paragraphs (i) and (ii) of paragraph (b) above.

(4) The sheriff may, on an application being made to him, at any time before the disposal of the application made under this section, make an order for the appointment of an interim guardian.

(5) The appointment of an interim guardian in pursuance of this section shall, unless recalled earlier, cease to have effect—

(a) on the appointment of a guardian under section 44 of this Act; or

(b) at the end of the period of three months from the date of appointment,

whichever is the earlier.

Disposal of application.

44.—(1) Where the sheriff is satisfied in considering an application under section 43 of this Act that—

(a) the incapable adult is incapable of making or is incapable of communicating decisions about, or is incapable of acting to safeguard or promote his interests in, his property, financial affairs or personal welfare, and is likely to continue to be so unable; and

(b) the making of an intervention order would not be sufficient to enable the incapable adult's interests in his property, financial affairs or personal welfare to be safeguarded or promoted,

he may grant the application.

(2) Where the sheriff is satisfied that an intervention order would be sufficient as mentioned in subsection (1) above, he may treat the application under this section as an application for an intervention order under section 42 of this Act and may make such order as appears to him to be appropriate.

(3) Where the sheriff grants the application under the said section 43 he shall make an order (in this Act referred to as a "guardianship order") appointing the individual or office holder nominated in the application to be the guardian of the incapable adult for

a period of 3 years or such other period (including an indefinite period) as, on cause shown, he may determine.

(4) Where more than one individual or office holder is nominated in the application, a guardianship order may, without prejudice to the power under section 47(1) of this Act to appoint joint guardians, appoint two or more guardians to exercise different powers in relation to the incapable adult.

(5) Where the sheriff makes a guardianship order the applicant shall forthwith send a copy of the interlocutor containing the order to the Public Guardian who shall—

    (a) enter prescribed particulars of the appointment in the register maintained by him under section 4(2)(c)(iv) of this Act;

    (b) except where he is the guardian, when satisfied that the guardian has found caution, issue a certificate of appointment to the guardian; and

    (c) notify the incapable adult of the appointment of the guardian.

Who may be appointed as guardian.

45.—(1) The sheriff may appoint as guardian—

    (a) where the powers to be conferred on the guardian include powers relating to the personal welfare of the incapable adult, the chief social work officer of the local authority;

    (b) where the powers to be conferred on the guardian relate only to the property or financial affairs of the incapable adult, the Public Guardian;

    (c) any individual whom he considers to be suitable for appointment and who has consented to being appointed.

(2) The sheriff shall not appoint an individual as guardian to an incapable adult unless he is satisfied that the individual is aware of—

    (a) the incapable adult's circumstances and condition and of the needs arising from such circumstances and condition; and

    (b) the functions of a guardian.

(3) In determining if an individual is suitable for appointment as guardian, the sheriff shall have regard to—

    (a) the accessibility of the individual to the incapable adult and to his primary carer;

    (b) the ability of the individual to carry out the functions of guardian;

    (c) any likely conflict of interest between the incapable adult and the individual;

    (d) any undue concentration of power which is likely to arise in the individual over the incapable adult;

    (e) such other matters as appear to him to be appropriate.

(4) Paragraphs (c) and (d) of subsection (3) above shall not be regarded as applying to an individual by reason only of his being a close relative of, or person residing with, the incapable adult.

(5) In this Act, "office holder" in relation to a guardian means the chief social work officer or the Public Guardian.

Renewal of guardianship order by sheriff.

46.—(1) At any time before the end of a period in respect of which a guardianship order has been made or renewed, an application may be made to the sheriff under this section by the guardian for the renewal of such order, and where such an application is so made, the order shall continue to have effect until the application is determined.

(2) Subsection (3) of section 43 of this Act shall apply for the purposes of an

application made under this section as it applies for the purposes of an application made under that section; and for the purposes of so applying that subsection—

    (a) references to the appointment of a guardian (however expressed) shall be construed as references to the continuation of appointment;

    (b) for paragraph (a) of subsection (3) there shall be substituted—

        "(a) a report of an examination and assessment of the incapable adult carried out not more than 30 days before the lodging of the application by a medical practitioner or other person suitably qualified in the assessment of incapacity;".

(3) Section 44 of this Act shall apply to an application under this section as it applies to an application under section 43 of this Act; and for the purposes of so applying that section—

    (a) references to the making of a guardianship order and the appointment of a guardian (however expressed) shall be construed as references to, respectively, the renewal of the order and the continuation of appointment;

    (b) for subsection (3) there shall be substituted—

        "(3) Where the sheriff grants an application under section 46 of this Act, he may continue the guardianship order for a period of 5 years or for such other period (including an indefinite period) as, on cause shown, he may determine.".

(4) Where the sheriff refuses an application under this section, the sheriff clerk shall forthwith send a copy of the interlocutor containing the refusal to the Public Guardian who shall—

    (a) enter prescribed particulars in the register maintained by him under section 4(2)(c)(iv) of this Act; and

    (b) notify the incapable adult.

Joint and substitute guardians

Joint guardians.

47.—(1) An application may be made to the sheriff—

    (a) by two or more individuals seeking appointment, for their appointment as joint guardians to an incapable adult; or

    (b) by an individual seeking appointment, for his appointment as an additional guardian to an incapable adult jointly with one or more existing guardians.

(2) Joint guardians shall not be appointed to an incapable adult unless—

    (a) the individuals so appointed are parents, siblings or children of the incapable adult; or

    (b) the sheriff is satisfied that, in the circumstances, it is appropriate to appoint as joint guardians individuals who are not related to the incapable adult as mentioned in paragraph (a) above.

(3) Where an application is made under subsection (1)(a) above, sections 44 and 45 of this Act shall apply for the purposes of the disposal of that application as they apply for the disposal of an application under section 43 of this Act.

(4) In deciding if an individual is suitable for appointment as additional guardian under subsection (1)(b) above, the sheriff shall have regard to the matters set out in subsections (2) to (4) of section 45 of this Act.

(5) Where the sheriff appoints an additional guardian under this section, the applicant shall send a copy of the order appointing him to the Public Guardian who shall—

(a) enter prescribed particulars in the register maintained by him under section 4(2)(c)(iv) of this Act;

(b) when satisfied that the additional guardian has found caution issue a certificate of appointment to the additional guardian and a new certificate of appointment to the existing guardian;

(c) notify the incapable adult.

(6) Joint guardians may, subject to subsection (7) below, exercise their functions individually, and each guardian shall be liable for any loss or injury caused to the incapable adult arising out of—

(a) his own acts or omissions; or

(b) his failure to take reasonable steps to ensure that a joint guardian does not breach any duty of care or fiduciary duty owed to the incapable adult,

and where more than one such guardian is so liable they shall be liable jointly and severally.

(7) A joint guardian shall, before exercising any functions conferred on him, consult the other joint guardians, unless—

(a) consultation would be impracticable in the circumstances;

(b) the joint guardians agree that consultation is not necessary.

(8) Where there are joint guardians, a third party in good faith is entitled to rely on the authority to act of any one or more of them.

Substitute guardian.

48.—(1) In any case where an individual is appointed as guardian under section 44 of this Act the sheriff may, on an application, appoint to act as guardian on the death, resignation, incapacity or removal by the sheriff of the guardian so appointed any individual or office holder who could competently be appointed by virtue of section 45 of this Act.

(2) In this Act an individual appointed under section 44 of this Act and an individual or office holder appointed under this section are referred to respectively as an "original guardian" and a "substitute guardian".

(3) An application for appointment as a substitute guardian may be made at the time of the application for the appointment of the original guardian or at any time thereafter.

(4) Subsection (1) above shall apply to an individual who, having been appointed as a substitute guardian subsequently, by virtue of this section, becomes the guardian as it applies to an individual appointed under section 44 of this Act and, for this purpose, any reference in this section to the "original guardian" shall be construed accordingly.

(5) Where the sheriff appoints a substitute guardian (other than a substitute guardian appointed in the same order as an original guardian) under subsection (1) above, the substitute guardian shall send a copy of the interlocutor containing the order appointing him to the Public Guardian who shall—

(a) notify the incapable adult and the original guardian;

(b) enter prescribed particulars in the register maintained by him under section 4(2)(c)(iv) of this Act.

(6) On the death or incapacity of the original guardian, the substitute guardian shall, without undue delay, notify the Public Guardian—

(a) of the death or incapacity and—

(i) where the original guardian has died, shall provide the Public Guardian with documentary evidence of such death; and

      (ii) on the incapacity of the original guardian, shall provide the Public Guardian with a certificate of such incapacity signed by a medical practitioner suitably qualified in the assessment of incapacity; and

  (b) whether or not he is prepared to act as guardian.

(7) The Public Guardian on being notified under subsection (6) above shall, if the substitute guardian is prepared to act—

  (a) enter prescribed particulars in the register maintained by him under section 4(2)(c)(iv) of this Act;

  (b) except where he is the substitute guardian, when satisfied that the substitute guardian has found caution, issue the substitute guardian with a certificate of appointment;

  (c) notify the incapable adult that the substitute guardian is acting.

(8) Unless otherwise specified in the order appointing him, the substitute guardian shall have the same functions and powers as those exercisable by the original guardian immediately before the event mentioned in subsection (1) above.

Functions etc. of guardian

49.—(1) Subject to the provisions of this section, an order appointing a guardian may confer on him—

  (a) power to deal with such particular matters in relation to the property, financial affairs or personal welfare of the incapable adult as may be specified in the order;

  (b) power to deal with all aspects of the personal welfare of the incapable adult, or with such aspects as may be specified in the order;

  (c) power to pursue or defend an action of divorce or separation in the name of the incapable adult;

  (d) power to manage the property or financial affairs of the incapable adult, or with such parts of them as may be specified in the order.

(2) A guardian may not—

  (a) place the incapable adult in a hospital for the treatment of mental disorder against his will;

  (b) consent on behalf of the incapable adult to anything mentioned in section 37(3), (4) or (5) of this Act;

  (c) revoke or overrule an advance statement.

(3) A guardian shall (unless prohibited by an order of the sheriff and subject to any conditions or restrictions specified in such an order) have power by virtue of his appointment to act as the incapable adult's legal representative in relation to any matter within the scope of the power conferred by the guardianship order.

(4) The guardian shall not later than 7 days after any change of his own or the incapable adult's address notify the Public Guardian of the change, and the Public Guardian shall—

  (a) enter prescribed particulars in the register maintained by him under section 4(2)(c)(iv) of this Act; and

  (b) where the guardian has powers relating to the personal welfare of the incapable adult, notify the Mental Welfare Commission and the local authority.

(5) A guardian having powers relating to the property or financial affairs of the incapable adult shall, subject to—

(a) such restrictions as may be imposed by the court;

(b) any management plan prepared under paragraph 1 of Schedule 2 to this Act; or

(c) paragraph 6 of that Schedule,

be entitled to use the capital and income of the incapable adult's estate for the purpose of purchasing assets, services or accommodation so as to enhance the incapable adult's quality of life.

(6) The guardian may arrange for some or all of his functions to be exercised by one or more persons acting on his behalf but shall not be entitled to surrender or transfer any part of them to another person.

(7) The guardian shall comply with any order or demand made—

(a) by the local authority in relation to the personal welfare of the incapable adult; or

(b) by the Public Guardian in relation to the property or financial affairs of the incapable adult,

in so far as so complying would be within the scope of his authority; and where the guardian fails to do so the sheriff may, on the application of the local authority or the Public Guardian, as the case may be, make an order to the like effect as the order or demand made by the local authority or Public Guardian.

50.—(1) A guardian having powers relating to the property or financial affairs of an incapable adult may make a gift out of the incapable adult's estate only if authorised to do so by the Public Guardian.

Gifts.

(2) On receipt of an application in the prescribed form for an authorisation to make a gift, the Public Guardian shall intimate the application to the incapable adult, his nearest relative, his primary carer and any other person who the Public Guardian considers has an interest in the application and advise them of the prescribed period within which they may object to the granting of the application; and he shall not grant the application without affording to any objector an opportunity of being heard.

(3) Having heard any objections as mentioned in subsection (2) above, the Public Guardian may grant the application.

(4) Where the Public Guardian proposes to refuse the application he shall intimate his decision to the guardian and advise him of the prescribed period within which he may object to the refusal; and he shall not refuse the application without affording to the guardian, if he objects, an opportunity of being heard.

(5) The Public Guardian may at his own instance or at the instance of the guardian or of any person who objects to the granting of the application remit the application to the sheriff for determination.

(6) A decision of the Public Guardian—

(a) to grant an application under subsection (2) above or to refuse an application; or

(b) to refuse to remit an application to the sheriff under subsection (5) above,

may be appealed to the sheriff, whose decision shall be final.

51.—(1) The incapable adult shall have no capacity to enter into any transaction in relation to any matter which is within the scope of the authority conferred on the guardian; but nothing in this subsection shall be taken to affect the capacity of the incapable adult in relation to any other matter.

Effect of appointment and transactions of guardian.

(2) Where the guardian has powers relating to the property or financial affairs of the

incapable adult, the certificate of appointment issued to him by the Public Guardian or the order appointing the Public Guardian as guardian shall, subject to the terms of the order appointing him, have the effect of—

(a) authorising the guardian to take possession of, manage and deal with any moveable or immoveable estate (wherever situated) of the incapable adult;

(b) requiring any payment due to the incapable adult to be made to the guardian,

in so far as the estate, payment or matter falls within the scope of the guardian's authority.

(3) A guardian having powers relating to the personal welfare of an incapable adult may exercise these powers in relation to the incapable adult whether or not the incapable adult is in Scotland at the time of the exercise of the powers.

(4) The guardian shall be personally liable under any transaction entered into by him—

(a) without disclosing that he is acting as guardian of the incapable adult; or

(b) which falls outwith the scope of his authority,

but where a guardian has acted as mentioned in paragraph (a) above and is not otherwise in breach of any requirement of this Act relating to such guardians, he shall be entitled to be reimbursed from the estate of the incapable adult in respect of any loss suffered by him in consequence of a claim made upon him personally by virtue of this subsection.

(5) A guardian may, with the consent of the Public Guardian (if he is not, himself, the guardian) permit the incapable adult to enter into any transaction relating to his property or financial affairs which falls within the scope of the guardian's authority.

(6) Where a third party with whom the incapable adult entered into a transaction was aware at the date of entering into the transaction that permission had been granted by the guardian under subsection (5) above, the transaction shall not be void only on the ground that the incapable adult lacked capacity.

(7) A transaction for value between the guardian purporting to act as such and a third party acting in good faith shall not be invalid on the ground only that the guardian acted outwith the scope of his authority or failed to observe any requirement, whether substantive or procedural, imposed by or under this Act, the sheriff or the Public Guardian.

(8) A refusal of the Public Guardian to give consent under subsection (5) above may be appealed by the guardian to the sheriff, whose decision shall be final.

(9) In subsections (3) and (4) above any reference to a guardian shall include a reference to a guardian (however called) appointed under the law of any country to, or entitled under the law of any country to act for, an adult during his incapacity, if the guardianship is recognised by the law of Scotland.

52.—(1) A guardian shall be entitled to be reimbursed out of the estate of the incapable adult for any outlays reasonably incurred by him in the exercise of his functions.

(2) In subsection (1) above "outlays", in relation to a guardian—

(a) who is someone other than the chief social work officer of a local authority, includes payment for items and services other than those items and services which the guardian is expected to provide as part of his functions;

(b) who is the chief social work officer of a local authority, includes payment for items and services only if they would not normally be provided free of charge by the local authority to a person who is in similar circumstances but who does not have a guardian.

(3) The local authority shall, in relation to the cost of any application by them for appointment of their chief social work officer as guardian or of any subsequent application by that officer while acting as guardian—

(a) where the application relates to the personal welfare of the incapable adult, meet such cost;

(b) where the application relates to the property or financial affairs of the incapable adult, be entitled to recover such cost from the estate of the incapable adult,

and where the application relates to the personal welfare and to the property or financial affairs of the incapable adult the sheriff shall, in determining the application, apportion the cost as he thinks fit.

(4) Remuneration shall be payable out of the incapable adult's estate—

(a) in respect of the exercise of functions relating to the personal welfare of the incapable adult, only in a case where special cause is shown;

(b) in respect of the exercise of functions relating to the property or financial affairs of the incapable adult, unless the sheriff directs otherwise in the order appointing the guardian,

but shall not be payable to a local authority in respect of the exercise by their chief social work officer of functions relating to the personal welfare of the incapable adult.

(5) In determining whether or not to make a direction under subsection (4)(b) above, the sheriff shall take into account the value of the estate and the likely difficulty of managing it.

(6) Any remuneration payable to the guardian and the amount of outlays to be allowed under subsection (1) above shall be fixed by the Public Guardian—

(a) in a case where the guardian is required to submit accounts, when the guardian's accounts for that period are audited;

(b) in any other case, on an application by the guardian.

(7) The Public Guardian may allow payments to account to be made by way of remuneration during the accounting period if it would be unreasonable to expect the guardian to wait for payment until the end of an accounting period.

(8) A decision by the Public Guardian—

(a) under subsection (6) above as to the remuneration payable and the outlays allowable to the guardian may be appealed to the sheriff;

(b) under subsection (7) above as to payments to account to the guardian may be appealed to the sheriff, whose decision shall be final.

Forfeiture of guardian's remuneration.

53. Where a guardian is in breach of any duty of care, fiduciary duty or obligation imposed by this Act the sheriff may, on an application being made to him by any person claiming an interest in the property, financial affairs or personal welfare of the incapable adult, order the forfeiture (in whole or in part) of any remuneration due to the guardian.

Management of estate of incapable adult.

54. Schedule 2 to this Act shall have effect for the purpose of the management of the estate of an incapable adult by a guardian having powers relating to his property or financial affairs.

Non-compliance with decisions of guardian with welfare powers.

55.—(1) Where any decision of a guardian with powers relating to the personal welfare of the incapable adult is not complied with, the sheriff may, on an application by the guardian—

(a) make an order ordaining any person named in the order to implement the decision of the guardian;

(b) grant a warrant authorising a constable—

(i) to enter any premises where the incapable adult is, or is reasonably supposed to be;

(ii) to apprehend the incapable adult and to remove him to such place as the guardian may direct.

(2) A constable executing a warrant under subsection (1)(b) above may use such force as is reasonable in the circumstances and shall be accompanied by the guardian or such person as the guardian may authorise in writing.

(3) Where an incapable adult has a guardian and absents himself without the leave of the guardian from the place at which he is lawfully required by the guardian to reside, he may be returned to that place by the guardian or by a person authorised in writing by the guardian.

(4) In this section any reference to a guardian shall include a reference to a guardian (however called) appointed under the law of any country to, or entitled under the law of any country to act for, an adult during his incapacity, if the guardianship is recognised by the law of Scotland.

Termination and variation of guardianship and replacement, removal or resignation of guardian

Replacement or removal of guardian or recall of guardianship by sheriff.

56.—(1) The sheriff, on an application made to him by an adult subject to guardianship or by any other person claiming an interest in the adult's property, financial affairs or personal welfare, may—

(a) replace a guardian by an individual or office holder nominated in the application if he is satisfied, in relation to an individual, that he is suitable for appointment having regard to the matters set out in subsections (2) to (4) of section 45 of this Act;

(b) remove a guardian from office if he is satisfied —

(i) that there is a substitute guardian who is prepared to act as guardian; or

(ii) in a case where there are joint guardians, that the remaining guardian is or remaining guardians are prepared to continue to act; or

(c) recall a guardianship order or otherwise terminate a guardianship if he is satisfied—

(i) that the grounds for appointment of a guardian are no longer fulfilled; or

(ii) that the interests of the adult in his property, financial affairs or personal welfare can be satisfactorily safeguarded or promoted otherwise than by guardianship,

and where an application under this subsection is granted, the sheriff clerk shall send a copy of the interlocutor to the Public Guardian.

(2) The Public Guardian on receiving a copy of the interlocutor under subsection (1) above shall—

(a) enter prescribed particulars in the register maintained by him under section 4(2)(c)(iv) of this Act;

(b) where the sheriff—

(i) replaces the guardian by the individual or office holder nominated in the application, when satisfied that, in the case of an individual, the individual has found caution, issue him with a certificate of appointment;

(ii) removes a guardian from office and a substitute guardian is prepared to act, when satisfied that the substitute guardian has found caution, issue the substitute guardian with a certificate of appointment;

(iii) removes a joint guardian from office and there is a joint guardian who is prepared to continue to act, issue a remaining joint guardian with a new certificate of appointment;

(c) notify the adult.

(3) Where the sheriff recalls the guardianship order he may at the same time make an intervention order.

(4) In this section any reference to a guardian shall include a reference to a guardian (however called) appointed under the law of any country to, or entitled under the law of any country to act for, an adult during his incapacity, if the guardianship is recognised by the law of Scotland; and "guardianship order" shall be construed accordingly.

Discharge of
guardian with
financial powers.

57.—(1) At any time after—

(a) the recall of a guardianship order appointing a guardian with powers relating to the property or financial affairs of an adult; or

(b) the resignation, removal or replacement of such a guardian,

the Public Guardian may, on an application by the former guardian or, if the former guardian has died, his representative, grant a discharge in respect of the former guardian's actings and intromissions with the estate of the adult.

(2) On receipt of an application in the prescribed form, the Public Guardian shall intimate the application to the adult, his nearest relative, his primary carer and any other person who the Public Guardian considers has an interest in the application and advise them of the prescribed period within which they may object to the granting of the application; and he shall not grant the application without affording to any objector an opportunity of being heard.

(3) Having heard any objections as mentioned in subsection (2) above the Public Guardian may grant the application.

(4) Where the Public Guardian proposes to refuse the application he shall intimate his decision to the applicant and advise him of the prescribed period within which he may object to the refusal; and he shall not refuse the application without affording to the applicant, if he objects, an opportunity of being heard.

(5) The Public Guardian may at his own instance or at the instance of the applicant or of any person who objects to the granting of the application remit the application to the sheriff for determination.

(6) A decision of the Public Guardian—

(a) to grant an application under subsection (3) above or to refuse an application may be appealed to the sheriff;

(b) to refuse to remit an application to the sheriff under subsection (5) above may be appealed to the sheriff, whose decision shall be final.

Recall of
guardianship by
Public Guardian,
Mental Welfare
Commission or local
authority.

58.—(1) The Public Guardian, at his own instance or on an application by any person claiming an interest in the property, financial affairs or personal welfare of an adult in respect of whom a guardian has been appointed, may recall the powers of a guardian relating to the property or financial affairs of the adult if it appears to him that—

(a) the grounds for appointment of a guardian are no longer fulfilled; or

(b) the interests of the adult in his property, financial affairs or personal welfare can be satisfactorily safeguarded or promoted otherwise than by guardianship.

(2) Where the Public Guardian recalls the powers of a guardian under subsection (1) above he shall—

    (a) enter prescribed particulars in the register maintained by him under section 4(2)(c)(iv) of this Act;

    (b) notify the adult and the guardian.

(3) The Mental Welfare Commission or the local authority in whose area an adult in respect of whom a guardian has been appointed habitually resides, at their own instance or on an application by any person claiming an interest in the property, financial affairs or personal welfare of the adult, may recall the powers of a guardian relating to the personal welfare of the adult if it appears to them that—

    (a) the grounds for appointment of a guardian are no longer fulfilled; or

    (b) the interests of the adult in his property, financial affairs or personal welfare can be satisfactorily safeguarded or promoted otherwise than by guardianship.

(4) Where the Mental Welfare Commission or the local authority recall the powers of a guardian under subsection (3) above they shall notify the Public Guardian who shall—

    (a) enter prescribed particulars in the register maintained by him under section 4(2)(c)(iv) of this Act;

    (b) notify the adult and the guardian.

(5) The Public Guardian, Mental Welfare Commission or local authority, as the case may be, shall—

    (a) where acting on an application, on receipt of the application in the prescribed form intimate it;

    (b) where acting at his or their own instance, intimate the intention to recall the powers of a guardian,

to the adult, his nearest relative, his primary carer and any person who he or they consider has an interest in the recall of the powers and advise them of the prescribed period within which they may object to such recall; and he or they shall not recall the powers without affording to any objector an opportunity of being heard.

(6) Having heard any objections as mentioned in subsection (5) above the Public Guardian, Mental Welfare Commission or local authority may recall the powers of a guardian.

(7) Where the Public Guardian, Mental Welfare Commission or local authority proposes or propose to refuse the application he or they shall intimate the decision to the applicant and advise him of the prescribed period within which he may object to the refusal; and he or they shall not refuse the application without affording to the applicant, if he objects, an opportunity of being heard.

(8) The Public Guardian, Mental Welfare Commission or local authority may at his or their own instance or at the instance of an applicant or of any person who objects to the recall of the powers of the guardian remit the matter to the sheriff for determination.

(9) A decision of the Public Guardian, Mental Welfare Commission or local authority—

    (a) to recall the powers of a guardian under subsection (6) above, may be appealed to the sheriff;

    (b) not to remit the matter to the sheriff under subsection (8) above, may be appealed to the sheriff, whose decision shall be final.

(10) The Secretary of State may prescribe the forms and procedure for the purposes of any recall of guardianship powers by the Mental Welfare Commission or the local authority.

Variation of guardianship order.

59.—(1) The sheriff, on an application by any person claiming an interest in the property, financial affairs or personal welfare of the incapable adult, may vary the guardianship order and any existing ancillary order.

(2) Where the sheriff varies a guardianship order or an ancillary order under this section, the applicant shall send a copy of the interlocutor containing the order to the Public Guardian who shall—

>   (a) enter prescribed particulars in the register maintained by him under section 4(2)(c)(iv) of this Act;

>   (b) notify the incapable adult; and

>   (c) if he is satisfied that the guardian has caution which covers the varied order, issue a new certificate of appointment where necessary.

Resignation of guardian.

60.—(1) A joint guardian, or a guardian in respect of whom a substitute guardian has been appointed, may resign by giving notice in writing of his intention to do so to the Public Guardian.

(2) The resignation of a guardian as mentioned in subsection (1) above—

>   (a) shall not take effect unless—

>>   (i) the remaining joint guardian is willing to continue to act; or

>>   (ii) the substitute guardian is willing to act;

>   (b) shall take effect on the receipt by the Public Guardian of notice in writing under subsection (1) above together with evidence as to the matters contained in paragraph (a)(i) or (ii) above.

(3) On receiving notice in writing and evidence as mentioned in subsection (2)(b) above, the Public Guardian shall—

>   (a) enter prescribed particulars in the register maintained by him under section 4(2)(c)(iv) of this Act;

>   (b) if satisfied that the substitute guardian has found caution, issue him with a new certificate of appointment;

>   (c) issue a remaining joint guardian with a new certificate of appointment;

>   (d) notify the incapable adult.

(4) A substitute guardian who has not subsequently become guardian by virtue of section 48 of this Act may resign by giving notice in writing to the Public Guardian and the resignation shall take effect on the date of receipt of the notice by the Public Guardian; and on its becoming effective, the Public Guardian shall—

>   (a) notify the guardian and the incapable adult; and

>   (b) enter prescribed particulars in the register maintained by him under section 4(2)(c)(iv) of this Act.

(5) A guardian—

>   (a) who has no joint guardian; or

>   (b) in respect of whom no substitute guardian has been appointed; or

>   (c) being a joint guardian or guardian in respect of whom a substitute has been appointed who cannot effectively resign by reason of subsection (2)(a)(i) or (ii) above,

shall not resign until a replacement guardian has been appointed under section 56 of this Act.

Change of habitual residence.

61. Where the guardian is the chief social work officer of the local authority and the incapable adult changes his place of habitual residence to the area of another local authority, the chief social work officer of the first mentioned local authority shall notify the chief social work officer of the second mentioned local authority who shall become guardian on receipt of the notification and shall notify the Public Guardian, who shall—

(a) enter prescribed particulars in the register maintained by him under section 4(2)(c)(iv) of this Act and issue a certificate of appointment to the new guardian; and

(b) notify the incapable adult.

Termination of guardianship on death of incapable adult.

62.—(1) A guardianship order in respect of an incapable adult under this Part of this Act shall cease to have effect on his death.

(2) A guardian having powers relating to the property or financial affairs of the incapable adult shall, until he becomes aware of the death of the incapable adult or of any other event which has the effect of terminating his authority, be entitled to act under those powers if he acts in good faith.

(3) Where the authority of a guardian (including a joint guardian) is terminated or otherwise comes to an end, a third party in good faith is entitled to rely on the authority of the guardian if he is unaware of the termination or ending of that authority.

(4) In this section any reference to a guardian shall include a reference to a guardian (however called) appointed under the law of any country to, or entitled under the law of any country to act for, an adult during his incapacity, if the guardianship is recognised by the law of Scotland.

Part VII

Miscellaneous

Future appointment of curator bonis *etc.* incompetent.

63. In any proceedings begun after the commencement of this Act it shall not be competent to appoint a curator bonis, tutor-dative or tutor-at-law to a person who has attained the age of 16 years.

Limitation of liability.

64.—(1) No liability shall be incurred by a guardian, a continuing attorney, a welfare attorney, a person authorised to act under an intervention order, a withdrawer or the managers of an establishment for any breach of any duty of care or fiduciary duty owed to the incapable adult if he has or they have—

(a) acted reasonably and in good faith and in accordance with the general principles set out in section 1 of this Act; or

(b) failed to act and the failure was reasonable and in good faith and in accordance with the said general principles.

(2) In this section any reference to—

(a) a guardian shall include a reference to a guardian (however called) appointed under the law of any country to, or entitled under the law of any country to act for, an adult during his incapacity, if the guardianship is recognised by the law of Scotland;

(b) a continuing attorney shall include a reference to a person granted, under a contract, grant or appointment governed by the law of any country, powers (however expressed), relating to the granter's property or financial affairs and having continuing effect notwithstanding the granter's incapacity; and

(c) a welfare attorney shall include a reference to a person granted, under a contract, grant or appointment governed by the law of any country, powers (however expressed) relating to the granter's personal welfare and having effect during the granter's incapacity.

PART VII
Offence of ill-
treatment and wilful
neglect.

65.—(1) It shall be an offence for any person exercising powers under this Act relating to the personal welfare of an incapable adult to ill-treat or wilfully neglect that adult.

(2) A person guilty of an offence under subsection (1) above shall be liable—

(a) on summary conviction, to imprisonment for a term not exceeding 6 months or to a fine not exceeding the statutory maximum or both;

(b) on conviction on indictment, to imprisonment for a term not exceeding 2 years or to a fine, or both.

Regulations.

66. Any power of the Secretary of State to make regulations under this Act shall be exercisable by statutory instrument subject to annulment in pursuance of a resolution of either House of Parliament.

Interpretation.

67.—(1) In this Act, unless the context otherwise requires—

"adult" means a person who has attained the age of 16 years;

"advance statement" shall be construed in accordance with section 40 of this Act;

1987 c. 22.

"bank" means an institution authorised by the Bank of England under Part I of the Banking Act 1987 and includes the National Savings Bank;

1986 c. 53.

"building society" means a building society within the meaning of section 5 of the Building Societies Act 1986;

"continuing attorney" shall be construed in accordance with section 11 of this Act;

"guardianship order" shall be construed in accordance with section 44 of this Act;

"intervention order" shall be construed in accordance with section 42 of this Act;

1994 c. 39.

"local authority" means a council constituted under section 2 of the Local Government (Scotland) etc. Act 1994, and references to a local authority shall be construed as references to the local authority for the area in which the incapable adult resides;

"managers of an establishment" shall be construed in accordance with Schedule 1 to this Act;

"Mental Welfare Commission" means the Mental Welfare Commission for Scotland continued in being by section 2 of the 1984 Act;

"nearest relative" means the person who would be, or would be exercising the functions of, the adult's nearest relative under sections 53 to 57 of the 1984 Act if the adult were a patient within the meaning of that Act;

"office holder" shall be construed in accordance with section 45 of this Act;

"person claiming an interest" includes the local authority, the Mental Welfare Commission and the Public Guardian;

"power of attorney" includes a factory and commission;

"prescribed", except for the purposes of anything which may be or is to be prescribed by the Public Guardian, means prescribed by regulations made by the Secretary of State;

"primary carer" in relation to an adult, means the person primarily engaged in caring for him;

"Public Guardian" shall be construed in accordance with section 4 of this Act;

1978 c. 29

"State hospital" shall be construed in accordance with section 102 of the National Health Service (Scotland) Act 1978 ;

"substitute guardian" shall be construed in accordance with section 48 of this Act;

"welfare attorney" shall be construed in accordance with section 12 of this Act;

Part VII

1984 c.36

"withdrawer" shall be construed in accordance with section 21 of this Act;

"the 1984 Act" means the Mental Health (Scotland) Act 1984.

(2) For the purposes of this Act, unless the context otherwise requires—

    (a) "incapable" means incapable of—

        (i) acting; or

        (ii) making decisions; or

        (iii) communicating decisions,

as mentioned in any provision of this Act, by reason of mental disorder or of inability to communicate because of physical or other disability and "incapable adult" and "incapacity" shall be construed accordingly; and

    (b) "mental disorder" means mental illness or mental handicap however caused or manifested; but an adult shall not be treated as suffering from mental disorder by reason only of promiscuity or other immoral conduct, sexual deviancy, dependence on alcohol or drugs, or acting as no prudent person would act.

1985 c. 66

(3) For the purposes of this Act, a person is bankrupt if his estate has been sequestrated for insolvency or he has granted a trust deed which has become a protected trust deed under Schedule 5 to the Bankruptcy (Scotland) Act 1985, or he has been adjudged bankrupt in England and Wales, or he has become bankrupt (however expressed) under the law of any other country.

Continuation of existing powers, minor and consequential amendments and repeals.

68.—(1) Schedule 3 to this Act, which contains provisions relating to the continuation of existing powers, shall have effect.

(2) Schedule 4 to this Act, which contains minor amendments and amendments consequential on the provisions of this Act, shall have effect.

(3) The enactments mentioned in Schedule 5 to this Act are hereby repealed to the extent specified in the third column of that Schedule.

Citation, commencement and extent.

69.—(1) This Act may be cited as the Incapable Adults (Scotland) Act 1995.

(2) This Act shall come into force on such day as the Secretary of State may by order made by statutory instrument appoint and different days may be appointed for different purposes.

(3) The amendments and repeals contained in Schedules 4 and 5 to this Act have the same territorial extent as the enactments to which they apply but, subject to that, this Act extends to Scotland only.

Incapable Adults (Scotland) Bill

SCHEDULES

MANAGERS OF AN ESTABLISHMENT

1. For the purposes of Part IV of this Act "the managers" of an establishment means—

1978 c. 29.

(a) in relation to a hospital vested in the Secretary of State under the National Health Service (Scotland) Act 1978, the Health Board responsible for the administration of that hospital;

(b) in relation to a hospital managed by a National Health Service trust established under section 12A of the said Act of 1978, the directors of the trust;

(c) in relation to a State hospital—

(i) the Secretary of State; or

(ii) if the Secretary of State has appointed a State Hospital Management Committee to manage that hospital, that Committee; or

(iii) if the management of that hospital has been delegated to a Health Board or to the Common Services Agency for the Scottish Health Service, that Board or Agency, as the case may be;

(d) in relation to a private hospital registered under Part IV of the 1984 Act and an unregistered hospital, the person or persons carrying on the hospital;

1968 c. 49.

(e) in relation to a residential establishment provided by a local authority under section 59 of the Social Work (Scotland) Act 1968, the local authority;

(f) in relation to an establishment in respect of which there is registration under section 62 or 63 of the said Act of 1968, the person registered in respect of it;

1938 c. 73.

(g) in relation to a nursing home in respect of which there is registration under the Nursing Homes Registration (Scotland) Act 1938, the person registered in respect of it.

2. The Secretary of State may by regulations amend paragraph 1 above for the purpose of adding to, removing or altering the establishments and persons specified as managers thereof.

SCHEDULE 2

Section 54

MANAGEMENT OF ESTATE OF INCAPABLE ADULT

Management plan

1.—(1) A guardian with powers relating to the property and financial affairs of the incapable adult (other than the Public Guardian when so acting) shall, unless the sheriff otherwise directs, prepare a plan (a "management plan"), taking account of any directions given by the sheriff in the order appointing him, for the management, investment and realisation of the incapable adult's estate and for the application of the estate to the incapable adult's needs, so far as the estate falls within the guardian's authority.

(2) The management plan shall be submitted in draft by the guardian to the Public Guardian for his approval along with the inventory of the incapable adult's estate prepared under paragraph 3 below or not more than 1 month, or such other period as the Public Guardian may allow, after the submission of the inventory.

(3) The Public Guardian may approve the management plan submitted to him under sub-paragraph (2) above or he may approve it with amendments and the plan as so

approved or as so amended shall be taken account of by the guardian in the exercise of his functions in relation to the incapable adult.

(4) Before the management plan is approved, the guardian shall, unless the sheriff on appointing him has conferred wider powers, have power only to—

(a) ingather and take control of the assets of the incapable adult's estate so as to enable him, when the management plan has been approved, to intromit with them;

(b) claim any benefit or other sum due to the incapable adult;

(c) make such payments as are necessary to provide for the incapable adult's day to day needs.

(5) The Public Guardian may authorise the guardian to exercise any function within the scope of his authority before the management plan is approved, if it would be unreasonable to delay him exercising that function until the plan had been approved.

(6) The guardian shall keep the management plan under review and shall put forward to the Public Guardian proposals for variation of it whenever it appears to him to be appropriate.

(7) The Public Guardian—

(a) may at any time propose any variation to the management plan; and

(b) shall review the plan whenever the guardian submits his accounts for audit.

(8) The Public Guardian shall notify the guardian of any variation which he proposes to make to the management plan and shall not make any such variation without affording the guardian an opportunity to object.

(9) Having heard any objections by the guardian as mentioned in sub-paragraph (8) above the Public Guardian may make the variation with or without amendment.

Directions from sheriff

2.—(1) Where the guardian disagrees with any decision made by the Public Guardian in relation to a management plan prepared under paragraph 1 above, he may apply to the sheriff for a determination in relation to the matter.

(2) The sheriff's decision in a determination under this paragraph shall be final.

Inventory of estate

3.—(1) A guardian with powers relating to the property or financial affairs of the incapable adult (other than the Public Guardian when so acting) shall, as soon after his appointment as possible and in any event within 3 months of the date of registration of his appointment or such other period as the Public Guardian may allow, submit to the Public Guardian for examination and approval a full inventory of the incapable adult's estate in so far as it falls within the scope of the guardian's authority, along with such supporting documents and additional information as the Public Guardian may require.

(2) The inventory shall be in a form, and contain information, prescribed by the Public Guardian.

(3) Errors in and omissions from the inventory which are discovered by the guardian after the inventory has been approved by the Public Guardian shall be notified by him to the Public Guardian within 6 months of the date of discovery or when submitting his next accounts to the Public Guardian, whichever occurs sooner.

(4) The Public Guardian may dispense with the need for the guardian to submit an inventory under sub-paragraph (1) above or may require the guardian to take such other action as he thinks appropriate in lieu of submitting an inventory.

(5) Where the Public Guardian is acting as guardian he shall prepare an inventory of the incapable adult's estate in so far as it falls within the scope of his authority and shall, if the sheriff on the application of any person with an interest in the incapable adult's estate so orders, submit the inventory to the sheriff.

Money

4. The guardian shall deposit all money received by him as guardian in a bank or a building society in an account in the name of the incapable adult and shall ensure that all sums in excess of £500 (or such other sum as may be prescribed) so deposited shall earn interest.

Powers relating to investment and carrying on of business by guardian

5.—(1) Subject to the following provisions of this paragraph, a guardian with powers relating to the property or financial affairs of the incapable adult shall be entitled—

  (a) after obtaining and considering proper advice, to retain any existing investment of the incapable adult;

  (b) to use the incapable adult's estate to make new investments—

1961 c. 62.

      (i) in the name of the incapable adult in any of the items specified in Schedule 1 to the Trustee Investments Act 1961; or

      (ii) in a personal equity plan comprising investments in such items in an account in the name of the incapable adult.

(2) Before investing, whether directly or by means of a personal equity plan, in any item specified in Part II or III of the said Schedule (other than a deposit with a building society), the guardian shall obtain and consider proper advice as to whether the investment is satisfactory having regard to the principles set out in sub-paragraphs (a) to (c) of sub-paragraph (5) below.

(3) For the purposes of sub-paragraphs (1) and (2) above—

1986 c. 60.

  (a) proper advice is the advice of a person authorised to carry on investment business in the United Kingdom for the purposes of the Financial Services Act 1986 who is not the guardian or any person who is an employer, employee or business partner of the guardian; and

  (b) the advice must be given or subsequently confirmed in writing.

(4) The Public Guardian may, at any time, authorise the guardian to invest in any item not specified in the said Schedule.

(5) The guardian shall keep every investment under review and in doing so shall have regard to the following principles—

  (a) that the investment must be prudent;

  (b) that there must be diversification of investments; and

  (c) that the investment must be suitable for the incapable adult's estate.

(6) The Public Guardian may at any time direct the guardian to realise any investment.

(7) The guardian may, subject to any direction given by the Public Guardian, carry on any business of the incapable adult.

(8) Where the guardian is the Public Guardian this paragraph shall have effect subject to the omission of—

  (a) sub-paragraph (4);

  (b) sub-paragraph (6);

  (c) in sub-paragraph (7), the reference to any direction given by the Public Guardian.

(9) Any decision by the Public Guardian—

(a) under sub-paragraph (4) above as to authorising the guardian to invest;

(b) under sub-paragraph (6) above as to directing the guardian to realise investments;

(c) under sub-paragraph (7) above as to giving directions to the guardian in carrying on the business of the incapable adult,

may be appealed to the sheriff, whose decision shall be final.

(10) In this paragraph "personal equity plan" means an investment plan which conforms to regulations made under section 333 of the Income and Corporation Taxes Act 1988.

Purchase or disposal of accommodation

6.—(1) The guardian shall not, without the consent of the Public Guardian, purchase accommodation for, or dispose of any accommodation used for the time being as a dwelling house by, the incapable adult.

(2) On receipt of an application for consent under sub-paragraph (1) above in the prescribed form, the Public Guardian shall intimate the application to the incapable adult, his nearest relative, his primary carer and any person who the Public Guardian considers has an interest in the application and advise them of the prescribed period within which they may object to the granting of the application; and he shall not grant the application without affording to any objector an opportunity of being heard.

(3) Having heard any objections as mentioned in sub-paragraph (2) above the Public Guardian may grant the application.

(4) Where the Public Guardian proposes to refuse the application he shall intimate his decision to the applicant and advise him of the prescribed period within which he may object to the refusal; and he shall not refuse the application without affording to the applicant, if he objects, an opportunity of being heard.

(5) The Public Guardian may at his own instance or at the instance of any person who objects to the granting or refusal of the application remit the application to the sheriff for determination.

(6) A decision of the Public Guardian—

(a) to grant an application under sub-paragraph (3) above or to refuse an application; or

(b) to refuse to remit an application to the sheriff under sub-paragraph (5) above,

may be appealed to the sheriff, whose decision shall be final.

Accounting and auditing

7.—(1) A guardian with powers relating to the property or financial affairs of the incapable adult (other than the Public Guardian when so acting) shall submit accounts in respect of each accounting period to the Public Guardian within one month from the end of the accounting period or such longer period as the Public Guardian may allow.

(2) There shall be submitted with the accounts under sub-paragraph (1) above such supporting documents as the Public Guardian may require, and the Public Guardian may require the guardian to furnish him with such information in connection with the accounts as the Public Guardian may determine.

(3) For the purposes of this paragraph, the first accounting period shall commence with the date of appointment of the guardian and end at such date not later than 18 months after the date of registration of the guardian's appointment as the Public Guardian

may determine; and thereafter each accounting period shall be a year commencing with the date on which the immediately previous accounting period ended.

(4) Notwithstanding the foregoing provisions of this paragraph, the Public Guardian may at any time—

(a) give directions as to the frequency of accounting periods;

(b) dispense with the need for the submission of accounts by the guardian; or

(c) require the guardian to do anything which the Public Guardian thinks appropriate in lieu of submitting accounts.

(5) The accounts shall be in such form as is prescribed by the Public Guardian and different forms may be prescribed for different cases or descriptions of case.

(6) The accounts submitted to the Public Guardian under sub-paragraph (1) above shall be audited by the Public Guardian or by an accountant appointed by, and responsible to, the Public Guardian for that purpose.

Approval of accounts

8.—(1) After the accounts of the guardian have been audited, the Public Guardian shall, if the accounts appear to him—

(a) to be a true and fair view of the guardian's management of the incapable adult's estate, approve them and fix the remuneration (if any) due to the guardian;

(b) not to be a true and fair view of the guardian's management of the incapable adult's estate, prepare a report as to the extent to which they do not represent such a true and fair view and adjusting the accounts accordingly.

(2) The Public Guardian may approve the accounts, notwithstanding any minor inconsistencies or absence of full documentation in the accounts, if he is satisfied that the guardian acted reasonably and in good faith.

(3) The Public Guardian shall send any report prepared by him under sub-paragraph (1)(b) above to the guardian, who may object to anything contained in the report within 28 days of it being sent to him.

(4) If no objection is taken to the report, the accounts as adjusted by the Public Guardian shall be regarded as approved by him.

(5) Where any objection taken to the report cannot be resolved between the guardian and the Public Guardian, the matter may be determined by the sheriff on an application by the guardian.

(6) Without prejudice to sub-paragraph (7) below, the guardian shall be liable to make good any deficiency revealed by the accounts as approved by the Public Guardian under sub-paragraph (1)(a) above.

(7) Where a deficiency is revealed as mentioned in sub-paragraph (6) above, the Public Guardian may require the guardian to pay interest to the incapable adult's estate on the amount of the deficiency at the rate fixed by Act of Sederunt as applicable to a decree of the sheriff in respect of the period for which it appears that the deficiency has existed.

Accounting where Public Guardian is guardian

9.—(1) Where the Public Guardian is acting as guardian, he shall prepare accounts in respect of each accounting period and shall send a copy of the accounts within 30 days of their completion to the incapable adult and to the nearest relative and the primary carer of the incapable adult.

(2) For the purposes of this paragraph the first accounting period shall end 12 months after the date of registration of the Public Guardian's appointment as guardian.

(3) Any person to whom a copy of the accounts has been sent under sub-paragraph (1) above may within 28 days of it being sent to him object to anything contained in the accounts.

(4) Where any objection taken by any person to the accounts cannot be resolved between that person and the Public Guardian, the matter may be determined by the sheriff on an application by that person.

(5) Nothing in sub-paragraph (1) above shall require the Public Guardian to send a copy of the accounts to any incapable adult who, in the opinion of the Public Guardian, would be unable to understand them.

Section 68

SCHEDULE 3

CONTINUATION OF EXISTING CURATORS, TUTORS, GUARDIANS AND ATTORNEYS UNDER THIS ACT.

Curators and tutors

1.—(1) On the relevant date, any person holding office as curator bonis to an adult shall become guardian of that adult with power to manage the property or financial affairs of the adult.

(2) Where any proceedings for the appointment of a curator bonis to an adult have been commenced and not determined before the relevant date, they shall be determined in accordance with the law as it was immediately before that date; and any person appointed curator bonis shall become guardian of that adult with power to manage the property or financial affairs of the adult.

2.—(1) On the relevant date, any person holding office as tutor-dative to an adult shall become guardian of that adult and shall continue to have the powers conferred by the court on his appointment as tutor-dative.

(2) Where any proceedings for the appointment of a tutor-dative to an adult have been commenced and not determined before the relevant date, they shall be determined in accordance with the law as it was immediately before that date; and any person appointed tutor-dative shall become guardian of that adult with such power to manage the property, financial affairs or personal welfare of the adult as the court may determine.

3.—(1) On the relevant date, any person holding office as tutor-at-law to an adult shall become guardian of that adult with power to manage the property, financial affairs or personal welfare of the adult.

(2) Where any proceedings for the appointment of a tutor-at-law to an adult have been commenced and not determined before the relevant date, they shall be determined in accordance with the law as it was immediately before that date; and any person appointed tutor-at-law shall become guardian of that adult with power to manage the property, financial affairs or personal welfare of the adult.

Guardians

4.—(1) On the relevant date, any person holding office as guardian of an adult under the 1984 Act shall become guardian of that adult under this Act and shall continue to have the powers set out in paragraphs (a) to (c) of section 41(2) of that Act notwithstanding the repeal of that section by this Act.

(2) Where any proceedings for the appointment of such a guardian of an adult have been commenced and not determined before the relevant date, they shall be determined in accordance with the 1984 Act as it was in force immediately before that date; and any person appointed guardian shall become guardian of that adult under this Act with the powers set out in the said paragraphs (a) to (c) of section 41(2) of the 1984 Act.

Proceedings relating to existing appointments

5. Where any proceedings in relation to the functions of an existing curator bonis, tutor-dative, tutor-at-law or guardian, have been commenced and not determined before the relevant date, they shall be determined in accordance with the law as it was immediately before that date.

Attorneys

6.—(1) On the relevant date, any person holding office as a continuing attorney under a contract of mandate or agency shall become a continuing attorney under this Act.

(2) Sections 4(2)(c)(i), 11, 14, 15(3)(a), 16 and 17 of this Act shall not apply to a person who has become a continuing attorney by virtue of sub-paragraph (1) above.

Managers

7.—(1) Any managers of a hospital who have received and hold money and valuables on behalf of any person under section 94 of the 1984 Act may continue to do so in relation to that person on and after the relevant date under this Act.

(2) This Act applies to managers as mentioned in sub-paragraph (1) above notwithstanding that the owner of the money or valuables has not been certified under section 29 of this Act.

(3) Sections 27 and 28 of this Act shall not apply in the case of managers who continue to hold money by virtue of sub-paragraph (1) above.

(4) Where the managers have authority from the Mental Welfare Commission to hold and manage money and other property in excess of the aggregate value mentioned in section 32 of this Act they may do so in relation to the money and valuables of any person which they continue to hold under sub-paragraph (1) above.

Application of Act to persons who become guardians by virtue of this Schedule

8.—(1) For the purposes of their application to persons who have become guardians by virtue of this Schedule to this Act, the following provisions of this Act shall have effect as modified or disapplied by this paragraph.

(2) In section 51, in subsection (2) the reference to the certificate of appointment issued under section 44 of this Act shall be construed as a reference to the order of the court appointing the person as curator bonis, tutor-dative, tutor-at-law or guardian under the 1984 Act, as the case may be.

(3) Section 46 shall not apply to a person who has become a guardian to an adult by virtue of this Schedule to this Act and who was—

    (a) a curator bonis or tutor-at-law to that adult, in which case the powers shall continue in force indefinitely;

    (b) a tutor-dative to that adult, in which case the powers shall continue for the period specified in the order appointing him or, if no period is specified, indefinitely;

    (c) a guardian of that adult under the 1984 Act, in which case the powers shall continue until such time as they would have continued had he not become a guardian by virtue of this Schedule to this Act.

(4) In section 52, in subsections (2) and (3) and in section 61 the references to the chief social work officer of the local authority shall be construed as including references to the local authority.

(5) Schedule 2 shall apply only—

(a) in a case where; and

(b) to the extent that,

the Public Guardian has determined that it should apply.

(6) Any determination by the Public Guardian under sub-paragraph (5) above, or a decision by him not to make such a determination, may be appealed to the sheriff, whose decision shall be final.

(7) No reference in this Act to registration shall have effect in relation to any person who becomes a guardian by virtue of this Schedule to this Act.

Interpretation

9. In this Schedule the "relevant date" in relation to any paragraph in which it appears means the date of coming into force of that paragraph.

Section 68

SCHEDULE 4

Mɪɴᴏʀ ᴀɴᴅ Cᴏɴsᴇǫᴜᴇɴᴛɪᴀʟ Aᴍᴇɴᴅᴍᴇɴᴛs

General

1. With effect from the commencement of this paragraph any reference in any enactment or document to a curator bonis or a tutor or curator of a person of or over the age of 16 years shall be construed as a reference to a guardian with similar powers appointed to that person under this Act.

Defence Act 1842

1842 c. 94.

2.—(1) In section 15 of the Defence Act 1842—

(a) after the word "nonage" in both places where it occurs there shall be inserted the words "or mental incapacity";

(b) the words "or not of whole mind" shall be repealed;

(c) for the words "out of prison, within this land, or of whole mind" there shall be substituted the words "within this land".

(2) In section 27 of that Act for the word "lunacy" there shall be substituted the words "mental incapacity".

Judicial Factors Act 1849

1849 c. 51.

3.—(1) In section 10 of the Judicial Factors Act 1849 for the words "guardians and tutors and curators" there shall be substituted the words "and guardians".

(2) In section 27 of that Act—

(a) the words "or Court of Exchequer, as the case may be," shall be repealed;

(b) for the words "guardians and tutors and curators" there shall be substituted the words "and guardians".

(3) In section 33 of that Act for the words "guardian or tutor or curator" there shall be substituted the words "or guardian".

(4) In section 34 of that Act for the words "guardian, tutor, or curator" in both places where they occur there shall be substituted the words "or guardian".

(5) In section 34A of that Act—

(a) the words "tutors and curators" and "tutory or curatory" shall be repealed;

(b) for the words "recovery, death or coming of age of the ward" there shall be substituted the words "coming to an end of the situation giving rise to it".

(6) In section 36 of that Act for the words "guardianships, tutories, and curatories" there shall be substituted the words "and guardianships".

(7) In section 37 of that Act for the words "guardian, tutor or curator" there shall be substituted the words "or guardian".

(8) In section 40 of that Act—

(a) the words "tutors and curators" where they first occur shall be repealed;

(b) for the words "factors, guardians, tutors and curators" there shall be substituted the words "factors and guardians".

1864 c. 114.

Improvement of Land Act 1864

4.—(1) In section 24 of the Improvement of Land Act 1864—

(a) the words "tutors,", "curators," "tutor," and "curator," shall be repealed;

(b) for the words "persons suffering from mental disorder within the meaning of the Mental Health (Scotland) Act, 1960" there shall be substituted the words "adults who are incapable within the meaning of the Incapable Adults (Scotland) Act 1995".

(2) In section 68 of that Act for the words "Mental Health (Scotland) Act 1984" there shall be substituted the words "Incapable Adults (Scotland) Act 1995".

1868 c.101.

Titles to Land (Consolidation) (Scotland) Act 1868

5.—(1) In section 24 of the Titles to Land (Consolidation) (Scotland) Act 1868 for the words "mental disorder within the meaning of the Mental Health (Scotland) Act 1960" there shall be substituted the words "mental or other incapacity".

(2) In section 62 of that Act for the words "of insane mind" there shall be substituted the words "mental or other incapacity".

1880 c.4.

Judicial Factors (Scotland) Act 1880

6. In section 3 of the Judicial Factors (Scotland) Act 1880 after the word "guardian" there shall be inserted the words "of a person who is under the age of 16 years".

Judicial Factors (Scotland) Act 1889

1889 c. 39.

7.—(1) In section 2 of the Judicial Factors (Scotland) Act 1889 at the beginning there shall be inserted the words "Without prejudice to section 4(1) of the Incapable Adults (Scotland) Act 1995 (Accountant of Court to be Public Guardian)".

(2) In section 6 of that Act, in the proviso, after the words "apply to" there shall be inserted the words "guardians appointed under the Incapable Adults (Scotland) Act 1995, to".

Heritable Securities (Scotland) Act 1894

1894 c. 44

8. In section 13 of the Heritable Securities (Scotland) Act 1894—

(a) after the words "taken; and" there shall be inserted the words "the person entitled to act as the legal representative of any such person";

(b) the words "tutors, curators," shall be repealed.

Trusts (Scotland) Act 1921

9. In section 2 of the Trusts (Scotland) Act 1921, in the definition of "trustee", after the words "16 years" there shall be inserted the words "but not including a guardian holding office under the Incapable Adults (Scotland) Act 1995".

National Assistance Act 1948

10. In section 49 of the National Assistance Act 1948 as it applies to Scotland—

(a) immediately before the words "the council" where they last occur there shall be inserted the words "or applies for an intervention order or for appointment as a guardian under the Incapable Adults (Scotland) Act 1995";

(b) immediately before the words "in so far as" there shall be inserted the words "or his functions under the intervention order or as guardian".

Offices, Shops and Railway Premises Act 1963

11. In section 90(1) of the Offices, Shops and Railway Premises Act 1963, in the definition of "owner", for the words ", tutor or curator" there shall be substituted the words "or person entitled to act as legal representative of a person under disability by reason of nonage or mental or other incapacity".

Medicines Act 1968

12. In section 72 of the Medicines Act 1968—

(a) in subsection (1) for the words "curator bonis" there shall be substituted the word "guardian";

(b) in subsections (3)(d) and (4)(c) the words "curator bonis," shall be repealed.

Solicitors (Scotland) Act 1980

13. In section 18(1) of the Solicitors (Scotland) Act 1980—

(a) in paragraph (a) the words "or becomes subject to guardianship" shall be repealed;

(b) for paragraph (b) there shall be substituted—

"(b) a guardian is appointed to a solicitor under the Incapable Adults (Scotland) Act 1995;".

Law Reform (Miscellaneous Provisions) (Scotland) Act 1980

14. In group C of Part I of Schedule 1 to the Law Reform (Miscellaneous Provisions) (Scotland) Act 1980 for paragraphs (b) and (c) there shall be substituted—

"(b) persons for the time being subject to guardianship under the Incapable Adults (Scotland) Act 1995."

Mental Health (Scotland) Act 1984

15.—(1) In section 3 of the Mental Health (Scotland) Act 1984—

(a) in subsection (1) for the words from "or subject" to "this Act" there shall be substituted the words "under the following provisions of this Act or subject to guardianship under the Incapable Adults (Scotland) Act 1995";

(b) in subsection (2)—

(i) in paragraph (b) the words "or who are subject to guardianship" shall be repealed;

(ii) in paragraph (d) after the words "any local authority" there shall be inserted the words "or of the Public Guardian" and after the words "the local authority" there shall be inserted the words "or the Public Guardian";

(iii) in paragraph (e) for the words "or a local authority" there shall be substituted the words ", a local authority or the Public Guardian" and for the words "or the local authority" there shall be substituted the words ", the local authority or the Public Guardian";

(iv) in paragraph (f) after the words "local authority" there shall be inserted the words "the Public Guardian".

(2) In section 5(2) of that Act—

(a) in subsection (2) for the words "this Act" there shall be substituted the words "the Incapable Adults (Scotland) Act 1995";

(b) at the end there shall be added—

"(3) In subsection (2) of this section the reference to a guardian includes a reference to a guardian (however called) appointed under the law of any country to, or entitled under the law of any country to act for, an adult during his incapacity, if the guardianship is recognised by the law of Scotland.".

(3) In section 9(1) of that Act at the end there shall be added the words "or any other enactment".

(4) In section 10 of that Act, in subsection (1)(b) for the words "under the following provisions of this Act" there shall be substituted the words "or its chief social work officer under the Incapable Adults (Scotland) Act 1995".

(5) In section 19 of that Act—

(a) in subsection (1) for the words "either by the nearest relative of the patient or by a mental health officer" there shall be substituted the words "by the nearest relative of the patient, by a mental health officer, or by a guardian or welfare attorney of the patient who has powers to do so";

(b) in subsection (2) after the word "relative" there shall be inserted the words ", guardian or welfare attorney, as the case may be,";

(c) in subsection (3) after the word "relative" in both places where it occurs there shall be inserted the words ", guardian or welfare attorney, as the case may be";

(d) in subsection (5), in paragraph (b) after the word "relative" there shall be inserted the words "and any guardian or welfare attorney";

(e) at the end there shall be added—

"(8) in this section any reference to—

(a) a guardian includes a reference to a guardian (however called) appointed under the law of any country to, or entitled under the law of any country to act for, an adult during his incapacity, if the guardianship is recognised by the law of Scotland;

(b) a welfare attorney includes a reference to a person granted, under a contract, grant or appointment governed by the law of any country, powers (however expressed) relating to the granter's personal welfare and having effect during the granter's incapacity.".

(6) In section 20 of that Act—

(a) in subsection (1)(a) for the words "or his nearest relative" there shall be substituted the words ", his nearest relative, guardian or welfare attorney, as the case may be";

(b) at the end there shall be added—

"(4) In this section any reference to—

(a) a guardian shall include a reference to a guardian (however called) appointed under the law of any country to, or entitled under the law of any country to act for, an adult during his incapacity, if the guardianship is recognised by the law of Scotland;

(b) a welfare attorney shall include a reference to a person granted, under a contract, grant or appointment governed by the law of any country, powers (however expressed) relating to the granter's personal welfare and having effect during the granter's incapacity.".

(7) In section 21 of that Act—

(a) in subsection (2)(b)—

(i) after the word "relative" where it first occurs there shall be inserted the words ", guardian or welfare attorney, as the case may be";

(ii) after the word "relative" where it second and third occurs there shall be inserted the words "guardian or welfare attorney";

(b) at the end there shall be added—

"(6) In this section any reference to—

(a) a guardian shall include a reference to a guardian (however called) appointed under the law of any country to, or entitled under the law of any country to act for, an adult during his incapacity, if the guardianship is recognised by the law of Scotland;

(b) a welfare attorney shall include a reference to a person granted, under a contract, grant or appointment governed by the law of any country, powers (however expressed) relating to the granter's personal welfare and having effect during the granter's incapacity.".

(8) In section 22 of that Act—

(a) in subsection (4)(c) after the word "relative" there shall be inserted the words "and any guardian or welfare attorney";

(b) at the end there shall be added—

"(5) In this section any reference to—

(a) a guardian shall include a reference to a guardian (however called) appointed under the law of any country to, or entitled under the law of any country to act for, an adult during his incapacity, if the guardianship is recognised by the law of Scotland;

(b) a welfare attorney shall include a reference to a person granted, under a contract, grant or appointment governed by the law of any country, powers (however expressed) relating to the granter's personal welfare and having effect during the granter's incapacity.".

(9) In section 24 of that Act—

(a) in subsection (2) after the word "relative" there shall be inserted the words ", of any guardian or welfare attorney who has powers to do so,";

(b) in subsection (5) after the word "relative" there shall be inserted the words "and any guardian or welfare attorney";

(c) at the end there shall be added—

"(7) In this section any reference to—

(a) a guardian shall include a reference to a guardian (however called) appointed under the law of any country to, or entitled under the law of any country to act for, an adult during his incapacity, if the guardianship is recognised by the law of Scotland;

(b) a welfare attorney shall include a reference to a person granted, under a contract, grant or appointment governed by the law of any country, powers (however expressed) relating to the granter's personal welfare and having effect during the granter's incapacity.".

(10) In section 26 of that Act—

(a) in subsection (1)(b) after the word "patient" there shall be inserted the words ", by any guardian or welfare attorney of the patient who has power so to consent,";

(b) in subsection (4)(b) after the word "relative" where it first occurs there shall be inserted the words "and any guardian or welfare attorney " and after the word "relative" where it second occurs there shall be inserted the words ", guardian or welfare attorney, as the case may be";

(c) at the end there shall be added—

"(8) In this section any reference to—

(a) a guardian shall include a reference to a guardian (however called) appointed under the law of any country to, or entitled under the law of any country to act for, an adult during his incapacity, if the guardianship is recognised by the law of Scotland;

(b) a welfare attorney shall include a reference to a person granted, under a contract, grant or appointment governed by the law of any country, powers (however expressed) relating to the granter's personal welfare and having effect during the granter's incapacity.".

(11) In section 26A of that Act—

(a) in subsection (4) after the word "relative" there shall be inserted the words "or any guardian or welfare attorney who has powers to do so";

(b) in subsection (6)(b) after the word "relative" where it first occurs there shall be inserted the words "and any guardian or welfare attorney" and after the word "relative" where it second occurs there shall be inserted the words ", guardian or welfare attorney, as the case may be";

(c) at the end there shall be added—

"(10) In this section any reference to—

(a) a guardian shall include a reference to a guardian (however called) appointed under the law of any country to, or entitled under the law of any country to act for, an adult during his incapacity, if the guardianship is recognised by the law of Scotland;

   (b) a welfare attorney shall include a reference to a person granted, under a contract, grant or appointment governed by the law of any country, powers (however expressed) relating to the granter's personal welfare and having effect during the granter's incapacity.".

(12) In section 29 of that Act—

  (a) in subsection (2) after the word "relative" there shall be inserted the words ", to any guardian or welfare attorney";

  (b) in subsection (4) after the word "relative" there shall be inserted the words ", guardian or welfare attorney";

  (c) at the end there shall be added—

       "(5) In this section any reference to—

          (a) a guardian shall include a reference to a guardian (however called) appointed under the law of any country to, or entitled under the law of any country to act for, an adult during his incapacity, if the guardianship is recognised by the law of Scotland;

          (b) a welfare attorney shall include a reference to a person granted, under a contract, grant or appointment governed by the law of any country, powers (however expressed) relating to the granter's personal welfare and having effect during the granter's incapacity.".

(13) In section 30 of that Act—

  (a) in subsection (5) after the word "relative" there shall be inserted the words "and any guardian or welfare attorney of his";

  (b) at the end there shall be added—

       "(7) In this section any reference to—

          (a) a guardian shall include a reference to a guardian (however called) appointed under the law of any country to, or entitled under the law of any country to act for, an adult during his incapacity, if the guardianship is recognised by the law of Scotland;

          (b) a welfare attorney shall include a reference to a person granted, under a contract, grant or appointment governed by the law of any country, powers (however expressed) relating to the granter's personal welfare and having effect during the granter's incapacity.".

(14) In section 33 of that Act—

  (a) in subsection (5) for the words "or by the nearest relative" there shall be substituted the words ", by the nearest relative or by any guardian or welfare attorney who has powers to do so";

  (b) at the end there shall be added—

       "(7) In this section any reference to—

          (a) a guardian shall include a reference to a guardian (however called) appointed under the law of any country to, or entitled under the law of any country to act for, an adult during his incapacity, if the guardianship is recognised by the law of Scotland;

(b) a welfare attorney shall include a reference to a person granted, under a contract, grant or appointment governed by the law of any country, powers (however expressed) relating to the granter's personal welfare and having effect during the granter's incapacity.".

(15) in section 34—

(a) in subsection (1) after the word "relative" wherever it occurs there shall be inserted the words ", or guardian or welfare attorney with powers to do so";

(b) in subsection (2) after the word "relative" where it first occurs there shall be inserted the words "guardian or welfare attorney, as the case may be" and after the word "relative" where it second occurs there shall be inserted the words ", guardian or welfare attorney";

(c) in subsection (3) after the word "relative" there shall be inserted the words "or by any guardian or welfare attorney";

(d) at the end there shall be added—

"(4) In this section any reference to—

(a) a guardian shall include a reference to a guardian (however called) appointed under the law of any country to, or entitled under the law of any country to act for, an adult during his incapacity, if the guardianship is recognised by the law of Scotland;

(b) a welfare attorney shall include a reference to a person granted, under a contract, grant or appointment governed by the law of any country, powers (however expressed) relating to the granter's personal welfare and having effect during the granter's incapacity.".

(16) In section 35 of that Act—

(a) in subsection (1) for the words "or his nearest relative or both" there shall be substituted the words ", his nearest relative, his guardian or his welfare attorney or all of them";

(b) in subsection (3) after the word "relative" there shall be inserted the words "or any guardian or welfare attorney";

(c) at the end there shall be added—

"(5) In this section any reference to—

(a) a guardian shall include a reference to a guardian (however called) appointed under the law of any country to, or entitled under the law of any country to act for, an adult during his incapacity, if the guardianship is recognised by the law of Scotland;

(b) a welfare attorney shall include a reference to a person granted, under a contract, grant or appointment governed by the law of any country, powers (however expressed) relating to the granter's personal welfare and having effect during the granter's incapacity.".

(17) In section 95 of that Act—

(a) in subsection (1) after the word "tutor" there shall be inserted the word ", guardian";

(b) in subsection (2) after the word "tutor" there shall be inserted the word ", guardian".

(18) After section 119 of that Act there shall be inserted—

"Applications to 119A. All applications to, and proceedings before, the sheriff under
the sheriff. this Act shall be disposed of by a sheriff nominated for the time being
for that purpose by the sheriff principal, unless no such sheriff is
available to do so."

(19) In section 125(1) of that Act—

(a) for the definition of " "application for admission" and "guardianship
application" " there shall be substituted—

""application for admission" has the meaning assigned to it by
section 18 of this Act";

(b) in the appropriate place, there shall be inserted—

"Public Guardian" means the Public Guardian within the
meaning of the Incapable Adults (Scotland) Act 1995;".

Insolvency Act 1986

1986 c. 45.
16. In section 390(4)(c) of the Insolvency Act 1986 at the end there shall be added
the words "or has had a guardian appointed to him under the Incapable Adults (Scotland)
Act 1995.".

Financial Services Act 1986

1986 c. 60.
17. In section 45(1)(d) of the Financial Services Act 1986 at the end there shall be
added the words "or when acting in the exercise of his functions as Public Guardian
under the Incapable Adults (Scotland) Act 1995;".

Access to Health Records Act 1990

1990 c. 23.
18. In section 1 of the Access to Health Records Act 1990, in subsection (1) after
paragraph (e), there shall be inserted the following paragraph—

"(ee) where the record is held in Scotland and the patient is by
reason of mental or other incapacity unable to make or
authorise the application, any guardian or other person
entitled to act on behalf of the patient under the Incapable
Adults (Scotland) Act 1995;".

Child Support Act 1991

1991 c. 48.
19. In section 50 of the Child Support Act 1991, in subsection (8)(b), for paragraphs
(i) and (ii) there shall be substituted the words "a guardian or other person entitled to
act on behalf of the person under the Incapable Adults (Scotland) Act 1995.".

Social Security Administration Act 1992

1992 c. 5.
20. In section 123 of the Social Security Administration Act 1992, in subsection
(10)(c), for paragraphs (i) and (ii) there shall be substituted the words "a guardian or
other person entitled to act on behalf of the person under the Incapable Adults (Scotland)
Act 1995.".

Clean Air Act 1993

1993 c. 11.
21. In section 64 of the Clean Air Act 1993, in subsection (1) in the definition of
"owner", for the words "tutor or curator" there shall be substituted the words "or person

entitled to act as the legal representative of a person under disability by reason of nonage or mental or other incapacity".

Section 68

SCHEDULE 5

REPEALS

Chapter	Short title	Extent of repeal
1585 c.25 (S).	The Curators Act 1585	The whole Act.
12 & 13 Vict. c.51.	The Judicial Factors Act 1849	In section 1, the words "and curator bonis" and the words from "the word 'tutor'" to "Act 1960" where second occurring.
		In section 7, the words from "and if any factor" to "not subject to appeal".
		Section 25(1).
		Section 26.
		In section 27, the words "or Court of Exchequer, as the case may be,".
		Section 28.
		In section 31, the words "tutor or curator" and "or curator bonis".
		In section 32, the words "tutor or curator".
		In section 34A, the words "tutors and curators" and "tutory or curatory".
		In section 40, the words "tutors and curators" where first occurring.
27 & 28 Vict. c.114.	The Improvement of Land Act 1864	In section 24, the words "tutors,", "curators,", "tutor," and "curator,".
31 & 32 Vict. c.101.	The Titles to Land (Consolidation) (Scotland) Act 1868	In section 3, in the definition of "judicial factor", the words "or curators bonis".
43 & 44 Vict. c.4.	The Judicial Factors (Scotland) Act 1880.	In section 3, the words "a curator bonis".
52 & 53 Vict. c.39.	The Judicial Factors (Scotland) Act 1889	In section 13, the words "tutor, curator" in both places where they occur.
57 & 58 Vict. c. 44.	The Heritable Securities (Scotland) Act 1894	In section 13 the words "tutors, curators,".
11 & 12 Geo.5 c.58.	The Trusts (Scotland) Act 1921	In section 2, in the definitions of "trust", "trust deed" and "trustee" the words "tutor, curator" and in the definition of "judicial factor" the words "or curator".
12 & 13 Geo. 6 c.45.	The U.S.A. Veterans' Pensions Act 1949	In section 1, in subsection (4) the words "tutor, factor loco tutoris," and "curator bonis or".
1968 c.67.	The Medicines Act 1968	In section 72, in subsections (3)(d) and (4)(c) the words "curator bonis,".
1980 c.46.	The Solicitors (Scotland) Act 1980	In section 18(1) in paragraph (a) the words "or becomes subject to guardianship".
1984 c.36.	The Mental Health (Scotland) Act 1984	In section 3(2)(b) the words "or who are subject to guardianship".
		In section 7(1), in paragraph (b) the words "under the following provisions of this Act".
		In section 29, in subsection (1), paragraphs (b) and (c) and the word "or" which precedes them, in subsection (2) the words "or, as the case may be, by the local authority concerned", and in subsection (3), paragraph (b).
		Sections 36 to 52.
		In section 53(3) the words "or his reception into guardianship".
		Section 55(3).
		In section 57(4) the words "or subject to guardianship" and the words "or so subject" wherever they occur.

Chapter	Short title	Extent of repeal
1984 c.36.*(cont)*	The Mental Health (Scotland) Act 1984 *(cont)*	In section 59, in subsection (1), paragraph (b), subsection (2), and in subsection (3) the words "or 44".
		In section 92, subsection (1) and in subsection (2), in paragraph (a) the words "or subject to guardianship thereunder".
		Sections 93 and 94.
		In section 105(2) the words "subject to his guardianship under this Act or otherwise".
		In section 107(1), in paragraph (b) the words "under this Act" in both places where they occur.
		In section 108(1), in paragraph (a) the words "or being subject to guardianship".
		In section 110, in subsection (1) the words ", or in the case of a patient subject to guardianship, the local authority concerned", "or subject to guardianship", "or guardianship" in both places where they occur, "or his reception into guardianship" and in subsection (4) the words "or, as the case may be, the local authority concerned in relation to a patient subject to guardianship as aforesaid".
		In section 112 the words "or his reception into guardianship".
		In section 113(1) the words "or for reception into guardianship".
		In section 121, in subsection (1)(b) the words "or subject to guardianship", "or 44", in subsection (2) the words "or subject to guardianship", "or 44", "and subsection (2) of the said section 44" and in subsection (6) the words from "(in the case of" where they first occur to "guardianship)", the words "or section 44", the word "respectively", the words "or the said section 44 (as the case may be)".
		In section 125, in subsection (4) the words "or subject to guardianship" and in subsection (5) the words "or received, or liable to be received, into guardianship", "(other than under Part V of this Act)" and "or received or liable to be received into guardianship".
1990 c.40.	The Law Reform (Miscellaneous Provisions)(Scotland) Act 1990	Section 71.

INDEX TO INCAPABLE ADULTS (SCOTLAND) BILL

We indicate here where the various provisions of the Bill are discussed in the report.

BILL: CLAUSE	REPORT: PARAGRAPH
PART II CONTINUING AND WELFARE POWERS OF ATTORNEY	
11(1), (2)	3.6-3.10
11(3)(a)	3.11-3.12
11(3)(b)	3.6-3.10
11(3)(c)	3.13-3.19
12(1), (2)	3.6-3.10
12(3)(a)	3.11-3.12
12(3)(b)	3.6-3.10
12(3)(c)	3.13-3.19
12(4)(a)	3.20-3.26
12(4)(b)	3.41-3.42
12(5)	3.43-3.48
12(6)	3.20-3.26
12(7)	3.83
13	3.27-3.36
14(1), (2), (5)	3.27-3.36
14(3)	3.37-3.40
14(7)	7.3-7.5
15(1), (2)	3.57-3.72
15(3)	3.69-3.72
15(4)	7.3-7.5
15(5)	3.83
16	3.27-3.36
17	3.75-3.77
18(1), (2), (4)	3.78-3.79
18(3)	3.83
19	3.82
PART III ACCOUNTS AND FUNDS OF INCAPABLE ADULTS	
20(1), (2)(a), (3)	4.4-4.12
20(2)(b), (c)	4.26-4.27
21(1)	4.14
21(3)-(6)	4.15
21(7)	7.3-7.5
22(1), (2), (7)	4.16-4.18
22(3)	4.21-4.25
22(4)-(6)	4.19-4.20
22(8)	7.3-7.5
23	4.19-4.20
24(1)-(3), (5)	4.22-4.25
24(4)	7.3-7.5
24(6)	3.83, 6.225
25	4.28-4.32
26(1)	4.13, 4.28-4.32
26(2)	3.83, 6.225

BILL: CLAUSE	REPORT: PARAGRAPH

PART IV MANAGEMENT OF RESIDENTS' FINANCES

27(1)-(4)	4.42-4.45
27(5)	4.46-4.47
28(1)	4.42-4.45
28(2)	7.3-7.5
29	4.48-4.53
30	4.58-4.61
31(1), (2)	4.55
31(3)	3.83, 6.225
32(1), (2), (7)	4.62-4.64
32(3)	4.58-4.61
32(4)	4.66-4.70
32(6)	4.57
32(8)	7.3-7.5
33	4.65
34	4.71-4.74
35	4.48-4.53
36(1)	4.54
36(2)	3.83, 6.225

PART V MEDICAL TREATMENT, CARE AND RESEARCH

37(1), (2)	5.3-5.17
37(3)(a)	5.31-5.32
37(3)(b)	5.33
37(4)(a)	5.29-5.30
37(4)(b)	5.27-5.28
37(4)(c)	5.22-5.24
37(5)	5.25, 5.26, 5.29-5.30
37(6), (7)	5.33
38(1)-(5)	5.34-5.40
38(6)	3.83, 6.225
39(1)-(4)	5.63-5.76
39(5)	3.83, 6.225
40 generally	5.41-5.50
40(2), (3)	5.59
40(6)	5.51-5.53
40(7)(a)	5.54
40(7)(b)	5.55
40(7)(c)	5.56
40(7)(d)	5.57-5.58
40(10)	3.83
41(1), (2), (4), (5)	5.77-5.82
41(3), (6)	5.83-5.86

BILL: CLAUSE	REPORT: PARAGRAPH
56(4)	6.225
57(1)-(5)	6.216-6.217
57(6)	7.3-7.5
58(1)-(8)	6.187-6.196
58(9)	7.3-7.5
59	6.179
60	6.205
61	6.204
62(1)-(3)	6.186
62(4)	6.225

PART VII MISCELLANEOUS

63	6.1-6.12
64(1)	2.74-2.79, 4.66-4.70, 6.141-6.144
64(2)	3.83, 6.225
65	2.80
67(1)	
"adult"	2.2
"nearest relative"	2.60-2.73
"person claiming an interest"	2.37-2.39
67(2)	2.3-2.15

SCHEDULE 2 MANAGEMENT OF ESTATE OF INCAPABLE ADULT

Paras (1), (2)	6.157-6.162, 7.3-7.5
Para (3)	6.156
Para (4)	6.171
Para (5)	6.163, 6.165-6.170, 7.3-7.5
Para (6)	6.164, 7.3-7.5
Para (7)	6.172-6.174
Para (8)	6.175-6.178

SCHEDULE 3 CONTINUATION OF EXISTING CURATORS ETC

Paras (1)-(5)	7.6, 7.9-7.10
Para (6)	7.7
Para (7)	7.8
Paras (8), (9)	7.9-7.10

SCHEDULE 4 MINOR AND CONSEQUENTIAL AMENDMENTS

Para (1)	7.11
Paras (3), (6), (7)	7.13
Para (15)	2.28, 3.48, 6.99, 6.114-6.118, 7.14

Appendix B

List of those who submitted comments on No 94 Discussion Paper

Organisations

Accountant of Court
Alzheimer's Scotland
Alzheimer's Scotland, Perth Branch
Association of Directors of Social Work
Association of Reporters to Children's Panels
Ayrshire and Arran Health Board Units
Borders Health Board
British Medical Association, Scottish Office
The Building Societies Association
Care in the Community - Scottish Working Group
Centre for Studies in Mental Handicap
Church of Scotland Women's Guild
Clinical Services Group, Craig Phadraig Hospital, Inverness
The Committee of Scottish Clearing Bankers
Director of Finance, Strathclyde Regional Council
The Elms, Residential Care Home
Family Advice Information Resource
Inverness, Nairn and Lochaber Local Health Council
Joint Ethico-Medical Committee of the Catholic Union of Great Britain and the Guild of Catholic Doctors
Joint Planning in Lothian
The Law Society of Scotland
Lothian Area Division of Psychiatry
Lynebank Hospital, Psychologists (Mental Handicap), Dunfermline
Mental Welfare Commission for Scotland
National Board for Nursing, Midwifery and Health Visitors for Scotland
National Schizophrenia Fellowship (Scotland)
Refuge
Registers of Scotland
Royal College of General Practitioners - Scottish Council
Scottish Action on Dementia
Scottish Association for Mental Health
Scottish Down's Syndrome Association
Scottish Society for the Mentally Handicapped
The Senators of the College of Justice
Sense in Scotland
The Sheriffs' Association
The Sheriffs Principal
Social Work Department, Dumfries and Galloway Regional Council
Social Work Department, Strathclyde Regional Council
The Voluntary Euthanasia Society of Scotland
West Lothian Advocacy Project
Womens' National Commission

Individuals

Ms Norah Anderson
Mr Paul R Beaumont, University of Aberdeen
Mr and Mrs Birt

Dr C M Corser, Consultant Psychiatrist, St John's Hospital
Mrs Elizabeth Cotter, Solicitor
Mr J Dick, Director of Social Work, Highland Regional Council
Miss Helen Grant
Mrs J Harrison
Mr Forbes W Inglis
Professor Bryan Jennett, University of Glasgow
Mr M W Kelly, General Manager, Renfrew Priority Services Unit
Dr Kennedy and colleagues, Royal Edinburgh Hospital
Dr J A Larner, Solicitor, Central Regional Council
Mr David P Lessels, University of Aberdeen
Mr Michael Lowitt, Northern College, Aberdeen
Mr D A Lush, Solicitor
Dr Alasdair J MacDonald, Consultant Psychiatrist/Psychotherapist, Crichton Royal
  Hospital
Dr A V P Mackay, Physician Superintendent, Argyll and Bute Hospital
Mr A L Martin, Mental Health Officer, Fife Regional Council
Mrs Lynn Maxwell
Dr William McCrea and colleagues
Mrs Jane McInnes, Senior Social Worker, Strathclyde Regional Council
Mr M D Murray, Director of Finance, Fife Health Board
Dr Kenneth Norrie, University of Strathclyde
Mr Stephen Rowan, Mental Health Officer, Highland Regional Council
Mr Don Stead
Miss Sandra Sutherland, Solicitor, Central Regional Council
Dr Roger A D Sykes, Consultant Psychiatrist, Ravenscraig Hospital
Mr Lawrence Thomson
Dr and Mrs Tulloch
Mr James W Wallace
Mr Adrian Ward, Solicitor
Mr George Watson, Mental Health Officer, Central Regional Council
Mrs Kathleen M Wilson

Printed by HMSO Scotland Dd 0293225 9/95 (099286)